100

DAYS

FROM

TODAY

Bringing the
HERO inside
you to life
to realize
your fullest
potential

Table of Contents

INTRODUCTION

Hello! I'm so glad you're joining me on this journey! You'll be happy you did! Now I'm warning you; it's not an all-easy, all-fun journey. But it is the journey you were meant to follow. The journey will take you where you belong. There may be hardships, difficulties, and disappointments along the way. This is part of the journey. Effort is needed to help you attain your fullest potential.

This book will help you increase your awareness about how you are currently living. And when you are aware, you have the proper foundation to fulfill your desires and needs to the last detail.

Awareness changes how you understand and view your life. Eventually you become a different person, living a more wholesome existence. This approach can be seen as a triangle with a circle running through it. The circle that runs through the triangle is equally affected by each of the triangle's three sides. In our life, the three sides of the triangle are as follows:

Side A: The external/physical side

Side B: The mental-emotional side

Side C: The intuitive/spiritual side

Once all sides are connected and balanced, working together, there will be no more mental struggles that you cannot overcome, and any physical suffering will be minimized or eliminated.

All healing, happiness, satisfaction, and fulfillment happen within the area that forms both the circle and triangle. I call this the inner field.

The inner field is the connection between the external/physical, mental-emotional and intuitive/spiritual worlds. It happens when you are aligned in all areas of your life.

When this happens, life becomes whole, perfect, flowing, loving, and blissful, even though there may still be difficulties on the outside, you have all you need to cope with them easily..

This book will show you how to reconnect with your inner field, which you came connected with when you were born.

On this journey, we go through 100 days of transformation. Each of the 100 days is divided into three parts. Each part will help you master one side of the triangle. Each lesson, when followed through, will help you connect with your true essence and transform any struggle into an opportunity.

The Three Parts Of A Day's Lesson:

1. A practical plan—Each of the 100 days begins with a quote followed by a lesson to get you closer to reaching your fullest potential. Each lesson includes practical steps that help you take the right actions to improve your life.

2. A thinking plan—At the end of each lesson, you have a question or several questions to ask yourself. These will help you to understand where you currently stand. If you are going through hardship in any area, then you will see the root of your suffering. This knowledge will help you grow and progress from any struggle and become more fulfilled and happier.

3. A spiritual plan—At the very end of each lesson, there is an affirmation. These affirmations, when repeated as suggested, help to connect you to your intuition, an infinite source of intelligence, unlimited and in union with all that is. Through focus, you can imprint your desires onto the matter that fills the spaces of the universe, allowing your dreams to materialize also in the physical world.

More on these concepts will be revealed throughout this book, so no need to worry if this sounds confusing at this stage.

Now that you understand each lesson's real power, follow through with every lesson in full. The lessons are short and simple yet can have a profound impact on your life.

No one says you have only 100 days for this transformation. In fact, for most of us, it takes between half and a whole lifetime. So do the steps at your own pace. There is no rush. So long as you are making progress, you will be moving in the right direction.

I have come to these lessons through experience, knowledge, and meditation. By committing to learning and applying them, they have transformed my life.

These lessons will bring you to the blissful life you desire, as they did for me. Although you will still be prone to the same situations and experiences that everyone goes through, your attitude will be different, and your perspective will be enlightened.

Let's begin!

A MESSAGE FROM THE AUTHOR:

**"HOW LONG ARE YOU GOING TO WAIT BEFORE YOU DEMAND THE BEST FOR YOURSELF?" ~
EPICTETUS**

Life is precious, and you are worthy of the best life you can dream of. You deserve to be your best every moment of every day.

Yes, it will take some work, we all know that, and most people are willing to do the work.

But the main problem is that people are not aware of what needs to be done to become happier and more fulfilled.

According to the world happiness report, most people are not happy and not sure what needs to be done to live a life that will make them happy and fulfilled.

We were not born with an instruction manual, and often what we were exposed to at an early age is far from the ideal life we desire. But it will become our life, our way of doing things, and our way of living if we don't consciously choose to change. And this is why I wrote this book.

It is a book I wish I had when I knew I wanted something better for myself while walking the path of addictions, failed marriages, life-threatening disease, poverty, and raising my two disabled children. The lessons I learned with time, helped me reach a life of abundance, health, love, and joy, and these are the lessons I provide for you in this book, which will do the same for you.

It is a book to open you to your higher self and purpose through awareness of your true divine essence. It is a book to help you lead your best life. The French philosopher Teilhard de Chardin said, "You are a spiritual being having a human experience."

Although our connection with the immaterial/spiritual world, or infinite intelligence is always there, we are often unaware of it. But awareness can be supported, and this is the goal of this book for you.

This book is like a bridge that may take you 100 lessons to cross to reveal the inner field and allow vitality and purpose to lead your life.

There may be lessons that you are well aware of and incorporate them regularly in your life already. When you study these lessons, they will boost your self-esteem and show you that you are headed in the right direction.

There will be days when the lesson material may be foreign to your daily life. These days will help you progress to a higher level of consciousness, growth, fulfillment, and enjoyment of life and bring you closer to your soul's desire.

While everyone has their unique purpose in life, we also have a combined purpose, to advance consciousness, and to do this we must personally reveal our true potential.

We are always in the right place to learn the lessons that will help us reveal our purpose to the world and, in turn, progress life. Follow your intuition; it brought you to this book. Follow the path and make the most of this experience that you were granted.

Enjoy, live, and connect with your true divine nature while giving it expression in this material world.

YOUR HERO'S JOURNEY

"A hero is someone who has given his or her life to something bigger than oneself." ~ Joseph Campbell

We all have the potential to be the Hero of our world. But to do that, we must undergo change.

In 1949, Joseph Campbell published his book, *The Hero with a Thousand Faces,* where he discusses his theory of the Hero's journey, which is shared by all mythologies.

Basically there is only one myth, a mono-myth, so to speak, which was told repeatedly in different cultures. Yet, all share the same great story.

The movies *Star Wars, Harry Potter, The Matrix, Spider-Man, The Lion King, The Lord of the Rings*, and *Alice in Wonderland* all follow this mono-myth theory. All are based on the same myth.

Deep within us, we know that our goal in life is to follow our own Hero's journey leading us to become the Hero of our lives and our world. The end result is connectedness and awareness of truth and bringing your essence forth into this world.

But there is an ongoing battle between our ego and our soul's desire. This constant battle is ongoing.

We are all on this Hero's journey. The question is whether we will complete it and allow our true divine nature to win, thereby allowing truth, love, hope, peace, humility, empathy, kindness, and joy to rule our lives, or cave in to our ego and let hatred, greed, anger, guilt, jealousy, fear, self-pity, inferiority, lies, pride, superiority, sorrow, and resentment to rule our lives.

The Journey - The Story Behind Becoming A Hero:

All potential heroes come from the "ordinary world" where the dominant rule is the ego. Greed, jealousy, attention-seeking, manipulating others to get what you want, craving respect and recognition, defensiveness, constant comparison, impatience, resentment, indifference to suffering, and emphasis on materialism are all signs that the ego is running your life. In the first stage, the potential hero lacks awareness of their ego, their purpose, and their potential. They are conforming to societal norms and doing what they are told to do. But deep within them, there is a fire. Then they are given the opportunity to leave their ordinary world and go to another world where their dreams can be fulfilled. They are afraid, but they take a leap of faith. Here, in the other world, the potential hero can discover and release their fire, but they first need to pass through great suffering, difficulties and hardships to do this. The hardships, and challenges, must be overcome for them to fulfill their destiny. When they conclude their journey, after overcoming many challenges and hardships, where their soul has triumphed over their ego and continues to do so every moment afterward, they can return back to the "ordinary world", where ego and lack of awareness rule people. When back in the ordinary world, they come with the knowledge and wisdom and perhaps even gifts they gained on their journey. These gifts, knowledge, and wisdom are powerful enough to improve society and the world significantly.

Joseph Campbell said that we must be willing to get rid of the life we've planned so as to have the life that is waiting for us. I say we must release the life we've designed through our selfish, egotistical traits to have the life that our soul wants for us and has in it all we need to feel satisfaction and bliss.

We are all destined to do great things, but the question is whether we will follow through with our hero's journey to do them? Every moment in life, we have a choice. To either follow our Hero's journey, make the right choices, overcome our nature, and grant our soul victory over our ego, or fall prey to frustration, disappointment, guilt, and sadness of giving in to our egos.

Once we are consistent with our efforts day-in-and-day-out, we become the Hero of our world, and suffering and hardship are replaced with understanding and bliss.

THERE ARE 17 STAGES TO ANY HERO'S JOURNEY.

First, examine your life and the challenges you overcame, which, as a result, made you stronger, and the lessons you have learned on the way. This way you can examine how far you've come on the 17 steps of your Hero's journey.

The question is whether you will go through all steps of the Hero's journey, overcome the ego and fulfill your destiny to become one with your soul's desire and the Hero you were intended to be?

You certainly have the capacity; this is true for all of us. But you have to make a choice every moment. Will you become the Hero, allowing your highest potential to shine through, or will you be the slave of your ego?

Many people follow the path of the Hero's journey and then stop on the way or they don't even start. Yet, we all have the potential to become the Hero of our world and to reach victory over our day-to-day battles between the ego and our soul. We all have this potential within us, but whether we reveal this potential is our own free will.

If we choose not to follow our Hero's journey, we will suffer and cause much suffering because we are not true to ourselves. We build a false facade and need to live abidingly. The requirements of the ego know no satiety, so you cannot know happiness following the path of the ego.

Most people want to follow their Hero's journey. Still, they seem to make the wrong choices. This is because their choices are connected with their ego rather than with their true identity, limitless, content, and connected to all.

This book will help take you through your own Hero's journey in 100 days and help you understand your true divine identity and connect with it while understanding your meaning and purpose in life.

Before you begin your 100-day Hero's journey, I will outline the 17 steps of the journey so that you can contemplate your current position on the journey. It would help if you did this not to see how much more you have to go through, but to see how much you have already accomplished and how much fun you still have awaiting you on the journey where you will learn to enjoy every moment within your journey.

The 17 steps of the Hero's journey are separated into 3 acts. You may not understand the names or what these acts and steps are about quite yet, but don't worry, as you grow in awareness during this 100 day journey, a transformation in your understanding will occur, and you will recognize your current place on the path. You may ignore the names of the 17 steps if you find them confusing. Here are the 17 steps of a hero's journey:

First Act: Departure. The first act is a departure from what is familiar and comfortable, a departure from the ego driven world of blaming others, materialism, jealousy, pride, guilt, negativity, impatience, and searching for fulfillment externally—the departure is a release from the grip your ego has over your life There can be no real revelation of your superpowers if you remain where you are, in your comfort zone, with your usual thoughts, behaviors, and actions.

1. **Call to Adventure**. The potential hero learns some information that sets the stage for change. Here, the potential hero understands that he must do something different to reach their full potential. But, as with all change, it is not easy. It may trigger fear, or a sense of obligation, insecurity, or even a sense of inadequacy.

2. **Refusal of the Call**. The potential hero will find ways to refuse the calling for change. They learn but become disinterested. They do not want change; they fear it, they hide. But then life becomes meaningless, intolerable, sad, and even painful, so they decide, even unconsciously, to go ahead with the challenge and start the path towards change.

3. **Meeting the Mentor**. The potential hero meets someone who either becomes their mentor or offers them some help or reassurance that they *can* go ahead with the challenges ahead. This can also take the form of someone with no direct connection to the person, as in a book, movie, biography, etc.

4. **Crossing the First Threshold**. Here the potential hero takes a leap of faith and ventures into the unknown. They may believe the change is dangerous to their known egoic identity that they now hold, and they are right. The potential hero needs to take a risk, make the change, and adapt to other conditions fast and with competence. Through courage to take on the task, the danger subsides.

5. **Belly of the Whale.** This step is named after the story of Jonah being swallowed by a whale. This step represents rebirth and commitment to their soul's desire. In this step, the potential hero commits to the change needed to become closer to their true potential after undergoing some form of threat to their life, or rather to their egoic life. The potential hero is now willing to undergo a personal metamorphosis to become a better version of themselves.

Second Act: After the departure act, we come to the initiation act.

6. **The Road of Trials.** These are a series of tests (challenges and hardships), that the potential hero must undergo to transform into a better version of themselves. These tests and trials are meant to push the person to soul search, to work on themselves and to change and become better.

During this step, the potential hero will meet with many small victories, allowing them to gain small glimpses of the wonderland that awaits him.

7. **The Meeting with the Goddess**. This step means that the potential hero will get something that will be of value for them or will help them in the future. This may be meeting a goddess in the form of transcendent love, or money, or significant knowledge. This is a reward for the potential hero's current and past efforts so that they understand that they are on the right track.

8. **Temptations**. Here the potential hero meets physical temptations. They may feel some success following the gift they received, but the gift was really another test. The physical temptations may lead the potential hero astray from their genuine pursuit or even to abandon their journey altogether. At this stage, the potential hero must overcome the temptations and continue on their quest.

9. **Atonement with the Father/Abyss**. This is the center point of the journey. All the previous steps have been advancing the potential hero to this place. The potential hero meets with a father figure with life and death powers. At this stage in the journey, the potential hero may hit rock bottom or confront their greatest fear. When they survive it, they will emerge transformed. This is when the person becomes a real hero.

10. **Apotheosis**, or the summit. Here the new Hero achieves a great realization and understanding. With this new knowledge and perception, the Hero is ready for more hard work.

11. **The Ultimate Boon.** At this stage, the Hero achieves their goal after going through all the previous steps, which purified and prepared them for this. They have found their connection to their true self and are ready to fulfill their purpose.

Third Act: This moves us on to the next act, which is Return to the ordinary world.

12. **Refusal of the Return**. Here the Hero enjoys their rewards, the good life, happiness, and enlightenment, and they may not feel the urge or will to do anything more. They have again become too comfortable to want to initiate change once more. But the Hero feels burdened again at this stage. They know they have to pass on what they have learned to others.

13. **The Magic Flight**. The Hero must deal with one last obstacle before they can return home to the ordinary world. This final obstacle is there to ensure they've learned the lessons and reached an undeniable connection to their true divine nature, void of the ego. In this Final Battle, the Hero goes through one more "resurrection". This may be any kind of difficult situation, even a near-death experience, a major loss of money, or health, or love. But the hero is able to cope with it and in retrospect understands that this is necessary to move them towards their true destiny.

This stage may leave the Hero wounded and in a worse place than they were beforehand, but their faith is now be unwavering.

14. **Rescue from Without**. The Hero may need some outside support because they have been weakened by the prior experience in some way, either financially, physically, or mentally. And at this stage, they get this external help in the form of guides, assistants, or rescuers to bring them back to everyday life. This step provides the hero the help needed to put them back on track.

15. **The Crossing of the Return Threshold.** The Hero decides to return to the ordinary world with the wisdom they gained on their chaotic adventure. They're different people than when they started: they've changed, grown, and matured due to the journey they have traveled. They decide to return to the ordinary world to share their value in the ordinary world.

16. **Mastering of the Two Worlds**. Here the Hero has to survive in the ordinary egotistical world again. Of course, it's not easy to adjust to the everyday world after all they have been

through during the chaotic and enlightening adventure. They have to do the ordinary things of the mundane world, but they have a different perspective. The Hero intuitively knows now how to integrate and apply their newfound wisdom into their daily life in the ordinary world. Thus, they achieve a complete balance between the material, egotistical world and the spiritual, awakened realm.

This makes them the master of two worlds. They live that balance competently and pass on their wisdom and gifts to others. They have become much more capable and resilient. They've learned many lessons and brought what they learned home with them to the real world and are living it here and now. Unfortunately, not many people complete their hero's journey and show their true and full light to the world. You may need to pass several hero journeys before seeing the bigger whole hero journey, and reach this stage of becoming the best version of yourself.

17. **Freedom to Live.** After all the difficulties on different planes, the Hero no longer lives in fear. They are constantly connected to their true divine nature. There are no regrets of the past or worries of the future. This allows them to live in freedom. They have defeated different aspects of their character and are passing their important knowledge and gifts onto the world, fulfilling their purpose and becoming immortal, or legendary.

Any person seeking to achieve their fullest potential must go through their own Hero's journey. And only when you manage to balance the external, material, ego driven world with the internal, spiritual and all united world and pass on your knowledge to others will you become a true legend.

I have created this book for you potential Heroes, to ensure that you don't give up on your own Hero's journey and that you keep on going, no matter what tests, trials, and tribulations come up along the way. The universe has your back, and if you do what you came to this world to do, you will have much to give back to society and your loved ones as well. You and all those around you will benefit in ways unimaginable.

Question of The Day:

Before moving on to the daily lessons, I want you to introspect:

Where am I on my Hero's journey? You may have many heroes journeys and one big one that sums them all up together. Choose which Hero journey you want to advance now.

When you figure this out, do not fear what still lies ahead, this book is here to support you. The way may not be easy, but as you will see, it is definitely worth it.

Affirmation Of The Day

Now sit quietly for a few minutes before continuing with this book and repeat this affirmation to yourself:

STEP BY STEP, THROUGH EVERY DEFEAT AND VICTORY, THROUGH EVERY CONNECTION I HAVE WITH OTHER PEOPLE, AND THROUGH EVERY SITUATION THAT ARISES IN MY LIFE, I AM BECOMING THE HERO OF MY LIFE AND MY WORLD.

Now tell this affirmation to yourself as often as possible because, with repetition, an affirmation has the power to alter your consciousness so that you think and behave differently for a better, happier life.

Now let's continue your Hero's Journey…

DAY 1 - BECOMING AWARE

"No problem can be solved from the same level of consciousness that created it"

~ Albert Einstein

Most people fail to achieve their dreams not because they lack the intelligence, resources, or willpower, but because of lack of awareness that leads them to behave in ways that are not beneficial. These behavioral patterns repeatedly return in their lives and lead them to live a life they do not desire.

Holding non-beneficial behavioral patterns by lack of awareness keeps us in the same loop resulting in unhappiness. We are sleepwalking through life without realizing it.

We must transform our level of consciousness to create a different, better, and more fulfilling life for ourselves. This means that we have to change. But we can only change when we become more conscious, more aware of ourselves and what leads us to behave in detrimental ways.

Nature is constantly changing to adapt to the weather and the environment. The same is happening with the world around us. It is ever-changing. If we are not willing to welcome change into our lives, especially inner transformation, or if we are not ready to become more insightful of ourselves and our behaviors, then we will be living our lives with an ever-growing gap between where we want to be and where we are today.

This gaps leads to unhappiness and confusion in our lives.

I can tell you that this discontentment comes from a lack of awareness of who we really are and our true potential. It leads to fear of change.

Fear of change is natural. Even though we need to make changes for our benefit and for those around us, some prefer things to stay the same. Often, being in a difficult situation is more comfortable for us than change. But in reality, if we are not improving and changing for the better, we are going backward.

When you become aware that you want and even need to change your habits to live a more satisfying life, it *will* be hard at first, but if you don't make any change, your life will be much harder in the long run.

Often reaching this troublesome state is good for us. We need to suffer enough to be willing to grow. Therapy and medications try to stop our suffering, but it is through our discomfort that we grow.

I was living with bulimia, an eating disorder, for sixteen years. I obsessed about food, but no one knew about this. I was living a lie. I found the power to release this addiction and find a better path when I understood that not only did my habits need to change, but I did too. The way I perceived things needed to change. I had a distorted view of the world and myself within the world. I needed to become more aware.

Earlier in my life, I used to prefer the easy way of doing things, and in the case of my eating habits, I found it much easier to vomit the foods I ate than to change them and myself.

But I *had* to change from this childish behavior to one of a responsible adult. I had to become more aware of what was triggering my behaviors and how thoughts and beliefs led me to behave in this way.

I became aware that change is scary.

I was scared to gain weight because I was afraid that I would not be lovable if I looked bad. I was also scared to lose the false perception of control. I was afraid I couldn't control my life.

To make a long story short, I became aware of my power. I took responsibility for my situation. And when I changed myself (I changed my perspective, beliefs, thoughts, and physical actions), everything changed for me.

An external change can only follow an internal change. You can't succeed at life and be happy if you hold faulty beliefs, especially if you are unaware that your beliefs are inaccurate and false.

Awareness is where it all begins.

There is nothing that you can't succeed at. You have to change your thoughts and beliefs to ones that are beneficial to you. You have to become more aware of who you really are and the power that lies within you.

This may not be clear yet because you are still unaware of who you are, and what needs to change and how to go about these changes. But this will become clear for you during the next 99 days.

Meanwhile, print out the PDF journal that comes with this book and answer the questions for day one.

This PDF is your journal for change.

Every day for the next 100 days, at the end of each lesson you will receive a few questions to help you become more aware of yourself and your role in life.

Questions of The Day

So, now, on this first day, your questions of the day are:

Out of the eight critical fields of my life, which areas need improvement?

1. Mental health - Peace of mind or release from negative thoughts and emotions.
2. Financial freedom or financial independence
3. Friends for enjoyment and support
4. Family and parenting
5. Relationship for intimacy
6. Physical health
7. Goals, creativity, and vocational interest
8. Self-actualization, wisdom, and purpose

What may be stopping me from making this change or improvement?

Write down your answers in your journal. Your answers may be very revealing.

Affirmation of The Day

After answering the questions in your journal, sit quietly for a few minutes today and repeat this affirmation.

I AM BECOMING MORE AWARE OF MYSELF AND MY CHOICES.

Repeat this affirmation often. With repetition, it has the power to alter your consciousness so you build a better, happier and more purposeful life.

DAY 2 - BECOMING AWARE OF ENVY AND PERFECTIONISM

"Transform jealousy to admiration, and what you admire will become part of your life" ~ Yoko Ono

Even if it seems that some people have all that you desire, research shows that most people would never trade their life for someone else's. This is because deep inside us, we know it is best for us.

We are on our unique journey, and we have something special and vital to offer the world, and everything we have is what we need for our growth.

We, therefore, never need to compare ourselves with others. We can only compare ourselves to how we did things in the past with how we are doing them today.

The unfortunate truth is that most of us do not understand that we are each worthy, essential and unique.

Dr. Joseph Murphy, a new thought leader and author of over 30 books, his famous one being The Power of Your Subconscious Mind, goes deeper into the concept of the subconscious mind coined by Sigmund Freud in 1893.

Joseph Murphy states that we live our lives through beliefs implanted into our subconscious mind when we were young to become a part of society, but most of these beliefs are false.

Our thoughts and beliefs are often not ours; they come from society, caretakers, and family. And these thought patterns often lead us to the false impression that we are not good enough.

We each have our unique gifts, passions, and specific purpose, and we can lead a very happy and fulfilled life when we become aware of our gifts and our true identity.

It's easier said than done.

But through mastering your mind and becoming more aware and insightful, we often understand that this programming was false.

When you compare your achievements with other people's accomplishments and feel disappointed with yourself, I recommend a simple exercise: Ask yourself, Who do I find myself comparing my achievements with most often and why? Now turn this person into your pretend mentor instead.

Please make a list of what you admire about them. Now write why you like these character traits. Of course, not all things can be changed, and not all qualities can be yours.

Still, more often than not, you will see that what you admire in this person is something that you already have the potential for within you, and you can adopt this characteristic into your life with minimal effort. Focus on yourself.

You are the only place where you should be focusing. Focus on what you need to do to change and improve yourself, and go for it. You have everything you need for your fulfillment.

Nothing is stopping you but you!

You do not need to be perfect. Everyone has their view of perfection. Our attachment to specific results that we think we need to have to be happy is often false.

Perfectionism comes from the belief that things are not perfect now, and we must improve them for our happiness. Perfectionism comes from the false impression that you are not good enough as you are now.

In most cases, fear of not being good enough is not connected with reality and is truly unfounded.Not everything must be 100 percent ready and perfect for you to do what you want to do. And not everything must go exactly as you wish it to go so you can be what you desire to be. If your mind or ego is the judge, you will never be ready and never be good enough because most people share the limiting beliefs that they are not good enough and not worthy yet.

These beliefs drain away from your happiness because you are focused on finding fault regarding something within you. You are focused on lack instead of witnessing what you already have.

Sometimes outside help can show us what we should be grateful for. You may see others as being perfect and yourself far from. But this viewpoint is produced by your past experiences and your thoughts and feelings. When you take action on something you desire to do before you are ready, you gain knowledge, insight and push yourself through your limiting boundaries. What's on the other side is incredible.

When you change your outlook on something you think you need to be happy, you realize all is already well. Of course, you can still improve and go after your dreams, but don't put too much emphasis on the results. Enjoy the process instead.When I took loans to buy properties, I was never really ready to buy another property, from any standpoint, ever. But I took action before I was ready, and I always gained from this.

Also, I could have never been ready enough during my first lectures. But I gave them anyway, and even during my later lectures, I still had very embarrassing moments. If you don't believe me, see the first minute of my TEDx talk that received millions of views. That was a very awkward moment for me. But it doesn't matter as long as I put my message out there for people to benefit.

Bringing your light out to the world is all that matters.

You are already perfect. No one can be better than you at being you. So you are perfect at being you. And when you are authentic, you will naturally attract people to you. All you need to do is be the best version of yourself as best as you can be today, not tomorrow, and not ten years from now. When you are the best version of yourself today, you are already perfect, and when you create things from this ideal version of yourself as you are today, then what you make will also be fitting for enough people.

Perfectionism is procrastination in disguise. When you wait for perfection to start to do something, this is procrastination. You avoid doing what you should be doing in the rationalization that you do not want to do something that isn't perfect, so you would rather wait until you are good enough or never do it.

Expecting to be perfect in the beginning is only an obstacle to your success. Anyone who you envy was never perfect in the beginning.You may interpret obstacles and struggles as signs of incompetence, and this may lower your self-esteem, and so you further procrastinate. But obstacles and even failing at times and rejection and frustration are an inevitable part of the long journey towards mastery, growth, and progress. If you focus on your own competence, you will never have a minute to be envious of anyone else.

When you're hypercritical about yourself and envious of others, you are in a state of hatred. You are not in a state of love, and nothing good will come out of it. You are the one holding yourself back. Realize how much damage you're causing to yourself just by maintaining such a negative state of mind.Perfectionism and envy rob you of your dreams. You are focusing outwards instead of inwards. The media shows only the perfect outcome; they do not share the long hard hours perfecting any craft. This can lead to envy. But all people who have now reached what seems to be perfection and perfect creations also went through awful first drafts, losses, and failures. Allow yourself to do things in a less than perfect way for a while. Stop focusing on other people's results as something that hinders your path because you feel that you will never be as good as they are. I stopped studying architecture as my first degree after my uncle helped me with my homework, and I thought that I could never be as good as he was.

Happiness comes from accepting what is. You cannot be happy being hypercritical of yourself or focusing on other people's achievements. Aim to live your life in the best possible way. Reaching perfection in your own eyes can take a lifetime. You will, in the end, see the perfection in everything, this will perhaps take a lifetime, but there is a perfect order of things.

Enjoy the process. Don't be shy or be less than what you believe you are. You have everything you need to succeed and become the person your soul wants you to be. Live each moment as best you can.

Question of The Day

So, to end off this lesson and to help you stop envy and perfectionism, the question that you want to ask yourself today is:

Who do I find myself comparing my achievements with, and why? Turn this person into your mentor. Please think of the powerful characteristics that you like and admire in them. Write a list of these characteristics. Now decide that these traits can and will be yours as well.

I recommend writing your answers in the PDF journal that you have received with this book to look over your answers and ensure that you are improving your life and bringing forth your true divine nature.

Affirmation Of The Day

After answering the questions in your journal, and examining your answers, sit quietly for a few minutes today and repeat this affirmation to yourself as you think and dwell upon it:

I DON'T NEED TO COMPARE MYSELF TO ANYBODY; I AM UNIQUE AND SPECIAL AS I AM.

DAY 3 - BECOMING AWARE THAT YOU ARE A MASTERPIECE

"You are allowed to be both a masterpiece and a work in progress simultaneously"

~ Sophia Bush

The first step towards any improvement is to accept yourself as you are right now. You are a masterpiece as you are! Everything is perfect even if it may not seem so. Everything is ready to bring you to the next level of consciousness, so that you can know your power and worth. You will know true freedom and reveal your glory to the world.

The fact that you are here already makes you special. Adopting a positive mindset is a necessary stepping stone on your hero's journey. This mindset comes from an understanding that you are connected to infinite intelligence and your job is to show this connection to the world through your actions. When you show your connection, whatever it is, you are contributing to the greater good and pushing humanity forward.

This mindset is one of self-love, but it is not a self-love that comes from the ego, but rather one that unites you with the whole, with all that is around you.

To reach this mindset, there are a number of prerequisite stages.

1. **Think positively**. Self-esteem is needed to bring forth your spark to the world and it dependent on positive thinking. Without it you will be afraid to take chances and make progress. Building self-esteem requires small steps to making better habits that push you forward.

2. **Respect**. When you start respecting yourself, you will naturally want to treat yourself better. You will be more careful with the foods you eat, with how you spend your time and with whom you spend it. You will be more thoughtful with your behaviors and actions. You understand that you are worthy of the best you can do. You are slowly becoming more aware of your personal power.

3. **Like yourself**. As you slowly make better choices, you will see your power manifest. You know that you have worth to give back to this world. Once you respect someone, it is natural to start liking them more. The same happens with you. You will like yourself more and stop acting from a place of pleasing others. You will make better choices. Your soul will be winning over your ego almost every moment.

4. **Love yourself**. You know yourself as part of the whole, but you find your uniqueness. You will want to give off some of who you are to the world in a way that feels right for you.

You do not wish to waste your time here on earth anymore and you must get to work helping others improve their lives, even if only for a special few who are close to you. We are each a masterpiece in progress. So don't focus on your flaws.

Start becoming more aware of who you really are. Think positively about yourself from this moment on and choose your behaviors and make your decisions from this place of understanding.

When you truly love yourself, you also love all other people and species around you for you understand that all has its place and importance in this world.

Questions of The Day

So, to end off this lesson and to help you take the steps to understand that you are a masterpiece, and that you matter, the questions that you want to ask yourself today are:

Do I truly respect myself in all areas of life? Are there areas in my life that I am not showing respect for myself? Which steps do I think I should take to love and respect myself more?

At this stage we are still gaining awareness. This is the very first stage toward any progress. There is nothing to do except to become more insightful of your actions.

As usual, I recommend writing your answers in the attached journal.

Affirmation of The Day

After answering the questions in your journal, and contemplating your answers, sit quietly for a few minutes today and repeat this affirmation.

I HAVE A SPECIAL SPARK OF INFINITE INTELLIGENCE WITHIN ME AS DO ALL OTHER CREATIONS. I MATTER.

Repeat this affirmation often. With repetition, it has the power to alter your consciousness so you build a better, happier and more purposeful life.

DAY 4 - BECOMING AWARE OF YOUR EGO

"A bad day for your ego is a great day for your soul." ~ Jillian Michaels

There is a constant war inside every one of us. This war is between our ego and our soul. Every moment we have a choice, to cave into our ego or follow our soul's desire.

But to make the right choice we must understand these two players, the ego and our soul, that we have within us.

So what exactly is the ego?

The English word "ego" is the Latin word for "I."

The ego moves the person to focus on themselves, or their "I" and this type of focus will influence their thoughts, emotions, motives, and behaviors.

When acting from the ego, it means that one is operating from self-interest, focusing on what "I" want, what "I" need, and what "I" have.

The ego is the "I" that is not connected to the true self. It is an illusionary self that makes us believe it's essential for our survival through self-preservation. But, what we believe is good actually hinders our progress.

The ego sees the world through a person's previous experiences and beliefs, through self-invented biases and preferences. It is not easy to step outside one's perspective and see things differently.

There is no way for us to process information except our personal frame of reference unless we open ourselves to reality. We are more ONE than separate, and that we are more ALIKE than different.

But the ego keeps us in the mindset that we are different and separate. The ego makes us believe that we have to fight for ourselves and that other people are most often a threat to us.

When we think through our egoic mind, we separate ourselves from others and are thinking only about our desires, what other people think of us, and how things are going for us. This self-absorption will lead us to behave in ways that have negative consequences on our life. These behaviors remove us from a good, fulfilling, and happy life. The trickiest part of the ego is that it gives false confidence.

The ego gives us an unrealistic sense of superiority, making us think that our opinion is the truth. It creates a self-image from thoughts that are nothing more than illusions that we allow to influence our lives.

All our choices, thoughts, and behaviors can come from the ego if we let them, which distances us from our true purpose and distorts our view of reality. The ego prevents us from connecting with our true divine nature, a part of the unified field where we are all connected.

However, deep inside, our soul knows that our ego is masking our true self.

We lose our identity to our ego because it is the easiest way to live life.

To renounce the ego is challenging and goes against our survival instincts. Still, once we give up our ego, we become free to live our lives with meaning in a way that is in line with who we are while being of service to everything else around us. These bring us abundance and lasting happiness.

When you live from your ego, you are always in fear that you will lose your unique identity when you do things for others and not only for your own benefit.

Many research studies show that people are biased to view themselves more positively than others.

But true freedom happens when you renounce your ego and start to live from a place of connection.

When the work you do is very engaging for you, when you are feeling good and free to be yourself without worry, and when you are in the flow state, during meditation, or massage, or while listening to music or during exercise of any sort, then your ego is often set aside.

When your ego is set aside, you are not only concerned with yourself, with what you want, or with your personal gratification from a situation.

This state of not focusing on yourself and your needs wants and desires, will make you happier because it connects you with your soul. On the other hand, focusing only on yourself will often make you depressed or behave in ways that harm you and others.

The ego is also very limiting. It limits your options and possibilities to what you can or can't do or become. Even though the ego gives you a sense that you can do and become the best, it is a very limited best and far from your real potential in every field of life. Only when you are connected to your true essence that is united with infinite intelligence can you fulfill your true potential.

The ego seeks to divide and separate you from others while really, to be your best and achieve greatness, you must become one with others and help, serve, and heal others while also connecting and using their gifts.

When you follow your purpose and do your work or take action for its own sake, because you feel that this is what you want to do, and not for any resulting benefits, then you will be happiest. You leave anxiousness and fear aside.

When you live like this, you renounce your ego, stopping it from controlling your life and telling you to do it only for personal gain, for personal wealth, attention, and fame. When you renounce your ego, this is when *you* start to control your life.

When we were children, we were not scared to express our true divine nature. We were not afraid to say what we thought, show our true feelings, or feel certain emotions. We lived in the present moment until we learned how to adapt our behaviors to other people and different situations to feel accepted.

Our ego grew as we left childhood. We began to put on a show to be everything but our true selves to be liked and accepted by others or set us deliberately apart from others.

This ego is very tempting in that it holds the promise that you are unique and different and better than others. But when you think this way then figure out the truth that everyone is unique and special at something and that we are all pretty much the same, then there is a big letdown and a lot of frustration and maybe even depression.

With the ego, we take things personally, even when they are not personal. We let things control our future as if every relationship or experience will end up the same because the last one ended up in such a fashion.

Past disappointments lead to future fear of disappointment. Fear will not let you be who you really are or have what you truly desire, which eventually leads to disappointment.

A life that comes from the ego and is built on social status and possessions may satisfy briefly but will be overall empty.

When we die, material things disappear, and only our legacy is what is left behind, which is all about how we treated people, and the service we provided to others, whether through love, friendships, or business. And since the spiritual world is eternal and our soul belongs to this dimension, we will experience in some form whatever we leave or didn't leave behind.

A life built on ego will bring out anger, arrogance, and selfishness which clouds judgment. When your judgment is clouded, you cannot learn from past mistakes, and you will not become your best. You will waste your time and life and cause much suffering to yourself and others through this clouded judgment.

It's important to understand that we already possess everything that the ego promises to give us.

The ego will not let you rest in search of a way to leave a mark on the world, be it either a positive or negative mark. Often we don't even know what was pushing us to such behavior that we later regret. We fell into the trap of our ego and raised it above all values.

You already possess a positive legacy within you through every connection you build and through every person you meet and influence positively. Patience, love, a smile, and words of encouragement already leave your legacy for you.

Moreover, the ego wants to leave a legacy so that it will be remembered and considered great. But you are already immortal because your soul, which is the spark of true divine nature within you, is immortal.

It would be best if you strived to become a better human being and leave a good mark on as many people as you meet through connection with the true divine nature of your soul.

When you aim to do and be your best most of the time, you are already leaving the most incredible legacy for those close to you. When you are doing your very best, there is no such thing as failure.

If you listen to the ego, you will never be enough. There will always be someone doing something better and having something more than you. And no matter how much you have, you will still want more since nothing will ever be enough.

But when you do things for the sake of doing them, because you want to do them, and like to do them, then you will release all tension from becoming better than others and from achieving more and more because you know that you are enough right now.

When you renounce your ego, you live your life on purpose, connected to your true self and at peace. And when you have peace of mind, then you also have joy.

You do not need any external acknowledgment.

The best way to improve yourself, is at times, to look foolish in the face of others.

The end of the ego is self-acceptance. When you love and accept yourself just as you are, without the need to have more or do more for another person's acceptance, this is the death of the ego and the rebirth of life.

The ego wants us to stay in familiar territory. But personal development is to grow out of the state of "I" and "mine" and into union with all that is. Growth and progress is your soul's desire.

We all can consciously change our lives for the better by taking responsibility for our choices and actions. This positive change means moving away from our ego that says to us that we cannot change, and instead reconnect with our true higher self that wants to change and improve and become a better version of ourselves when we decide to be, because part of our soul's desire is to advance humanity in our unique way.

Remember that your ego is leading your thoughts and behaviors whenever you feel superior or inferior to anyone else. At this moment, you are not connected to your true divine nature. But you can change this and let your true self, which is connected to infinite intelligence, lead you instead.

When you renounce your ego of "I" and "mine," you unite with love, and this is how to live your best life and genuinely leave the best legacy.

Questions of The Day

So, to end off this lesson and to help you remove your egoic nature and connect with your true self, the questions that you want to ask yourself today are:

What is pushing me to achieve my dreams? Is it because I think I am not good enough as I am right now, or perhaps I think I am better than others? Or is it because I have this will inside of me that must come forth and show itself to the world even if I never gain any personal benefit from it?

When the last choice was your honest answer, then you have renounced your ego and are on track to leading the life of your dreams full of meaning and purpose.

As usual, I recommend writing your answers in the attached journal.

Affirmation Of The Day

After answering the questions in your journal, and examining them, sit quietly for a few minutes today and repeat this affirmation:

I RENOUNCE MY EGO AND LET MY TRUE SELF SHINE THROUGH. I AM PERFECT AS I AM, AND SO IS EVERYONE AND EVERYTHING ELSE.

With repetition, it has the power to alter your consciousness so you build a better, happier and more purposeful life.

DAY 5 - BECOMING AWARE OF YOUR WORDS

"Words are free. It's how you use them that may cost you." ~ J. Martin, Reverend

Words have power. Your words influence the people around you and your subconscious mind.

We act from default behaviors that come from our subconscious mind. Whatever your mind is thinking, and your mouth is speaking, your body and your subconscious mind makes your reality.

Words have the power to separate and disconnect people or to connect them through closeness, unity, and love. The reality is the connection between all creations. And words can either reveal this connection or express disconnection and alienation. The impact of words is tremendous.

Think of how much power gossip has over you.

Think of how much other peoples' words that you've heard about yourself have influenced your life. Think about how much your own words affect your life and the lives of others.

Your mind and your words influence all disease states. Whether you are looking in the mirror and thinking or saying: I am fat, or I look sick, or I am full of vitality, your subconscious mind hears it and creates this reality for you by holding onto these beliefs and by nudging your choices, actions, and behaviors to match your thoughts and your words.

Words are potent, yet you are more powerful since you have the freedom to choose your words. Positive words can uplift a person's soul and fill them with happiness, whereas negative comments said to another are often remembered long after they were told and can cause much pain and sadness.

The first step towards changing any physical condition is mastering your mind and mastering your words. It would be best to control your words and your mind like you control your car with two hands steady on the steering wheel. Otherwise, you will fail to achieve a blissful life.

You must be in control of your words and your mind and not let random thoughts control your life.

You are not your mind, nor are you your body. You are separate from your mind and body, which is why you can control them externally. You need to watch your chosen thoughts and words and make sure they are aligned with how you wish to be.

I remember the moment that I started observing the thoughts and the words I used. I was shocked to notice that most of my thoughts and words were very hostile towards me. I couldn't believe it. I was sleepwalking through life, behaving from my negative thought patterns without noticing that I was doing this.

Unfortunately, most of us are like this. We are unaware that we behave from inbuilt thought patterns that we took on from our ancestors and, our environment, the way we were cared for at an early age and even through genetics.

Words are like seeds; when you plant them either in your fertile mind or in the minds of others, these seeds will grow to produce the results based on whatever was planted.

Words of fear, uncertainty, blame, as well as judgmental words, lies, and words of hatred will all lead to devastation in your life since these words go against your true divine nature.

When we hear the words of others, they are most often the opinions of other people and indeed not truths. When you accept their words as being truths, then their words have power over you.

We know how words can change our beliefs about ourselves. Because of the power of words, I give affirmations at the end of each day's lesson in this book to connect you to the immaterial/spiritual world, or infinite intelligence, so that you can use positive words to make your life better, as you would like it to be.

When I noticed my negative words and thought patterns, I chose to control my thoughts and words. Whenever a negative thought entered my mind, I would cancel it out by saying "cancel, cancel, cancel," and afterward replace the negative thought or word with what I wanted to have instead. I would replace the negative thought or word with a positive thought or word.

Instead of seeing what I had in front of me, which in effect was the product of my previous negative thought patterns, I started to use my mind to create what I wanted to have in my life through the power of words in the form of repeated affirmations said out loud.

Through repeated affirmations is how I started my path towards my bliss.

Your life is precious. You don't want to waste your time thinking thoughts, talking words, and maintaining habits that do not get you to where you wish to be in this lifetime and keep you in a negative state. You must control your thoughts and the words you say about yourself, about how you see things in life, and about others because this is the starting point to everything you wish for your life.

Negative thoughts and words have the power to change your physiology and create disease within your body. It is never really enough to treat a physical condition without helping the person change their thoughts and words that brought them to this condition in the first place.

Whenever you use the power of words to spread love, this is what will come back to you.

Questions of The Day

So, to end this lesson and to help you master your words, the questions that you want to ask yourself today are:

Which thoughts does my mind entertain most of the day? Which words do I often speak about myself and my state to others? Which words do I most often use when I talk about others? What am I creating with the thoughts and words that I choose to entertain in my mind and my life?

Are your thoughts and words positive or negative? If they're mostly negative, ask yourself: Am I willing to work on replacing these negative thoughts and words immediately as they come towards positive ones instead? How can I change these thoughts and words to reflect what I want to have in my life?

If you are not in a state of bliss most waking hours of your life, you have negative thought patterns.

I recommend writing your answers in the PDF journal.

Affirmation Of The Day

After answering the questions in your journal, and contemplating on your answers, sit quietly for a few minutes today and repeat this affirmation:

ALL THAT I THINK AND SAY IS IN LINE WITH MY ULTIMATE SOUL'S DESIRE AND IS POSITIVE AND LIFE-ENHANCING.

Repeat this affirmation often. With repetition, it has the power to alter your consciousness so you build a better, happier and more purposeful life. Have a great day!

DAY 6 - BECOMING AWARE OF THE PHASES OF LIFE

"You need a name for every stage of your life. Butterflies don't go by 'caterpillar' forever, and they certainly don't go by 'pupa' one second longer than they have to." ~ Sasha Martin

We all grow, develop, and mature. But to make the most of life, we need to move through the natural phases of life and complete each phase in the best possible way for us.

All people go through four phases in life. For some people, the transition between the different phases is natural, while for others, the transition doesn't happen that easily, and they may get stuck in a particular phase for much longer than is good for them. For most people, the phases overlap, and there is a to and fro between the phases during the transition period.

So let's look into the four phases of our life cycle:

I call them the four Cs:

Conforming, Conquering, Consolidation, and Contribution

1. **Conforming.** The goal of this phase is to teach us how to function best in society. It teaches us which decisions are best and which actions are best to fit into society. This is a crucial phase ensuring that we can live with other people in the best possible way. In this phase, we copy other people's behaviors. We copy people who are older than us. We want to look like them, so we dress similarly. We learn how to behave through copying other people. In this phase, pleasing other people is the norm while we slowly learn some independence. At this stage, rejection and being judged by others is very hard on us. This phase lasts until the age of eighteen on average.

2. **Conquering**. This lasts up till the age of 27-38. In this phase, we focus on what makes us unique. Independence is very important. We are making our own decisions and learning to understand ourselves. This phase requires us to experiment with new people, in new places, and with new things. We feel that we want to and can conquer the world. We see no limitations. We think that we can do everything. We go after external success and materialism. But as we experiment, we see that some experiments go well for us and others don't. In this phase, we learn what we are good at and learn what we are not so good at. We understand what we should be doing and what we should not be doing. Regarding relationships, we learn which relationships are right for us and which are less supportive for us. And hopefully, we learn to settle into one relationship without feeling that there is always something better out there for us. In this phase, we learn to admit our failures, at least to ourselves, and see our limitations. At the end of this phase, we should know and slowly become more focused on what is right and what is good for us, and what matters most. In this phase, we realize that we can't have it all even if we really like something or want something. We learn that we should focus on what is a good fit for us and leave behind what is not right for us. By the end of this phase, we should carefully pick and choose what we have the best chance of success at and commit to it, be it a relationship, a career, a life mission or purpose, and a place to live.

3. **Consolidation**. This phase lasts until about age seventy. At this stage, you focus on certain things and improve on them and make them better and stronger. It is a phase in life when you work hard on things that have meaning and purpose for you. Everything that prevents this focus should be slowly removed or replaced. Hobbies, old dreams, friends, and partners may be

released or replaced if they disturb in this consolidation phase, while others will eventually take their place. Now you can focus on what is really important and good for you, and you can focus on your mission in life and get into full-fledged action. This is the phase of leaving your dent in the world. This is the stage that you can reach your full potential.

4. **Contribution.** It begins when you feel as though there's not much else you can accomplish, and you feel that you have enough and prefer to have more fun with friends and family doing the things you love. You arrive at this phase after working hard to achieve meaningful and important goals. I call this the contribution phase not because it is time to contribute but because it is time to make sure your contribution lasts beyond your lifetime. At this phase, you will pass on your projects to other people or your children. You are wise enough to advise your children from your experience at this phase, and you may help raise your grandchildren. At this phase, you may teach or advise others through lectures or politics. This phase ensures that your life means something.

At each phase of life, your priorities will change. Sometimes we need something big to push us forward and reevaluate our choices and move on. This can be a disease, the death of someone close, or a traumatic event. This reevaluation helps us move onto the next phase of life in search of a better way to pursue happiness.

In the end, we learn that it is what we choose to live for that will determine our level of happiness. We realize that when we base our happiness on internal, self-controlled values, we will be our happiest. The only reason we get stuck in a specific phase is when we think that what we did is not enough. To move from phase one to phase two, we must understand that we can never be enough for everybody all the time. This is why we must become independent of others.

To move on from phase two to phase three, we must understand we cannot accomplish everything we want to. We can't be all over the place. We must focus on what matters most and commit to it.

To move from phase three to phase four, we must understand that time and energy are limited, so we should now focus our attention on helping others take over our meaningful projects so that our projects have a life of their own.

To be at peace and move on from phase four, we must understand that we are part of a bigger picture and accept that what we gave to the world was perfect and was exactly what was needed.

Questions of The Day

So, to end off this lesson and to help you gain more awareness of where you currently are in life, please ask yourself:

At what phase of life am I supposed to be right now? Am I in the proper phase for me now? If not, in which area do I feel that I have not done enough yet? Have I really not done enough? Perhaps I have done enough, and I *am* enough just as I am to move forward in life.

As usual, I recommend writing your answers in the PDF journal that you have received with this book. Then look over your answers to ensure you improve your life and bring forth your true divine nature.

Affirmation Of The Day

After answering the questions in your journal, and contemplating on your answers, sit quietly for a few minutes today and repeat this affirmation:

I AM A BEAUTIFUL WORK IN PROGRESS.

Repeat this affirmation often. With repetition, it has the power to alter your consciousness so you build a better, happier and more purposeful life.

DAY 7 - BECOMING AWARE OF WHAT TO CHANGE

"One day or day one, you decide." ~ Paulo Coelho

We always have a choice to remain with the life we currently have or we can take a leap of faith and start taking steps towards a better life for ourselves. Every day we have the opportunity to start over in places where we're unfulfilled and unhappy. The same is true for all areas of our life.

We don't need to stay in the same place we are in today. As Jim Rohn, the personal development guru, said, "We are not trees." Start by making small changes that will lead you to a better path.

All too often, we're so caught up in our way of doing things that we believe our current way is the only way. But when we introspect and take a closer look at our daily habits, we see that we are not moving in the right direction to making our life fulfilling and happy for us.

Many of us do not notice that our daily rituals and habits slowly move us in the wrong direction. When we become aware of our results, we can course-correct, but when we are blinded or asleep, we will not see until it may be too late. Effects take time. If our teeth rotted immediately after drinking sugar-rich beverages or not flossing or brushing our teeth, then we would avoid sugar and always floss and brush our teeth, even several times a day. But the effects of our actions take time to show up. Not having immediate consequences is actually good for us to grow and make the necessary changes in time to unite with our true selves.

Even if you are enjoying your life now, you must introspect whether this is the result of your past efforts or will your past habits soon catch up and ruin your happiness by coming to haunt you.

What are your vices? Get acquainted with them consciously so that you can remove them and improve your life in all fields. Get familiar with your habits and see how much time you spend on moving yourself closer to your dreams, goals, and your soul's desire.

Are your daily habits benefitting you in the long run? What will be the consequences to your health, love life, career, and finances if you keep doing the things you are currently doing right now? Check your results according to your level of satisfaction and happiness with them.

You want to examine your numbers. Check your debts, check your weight, blood test results, the number of dates with your spouse, the numbers of drinks you consume, or cigarettes you smoke, or your time wasted in front of the television. Check your health, relationships, and financial numbers with the same rigor that you check the likes on your social media posts.

In the fig tree parable, Jesus cursed the fig tree that had only leaves and no fruit.

When there are no results, the effort you put in and the habits you held were not productive to yield sufficient progress towards your success. Something needs to change. Your behaviors, your perspective, and most often, your habits need to change.

The best way to ensure that you do have the results you want and won't look back two to three years from now and see that your life has moved in the wrong direction is to track your habits.

Take a small notepad with you wherever you go for the next week. If you are interested in your health, track what you eat and drink and when. Track the number of steps you make during the day through a health app, monitor your workouts, and the number of hours you sleep. When you look at the content of your notes after one week, you'll find your soft spots.

If you are interested in your finances, write down everything you spend your money on for one week along with the times you spend the money. Then check your notes for soft spots. You can also check your monthly credit card bills to see where most of your money is going. See where your habits are leading you away from financial freedom. Perhaps you can eat less out, or at least have your coffee at home.

Do the same for your career. How many hours a day are you spending on education and work towards your career goals. How many times a day or week are you solely focused on your career goals?

In your relationships, how much time are you making for yourselves as a couple? How many times do you go out just the two of you on a date?

Once you take an earnest look at your notes, you will see where your problematic habits, behaviors, thoughts, and beliefs lie and what needs to be changed to get the results that you *do* desire in a few months or a few years. Do the work that will bring you to where you desire to be. Time is less critical because just as it takes time to turn a roundabout at first, you can hop on and enjoy the ride once you get it moving. The most important thing is to take the right actions regularly.

Even minimal actions in the right direction done daily will have a significant positive effect in the long run. If you incorporate good habits into your life, then the results will surely be good in the long run.

For example, if you look at a map and see that a particular road leads to a specific destination that you want to reach, you will eventually reach your desired destination if you walk down that road. The time it takes to get there is less critical. You merely need to make sure that you are headed down the right road that leads to your desired destination.

Helping you know where you want to go is part of the subject of many lessons on this 100 day to self-awareness journey.

This lesson helps you clarify where you currently are so you know what you have to change to get you to where you desire to be. After truthfully acknowledging and taking responsibility for where you currently are in your life and where your current habits are leading you, then you will only have the choice of deciding that it is either "day one" for you or one day. Will you do what needs to be done to reach your goals and live with happy results, or will you decide not to do what needs to be done today and move off course from your dreams, making you unhappy and unsatisfied.

Winston Churchill said, "However beautiful the strategy, you should occasionally look at the results." Always examine where your strategy is taking you with the knowledge and evidence that you have gathered. Your future is your choice. When you follow the proper habits, success will be yours to keep.

In 2006 I fully grasped that it could be "day one" or "one day" for me. So I put in the effort and finished my master's degree. It was not easy, but I did it. I was so happy with myself. That year I also moved to a home with a garden. My new home was big enough for me to open a nice clinic. I wanted to have my clinic at home so I could be near my children. I was always afraid to do what I wanted to do because I let fear dictate my life. I was fearful that I couldn't afford the house. I was afraid that the risk was too considerable, but then I decided to try, and I took a leap of faith anyway. I changed my life. All I needed to do was examine what wasn't working. I needed to figure out which behaviors and beliefs were not getting me the results I desired and take the first steps to make the necessary changes to better results in my life.

Is it day one for you or just another day? If you want improvement in your life, then you have the power to decide that today is day one of your new life. And after making that decision, which, as Tony Robbins says, is like an incision, then, on this first day, write out a plan for the life you desire.

Write down five to ten desires for your life. What do you think you would need to have in your life to make it a life worthwhile for you? What would make you truly happy? What would make you proud? Think about what you would regret if you did not do.

We are still at the beginning of the journey, so please only write down your desires. Later we will transform these desires into an action plan, but introspection is crucial for your success.

I want to tell you that leading a genuinely joyful and fulfilled life is possible for everyone, but it takes dedication, and it will take an overcoming of fears of not being good enough and not having what it takes. But I am here to tell you that you do have what it takes to succeed and fulfill your dreams because they are YOUR dreams. They are your soul's desire, so you CAN achieve them.

Sometimes, dreams may change, but what I have found is that most people have dreams with them from the time they were young. These are really where you want to focus your introspective energy. What interests did you have when you were a teenager? How do you want to see your life unfold?

Now I can tell you that creating the life of your dreams does take effort, but the effort is actually fun. It also requires surrender. It is allowing what needs to happen to happen. I will talk about this in another lesson, but in the meantime, focus on becoming aware of what you really want for yourself and not what others have implanted in your mind that is good for you.

Questions of The Day

To end this lesson and to help you understand your needs and desires best, the question that you want to ask yourself today is:

What area of life would I like to have a fresh start to get me to a better place?

The answer could be in the field of relationships, finances, health, mental well-being, or self-actualization. You know which area you would like to improve most in your life.

Then, if you wish to, decide that this is not just another day in this field; this is day one, and write out your dreams and which steps you may need to take to get you to where you desire to be.

Don't forget to write in your journal.

Affirmation Of The Day

After answering the questions in your journal, and examining them, sit quietly for a few minutes today and repeat this affirmation:

I BELIEVE IN MY ABILITY TO SUCCEED! MY HABITS LEAD ME TO MY DREAMS ONE STEP AT A TIME.

Repeat this affirmation often. With repetition, it has the power to alter your consciousness so you build a better, happier and more purposeful life.

DAY 8 - BECOMING AWARE OF YOUR SOUL'S DESIRE

"Follow your heart and intuition. They somehow already know what you truly want to become. Everything else is secondary." ~ Steve Jobs

Sometimes you may ponder whether the path you want to follow is the right path for you. So how will you know?

Simply follow your heart. To be clear, I am not saying to follow your emotions. Absolutely not. When I suggest following your heart, it is because your heart is a means by which your soul expresses itself.

When we follow our heart or our soul's desire, we convince our heads to join in, but when we follow our head, no amount of convincing will bring our hearts into it.

Your head will want you to remain safe and secure. Your head may constantly be thinking, "What will happen if…" while your heart may be more adventurous and push you to go after your dreams.

Your heart relies on instinct while your head goes according to what happened in past experiences. Therefore the head is not free. It is also scared to try new things that are untapped by others.

When you make your decisions so that your heart leads the way, you can use your head for what it's good at, such as making the proper adjustments to your actions and plans so they will go smoothly and in the best way for you.

When Jeff Bezos bought the Washington Post, it was a decision that came from his heart. He said that it had nothing to do with logic. Instead, he wanted to give for the sake of freedom of speech. Your heart will steer you in the right direction of your soul's desire if you follow it. It will help you stay on track with your beliefs and values. It will help you remain true to your soul.

Then, you will genuinely reach success as you define it. When you follow your soul by following your heart, you will leave a meaningful legacy that you and your loved ones will all be proud of.

On the other hand, when you follow your head, you will see that what you are doing conforms to what may seem acceptable by others, or worse yet, adhering to your ego.

You will be busy seeking legitimacy from other people and society, and you will become self-centered. As a result, you will often feel that you are living a lie. You are also much more likely to do things that are not aligned with your values and ideals. And then, you are also more likely to give up on the way.

When you follow your head, you will never really know what is truly right for you. You are blocking out your soul from your decision-making process. Your emotions will confuse you, and you will not know whether this is really what you want or don't want to do. Fear will creep in and affect your thinking.

With this confusion, you cannot generate much passion, which will hinder your success.

Your head may tell you *not* to do something because of fear of rejection, fear of failure, or even fear of success. Or your head may advise you to go ahead and do something that is not right for you just because it is the logical thing to do or that this is what everyone else is doing.

When you act from your head, it most often won't lead to your happiness, but following your heart and soul *will* lead to happiness.

You will be doing what is best not only for you but what is right in general. You will simplify your life and make critical choices more easily. You will also naturally have passion for what you are doing. And you will want to work harder on your goals. Everything will seem easier for you. You will naturally be willing to do what is necessary to succeed because you are true to yourself and your soul.

Your heart knows where you should be and with whom. Follow your heart and trust that it has the correct answers. Your soul knows better as to what is good for you.

Warren Buffet says that you should take the job you would take if you were independently wealthy.

Following your heart is not always straightforward because emotions and logic seep in. These must be quieted so that you can hear your soul calling. You can connect with what is natural for your soul by following this simple formula whenever you are up against a difficult decision.

In your head, follow through with your idea as if you had already made the decision. Then examine your first feelings before fear enters the equation. If you allow anxiety to govern your choices, you will not get very far. Disregard embarrassment of what other people will think, as this may also stop your connection to your heart and soul. Recognize positive or negative core feelings, and then you will know what to do.

This is how to connect with the pure feelings of what your soul wants you to do. Make the decision and then sleep on it. After a good night's sleep, your feelings towards your choice will be evident. The mood you are in the first moment you wake up will tell you if your choice was the right one for you or not.

You can also connect to your heart when you are in the flow state, either during meditation, or a walk by yourself in nature or by listening to calm music or theta waves on YouTube, or when driving a long drive to a familiar place by yourself. When you let your mind relax, you will tend to get answers from your soul.

Once you have decided, know that it will be right for you, and even if you make a mistake, it's the right mistake for you at this time which you can learn from and improve yourself.

When you follow your soul through your heart, you will be faithful to your purpose and your soul's desire. Follow the path that is guided by your heart, and everything will open up for you.

Questions of The Day

To help you connect with your heart and soul when choosing your goals or when making a decision, the questions that you want to ask yourself today are:

What does this choice feel like to me after I've committed to it in my mind? Does it make me feel stronger or does it weaken me? What does my intuition say? Am I doing what I know to be right for me, or am I simply doing what everyone else is doing? Am I doing what I believe I should be doing? Have the courage to follow your heart which will lead you to your soul's desire. Yes, it does take courage, but without courage, not much good can be accomplished.

As usual, I recommend writing your answers in the PDF journal.

Affirmation Of The Day

After answering the questions in your journal, and examining them, sit quietly for a few minutes today and repeat this affirmation:

I LEAD A PURPOSEFUL LIFE BECAUSE I ALLOW MY HEART AND SOUL TO LEAD THE WAY FOR ME.

Repeat this affirmation often. With repetition, it has the power to alter your consciousness so you build a better, happier and more purposeful life.

DAY 9 - BECOMING AWARE OF NEGATIVITY

"Remove all the self-doubt, worry, jealousy, regret, anger, guilt, or any other negative emotions that are holding you back from your happy, fulfilled life." ~ Nanette Mathews

Negativity can sometimes creep up on you, even if you are generally happy. You may have woken up to a negative thought, had a negative encounter with someone, or had a negative experience.

We all have days or periods like this. The key is not to let this negativity spread to more and more days or areas of your life. At times, we all have negative feelings, but they must be stopped, or they can take control over your life.

Things tend to get worse and worse, like a downward spiral when negativity runs out of hand. It can negatively affect your family life, relationships, business or career, and health.

But why does negativity happen?

Negativity happens when your beliefs and reality are not the same. When you believe that something should be one way or that someone should behave in one way, but the situation is different from what you want or expect it to be, you will feel negativity.

And if someone does something disturbing to you, know that it is because they are hurting inside, and they have many negative feelings.

Remember, you are the one who is supposed to be choosing your emotions. Don't give that power away to someone else. Keep your power with you and if someone focuses their negativity towards you, ignore it and let them suffer the consequences of their own negativity.

A downward spiral can also happen when you feel negative feelings towards yourself. When your expectations for yourself do not match reality, negativity creeps in and leads to self-sabotaging behaviors.

Self-sabotaging behaviors are the reason why so many people live unhappy lives. Many people hurt and punish themselves because of negative emotions. Negativity must be acknowledged and released before it ruins your dreams. Don't hold onto negative emotions. Release them. Ask yourself, "Are things as bad as they seem?"

I have found that sharing your thoughts with someone is helpful in getting rid of negativity. It is said that when you share your problems, you halve them and when you share your successes, you double them. Now it's not always comfortable to share negativity. Personally, I'm not particularly eager to spread any negativity I am feeling, so on days that something spins me off to a negative start, I call the free hotline and talk about my problems. You feel much better, and when you dump this negativity somewhere where the other person doesn't know you, then after the conversation, they move on without it affecting them in any negative way, and you feel so much better. In this way, no one is harmed by the negativity.

You can also exercise and release some endorphins to make you feel better. You can get a massage, listen to energetic and happy music, or do a meditation to shift your negative state and focus on what you can do to improve your feelings and your life.

But the first step is recognizing negative feelings and understanding that they must be stopped quickly for your benefit. Whatever the trauma you went through in the past is irrelevant because now you are no longer suffering from the trauma but rather from your distorted views. Remember, negative feelings can ruin your health, relationships, job, career and even your life.

Negative actions such as complaining follow negative thoughts. Your life is your creation, and when you complain, you are taking action on your negative thoughts and creating pain and suffering in your life.

When you complain, you act on the negative side of things, and you feel no control because you are not taking responsibility.

"The only thing complaining does is convince other people that you are not in control." ~Anonymous

If you look towards outside circumstances to become positive, you will wait forever. It would be best if you choose your attitude from within. There is always a possibility to see the positive side of things. It is your choice how you view anything.

I divorced my second husband because of his negativity. He was always complaining. I felt that this was draining my energy and my joy. When we divorced, we stayed good friends, and now we laugh at his negativity. A person who complains cannot be happy because they do not see what there is to be pleased about, and this is why complaining kills off any chances of your dreams coming true and a life of bliss.

Can you imagine how difficult it is to live a life when you constantly focus on what is not there, what is lacking, and what can and must be improved to be happy? Now can you imagine living life while seeing everything as a wonder, as something to celebrate, as something good for you and everyone even if it may seem otherwise in the moment?

You tell me which person you think will have a better life.

A person who complains sees the bad things that can happen and they become paralyzed, sticking to what is known to them. They are often acting from a place of not losing instead of acting to win. This is how they justify their non-action.

High achievers use their creativity to be successful. They don't complain, whine or blame others for their situation. They take responsibility and search for better solutions to their problems.

Not once did we hear complaints from Steve Jobs, Warren Buffett, Elon Musk, Bill Gates, or Jeff Bezos, to name a few people who have really succeeded.

We complain when we don't want to take responsibility for something in our lives or don't want to risk changing our difficult situations. These are the only times when we complain — when we are not willing to do what it takes to become the best version of ourselves. Yes, it takes courage, faith, optimism, and risk, but this is the only way to live your life fully.

Being near a complainer is quite contagious. So it would be best if you made sure that the people around you most of the time are people who see things either realistically or positively.

Complaining focuses on what you don't like, and this doesn't help achieve what you *do* want in life. You may feel that people owe you something. Then you become angry when you don't get what you want. But suppose you focus on what you do have instead of your lack and show appreciation for what you do have. In that case, you will automatically become happier and more grateful because everything that you do have today can be gone tomorrow.

Use your wisdom and imagination to find solutions to your problems instead complaining about them.

Here are a few ways to stop this harmful habit of complaining:

1. Become aware of your behavior. I thought I was an optimist until I noticed how much I was complaining. You must become more aware of your thoughts and words. Catch yourself whenever you are complaining.

2. Figure out what you complain about the most.

3. After you know the primary triggers that cause you to feel this negativity, see how you can take responsibility for this problem so that you can start to deal with it in the best possible way.

4. Take focused action. Talk with the people you need to talk with to change how you are feeling about them. If your spouse or boss leads you to complain, then speak with *them* about what they trigger within you that leads to your complaints instead of complaining to your friends about them. Your friends can't change anything about your situation. So talk with the people who *can* change your situation. Take full responsibility for your feelings and take the right actions to change your feelings.

5. As a metaphor, I will use sand and stone. I say to write on the sand all of your negative thoughts and write on stone all of your positive and grateful thoughts.

6. Do not give your negative emotions ground to grow. Whenever you feel that you need to let out some steam, do what I do, take a nap. It is unbelievable how differently you can wake up. Suddenly all those negative thoughts and complaints that you had running through your mind have stopped, and new, better thoughts of what could be will enter your mind instead.

7. You may also talk to someone about your negativity, as I mentioned earlier in this lesson.

Awareness and understanding bring change. On bad days, remind yourself that tomorrow will be better. Believe this and follow these steps that I mentioned to change your attitude to make your life better.

Questions of The Day

To end this lesson and to help you overcome negativity and stop complaining, the questions that you want to ask yourself today are:

What triggered my negative feelings? Why did I give away my power? How can I prevent this from happening again? What can I do right now to avoid this negativity? What do I complain most about? What actions can I take to change my situation and my feelings? Can I find something positive about my situation? And can I let go of this negativity, knowing it only brings bad things into my life?

As usual, I recommend writing your answers in the PDF journal.

Affirmation Of The Day

After answering the questions in your journal, and examining them, sit quietly and repeat this affirmation:

I RELEASE ALL OF MY NEGATIVITY BY TAKING FOCUSED ACTION THAT WILL LEAD ME TO BE CONTENT ABOUT MY SITUATION. I DESERVE GOOD THINGS IN MY LIFE, AND I DESERVE TO BE SUCCESSFUL IN MY ENDEAVORS.

Repeat this affirmation often. With repetition, it has the power to alter your consciousness so you build a better, happier and more purposeful life.

DAY 10 - BECOMING AWARE OF HOW PAIN CAN BE USEFUL

"There are two types of pain in this world: pain that hurts you, and pain that changes you."
~ Robert McCall

Pain will hurt us until we decide that it can change us. When we suffer from physical or emotional pain, all of our focus goes to the cause of the pain. And this is why the pain does not go away easily.

When the pain is physical, for some people, only taking pain relief will allow them to focus on something else, leaving the body the freedom to heal itself from within. But what do we do when the pain is not physical but mental. How is it possible to stop focusing on pain and suffering? Anyone who has suffered from any relationship, heartbreak, or other emotional crises can tell you that it is not easy to change focus. But using this pain to find something positive can lead to healing. Pain can be very motivating for change and for learning to take responsibility.

Change is never easy, but if there is no change, the pain will persist. Often the only way to relieve yourself of pain is to change something within you. It will help if you change your thought or behavioral patterns or your perspective or level of awareness regarding your power to relieve pain.

When I was married, I never realized how dependent I was on my first husband, who took care of all the bills, finances, and taxes. I never realized that he was caring for all of these things on top of his job while I was doing other things like cooking, cleaning, caring for the children, working part-time, and studying at university. So after divorcing, I had a real shock at what living in the real world involved. I needed to care for everything because no one else would do it for me. It was painful. It was a hard blow. I did not realize how difficult and expensive taking responsibility for everything was.

But after going through the pain and suffering of this new independence, I learned how to take care of everything. The bills, taxes, the car, the law, bureaucracy, and doing the regular housework and caring for the children.

I also got a job and started earning money, and started paying off my debts that I went into after the divorce. Finally, I was on my way to independence, and this seriously raised my self-esteem.

The pain changed me. I swore to myself that I would never again be in a position where I depended on someone for my livelihood. I would learn how to do everything I needed to know to care for my family's and my own needs, even if I would let some help in, but not without knowing how to do what they were doing myself and cope with it just in case.

This pain of being so vulnerable brought me to the decision to change and take responsibility for all areas of my life, which has helped me lead a calmer, happier, and more successful life.

Pain is an excellent motivator for change. Whether you are suffering from any physical condition, or are in a destructive relationship, or are in no relationship, and desire one considerably, or in financial despair, these are all pain.

The pain may be physical or mental, or even both.

You can use pain by focusing its energy towards making the change within you that will help you heal yourself and become better equipped to deal with life's challenges.

When pain is a teacher, we learn to become better at life, but when pain is just pain, we grow deeper into depression and self-deprecation.

Suppose you take a look at physical pain following exercise. This pain shows you that you have improved your muscle tone and that you are growing stronger. This leads, in the end, to more pleasure. You become more powerful, and feel better, and are more relaxed and healthier. When you have no pain following exercise, you know you didn't do enough. The same goes with life. When you go through some pain and surrender to the change you need to make within you and do it, you become stronger and better equipped to deal with whatever the world throws at you.

You are overall more satisfied with yourself after overcoming the cause of the pain, which increases your self-love.

On the other hand, if you suffer some setback which is painful, for example, in a relationship or a business venture, and instead of learning from your mistakes and improving yourself, you sit there sulking and feeling sorry for yourself, you have not learned the lesson, and the mental or emotional muscle has not improved. You will continue to suffer, perhaps even more, until this pain moves you to take action and change. In the end, the pain WILL lead you to act, whether now or in the future, because eventually, the pain of not changing will become more substantial than the pain of changing.

If you suffer from something that is causing you pain, a different approach should be taken, changed from your current approach to the subject.

Bob Marley once said, "You never know how strong you are until being strong is your only choice."

Understand that the pain you feel is actually what points you in the direction towards healing, learning, coping, growing, and making better choices and becoming a better, stronger version of yourself.

The Dilution Method:

However, often these feelings of pain may arouse more negative feelings, which may attract more unhappiness into our lives. It is important to stop these negative feelings before they run out of hand.

Therefore, I would like to introduce you to the dilution method.

You can dilute the effects of what you are not happy about in your life.

It may be something small, but still brings down all of the other areas of your life so much so that you cannot feel appreciative.

* Think of what it is that is making you unhappy. Envision it in your mind.

* See the image of this situation, person or thing becoming blurry and diluting.

* See the negative image in your mind slowly lose its color and become colorless.

* If there are sounds involved with the negativity, turn down the volume until there is quiet.

This will help you take any situation and dilute the effect it has on you. When we dilute the effects something has on us then it will naturally not affect us as much and we can see things in a different perspective. We become more aware.

It is like the popular story of the goat, whereby a family with four children was complaining of their small house. They were living in a small one bedroom house. So the father went to his religious advisor and told him how they were suffering. The advisor told the man to get a goat and put the goat in the house with them and come back for more advice in two months' time. The man asked his advisor: were you not listening to what I said? I said that we don't have enough room in the house, and that we are crowded. The advisor remained silent. The man came home with a goat. Living in the house was now even more of a punishment. The goat was eating everything in the house and leaving excrement all over the floor and beds. It was horrible. After two months the man came back to his religious advisor who now told him, sell the goat and come back in two weeks. After two weeks the man came back all smiles, telling the advisor how happy they all were now in their house and how he had made a profit from the goat which, during those two months, had become very fat.

Sometimes we need things to get worse before we can appreciate what we really have. This increases our awareness. When you remain in your comfort zone, soon you will be complaining about your current situation even if you consider it comfortable today. Now let's be clear, appreciation of something does not mean that we must be completely satisfied with what we have, but it does mean that our vibration is high and then something better can enter our life. When we are dissatisfied, then the vibrations we emit will not be very high and this is what we will attract to ourselves. Keeping a high vibration will allow you to accept more goodness into your life.

Dampen and dilute the power of anything negative that is bringing you down in your life. Do this with your imagination and you will have much more joy in your life.

Questions of The Day

To help you understand the benefits of pain, ask yourself:

Where in my body do I feel pain? Where in my life do I feel pain? In which relationships or environments do I have pain? What actions led me to suffer from this pain? What changes should I take on to help me relieve myself from this pain? In which area of my life do I find myself complaining? Can I dilute the effects of this issue in my imagination?

Now the answers you get will give you hints about what needs to change in your life for you to be happier and more fulfilled. Trust me; I can tell you that even once the lesson is learned and small action steps are taken, the pain will subside. Yet, if the negativity is impacting your life, dilute its effects by using the dilution method, and start to live a happier life.

As usual, I recommend writing your answers in the PDF journal.

Affirmation Of The Day

After answering the questions in your workbook, and contemplating your answers, sit quietly for a few minutes today and repeat this affirmation:

I HAVE THE POWER TO MAKE CHANGE FOR A BETTER LIFE FOR ME AND THOSE AROUND ME! I AM HAPPIER EVERY DAY.

Repeat this affirmation often. With repetition, it has the power to alter your consciousness so you build a better, happier and more purposeful life.

DAY 11 - BECOMING AWARE OF YOUR TRUE SELF

"You are a spiritual being having a human experience" ~ Teilhard de Chardin

Although I been formally educated by universities, I also studied multiple alternative teachings, including mindfulness, meditation, yoga, and spiritual teachings. In one Kabbalah lesson, I learned a concept that I found very interesting. The teacher said that we are like rocks taken off a mountain.

This wisdom resonated with me. My life transformed through that brief sentence.

You see, all of the rocks are OF the mountain; they are part of the mountain each one necessary. The rocks have been separated from the mountain, but they are still an essential part of the whole.

Now let's take this one step further and say that when the rocks are separated from the mountain, they form an ego that differentiates them from all of the other rocks so that, now living all on their own, they will be able to survive.

This ego instills separation from all that is around them to ensure their survival.

The ego, created for survival, is really a hindrance on the path to truth. Because when we think only of ourselves, we are not really caring for survival.

The ego forgot that we all come from the mountain. We are all rocks temporarily separated from all other creations. We can choose to understand our unity or to reveal our ego and emphasize our differences and separateness.

When your desires align with consciousness, which includes unity, acceptance, progress and creativity, then we will have the help of infinite intelligence to fulfill our desires. But when our desires are not aligned with our true purpose, our soul's desire, and our higher self, and seek only to benefit ourselves at the expense of others, we will suffer hardship to realign us with our true path, connected to an overall higher purpose.

One of my clients in her advanced stages of cancer told me that she felt as if the cancer was a wake-up call to change her direction in life. I told her that this was probably true. We get subtle messages during our life, and when we do not listen, the messages get stronger and louder until we finally understand them and make the changes needed. We get calls to wake up from the slumber that we live our lives in to wake up to our true divine nature of being part of all that is.

Each rock may have its own desires, but when we understand that we are all essential parts of the mountain, we are no longer attached to results. There is an awareness that whatever will come of our work and our effort is perfect for us and the good of all.

This is non-attachment or surrendering. And when we surrender to our higher self, being a part of the mountain, then we will reach much more than we ever imagined possible.

When our desires come from the false self, separation, or from the ego, we can only reach so much, and peace of mind and bliss will never come from our accomplishments because we are not connected to our true selves. Whereas when we take action from our soul's desire, and do our best, and surrender the outcomes with the belief that if something is appropriate for the good of all, then it will succeed, and if it is not, it will not succeed, then whatever happens is right just as it is, and will give you bliss.

Do everything you do through alignment with your higher self, and ultimately release any result you desire from the picture because whatever will come of your effort is perfect.

As Buddha says, "Peace comes from within. Do not seek it without." Peace is happiness. When you are in the right spot for yourself and all areas of your life align with your higher self, you will know and see understanding and peace. And the only job you will want to do is bring others to a higher level of consciousness in your unique way, through your unique gifts as being a special unique rock that is part of the mountain. We are all part of the complete, and we all have our uniqueness for which the whole is not complete without.

We may desire beautiful things—a beautiful home, a loving relationship, and good health, and this is not wrong to want these things if the purpose of all of these desires is not just for the accomplishment of them, but rather as a means to bring you closer to your true purpose of being a creator and sharing your gifts and creations for the good of those closest to you and the world.

You are a loving creator in union with all that is.

Everything is part of this mountain but has been separated only from our perspective, but not in reality. We are all interconnected with all life forms around us because we are all part of the same mountain. All creatures and everything we are aware of in this world is part of the mountain but has taken on a separate form.

Therefore, when we reunite with mountain consciousness, our behaviors will change. We will become the best version of ourselves that we have always been, but our ego has caused us to forget this through feelings of separation, limitedness and disconnection, which lead to much suffering.

Questions of The Day

To end this lesson and help you connect with your true divine self and leave any attachments behind, please ask yourself: Where in my life do I keep getting messages that I am ignoring? These messages could be in the form of poor health, poor relationships, failure, lack of money, etc. What is really suitable for me when I remove my ego and think from my true identity as being part of the mountain? What is my true purpose? Do I desire certain people, situations, or things so I can forget or procrastinate on my authentic work in this world, and so I can stay in my prison and continue to conform? Or do I desire from a will to do more and be the best version of my true self?

Examine your thoughts, emotions, beliefs, and attachments. Examine your prison walls so you can free yourself and start to live. Once you understand your attachments, you will free yourself from them.

As usual, I recommend writing your answers in the PDF journal.

Affirmation Of The Day

After answering the questions in your journal, and contemplating your answers, sit quietly for a few minutes today and repeat this affirmation:

EVERYTHING IS HAPPENING ONLY FOR THE HIGHEST GOOD OF ME. I AND EVERYTHING IN MY LIFE IS CONNECTED TO INFINITE INTELLIGENCE.

Repeat this affirmation often. With repetition, it has the power to alter your consciousness so you build a better, happier and more purposeful life.

DAY 12 - BECOMING AWARE OF ATTACHMENT

"Peace comes from within. Do not seek it without. Attachment is the source of all suffering." ~ Buddha

———————✦✦✦———————

There is a belief that if you get what you want, you will be happy, but this is not true as we have all experienced in life. When we fulfill our desires, they will only give us relief for a brief moment in time. We will then find something else to desire that we think we need to help us feel satisfied and happy.

But what if it didn't matter to you whether you reached the results you desire or not?

What if you could detach yourself from the results?

What if you could be happy and live in the world at peace, true peace with yourself, independent of whether you get your desires or not?

When we are in a constant frenzy to achieve our desires, at times, we behave in a somewhat violent way, littered with much effort and intensive work in search of control over our situations so that we can reach our desires.

Well, what if instead of this path, we could choose a way that releases this effort and allows what is there for us to enter into our lives?

When we are living in a state of allowing, things are not so difficult. Much less effort is required, and there is much less stress in our life, and the results are also superior.

So how can we achieve peace of mind while also moving towards a happier and more successful life? The answer lies in your level of attachment to things that you think you need in your life to be happy. You become unhappy because you believe that you will not get your desires or believe that you can't live without your desires. You are attached to the results.

And even if you do happen to achieve your desires, you will still not be happy since your attachment to them then changes form, and you become afraid to lose them.

Anger is presented towards anyone in the way of you reaching your desires. Your perspective on life comes from your attachments. You do not see reality as it really is.

All unhappiness comes from an attachment to results. You think life will not give you what you desire, so you are angry, depressed, frustrated.

The only way to get rid of attachments is through awareness of the hold that attachments have on your life. An attachment is everything you think you need to have to be happy. You were brainwashed to think that you need certain things, so you cling to them.

Attachments threaten your peace of mind and bring emotional turmoil. Any single attachment that is not met will ruin your mood no matter what else you succeed with throughout any given day.

Your attachments are a form of prison that most people adapt to. Some people may fight for better living conditions in their prisons, but they are still in prison. Only a few people who break free from their attachments are free and released from the prison of their minds.

The only way to break free from your prison is first to become aware that you are in jail.

Once you understand that you can be free and happy right now under any circumstance, then you can see how blessed you really are, and you can start to live your life in freedom finally.

Desires are not what cause suffering. We all are born with desires, and this is what moves our evolution forward. It is attachment to specific results that causes suffering.

When you have a desire but you are not attached to the results of your actions, but rather, you are just doing your best to serve your higher purpose, your soul's desire, then you are at peace in this world. You are enjoying the moment. As a result of this allowing state of mind, better ideas, more abundance, and happiness will enter your life without effort, naturally.

When you surrender to the results, there is also no rush, and there is also no anger or frustration when things do not work out exactly according to your plans. Instead, you keep going because it is the progress and the movement towards what you believe is necessary and correct that motivates your actions, not the results.

This steers away from all aggression, violence, and anger because there is patience and pleasure found on the way.

When you do something for the sake of doing it, just because it is the right thing to do, and not for your personal benefit, while surrendering any specific results, then you are free.

This is the key to spiritual living.

Serving your higher purpose allows you to take part in the experience of life with a connectedness to who you truly are; consciousness in material form united with all consciousness.

You do not need to renounce the things you desire, just your attachment to them. You can still enjoy them without being attached to the results. Then you will enjoy them even more because all the stress is gone.

Imagine a couple wanting to build a family, but they do not get pregnant. They can still enjoy their intimate time together and search for other solutions. Research published in the Dialogues of Clinical Neuroscience in 2018 shows that often women will get pregnant once the stress is removed.

In your imagination, only that specific person, situation, or thing can make you happy. If you widen your horizons, you will see that you *can* enjoy many other people, situations, and things.

When you know that whatever needs to happen will happen, all you need to do is your best at all times. Then you have released yourself from attachments.

Of course this does not mean that you should not take action and wait for things to come to you. This is not the way of creation. All creation take on a life of their own.

Make your actions come from your true self, from your soul's desire rather than from your ego.

Rather than coming for your personal good, from separation, come from a place of oneness with all of creation.

When you live like this, in union with all creations, then your life will be whole and blessed because the present moment becomes most important, rather than any future outcome. In effect, success is the path and not the achievement of any goal.

This is how most of the highest achievers have succeeded with their dreams. They did what they believed was necessary and right, and they did whatever needed to be done to advance their beliefs. They enjoyed the process, and the process itself formed their most notable success.

When you think of your soul as eternal, you understand that you will never reach the end. This is when you understand that the process is the most important factor in life. By following the right path for you, you will benefit yourself and all those around you. This is the right way to live life.

When you surrender the results but try always to do your best, without need for personal gain, you will not waver when difficulties come. You will continue on the path towards your goals.

And one day, you will achieve your goals, whether by you personally or by being the stepping stone for the advancement of humanity. As an eternal entity, your soul will be a witness to this success, and your life will have been worthwhile to you in any case when you have passion in the process and enjoy the way.

It is important to note that non-attachment is not apathy, it is not laziness, and it is not giving up. No! It is involvement in what is seen as important.

Non-attachment to results is a state of mind that refers to the results of your actions and to your opinions.

Attachment to any opinion of how things should be and how people should behave will also lead to suffering. When you have expectations from other people to behave in explicit ways, you will often be disappointed when they don't behave in that specific way, and then you will suffer frustration.

When you want nothing for yourself, you also have no expectations from others, and then you can see clearly other people's needs and see how you can serve them best or, if necessary, steer away from them.

When you have attachment issues for specific results, you forget your overall mission and become obsessed with the obstacles on the way to the results that you desire. You get wrapped up in the difficulties and may give up or lose yourself in anger.

If you engage in action for the sake of reward, then the ends will always be more important than the means, and all ways to achieve the end will become acceptable. You will not care if you hurt others to get your results; you will do everything you need to get the desired results. But when you act in this way, even if your results are achieved in the end, you will never be happy, nor will you have any peace of mind. You will be angry, and you will feel guilty, and you will also live in fear of losing your possessions.

As I mentioned before, we each have gifts and unique abilities. We have to bring forth these gifts and use them to benefit ourselves and others. This is our purpose in life. Life is not results-based but action-based.

When you live your life in this way, peace will most often fill your life. Whatever happens in life around you, whether good or bad, will not move you from your course of doing what you need to do. You will continue on your path, satisfied with the opportunity to do rather than anything else.

When you do your best and work on your life's purpose, then other people's reactions to your work will not matter.

You will, of course, still want to learn and improve yourself and your products, but you surrender to what other people do or think about your choices.

Sri Chinmoy, the famous Indian spiritual leader, said that "Non-attachment is not indifference. When you are indifferent, you don't look at a person. You are walking along the street, and somebody is dying of thirst, but you will not look at him. If you are non-attached, your inner being will compel you to give him a glass of water. But if he doesn't drink it, you will not feel sad or angry."

I find this to be the perfect description of non-attachment or surrender. You do what is right and what you are compelled to do no matter how other people react to it without expecting anything in return.

When you are results-focused, you actually make yourself smaller than what you can be when you dissociate yourself from the results. When you free yourself from results, you also free yourself from competitiveness and likes and dislikes.

Your heart fills with joy when you act generously and with compassion without expecting anything in return. Also, peace of mind comes your way when you surrender the results because you can never really control outcomes or results anyway.

Any form of overthinking about something also comes from attachment to results. Relax. Allow your mind to think these thoughts, but remember that you are not your thoughts. You are the observer of your thoughts, so do not confuse your role.

There is no need to get anxious or worried because of your thoughts. Most of the time, worrisome thoughts never come to fruition, and often lead to anxiety disorder according to StatPearls 2021, so do not judge. Just relax and live your life on purpose, with passion, and surrender to what is.

Do not identify with the things happening outside of your control, and do not try to interfere with things happening outside of your control. This will only lead you to unhappiness.

And the same with people. Do not try to control people. This will only eventually lead to your suffering.

Not all things will go according to your plans, but when you give your best to what you love doing and what you feel is right and worthwhile while not causing harm to another and while emotionally letting go of the results, then you are living in the now, and this is bliss.

When you understand that you really need nothing in return for doing what you love and feel is right to do, then you know that you are already rich, and you already have peace, abundance, and prosperity.

Non-attachment is very much a conscious choice rather than a typical reaction. In the beginning, this practice may not come naturally to you. But when you keep going over this lesson and start to implement this outlook into your life, you will have so much joy just from doing what you are meant to do, and the worry and anxiety you may have had will all naturally dissipate from your life leaving you fulfilled and joyful.

Questions of The Day

To end this lesson and help you remove attachments from your life, ask yourself:

Where in my life are the results of my actions more important to me than the actions themselves?

Once you know this, change your attitude. Do what you love for the sake of doing it, without tension or worry. Give thanks for the opportunity to do, and your life will be much happier and much more fulfilling.

As usual, I recommend writing your answers in the PDF journal.

Affirmation Of The Day

After answering the questions in your journal, and examining them, sit quietly for a few minutes today and repeat this affirmation:

MAY MY ATTACHMENT TO TRANSITORY THINGS SUCH AS WEALTH, FAME, AND COMFORTS DECREASE EVERY DAY, SO I CAN DO WHAT I LOVE WITHOUT ATTACHMENT TO WHAT WILL BE.

Think of how much freer and happier you can be with this line of thought guiding your actions.

Repeat this affirmation often. With repetition, it has the power to alter your consciousness so you build a better, happier and more purposeful life.

DAY 13 - BECOMING AWARE OF EVOLUTION

"Perhaps our greatest distinction as a species is our capacity, unique among animals, to make counter-evolutionary choices." ~ Jared Diamond

We are the only species that has free will. We can choose a good path, and we can choose a path that is detrimental to us. Craig D. Lounsbrough said, "It's not that I've been invited to the hole I'm standing in. It's that I accepted the invitation."

There are many times when we have to choose to take specific action or not, so how do we know that what we are choosing is really the right path for us and that we are making the right choice?

We can listen to our intuition, but for many, we have not yet developed this gift because we are not aware of our true divine nature. To help you in choice-making, we can look at choices in two distinct ways:

The first way is the 4:1 method. Take a look at your hand and your five fingers. Make all choices so that four fingers represent your selection's effect on your future, and only one finger represents the impact your choice has on your current level of happiness.

What does this mean?

It means that ⅕ of the weight of any decision should provide immediate gratification, while ⅘ of the decision-making process should consider the long-term implications for you, your loved ones, and the world around you.

Although we can make choices counter to our evolution, we want to make sure that we are not making such choices. Choices that go against us are often choices that come from our ego, which has a false image of our identity and pushes us to fulfill our mistaken identity rather than our true divine nature.

Choices that come from our ego are usually choices fueled by selfishness, greed, and an immature line of thinking.

By examining the effect your choice may have on yours, your loved ones, and the world's future much more than exploring the impact it will have on your level of immediate pleasure, you learn to take a look at the decision through a different perspective. You have a clearer perspective of the situation, which is not affected by your present mindset or current emotions. So your choice will not be influenced by petty things that are of less importance to the bigger picture of your life.

A few examples of this are:

1.   When choosing your partner for life, you want to have in mind ⅕ attraction and ⅘ sharing values and moral code. If you have similar values and ethical principles, your future together as parents and friends will be much more satisfying and fulfilling for you and everyone around you.

2. When choosing your line of work, you should give ⅕ power for your current salary and 4/5 power if the job can offer you a place to grow and develop new skills and become a better person in the future.

3. With health, it is the same. Once every five days, you can indulge in comfort food, something that is not the healthiest of foods, but on the other four days, you want to make sure that you are feeding your body nourishing foods that support your health. And when doing exercise, you should have four days of practice and one of less physical exertion.

The 4:1 method is the best way to make any decision, but there is also another way. The way I will introduce now is best for significant decisions. The second method for making the right decisions is to think of your decision's effect on the next two generations of your lineage. For example, consider how this choice you are now making will impact lives 40-80 years down the line. Now I know this sounds crazy, but if you think of it, this type of thinking has led us to where we are today as a species.

Our previous generations made most of their decisions to allow us to live the free life that we currently have to enjoy. We must also care for our future generations in the same way we were cared for by our previous generations. This is why every choice we make must consider the future to ensure the vitality of humanity.

Remember that not only will you have to live with the outcomes of your choices, but so will your future generations.

This line of decision-making led me to consider my knowledge of health, sustainability, and global warming before deciding where to invest my money, which car and clothes to buy, which foods to consume, and my lifestyle.

Now, you want to have a little enjoyment from your decisions, but only 20 percent of the thought process should be for current pleasure, while you should focus 80 percent of the thought process on the future consequences of your decisions.

Every action we take will affect the world around us whether we like it, believe it, or not. So it is wise to consider the consequences of our actions before taking them.

Questions of The Day

To help move you towards making better decisions for yourself, ask yourself:

Where do I need to make a decision in my life at the moment, and what would I choose if I thought in the 4:1 method of four thoughts for the future and one thought for the present? Now can I take this decision process even further and think of my choice's effects on my future generations. What decision would I make if I took the future into major consideration?

As usual, I recommend writing your answers in the PDF journal that you have received with this book. Then look over your answers to ensure that you improve your life and bring forth your true divine nature.

Affirmation Of The Day

After answering the questions in your journal, and contemplating on your answers, sit quietly for a few minutes today and repeat this affirmation:

I MAKE THE BEST CHOICES AND DECISIONS FOR MYSELF, MY FAMILY, AND THE WORLD, AND I TAKE FULL RESPONSIBILITY FOR ALL OF THE CHOICES AND DECISIONS I MAKE.

Repeat this affirmation often. With repetition, it has the power to alter your consciousness so you build a better, happier and more purposeful life. Have a wonderful day

DAY 14 - BECOMING AWARE OF PEOPLE PLEASING

"I can't tell you the key to success, but the key to failure is trying to please everyone."

~ Ed Sheeran

You can never fail more and make your life more miserable than when you are trying to please everyone. It is an impossible task to be liked by everyone. The most challenging part of living as a people pleaser is that you have a continuous battle inside your mind of how you should have behaved and what you could have done or said differently, making you miserable.

The typical behaviors of people pleasers include:

- Fear of being rejected by anyone in any way
- Being occupied with what others think and feel about you
- Being hungry for the approval of others
- Giving more than you get in relationships while being neglectful of your own needs
- Fear of saying no to people and not setting boundaries
- Being afraid of seeming "mean" towards others

People pleasers feel rejected by other people even when other people may not be offended by something they have said or done.

We tend to have these people-pleasing tendencies because getting along with other people was essential for our survival as ancient humans. But now things have changed. There are many more people around you than there ever were for our ancestors. This makes people pleasing everyone, something that is not in favor of our survival anymore and impossible to achieve.

Some people have remained people-pleasers, even if it does not serve them anymore. People-pleasing is a sure way to fail in life and become very unhappy.

An example from my life comes from my clinic. As a natural-born people pleaser, helping people through dietary changes to heal themselves is probably the worst career choice I could have made. Why? Because people get great enjoyment from eating junk food. They get a high when they eat sugar-rich foods with fats, making them feel great, but just for a few minutes. But they still don't like to hear that their food choices and habits brought them to where they are today; sick, overweight, unhappy, and with many other issues.

In my clinic, I have to be the party pooper, which is no fun thing for a person who grew up as a people pleaser. You see, most of these people-pleasing tendencies are so deeply ingrained within us and follow us from childhood. This behavior often comes from our family dynamics. In many cases children who received conditional love from their parents, meaning that the child would receive love and acceptance only when they behaved in a certain way, or did not receive enough affection, moved the child to want to behave in a way that would please their parent, and allow them to receive attention. So the child may start as parent pleaser and then take it up a notch to become an everyone pleaser.

Of course, people do not like to leave their comfort zone. People do not always willingly change their habits. I used not to like leaving my comfort zone and talking to people about their eating habits and why they need to change them for their own benefit, but, with time, I learned to do it anyway, since it was the right thing to do and they really needed to hear it. Some people were just not aware of the effects of their choices or from where their choices came. In the end, I understood that I was not changing their eating habits but waking them up to reality.

Know that love does not need to be earned. People who genuinely love you will love you and accept you just as you are. You may want to change or improve yourself, but those who love you will still accept you as you are today.

Instead of trying to make up problems in your mind, allow others to tell you if there is a problem, and if they don't say there is a problem, then stop making the problem up in your head.

Stay true to yourself and let your light shine.

Changing behaviors is never easy, and to this day, I still find myself sometimes going back to my people-pleasing ways, but I am more aware of this and change it immediately.

A fundamental key to making the change is to work on your self-esteem.

The simplest way to do this is by learning not to tie your self-worth with what others think of you, but rather with just doing the best you can in any given situation.

If you can say to yourself that you love yourself and appreciate yourself by doing the best you can in the given situation, no matter what the outcome is, and no matter what other people think or say, your self-esteem will grow. Soon enough, you will be capable of saying no and placing boundaries, and doing what is suitable for you in the time you have.

I work in the mornings on my writing. If people call me during this time, I will not answer unless it is a call from my daughters' school. No one else will be able to reach me until I finish my writing for the day. This helps me do the best I can with my writing. If I allow people to interfere, I lose my focus and cannot do the best to spread my knowledge with the time I have, so I don't permit it anymore.

Learn what you need to do to place boundaries to do your best in the areas of life that are most important to you.

Questions of The Day

To end this lesson and to help you stop people-pleasing and help you become true to yourself, ask yourself these questions:

Where in my life am I forsaking my truth for the validation of others, and where am I putting the desires of others before my own needs?

The answers you write for these questions will be pretty revealing for you, I am sure.

As usual, I recommend writing your answers in the PDF journal that you have received with this book to look over your answers and ensure that you improve your life and bring forth your true divine nature.

Affirmation Of The Day

After answering the questions in your workbook, and contemplating your answers, sit quietly for a few minutes today and repeat this affirmation:

I HAVE HIGH SELF-ESTEEM TO DO WHAT IS RIGHT, AND I TREAT MYSELF WITH KINDNESS.

Repeat this affirmation often. With repetition, it has the power to alter your consciousness so you build a better, happier and more purposeful life.

DAY 15 - BECOMING AWARE OF DISAPPROVAL

"Disapproval is a very important factor in all progress. There has really never been any progress without it." ~ James H. Breasted

When you do something greater than yourself, there will always be disapproval of you and your thoughts and actions by other people. This is human nature. We are all different, and there will be people who disapprove of your way, which gets more profound the higher up you go on the ladder of influence and power.

The more chances you take, the more disapproval you will get.

But it is possible to stay happy and calm even if people disapprove of you.

First, you must understand that people view qualities differently. For example, one leader may be considered stubborn, domineering, reckless, and even foolish, while other people may view this person as decisive, progressive, open to change, and strong.

This is what is going on in my country at the moment. A little less than half of the population views our current prime minister as a very negative person, and they go out and demonstrate and rally against him almost every day. On the other hand, over 50 percent of the population loves and adores him and thinks he is the very best. They keep voting for him, and he keeps winning elections.

We all make different impressions on different people. People interpret behaviors in different ways.

No matter what you do, there will be people who will disapprove of your way of life, and this is very important to understand. You will never get 100 percent of people to like you. It is impossible to avoid disapproval. We must have some objection. Parents who always approve, affirm, and praise their children hinder their spiritual growth.

The only way to stay happy despite disapproval is to accept yourself fully and see it as a natural part of life. When disapproved of, you should first consider whether you should make any improvements or changes to your line of thought and behaviors. Perhaps you need to make a change and learn to become a better version of yourself. This is especially true if the disapproval comes from someone close to you who usually has your best interest in mind. You should consider what they are saying, but you also should make any decisions from your internal compass. Even close people may disapprove of something you do even if they think they have your best interest in mind, and they may not always be correct.

When you are internally controlled and you follow your internal compass, you can stand up for your beliefs and values no matter what other people think or say.

When you have disapproval from others but honestly believe that your way is the right way to think and act and are not apologetic, then you are more internally controlled, which means that you are the master of your mind whereby you are more in control of your thoughts and feelings rather than having your thoughts and feelings controlled by sources outside of you.

When you are externally controlled, it is a sign of low self-esteem. You may think that you are not competent enough to make the right choices for yourself and are constantly apologetic for things, even when there is nothing to apologize for.

Of course, your actions should not deceive people or cause intentional harm to others. But if you are coming from your highest self, this will never be the case. When you are aware, you will not hurt others with your actions and choices.

After I gave my TEDx talk on the ideal diet for humans, it was seen by millions of people around the world. I understand that changing food choices is not comfortable for most people, and our food choice habits are embedded into our consciousness for generations, even if they are not healthy. I knew that there would be some disapproval even though I knew that what I was saying was based on a substantial body of research and that it was the truth. One day I went into the comments and decided to read them as if they were not talking about me as the speaker. Some people disapproved of my talk, and others were fighting for me. I distanced myself and became an observer instead of coming from a place of involvement. I didn't take any of the comments personally.

Not taking things personally will help you handle any disapproval. When you stand up for your beliefs, the walk may not be easy, but people will come around to the truth in the end. There is a saying that goes: First they ignore you, then they laugh at you, then they fight you, then you win. Think of what happened to Galileo Galilei; he was condemned during the Roman Catholic inquisition for his support of the model that the earth and planets revolve around the sun rather than Earth being the center of the universe.

They say that all truth passes through three stages. First, it is ridiculed. Second, it is violently opposed. Third, it is accepted as being self-evident.

If people were always seeking the approval of others, we would have never come this far as a species. Catch yourself apologizing for something that you know is right, and stop doing it. Stop steering away from disapproval at all costs.

Follow what you believe, and apologize only if you internally verify your mistake.

Maintain internal control and trust yourself.

Remez Sasson, the self-improvement author, said, "Your mind is your instrument. Learn to be its master and not its slave."

Your mind was intended as a tool to help you see reality and to create what it is that you desire by gathering knowledge and being creative. But, when you let your mind lead, then you will know much suffering.

The meanings our mind gives to things often distorts our view of reality as it is. We start confusing between what we want to be real and what *is* real. And then, to reduce the confusion, we build up stories to support mistruths that we believe to be real.

And when we go further from reality, we will suffer much disappointment and frustration in our lives.

To lead a happy and fulfilled life, you must have control over your mind. If you allow your mind just to run rampant, it will start a downward spiral of thoughts that will lead to depression, addictions, misery, and lack in all fields of life.

When you understand that you are not your thoughts and feelings, then you can control them and direct them in the direction of your desires. You can see that most of what you thought was imagined and did not come from truth, which never considers feelings, or beliefs about a thing, just plain truth or reality.

Your mind is in constant chatter, trying to make sense of things to match your beliefs and thoughts. But what if your thoughts and beliefs are wrong. Your mind will still try to make sense of them and elude you further and further from the truth.

This is why many wise people meditate. They stop the non-stop running of thoughts through the mind, and by doing this, they can clear up the fog and allow themselves to be more connected with life as it really is in the present moment.

Our mind also forms the false identity of our ego and is constantly trying to hold this mistaken identity together. But all we need to do is understand that we are not our mind but rather the observer of our mind. We are part of source, and our mind is a powerful tool that we have to make the most we can with our human experience.

We cannot reach our fullest potential when we do not have control over our mind. Our mind will lead us to anxiety, fear, worry, victimhood, and all of these negative feelings and beliefs that we hold when we do not control them. But control over our minds will only happen when we hold the reins of our thoughts, beliefs, and perspective and put our minds on the right track for us.

The amount of control you have over your mind determines the quality of your life.

You think that what goes on around you determines the quality of your life, but this is not true.

Michael Singer said, "Your mind is the biggest bully that has ever walked the face of the earth." Think of what your mind is constantly chattering about. Think of the uncontrolled inner conversation that is going on in your mind, and you will most often agree with this statement.

So now that you see how your mind can either make or break you, how do you control it?

The answer to that is simple, but its practice may take years to accomplish. You connect with who you truly are, and then you don't need anything outside of you to be happy, loved, and abundant.

You have to look inward for truth, happiness, and fulfillment.

When you quiet the mind, you can tap into your intuition, and you will know who you really are, an irreplaceable part of the puzzle of consciousness. An important rock from the mountain.

The funny thing is that controlling the mind is not done through force or effort. We can only do it by releasing who we think we are to reveal who we really are. Release your unwanted baggage held in your mind blocking you from reaching your fullest potential.

Following the spiritual path is always about getting rid of something, not adding something. We already have all we need to be happy and fulfilled within us. We just need to remove the blockages that block us from knowing and feeling this. When we release our limiting thoughts and beliefs, we become free to enjoy life as it is, an opportunity to be who we are and give from our true divine nature to the world.

Once you get rid of what doesn't serve you in the form of limiting thoughts and beliefs, then you will not hide your true highest nature behind the fog, and you will shine your light in the world.

Through practice, your self-reflective capacity increases. Just make sure to maintain the right relationship with your mind, where you are the master, and your mind is your servant.

Questions of The Day

To end this lesson and help you maintain internal control of your mind and your choices, ask yourself:

What chatter is going on in my mind that is blocking my path to unlimited joy? What thoughts and beliefs am I holding that makes me think of my limitations instead of my gifts? Where in my life have I encountered the most disapproval? How did I react? Do I think I did the right thing without harming others intentionally? Did I do my best? What can I do differently so that next time I accept disapproval as a natural part of life?

If you have not encountered disapproval, perhaps you are behaving in such a way that is too people-pleasing, and you are leaving your true self out. If this is your situation, then ask yourself, what do I believe to be accurate, but instead of following this truth, I am conforming to other people's points of view?

Now that you understand what is blocking you from mastering your mind and life go out and release these burdens from your life and allow your true divine nature to shine through. All you need to do is to be present. Allow your true nature to reveal itself. Release the tension, anxiety, stress, frustration, unhappiness, and disappointment, and just live. Do your best to show your light and remove from your life whatever is blocking your light from showing up. Just by recognizing your limiting thoughts, you will already release some of their effect on you. Do this persistently, and you will succeed.

As usual, I recommend writing your answers in the PDF journal.

Affirmation Of The Day

After answering the questions in your journal, and contemplating on your answers, sit quietly for a few minutes today and repeat this affirmation:

I ACCEPT MYSELF AND MY BELIEFS. I AM WHOLE AND COMPLETE. I AM THE MASTER OF MY LIFE. I HAVE ALL I EVER DESIRE RIGHT WITHIN ME.

Repeat this affirmation often. With repetition, it has the power to alter your consciousness so you build a better, happier and more purposeful life.

DAY 16 - BECOMING AWARE OF REALITY

"Reality is only a reflection of our own intentions, biases, knacks and desires." ~ Abhijit Naskar

So, how do we know what is real and what is not? Some say that we need to create our own reality and other people say that we need to live in reality as it is so that we are connected to what is happening around us and not living with pink glasses on.

So what's the verdict? And how can we tell if we are living in reality or are living in some made up reality that we have invented in our minds?

Reality is simply what is. Without having any meaning behind it. Without it being defined as good or bad. It is just what is—nothing more and nothing less.

Often we may think something is real because we believe we "know" it. To give something meaning, we need to judge it. And we assess things by whether they are good or bad for us at that moment. In nature, there is no bad or good. There just is. The meanings we give to things are only in our minds. If you think about it, there are many meanings that something can have. It depends on the onlookers'. The onlooker determines the meaning and, thus, whether something is good or bad, comfortable or uncomfortable, etc.

The meanings we give everything in life form our reality. We choose the meanings; therefore, we basically create our reality, really just as if we are writing a story. The fact is that most people do not see reality as it is. We give meanings to what we hear and to what we think we hear. We give meanings to what we see and to what we think we are seeing.

We may give meanings to things, and situations or come to conclusions to match our sometimes extraordinarily distorted view of reality.

But even when we positively distort our reality, is this good? Well, it is certainly better than when we give negative meanings to things through negative emotions. But even if you are creating a pink picture of reality and don't see reality as it is, it may be comfortable in the short term, but it may lead to much suffering in the long term.

The meanings we give to things become the beliefs that can stay with us forever unless we understand and become aware that the meanings we give to things are not truths. We cannot change truths or facts, but we may change the meanings we give to things. The reality we formed due to the meanings we gave to things can be changed by changing our beliefs about something.

For example, when my mother married her second husband after divorcing my father, her new husband said to me, now your mother has a new family, so go and find something else to do. I was only sixteen. When my mother didn't intervene, I thought it meant she didn't love me. This event ruined my self-esteem and led me down a path of addictions. But in reality, many years later, my mother told me that she had never heard her husband tell me this. Whether this is true doesn't matter. It changed my view of reality.

Since we all have an imagination, we can create meanings to situations through our thoughts. So basically, every human can live in a different reality. Any two people may have different views of reality because no two people went through the same experiences and gave the experiences the same meanings. Even twins, who grew up with the same parents in the same environment, may interpret situations and experiences differently depending on their previous interpretations and mindset.

But why do we give meaning to things?

Because usually, the reality is more painful than the vision we have created for ourselves of reality. But seeing things in a distorted way will not clear away the future consequences and suffering of a distorted image of reality.

Only when you see reality as it is will you learn to thrive in the real world.

Only when you face reality as it is, will you become strong enough to face the world and thrive in it, and create new possibilities for yourself in life. You are also more capable of seeing opportunities for solving any given problem and taking better action. You do not need to give something meaning to act.

For example, during the coronavirus lockdowns in 2020, many people lost their jobs. If we give a meaning that being laid off means we cannot survive or care for our family, then we become overwhelmed with fear and cannot think straight or find better strategies to cope with the situation. Living a simpler life and cutting unnecessary expenses during that period until things changed could only be a strategy if we see reality as it is and accept it.

What is, simply is, without having any meaning.

A fly is just a fly, but if the fly disturbs us, we give the fly meaning, and we immediately view the fly as a nuisance.

Or we can give meaning that sunshine is not good because it can cause skin cancer, and then we suffer the consequences of vitamin D deficiency such as lowered immunity, depression, hair loss, and more.

We can choose to eat unhealthy foods believing that they are good or that health is all in our minds, but physical laws all have consequences.

When we distort reality, we will suffer the consequences whether we had a positive mindset or not.

When you remove the meaning that you gave to something, good or bad, you instantly remove the feelings that come with it, and then you clear your mind from it. When you are free from having an emotion about something, you see things more clearly and make better choices for yourself today and in the future.

Questions of The Day

To end this lesson and to help yourself see reality with a clearer lens, please ask yourself:

In which area of my life am I distorting reality and choosing a view that is not real to make me feel better in the moment and justify my actions? Can I change my opinion of the situation, person, or feeling in any field to a view of reality without judging anything, just seeing the situation, person, or feeling as they are? As usual, I recommend writing your answers in the PDF journal.

Affirmation Of The Day

After answering the questions in your journal, and contemplating on your answers, sit quietly for a few minutes today and repeat this affirmation:

I AM SUCCEEDING IN THE WORLD BECAUSE I AM CONNECTED TO REALITY, AND I CHOOSE MY ACTIONS IN ACCORDANCE WITH REALITY.

Repeat this affirmation often. With repetition, it has the power to alter your consciousness so you build a better, happier and more purposeful life.

DAY 17 - BECOMING AWARE OF SELF ESTEEM

"You can never have too much self-esteem." ~ Nathanial Branden

Some people mistake self-esteem with boasting or arrogance, but these are not signs of self-esteem. These are, in fact, evidence of a lack of self-esteem and lack of security in a person. A lack comes from the need to receive some positive feedback from the environment.

So what is self-esteem?

Self-esteem is what a person **really** thinks about themselves and how a person feels about themselves. Self-esteem has nothing to do with what other people think or feel about you. Only what you think and feel about yourself. Although other people can influence your self-esteem, they have much less influence than we have on our level of self-esteem, which we influence through the internal dialogue that we have going on in our heads.

Self-esteem is being confident and trusting in your ability to care for yourself and to choose the best for yourself, and to believe that you can cope with whatever lies in front of you in the best possible way. It is a feeling that you are worthy and deserve good in your life. Self-esteem is the basis for a favorable outcome. It builds self-respect, which is essential for all of your relationships.

Having high self-esteem allows you to treat others with more respect and acceptance, which leads to even more self-respect coming back to you. It is an escalating spiral that gets better and gives you more as you gain more self-esteem. Self-esteem rises when you succeed at something, but it also begins the process of success because you will fail to act in the right way if you lack self-esteem in the first place.

You cannot be happy even if you succeed when you lack self-esteem. You can push to success without having much self-esteem to prove your worthiness to someone else. But this success will never make you happy or satisfy you because you do not feel that you are worthy of it or are enough. You will always feel that you need more and more to prove yourself to others. No joy will come from such a situation.

When you develop some self-esteem, this allows you to persist even during challenging and difficult times and respond to challenges that life throws at you more positively. Developing self-esteem also makes you happier, which is another basis for a favorable outcome in all fields of life. Denis Waitley, the motivational speaker, said, "It's not what you are that holds you back, it's what you think you are not."

A person cannot have "too much" self-esteem, just as a person cannot be "too happy" or "too healthy". There is no such thing as too much self-esteem. When you trust yourself and your choices, you can expand your limits. You can seek new challenges, and you are more capable of achieving your desires. Overall this is a healthy state of mind when compared to motivation that comes from fear. Fear is a motivating force that shows low self-esteem, which leads to self-doubt and anxiety. And when you justify your fears, this may lead to real tragedy for you and everyone in your surroundings. This is not genuine self-esteem. This is showing a false identity. When we look outside of ourselves to build our self-esteem, we will not succeed, and as I stated, it often leads to much tragedy in peoples lives.

The first step is always the most difficult; that's why it is good to build your self-esteem at school age, where small successes at school and in social situations start the elevation process of self-esteem. But even if you are past school age, you can still develop self-esteem at any age throughout your lifetime. We can improve our self-esteem in the following five ways:

1. Self-esteem rises when we show integrity when the behaviors that dominate our character are assertiveness, honesty, and kindness.
2. Self-esteem comes from self-acceptance, and this can be achieved easily when you cultivate the self-discipline to behave in the right way, and cultivate good habits that will ensure you make the right choices automatically.
3. Self-esteem comes from taking on responsibilities and not shying away from responsibilities. It would be best if you also took on responsibility for your actions and the consequences of your actions, both actions from the past and in the present, as well as future results.
4. Self-esteem comes by taking conscious actions against our fears.
5. It is also essential to cultivate the habit of gratitude which we will cover later. Being happy with a half-full cup instead of focusing on a half-empty cup is crucial.

These five ways build more self-esteem. When you are authentic, honest, and have the self-discipline to behave correctly, you achieve high self-esteem, which will help you in every field of life.

It would help if you lived your life intentionally to improve and grow as a person every day. Focus on growth as a person, which will lead you to take on more challenges and more significant goals that are all in line with your true purpose and who you really are. And very importantly, eliminate any negative self-talk about yourself and don't tolerate negative talk from others about you or other people. Do not delve into gossip. Gossip may appear to increase your self-esteem because you see yourself as "better than". But in reality, gossip, which comes from the ego, will make you very unhappy and lower your self-esteem.

When your self-esteem is high, you will naturally be more open, honest, less anxious, fair, and will not feel threatened by other people, and you will welcome clarity rather than uncertainty.

High self-esteem will help you enjoy life because you appreciate who you are, and you reap the benefits of your actions.

You can be either your best friend or your worst enemy, depending on your self-esteem level.

Questions of The Day

To end this lesson and help you increase your self-esteem, ask yourself:

What makes me feel good about myself? What would make me love and accept myself more? Who are the positive people in my life? What successes am I proud of? What am I grateful for in life? As usual, I recommend writing your answers in the PDF journal.

Affirmation Of The Day

After answering the questions in your workbook, and contemplating your answers, sit quietly for a few minutes today and repeat this affirmation:

I AM WORTHY OF HAPPINESS, I AM LOVABLE JUST AS I AM, AND I LOVE AND ACCEPT MYSELF AS I AM. I TAKE FULL RESPONSIBILITY FOR MY ACTIONS AND CAN IMPROVE WHATEVER NEEDS IMPROVEMENT IN MY OWN EYES.

Repeat this affirmation often. With repetition, it has the power to alter your consciousness so you build a better, happier and more purposeful life.

DAY 18 - BECOMING AWARE OF SELF-CONTROL

"In that power of self-control lies the seed of eternal freedom." ~ Paramahansa Yogananda

Self-control is the equivalence of freedom and mental health. Psychology shows that the amount of self-control we have is in direct proportion to our mental health.

Can you remember a time when you were madly in love with someone? You may have lost all self-control and felt despair when things took too much time or did not go as you wish. This is a time when mentally, you were less stable.

There is a direct connection between the amount of self-control we have and how good we feel about ourselves, and this goes in both directions.

When we feel that we are holding the steering wheel of our lives, we feel happy with ourselves. We will feel bad with ourselves when we feel controlled by someone or something external to us.

If we truly want to control our destiny and be happy with ourselves, we need self-control. But what exactly is self-control? According to the dictionary, self-control is "the ability to control oneself, particularly one's emotions and desires, especially in difficult situations."

To attain self-control, we need awareness that we can control and change our feelings and emotions at any moment. When you have control, especially in difficult situations, you also control your destiny.

Having self-control allows you to control your destiny because of the law of cause and effect, which Ralph Waldo Emerson called the "**law** of **laws.**" He said it is the most crucial lesson involving human conduct and interaction. This law states that we reap what we sow. We always control what we sow; at all times. We control the causes (thought, beliefs, words and actions); therefore, we control the effects (the physical manifestations or results). People who live a harmonious life with peace of mind, happiness, health, and abundance have self-control. They have the discipline to rule the causes, and thus they can control most of the effects or the results they have in their lives.

When I first learned this law I was shocked. It transformed my life because I realized that I am the creator of my life. I have power over my life and my destiny. I understood that we are all very powerful.

When you have control over your thoughts, beliefs, words, and actions, you control the physical manifestations in your life or your reaction to them. The causes in your life are the thoughts and beliefs that you hold. These form your words and actions that lead to specific physical manifestations.

Now it is essential to state that you may not get the exact results you desire. You may think that you are doing everything right but are still not getting the results you want. As I mentioned in the non-attachment lesson, relax and do your best to control your mind and actions, and what you will reap may be much better than you could ever imagine, and it will come at the right time for you. Maintain complete control over your mind and actions and continue on your path while enjoying the work. You will be rewarded when the time comes in the most perfect way you could ever imagine.

If you want to live a life of bliss, you will have to take control over your thoughts, beliefs, words, and actions today. This will change the direction of your life. You see your life through your beliefs, and you will not let thoughts that negate your beliefs enter your mind, even if your beliefs are false. Limiting beliefs are often wrong, yet if we believe in them, we will only allow things into our lives that correspond to these beliefs, even when they are mistaken.

We live in accordance with our beliefs. If, for example, we don't believe we are good at something, even if we are, we will no longer participate in that activity.

When I was a student during my first degree at university, six months after I began studying, I was involved in a serious car accident, a head-on collision with another car. It happened right after my first semester exams. I was in the hospital and missed three months of the second semester. Because I missed so much, I would have to wait until the next semester to resume my studies. I was sure that I was not good enough to continue, so I decided to leave university after healing. Then one day, I received a phone call from the head of the faculty where I was studying. He asked me when I planned to return to university. I told him that I did not intend to return because I was not a good student anyway. He told me that my grades were of the highest in the class. I was shocked. I did not believe it. He told me that I excelled in all sciences and that it would be a great injustice if I did not go back to my studies.

From that moment, my beliefs changed about my studying abilities, and I finished my first degree in two and a half years instead of three. Suddenly, I believed in my abilities to study, and I managed to study more than everyone else did during every semester. After finishing my first degree, I studied for two master's degrees and then a doctorate. This shows the power of beliefs.

When we take control over our thoughts, beliefs, words, and actions, and ensure that they are pointing us in the right direction for our fulfillment, then we determine the quality of our life and our destiny. Michael Altshuler said that the bad news is that time flies; the good news is that you are the pilot. You will create the destiny you desire through self-control over your thoughts, words, beliefs, and actions.

Questions of The Day

To end this lesson and help you increase your level of self-control, ask yourself:

What do I have in my life that I am not happy with at this time? What thoughts, beliefs, words, or actions have created my current situation, and what thoughts, beliefs, words, and actions can bring me towards my desired life of bliss?

Now all you have to do is take control over your thoughts, beliefs, words, and actions, to point you in the right direction. As usual, I recommend writing your answers in the PDF journal.

Affirmation Of The Day

After answering the questions in your journal, and contemplating on your answers, sit quietly for a few minutes today and repeat this affirmation:

I AM POWERFUL. I AM THE MASTER OF MY DESTINY. I CHOSE MY THOUGHTS, BELIEFS, WORDS, AND ACTIONS WISELY AND PERSISTENTLY.

Repeat this affirmation often. With repetition, it has the power to alter your consciousness so you build a better, happier and more purposeful life.

DAY 19 - BECOMING AWARE OF YOUR THOUGHT PATTERNS

"The primary cause of unhappiness is never the situation, but your thoughts about it. Be aware of the thoughts you are thinking." ~ Eckhart Tolle

To be aware of your thoughts, you must know what to look for. It would be best to recognize faulty thought patterns that hinder your development and stop you from reaching your dreams. So today we will talk about the twelve faulty thought habits that hamper growth and what you can do to change them.

1. **Jumping to conclusions.** How many times do we reach an assumption without having the relevant information? We do this so often, but this hinders our growth. For example, how many times have you thought that some goal was not attainable? How often did you think you had to do something or have something to reach a goal and found out someone else did it without having what you thought was necessary. Our assumptions may or may not be accurate. Ask yourself: where is the evidence for this belief? Ask yourself: could I be jumping to conclusions? People say that you need to have money to make money. This is not true. You have to have an idea to make money. We tell ourselves so many stories that are simply not true, but these stories actually block our path to success. Where in your life are you jumping to conclusions and thereby preventing advancement for yourself?

2. **All or nothing thinking.** This black or white pattern of thinking blocks out so much potential. Where in your life are you thinking in all-or-nothing terms? Perhaps there are other colors on the spectrum that you are blocking out. Perhaps there are different ways to reach your goal. Thinking in terms of black or white blocks out a lot of opportunities.

3. **Placing the blame on others.** This happens when you do not take full responsibility for your actions or the results of your actions. You blame others for your situation. How can you move forward when you think others are to blame for your current situation? You can only move forward and advance towards your dreams when you take full responsibility for your current situation. Only from this step will you make the necessary changes needed to move forwards towards your goals.

4. **Using derogatory tags, labels, or names.** A competent person will stay competent as long as their mind forces them not to believe otherwise. You are in control of your words, so use them wisely. Be aware of your words and their power, as we talked about on day 5. Do not talk badly about yourself just because you may have made a mistake. Ask yourself whether you are focusing on your weaknesses instead of focusing on your strengths? Your subconscious mind should never hear you say anything critical about yourself because this is much more damaging to your self-esteem than having other people say something bad about you. When you start to believe it, it becomes a self-fulfilling prophecy.

5. **Negative expectations.** How many times have you spoken negatively about what the future holds for you? I had a client who showed me messages that she sent to her friends two years prior, saying that she will probably get cancer from all her stress. Two years later, she was battling cancer. Think about whether you are expecting adverse outcomes for yourself. You do not want to be telling yourself anything that you do not wish to have

happen in your life, ever! Ask yourself whether you are predicting an outcome instead of experimenting and seeing what is possible.

6. **Low tolerance levels**. You may find yourself saying, I can't stand stupid people, I can't stand slow drivers, I don't like X,Y, and Z. I can't tolerate X, Y, or Z. This thinking limits your coping abilities and limits opportunities from growing and increasing your self-esteem. This is a genuine limiting belief. What you can't tolerate in others is often something you need to fix within you. Where are you impatient? Where are you less understanding? And how can you become aware that all people have annoying behavior at times, including yourself. Being more patient and accepting of others is a crucial step towards awareness and bliss.

7. **Fear of what others think of you.** This type of fear comes when you fear that other people will see your authentic self instead of the mask you put up. This belief disrupts any chance for meaningful relationships, and this causes significant problems in the work environment. We are all humans, and we all have faults. Suppose you remain authentic and understand that you also have shortcomings. In that case, you can remove this fear and start to live life to your full potential without fearing making mistakes.

8. **Personalization.** It is taking an event personally. Taking something personally is a negative thought pattern that has a major effect on your well-being. This leads to many negative emotions. There are endless examples for this faulty thought pattern. Ask yourself if you are taking things too personally. Not everything has to do with you. When you take things personally, you simply add stress and anger to your life without reason. Ask yourself whether this has to do with you before you take on any consequences personally.

9. **Disproportionate thinking**. This happens when you overreact. Your expectations are based on assumptions without any accurate proportions. This leads to excessive anxiety and worry. Stress, anxiety, and worry in any field of life will prevent progression and prevent you from reaching what is best for you.

10. **Minimizing your achievements**. Making excuses for your achievements, like saying that the competition was easy today and so that's why you won, lowers your self-esteem. This is unfortunate since all your actions success come from what you believe about yourself. Do other people agree with these assumptions? Is this real? Celebrate your successes no matter how small they may seem to you.

11. **Mistaking feelings for facts.** You are in love with someone and feel he is the only person who can ever make you happy. You think you cannot take one more day, or you cannot continue with this even though the benefits you will reap if you continue will be immense. These are examples of mistaking feelings for facts. You may say things like I feel like I'm losing my mind, or I know this will never succeed, I know I can't get a higher price. All of these feelings are not connected with reality. They are assumptions, and they limit you from ever really trying, which will undoubtedly limit you from reaching any success. Ask yourself if this what you are feeling or if this is real.

12. **Too high demands for yourself and others.** This very rigid pattern of thinking puts a heavy weight on your shoulders and on all the people you come in contact with. "I must do this, I should have done this, he should have done that." This type of thinking lowers your self-esteem, especially when you don't stand up to your expectations, and this leads to resentment when other people don't stand up to your expectations. It burns you out and leaves you tired and frustrated. To be happy, you need to recognize your accomplishments,

your advancements, and other peoples' efforts.

I will now conclude with a 7 step action plan that can help you improve your thought patterns.

1. Ask yourself if this is real. Is what I'm feeling an accurate indication of what is or was going on? Do not make assumptions based on your feelings. Look for evidence. Ask colleagues what they think. Perhaps you CAN break the habit and prove it was wrong.

2. Learn self-acceptance. Accept yourself as you are. Nobody is forcing you to improve yourself. Do it only if this is what you desire to do. Improve yourself and your situation only if this is your wish.

3. Be kinder to yourself. Would you judge others as you judge yourself? Probably not as harshly. Treat yourself with more courtesy and dignity.

4. If you have the habit of taking on all of the blame for situations, ask yourself if really only you were to blame. Were you the only one responsible for the result? It is essential to see things realistically. Divide responsibility in a pie chart to see your actual part in the responsibility for a situation. On the other hand, if you blame others for your situation, perhaps you also had a side in the results. Think about this and take responsibility to ensure it doesn't happen again.

5. See the grey. More often than not, things are not black or white. We are complex beings, and most situations are complex. This change of perspective will help you examine the problem through the right eyes, with less rigidity and more awareness.

6. Leave out the "should's" and "must's", and "I can't take this". This line of thinking increases stress levels. You want to down tones the extremes. For example, this is, or this is not **advisable**, **preferable**, or **desirable**. This will help reduce the pressure on your back and let you live life more happily.

7. Lastly, you may want to go over this list of negative thought patterns when you are under stress or in a negative mood to help you pinpoint the negative thought patterns you are using unconsciously. This will help you slowly become more aware of your thoughts and actions to prevent negative thought patterns from taking over your life in the future.

We will go into depth for some of these negative thought patterns in future lessons to support new habits more readily.

Questions of The Day

To end this lesson and to help you remove negative thought patterns from your mind, apart from the questions mentioned above, also ask yourself:

In which area of my life am I feeling stressed, or am I underperforming or procrastinating, and which thought patterns are behind these behaviors?

How can I learn to accept myself, be kinder to myself and replace these negative thought patterns with what I want to have in my life instead?

As usual, I recommend writing your answers in the PDF journal.

Affirmation Of The Day

After answering the questions in your journal, and contemplating on your answers, sit quietly for a few minutes today and repeat this affirmation:

I ABANDON ALL THOUGHTS THAT NO LONGER SERVE ME AND PREVENT MY GROWTH.

Repeat this affirmation often. With repetition, it has the power to alter your consciousness so you build a better, happier and more purposeful life.

DAY 20 - BECOMING AWARE OF YOUR BELIEFS

"A thing is not necessarily true because a man dies for it." ~ Oscar Wilde

Today we will talk about the beliefs we hold. Sometimes our beliefs about ourselves and our abilities are correct, but sometimes they are false. As Oscar Wilde said, false beliefs may lead us to death, even when we are physically alive. We can be dead on the inside when we hold certain beliefs. We see our life through our beliefs, and we will not let thoughts that negate our beliefs enter our minds.

Our thoughts and beliefs form a vision of the person we see ourselves to be. Now this vision we hold of the person we see ourselves to be is what controls our actions. We will always act in accordance with our beliefs. We will not be able to act differently than the person we see ourselves to be would behave.

The person we see ourselves to be is based on our former thoughts, beliefs, and experiences and the stories we tell ourselves in our minds. All our behaviors come from this vision of how we see ourselves.

However, scientific proof shows that human potential is much more than what we are currently bringing forth. Scientists say that we are only using a tiny percentage of our brain's capacity compared to what we can employ. Some say that we are using only between 1-10 percent of our brain's ability.

Our potential is so much higher than we believe it to be.

But we limit ourselves based on what we believe is real. This is why these beliefs are called limiting beliefs. They restrict our capacity because we now know that people will only reach the potential they believe they can achieve.

It's that simple. We won't be able to do something if we believe that we cannot do it.

As Henry Ford stated, "Whether you think you can, or you think you can't, you're right."

Did you know that you have a vision for your ability in every single field of life? And all of these visions come together to form the total image of who you see yourself to be.

You will always think, walk, talk, act and behave in absolute alignment with the person you see yourself to be—no less, but also no more.

By changing the small visions and beliefs we hold of ourselves in areas of importance for our success, we can change the image we have to a better, happier, aligned picture of ourselves. An image aligned with our true essence, connected to infinite intelligence.

We hold visions for our abilities from everything about how we look, cook, dress, drive, which sports we are good at, to even how good we are at reading, memorizing, parenting, weight management, how musical we are, how good we are in specific fields of study, how fast we can learn a language and which languages we can learn and which not, and even how good we are between the sheets.

There are countless small visions that we hold about ourselves and our abilities in every field of life.

Anything we have experienced in life, and we believe about it, will influence our behaviors and actions. Anything someone has told us about our abilities in a particular field during our growing years may have registered and become our belief about ourselves that formed our current vision of reality.

Our visions about every aspect of life influence our perceived abilities. These visions together, especially for essential areas, form our total concept of the person we are.

To change our beliefs, we will need to change this vision of the person we see ourselves to be one area at a time.

But to what should we change our vision?

Most of us hold a vision of the ideal person we would like to be, the person we could be when we reach our highest potential. This vision comes from our soul, and we shed light on our ideals through the people we admire throughout our life, through the books or biographies we read, through movies we watched, and through seminars we attended, etc.

Together, the characteristics of the heroes we admire, form a vision of our ideal self, our soul's desire. This helps point us in the right direction to where we truly want to be in life. You see, not all people admire the same people, and not all people have the exact wishes or desires.

If we choose to, we can slowly change our beliefs and thus our behaviors to become more in line with the ideal vision we hold of ourselves.

This ideal vision is one that we *can* reach when we have self-control over our thoughts, beliefs and actions. This was covered in a previous lesson.

To change our behaviors in any field of life, we will need to change our vision of the person we see ourselves in that area of life.

So how can we do it?

We can change a very negative field of life to a very positive one by practicing positive thoughts and beliefs for that area of our life. Our thought patterns are as they are through repetitive practice of thinking them over and over again. To change our thought patterns, we must think of new, more beneficial thought patterns over and over again. A new thought held in your mind only once is not enough to change deeply ingrained thought patterns.

Only with time and repetition can new neural networks form. Then new thought patterns will become your new default thought patterns, bringing you to a much better place in life.

You choose to see every situation in a negative or positive light. Positive people form the habit of seeing things in a positive light. Very simple. This allows them to relate better with other people, they interact better with other people and find the good in everything, so they are willing to take more risks because they care less about rejection. They believe that everything is in their favor, always.

This line of thinking is a habitual thought pattern that they have formed by practicing it for long enough for it to become a habit.

Positive thinking is basically the habit of seeing **ourselves as winners in every field.** Holding the vision that you are a winner in every area necessary for your advancement is the basis of positive thinking. Positive thinking is the basis for creating the beneficial habits that lead you to become the ideal version of yourself.

Once you see yourself as a winner, you will have an overall vision of you being a winner, which in essence, you are, and this will lead you to a life of bliss.

But the key towards changing your vision from the person you are today to your ideal version of yourself is by doing it in a relaxed manner, not forcefully.

When you make these mental changes with love and in a relaxed way, you will have a much better chance for success at embedding these new thought patterns into your life. Effort, stress, and force will only delay or ultimately hinder this developmental process.

The more effort you put into changing your thought patterns, the further you move your desires away.

If you try to force things to happen faster than they should, especially when the change is mental or emotional, you may bring on to yourself deep frustration, stress, and confusion. Relax, believe in yourself and your abilities, and continue to focus on your ideal. Take action, but you allow the change by relaxing your mind on the mental plane.

Questions of The Day

To end off this lesson and help you make the mental and emotional changes necessary for you to live a life in bliss, ask yourself:

What areas of life do I hold limited visions for myself, and what is my ideal in these areas of life?

As usual, I recommend writing your answers in the PDF journal.

Affirmation Of The Day

After answering the questions in your journal, and examining them, sit quietly for a few minutes today and repeat this affirmation:

I ENTERTAIN ONLY SELF-NURTURING BELIEFS OF ME BEING A WINNER!

Repeat this affirmation often. With repetition, it has the power to alter your consciousness so you build a better, happier and more purposeful life.

DAY 21 - BECOMING AWARE OF LIMITING BELIEFS

"All things are possible if you never give up". ~ Jesus

If your goal is meaningful to you, you should go out and do your best to achieve it. Otherwise, you may regret not doing whatever was possible for you to do at the time.

My ex-husband's mother was in hospital following a stroke. She was intubated and anesthetized twice. My ex-husband and his brother had a difficult decision to make. Her blood oxygen saturation levels were going down, and they had to decide whether to intubate and anesthetize again. His brother said they must try, whereas my ex-husband didn't want to go through this torture again. He did not believe it would help. He had lost hope, but in the end, they agreed to try. After three days of intubation and sedation, they extubated her. Suddenly while coming out of sedation, she recognized her boys and expressed her love to them. They were together for one more day. She was smiling and happy during that day, and they all had the opportunity to express their love to each other before she died a natural death the following day. It was clearly worthwhile that they tried. For a short time, she was still there with them, and they could lovingly say their final goodbyes. She understood what they were talking about, and it was something so beautiful to see.

What we have today in the world all around us would have seemed impossible to a person living only a short while back. Supermarkets, smartphones, cars, toilets, electricity, and refrigerators would have seemed like an impossible dream to most people until it became possible.

Only our limiting beliefs are holding us back from achieving what we desire in life. Even if we do not want much, just to have a family, and have enough income to support our lives and have health, this may seem basic for some, but it seems the world for others. Everything is possible, and if the usual route to having something specific is not an option, nowadays there are so many other routes to achieving what we desire. For example, having children; now there is in vitro fertilization to help women become pregnant, and if the woman doesn't have a husband, she can choose a mate in a sperm bank to help her have a child. And if she is too old to have children, she can adopt or have an egg donor.

The same goes for earning an income. There is no need to have a university degree. Today there are countless opportunities to study something you like, and within a few months, you can already be working in that field. You can work for yourself online or open anything with practically no financial investment doing something you love. The only person stopping you is you. Only you are blocking your abundance because of the stories you tell yourself. You may believe that you have no control over this internal dialogue going on in your head-well, you do. When you choose to become a little more flexible in the way you view life, you become more open to different opportunities and lines of thought. Look at Oprah's story. It is truly astonishing what she became. And the secret is that she did not put herself in a box. If you find yourself in a box, you can come out just by opening the lid and opening yourself to what is possible for you.

In life, our beliefs change as we grow older. We may have believed in fairy tales, tooth fairy's and Santa's reindeer's when we were younger, but we outgrow these beliefs. We can do the same with our limiting beliefs. We can outgrow them.

See how many times you say the word "But". As the renowned speaker Les Brown says, "but" is a dream killer. There are places we want to go, things we want to do or have, and then there is the but word, arguing with our mind about our limitations. This is a daily war between our soul and our ego. But comes from our ego, and our mind finds excellent arguments for our limitations. And when we have such profound evidence for our limitations, we get to keep them.

Be mindful of your internal dialogue. Be conscious about what you are trying to spare yourself from this negativity. Are you trying to spare yourself rejection, embarrassment, or disappointment? Thank your mind and ego for the effort but release these negative limiting beliefs.

In a simple method, we can leap out of our limiting beliefs. I call it "The Wall" meditation. The first step is to know where you want to go. Create an image or movie in your mind of what each area of your life would look like if it were perfect. Once you have created this movie, you have opened doors of possibility.

You will never be able to get anywhere that you cannot see as a possibility in your mind. However, you CAN get anywhere that you can envision in your mind. If you see something in your imagination, you can reach or attain it.

Once you have visualized your ideal version for any area of life, and you would need to improve to get there, imagine a massive wall between where you are today and the ideal you. See yourself standing there as you are today on one side and the ideal version of yourself on the other side of this vast and endless wall.

Now imagine yourself making a hole in the wall. Every day you come back and do the work to make a hole in the wall. This work becomes a habit, and every day you are there doing the work grinding away at the wall. Eventually, one day as you work, the wall begins crumbling, and before you know it, the whole wall has collapsed. You run towards your ideal self and become one with it. There you are now, standing in the place you desire to be. Now it is yours. You have become one with your ideal self, your soul's desire.

Do this visionary meditation at least once every few days, and soon your limiting beliefs are removed, and you will notice that you have changed for good. You will notice small things about you that were not there before. You will see that you have more courage and that you are more powerful and assertive. Your whole life will start to change after this short awareness meditation that you've achieved by guiding your imagination to where you want it to be.

You can do this! Know that any behavior or thought, or belief that you hold also influences the immaterial/spiritual world. And what you affect in the immaterial/spiritual world comes back to you. Direct your thoughts into positive directions, and doors you never imagined will open up for you.

Questions of The Day

Now, to help you with the visualization process, ask yourself the following question: What would my life be like if this area of my life was perfect? Imagine this ideal situation in your mind when you have some quiet time alone time for yourself. Imagine the ideal image in your mind and do the wall-crumbling meditation which I have recommended here. You will soon see yourself where you dreamed you would one day be.

Affirmation Of The Day

After answering the questions in your journal, and contemplating on your answers, sit quietly for a few minutes today and repeat this affirmation:

I VISUALIZE THE ATTAINMENT OF MY GOALS, AND I KNOW THAT MY SUCCESS IS REAL.

DAY 22 - BECOMING AWARE OF YOUR CHOICES

"All men are created equal, they are endowed by their Creator with certain unalienable Rights, that among these are Life, Liberty and the pursuit of Happiness.

~ Declaration of Independence, USA

———————⊘⊗⊗⊘———————

The declaration of independence was signed almost 250 years ago on the 4th of July 1776, making the thirteen states united, free, and independent, and no longer under British rule.

This is a compelling statement suggesting that all people are equal and have the freedom for life, liberty, and the pursuit of their happiness.

But do we really live our lives in freedom and see ourselves as equal.

The unfortunate answer is no.

We conform our behaviors to societal norms, often following what our parents and their parents did. With time, these norms become our identity. We conform to behave in specific ways, think in certain ways, and even react to things and situations in particular ways.

Television from an early age shows children how they should behave, what they should eat and what they should wear.

What we watch on television and social media dictates a conformative behavioral pattern.

This is how we are expected to behave, and anything outside of this norm is considered crazy, faulty, or wrong by people around us and even by ourselves.

So, are we really free?

In truth, we do have free will that is entirely in our own hands. We can choose our thoughts, beliefs, actions, and environment for the most part. We can live happily ever after or live in sadness, anxiety, and fear. The choice is always in our own hands.

But when we look at the world around us, we see that we are not really free. Most people put themselves into a comfortable box, and anything that threatens their presumed identity is seen as a threat.

And what about equality? Most of us spend our days belittling ourselves and feeling inferior to others. Our minds think that others are better than us. After all, they have studied more, they were in this or that job, they are married, they have more money, they are taller, thinner, stronger, and this list goes on and on.

Although we are entitled to life, liberty, and the pursuit of happiness, it is WE who get in the way of us having true freedom, having a life of bliss, and the joy that we desire in life.

We block the greatness and abundance that we deserve from entering our lives. We stay in bad relationships just because we don't want to be seen by society as failures. We stay in jobs we hate because we fear that we will not be accepted for anything better, and we stick with our bad habits because we love the comfort and fear the change.

We lock ourselves in a self-made prison, believing that we cannot get out. It is like the story of the elephants at the circus. The story starts with a boy who came to visit the circus with his grandfather who used to work there. After the show, he was curious and went around the back of the tent where he saw the elephants. They were tied with a thin rope to a small pole. The boy noticed the flimsy rope and asked his grandfather why the elephants didn't just walk away. The boy understood that the elephant was much stronger than the rope and the pole holding him. His grandfather explained that when the elephants were very young, they tied them to the ground with robust ropes and pegs. They tried over and over to escape but to no avail. As the elephants grew older, they were tied with lighter ropes, but the elephants did not try to break free ever again. This is what we tend to do in life. We take things as truth and never again examine whether what may have been valid years ago is still accurate and relevant for us today.

Most of us live in the prison of our minds, never having second thoughts about whether this is really the truth or just an opinion. These thought patterns form our life and determine whether we are happy or not, free or not, alive and awake or not.

It takes great courage to test the rope again to see if we are really tied down. And it takes even more courage when we recognize that we are really not tied down, to walk away and do what's right for us and those around us.

We can walk away from the confinements of our ego that we have created in our minds. We are all equal in our ability to choose what is suitable for us. All we have to do is stop conforming to other people's standards and beliefs and start living the life we were meant to live.

So how do you do this?

In Eastern traditions, people are taught to remove themselves from a situation by examining it from the outside. You separate yourself from the situation, which allows you to contemplate and make the right choice for you. Removing yourself from the situation will enable you to free yourself and follow your true, free nature.

You can take yourself out of any situation by becoming an *observer* of the situation instead of someone taking part in the situation. I mentioned this a few times before.

This will allow you to determine whether this behavior or emotion is still fitting for you. By distancing yourself from this behavior or feeling, you can see if this is really the right way for you to behave and act. To see if this is still your truth. Does this behavior resonate with your true being?

Societal norms will slowly have less power over you, and you will reveal your true self. You become free from the reigns of external forces and open to your true light and destiny.

So are you conforming, or are you free to be true to yourself? Do you feel a sense of equality with the people you admire?

All you have to do to have Life, Liberty, and the Pursuit of Happiness, is to distance yourself and separate yourself from any given situation and see how your true self would choose to behave and react in that situation.

Questions Of The Day

So, to become more aware of your reactions, please ask yourself:

Am I really free, and am I really living the way I would choose to live my life? Am I really doing what is suitable for me? Am I truthful to myself?

If I knew I could, what would I do differently? How would I choose to live my life if I knew I honestly had the freedom to choose?

You do have the freedom, so go and choose your destination and do what you can to get there. As usual, I recommend writing your answers in the PDF journal that you have received with this book. Then look over your answers to ensure that you improve your life and bring forth your true divine nature.

Affirmation Of The Day

After answering the questions in your journal, and contemplating on your answers, sit quietly for a few minutes today and repeat this affirmation:

I AM OPEN TO GIVING MYSELF THE FREEDOM TO BE ALL THAT I CAN BE.

Repeat this affirmation often. With repetition, it has the power to alter your consciousness so you build a better, happier and more purposeful life. Have a wonderful day!

DAY 23 - BECOMING AWARE OF YOUR BEHAVIORS

"You cannot change your destination overnight, but you can change your direction overnight." ~ Jim Rohn

We can't change where we are overnight. Still, in a minute, in one decision, we can choose a different and better direction for us.

So how do we make this change in direction? The first step is recognizing behavior that is not leading to your happiness. As I stated before, without awareness, there can be no change.

If we take eating as an example. About 90 percent of the time, we choose our food unconsciously. We are not aware of the choices we make. We are making our choices unconsciously and automatically, which is happening in all areas of our lives. So the first step is to become aware of what we are currently doing. In this example, we first want to realize how we are now eating. At which times are we eating? What are we eating, and what inspires our choices and food times. This awareness will reveal a lot to you about why you eat the way you eat.

The second step is to determine what you want to have instead of the existing behavior. With what would you like to replace the current behavior? What is the ideal behavior for you? For example, you would like to know which foods are healthy and nourishing for you and always have these foods readily available.

The third step is to imagine your reality when the new and desired behaviors become your habit. For example, you will have great days without thinking about food, weight, or health because these will come naturally to you. Instead, you will have the time and energy to focus on other things that make you fulfilled.

The fourth step may be surprising for you. Still, it is a crucial step for changing any unwanted behavior. You want to examine your current behavior that you wish to change and determine why you think you chose to behave in this way in the first place. We acquired most of our automatic behaviors through genetics or by copying significant figures during our early years of life, being told what is right to do or not. Our parents, siblings, important adults, caretakers, and teachers often influenced us while we were growing up.

Think about how these behaviors may have served you at a different time in your life. Maybe you were eating a lot because you were told that it would help you grow strong, or perhaps you were told that eating a lot will help you have more energy. Whatever the reasons were at the time you picked up these habits, usually from the time you were born till the age of about seven, these were real and relevant positive motives that led you to want this behavior. Figuring out what these positive motivators were at the time that led you to believe that these habits were good for you is a crucial step in becoming more aware of your current behaviors and what made them your default behaviors today.

Things change in life, and circumstances change. The behaviors that once served you may no longer be relevant.

As you become aware of why you chose these previous behaviors, you will respect yourself for caring for your needs at the time.

And now, to respect yourself and care for your current needs, you become aware that you need to change your behaviors to match your current needs, goals, and circumstances.

Now you are forming a new agreement with yourself to be responsible and care for your new needs.

And this is what you will be telling yourself whenever it is time to make a choice connected with what you wish to change.

These are the four first steps towards changing any behaviors that do not serve you anymore. You understand that you must replace old behaviors with new behaviors that help advance your soul's desire. Even though previous behaviors came from a version of self-love, now changing these behaviors also comes from a place of self-love.

Now there is also a fifth step, the implementation step.

To implement the new behavior, it must be embedded in your subconscious mind, which is responsible for its implementation. To do this, it is vital to hypnotize your mind through visualizations, repetition of affirmations, and control of your thoughts. Some of these were covered in previous lessons, and others will be covered in the coming weeks. Slowly, these practices will help you make the necessary changes to make significant progress in your life this coming year.

Questions Of The Day

To end off this lesson and help you become aware of your behaviors and where they are leading you, ask yourself:

Which behaviors am I holding that are no longer relevant for my current situation? And what is the positive aspect that made me form this habit in the first place? And why is it no longer relevant to my life? And which habits and behaviors should I take on to support my soul's desire?

As usual, I recommend writing your answers in the PDF journal.

Affirmation Of The Day

After answering the questions in your journal, and contemplating on your answers, sit quietly for a few minutes today and repeat this affirmation:

I GROW IN STRENGTH WITH EVERY FORWARD STEP I TAKE.

Repeat this affirmation often. With repetition, it has the power to alter your consciousness so you build a better, happier and more purposeful life.

Have a wonderful day!

DAY 24 - BECOMING AWARE OF YOUR FEELINGS

"What we feel is a choice." ~ Piyush Shrivastav

Our emotions are our choice, and we CAN control our feelings.

This is not an easy thing to do since the way we react to any situation is wired within our brain through neural networks firing in a specific way for a very long time. But we CAN change our emotional reactions.

As you know, the first step is always awareness. You have to be aware of your emotions, of what you are feeling, and when you tend to feel this way.

What are the triggers that set off this emotion within you? For example, you can get angry when your children do not listen to you, or you can deal with the situation in a more effective way.

You can get angry when you are stuck in a traffic jam, or you can choose to react differently and see it as quiet time for yourself. You can't change the situation; you can only change your reaction to it.

For every situation, some people will react differently than you. The way we react is not set in stone, and we know that neural patterns, and therefore also emotional states, can be changed.

When you examine your reactions, and become aware of what triggers them, and work to change them into more beneficial states of emotion, then you take responsibility for your feelings, reactions, and life.

I know how difficult it is to control your emotions as they come, but you can also manage your emotions after they arrive. You can choose not to stay in the negative state of emotion but to replace your state with a more positive one. So how do you do it?

Well, there are three steps towards changing your emotional state.

Since how we feel is a choice, let's make a better choice and choose the most beneficial emotional state for us.

If you find yourself in a depressed state because of your circumstances, you can change it by changing the physical state you are in. It is not difficult for us to see the physical difference between a person who is happy and a person who is depressed. First of all, they hold themselves differently. A depressed individual will have slumped shoulders, will look down, and will have a sad expression on their face that even their eyes will look slumped. On the other hand, a happy person will usually stand erect with their shoulders back and look more alert, with their eyes more open.

We can all tell the difference. So the first thing that you want to do to change your feeling state is to change your physical state. Stand or sit erect, shoulders back and smile, even forcing a smile on your face. I tell you that it is almost impossible to stand or sit upright with your shoulders back and head held high and feel depressed at the same time. It is a different neural network that allows a person to stand erect and allows feelings of depression and anxiety.

When I first learned this, it changed my life. I was depressed at the time. I lacked the money to support my family; being a single mother of two special needs children with no help from my family was extremely difficult. I was walking so slumped that someone at work told me that I should straighten my back. I immediately noticed I felt much better—that simple change in how I stood changed my mood drastically.

A day later, I was in a medical device shop through my work. There I came across a strap that helps you keep your back straight and belly tucked all day. I immediately bought it and used it daily. I was walking straighter, so I was also feeling better about myself and my life. This strap didn't let me fall back into my unconscious ways. The strap also helped me become more conscious of my feelings.

Change your physical state by changing your posture, your walk, and your face into those of a happy person even if you are not yet happy; this will help you change your emotional state as well.

The second step is language. We already talked about the power of words, which are indeed very powerful. During that period, I remember always asking myself "why me"? and "why did this have to happen to me"? These questions are common among depressed people. But what this question does is place you in a powerless position—one where you feel you have no control and cannot change.

These questions lead to loss of power. If the questions you ask yourself in your head change, your emotional state will also change. We will talk more about this in tomorrow's lesson.

The third step is changing your focus. When you are focused on what is not good, this will keep you in a depressed state. What you choose to focus upon is under your control. If you change focus from what is not currently working for you, you will have mastered a better emotional state.

You can replace negative thoughts of what you *don't* want to have in life with positive thoughts of what you *do* want to have in your life.

I remember flying to Israel from the UK right before getting divorced from my first husband. I went to live for a few weeks at my father's house with my daughters. He told me look at what you *do* have in your life and not only what you don't have. But, at that time, apart from being able to breathe, I couldn't find anything to be grateful for. But I slowly learned to change my focus and look at things differently. When I became aware of my negative emotions, I replaced them with positive thoughts of what I did want to have in my life.

Getting out of a negative emotional state such as depression is no easy task; however, it is a TASK that you must CHOOSE to do.

Depression prevents your progress. Things may not always work out as expected, but they are there to benefit you no matter how you currently view the situation.

Depression is a lack of belief that things will work out well. However, sometimes we may need to reach the lowest point whereby we see no other option but to open our heart and connect with our true identity, connected to Source. When we connect with our soul and our true identity, we can focus on others and raise ourselves from darkness.

The sooner we recognize the changes we need to make, the faster we spare ourselves of suffering.

You are always only one thought away from a positive thought, which leads to a positive mood and slowly also to a better life.

Questions Of The Day

To end this lesson and to help you master your emotions, ask yourself:

How can I change my emotions to make me feel better?

Can I add exercise into my life?

Can I become more aware of my posture?

Can I stop negative feelings by replacing them with positive emotions before they ruin my day?

As usual, I recommend writing your answers in the PDF journal.

Affirmation Of The Day

After answering the questions in your journal, and contemplating on your answers, sit quietly for a few minutes today and repeat this affirmation:

I FEEL JOY AND EASE AT THIS VERY MOMENT. I CHOOSE TO FOCUS ON THE POSITIVE.

Repeat this affirmation often. With repetition, it has the power to alter your consciousness so you build a better, happier and more purposeful life.

Have a wonderful day!

DAY 25 - BECOMING AWARE OF YOUR INTERNAL DIALOGUE

"The saddest summary of a life contains three descriptions: could have, might have, and should have." ~ Louis E. Boone

How many times have you said these words to yourself? This thinking will always bring you down.

Firstly, your way of thinking, or rather your attitude, shows much more than the words you say. Your attitude disturbs your path to happiness and fulfillment and it affects not only you but the people around you.

People choose to stay in your company or not because of your attitude. If your attitude is similar to theirs, they will stay, and if your perspective is different from theirs, they will tend to leave.

You want to make sure that your way of thinking is upbeat, overall optimistic, and positive. You can never hide your attitude from other people. The reason for this is that it shows through your body language, your expressions, and even your slightest movements.

People can pick up on your attitude whether you like it or not. People will know your state of mind because we, as humans, have lived for millions of years without having the ability to talk or communicate with words as we do today, but there still was communication between people.

This is why we can understand each other and know what another person is conveying just by their movements, expressions, and tone of voice. My two eldest daughters cannot speak, but they convey their needs very clearly to me through moans, groans, body, and facial movements. They can even hold a sort of conversation with me because they have learned a form of communication that I understand very clearly. I also noticed this with my ex-husband's mother. After she had a stroke and lost her ability to speak, she still got into real conversations only through slight hand and facial movements and grunts.

We all use this ability even when we are unaware and do not notice that we are using it. We use this ability to recognize what another person is thinking. There is even research that shows what a baby is requesting through different patterns of crying. A baby is communicating, and one can always understand if a baby is hungry, thirsty, tired, or just calling for attention by the pitch and pattern of their cry.

There is a whole science behind facial expressions and eye accessing cues. One celebrity decided to experiment and answer the question of "how are you doing today?" by smiling and behaving as if all was fine while saying the words, "I am fine, I just killed my wife, and now we are all happy," to see if anyone would notice. And what do you think happened? No one paid any attention to what he said, but only to his body language and facial expressions, which were calm and positive.

This story shows that we cannot hide our attitude, and a good attitude is a precursor to reaching peak effectiveness and good results in life. Having a good attitude will help you in your relationships and marriage, in your job and career, in your studies, and with your mental health and physical state.

An energetic and positive way of thinking will make you a magnet to positive people who will always want to hear what you have to say and want to spend time with you. If you are in business, a positive attitude will keep you busy and prosperous.

To change your self-talk from "shouldn't", "can't", "won't", and "impossible" to the more positive aspects such as, "it's possible", "I can", and "I will", you must change the internal conversation you are having in your mind to a more positive one. Changing your inner dialogue is something you want to do because your attitude is working like a magnet, bringing into your life whatever aligns with who you are and how you think.

So how do you change your internal conversation? You change the questions that you ask yourself. Asking yourself empowering questions will help you transform your internal dialogue very quickly.

Instead of asking yourself *"why"* questions, ask yourself *"what"* or *"what-if"* questions. Instead of asking *"Why* is this happening to me?", a much more powerful question to ask is, *"What* can I do to improve my situation and make me feel better?"

Instead of saying I can't do that, instead ask yourself *what can* I do?

Instead of saying I shouldn't do that, instead ask yourself what *should* I do?

Instead of saying I mustn't do that instead, ask yourself what *must* I do?

Or you can go even further and ask *'what-if"* questions,

Instead of saying I can't do it, instead, ask yourself *what if* I *can* do it?

Instead of saying I shouldn't do it, instead ask yourself, *what if* I *should* do it?

Instead of saying I mustn't do it instead, ask yourself, *what if* I *must* do it?

These examples of different sets of questions bring about different answers and different actions. You always want to ensure that your actions following your responses do not cause harm to anyone.

I talked with a teacher about custody of my two mentally disabled daughters. I never believed I was able and strong enough mentally, physically, and financially to have full custody. The only option I saw was joint custody, which was fine, to begin with, but became a real problem when my ex-husband refused to give our daughters their anti-epileptic medications. So they had grand-mal seizures every other day. My teacher asked me a question that changed my whole life. He asked: *What if* you *must* take them full time?

Before that moment, I had never thought of this option. By asking myself a different question, my whole life transformed. When my ex-husband offered me full custody I took it because I knew I was capable.

It is when we become aware of our internal dialogue and then change it to a more positive and supportive conversation that we can transform our way of thinking, and as a result, transform our lives.

Questions Of The Day

To end off this lesson and help you become aware of your internal dialogue, ask yourself:

What can I do that I am not doing now because of fear? What should I do, and what must I do that I am not doing now? Ask yourself *"What"* and *"What-if"* questions regarding your situation.

As usual, I recommend writing your answers in the PDF journal.

Affirmation Of The Day

After answering the questions in your journal, and contemplating on your answers, sit quietly for a few minutes today and repeat this affirmation:

MY POSITIVE ATTITUDE SUPPORTS MY DREAMS, AND I AM MOVING TOWARDS THE LIFE OF MY DREAMS.

Repeat this affirmation often. With repetition, it has the power to alter your consciousness so you build a better, happier and more purposeful life. Have a wonderful day!

DAY 26 - BECOMING AWARE OF REJECTION

"Rejection is the sand in the oyster, the irritation that ultimately produces the pearl."

~ Burke Wilkinson

As young children, two driving forces push our behaviors, and these are:

- To find connection
- To avoid rejection.

Avoiding rejection is very important for our survival since a child needs their parents to survive. Therefore the baby learns to avoid rejection at all costs.

Nature also ensured that the mother accepts the child through certain hormones released into the mother's bloodstream when breastfeeding. These hormones ensure good bonding between the mother and child. But what if the mother chooses not to breastfeed the baby and has difficulty bonding naturally with her baby, or suffers from postpartum depression?

Luckily, the baby will learn behaviors that will ensure that their mother will not reject them. But sometimes these behaviors can influence the child for the rest of their lives if not consciously changed by becoming aware of them.

Feeling accepted is of significant importance for the child's survival. A child would die if its mother rejected it, so we hold the belief that rejection kills. But this is not necessarily true at any age.

If our self-image is tied to what others think of us or how we relate to others, then fear of rejection becomes a major motivator. This creates a lot of stress and anxiety. If you define yourself by how popular you are or how liked you are by other people, then, any threat to how popular or liked you are becomes a major source of anxiety.

It all has to do with how confidant you are in your ability to care for your own needs and make yourself happy without needing anything external to make you happy.

When you reach the stage where you stop fearing rejection from others, then anxiety subsides. Then you become much more likely to attract the best relationship, job, and opportunities for you. You are less needy and fearful, so you become more attractive to others, be they potential friends, lovers, or business partners. You become more attractive to anyone when another person sees you as someone who can potentially contribute to their happiness.

Feelings of belonging and social support are critical for psychological and physical health. When we fear rejection, we try to change who we are to become more compatible with another person and more likable. But if you are not being true to your authentic self and are not showing your real self to the world, you are less likely to have satisfying relationships, business and personal.

Fear of rejection may also lead a person to more solitude because they fear rejection or failure. This is not so bad if you use this time of seclusion to improve yourself into the person you want to be.

Learning new skills will help you build your self-esteem. Think to yourself if you would be attracted to another person who behaves or reacts as you do now.

Ask yourself if you would want to form a relationship with *yourself* as you currently are. Why would you or why would you not? What would you find impressive about your character if someone else came with the same character traits as you? What wouldn't you find impressive about your character? Please be honest when you answer but not overly critical.

We are fixed in our behaviors, and most of our behaviors go unrecognized because they are so automatic.

We fear rejection because of emotional programming, not because we lack anything external. It is an internal job to remove feelings of rejection.

Your internal dialogue is feeding your feelings of rejection and must be stopped.

If you change your internal emotional programming, your fear of rejection will disappear.

When you see yourself as likable and are happy with yourself, then, even if you are not perfect, you will find many suitable matches for you. In fact, by being who you truly are and letting your light shine through, you will form an excellent filter for finding the perfect match for you in all relationships, business or personal.

Many people have less than you and do not feel fear of rejection. It is the programming that makes all the difference.

If you don't see yourself as likable, working on self-love to change your emotional programming is of utmost importance.

It is useless to change your feelings of rejection by changing anything external such as your hairdo, body, clothes, house, or car. If you change these, they may bring you some relief from fear of rejection, but it will be short-lived. You do not need to please other people to banish the fear of rejection. The fear of rejection is caused by you, in your mind, not by other people.

What if you knew that you cannot be rejected unless you choose to be.

Choose not to let rejection in, no matter what.

If someone says something mean to you and you feel rejection coming up, say to them:

"Thanks for sharing your opinion," and smile. Then give it no more thought. Release the feeling. What they think about you is their issue and has nothing to do with you. When you do this you can never be rejected again. The only rejection you can ever feel is when you decide to start believing it.

Think about any situation that came to you in the past, you have handled well. If you were rejected before, you survived. Any moment you go through in life will present the resources you need to overcome its difficulty. You cannot deal with any situation before it comes, only while it is happening. Therefore, a future fear of rejection is a waste of your time and energy. If there is something, you can do about the future, do it, and then release it to be while you enjoy the present moment. Any worry of rejection only weakens you in the present moment. Be yourself and enjoy the moment.

Find a way to ensure that your happiness is only dependent on you and what you can control.

You can control your level of effort, and you can manage your attitude; you can influence your perception. You do not need something external to be happy. Ensure your inner dialogue is empowering you.

You have a choice to do whatever you please with your life and with your money. Therefore you should not allow people to force you to do things you do not want to do or prevent you from doing something you do want to do just because of fear of rejection.

You did not come to this world to play it safe. You came to have fun, to enjoy your life, to be creative, and to make a difference in the world. Be independent in mind.

Nobody is perfect, but all together, all people in the world are one perfect entity. We are all parts of a big and perfect puzzle. Know that even if you are not perfect, you are still worthy of love. We are all worthy of love just by being ourselves. The only thing we can ever be perfect at is being who we are.

Be assertive and tell your genuine thoughts and feelings openly, even if you may be rejected. Practice makes perfect, and the more you speak openly about your feelings, the better at it you become. Being honest about your emotions allows the right people to move towards you and allows the people who are not suitable for you to drift away naturally. Most people prefer someone honest and open around them, so you will be more attractive to more people when you are honest about your emotions.

Introspect and learn from your feelings of rejection. Ask yourself, what is making you feel rejected? The more you understand what is pushing you to these feelings, the better you realize that you are not living in the present moment; you are either living in the past or the future. When you start to enjoy and make the most of your present moment, you can conquer all. You will always have what you need to bear the present moment, no matter how difficult it is.

Questions Of The Day

To end this lesson and help you understand and then slowly remove your fear of rejection to let your true light shine through, please ask yourself:

In which fields of life do I feel a fear of rejection?

What do I think is the reason behind my fear of rejection? Is it being alone or not being good enough?

Can I understand that there can never be any rejection if I do not allow for it?

Can I understand that I do not need to be perfect to be worthy of love?

Can I understand that I *am* good enough right now? Can I allow my authentic light to shine through? Can I let myself just be me?

You did not come to this world to play it safe. You came to bring forth your true light.

As usual, I recommend writing your answers in the PDF journal.

Affirmation Of The Day

After answering the questions in your journal, and contemplating on your answers, sit quietly for a few minutes today and repeat this affirmation.

I CAN DO WHAT IS SUITABLE FOR ME DESPITE MY FEAR OF REJECTION.

Repeat this affirmation often. With repetition, it has the power to alter your consciousness so you build a better, happier and more purposeful life.

DAY 27 - BECOMING AWARE OF THE NEED FOR SELF-LOVE

"It's not selfish to love yourself, take care of yourself, and to make your happiness a priority. It's necessary." ~ Mandy Hale

We are genetically coded to survive, and to do so we need to work together. As children, most of us are raised to be less selfish, which is crucial for finding our place in society. However, as adults, some of us may forget who we are because we are busy solely caring for other people's needs, wants, and desires.

Although it is crucial to help and care for other people's needs, we also need to care for our needs. This means that we have to find the fine line between being of service while also caring for our own needs and desires.

When we care for our needs and when we are true to ourselves, we fill up our cup, so to say, and when our cup is full, we will have abundance to give to others.

Being selfish is different from self-care. Being selfish means that you are not only caring for yourself, but also taking other peoples' resources for your own needs and desires. In this case, you are causing suffering to others as well as yourself. You do not want to be selfish, but you also do not want to be selfless.

We are each important and have our unique qualities that are needed in this world. There is no one else like you in the world. And if you go on giving of yourself to the point that your glass runs dry, you will not be able to give your unique gifts to the people around you who need you. You will not be providing your contribution to the world. You will not shine your needed light in the world.

I remember hearing a fictional story about a man who dies and comes before the angels who decide what will happen to his soul after death of the body. He tells them how he was a good person, how he was honest and law abiding. The angels looked at their papers and asked, where are all the books you were supposed to write? Where are the lectures you were supposed to give, and what about the transformation you were supposed to lead in so many people? The man looked at the angels and had nothing to say. The angels decided that he should have another round at life and sent him back to live an earthly material life again and do the work he was supposed to do in the world.

It is just not good enough to be a good and honest person. Yes, this is the basis of a good life, but it is not why we came here. We each have something to gift to the world, and it is our responsibility to do this. We must not only do what is needed and required of us, but we must also do what we like and want to do in our life (responsibly). This will help let our light shine through. Simple tasks of self-love will help us become happier and this, in and of itself, will make the world a better place for everybody. Make yourself happy to ensure that your cup is full.

You have to honor yourself. You have talents and gifts and passions, and it is your responsibility to find what those gifts, skills, and talents are and work on improving them so that you can give those precious gifts back to the world.

When you recognize and put forth your skills, your contribution to all life magnifies, and the value you provide to society will also magnify. As a result, you will get much reward as your gifts provide value for others.

When you become more self-accepting of who you are and your needs, you will see that, with time, the quality of people around you will match your self-welcoming image. When you are true to yourself, you will naturally have more people around you who accept you as you are.

From my experience I find that some people will not like this change of self-acceptance in you, They may be needy and dependent or may fear you becoming too independent and risk having you leave them. Some people will leave you, but others who are more suitable for you will take their place. This may be seen as proof to you that you are headed in the right direction for you.

During my research on the ideal diet for humans, I transformed our home into a healthier home based on the principles I had gained. After changing our diet and removing all unhealthy foods and products from the house, my husband was not pleased. I became more aware so I naturally wanted my environment to be part of my growing awareness.

Once aware, I could not go back to living as I did before. I also changed all of the cleaning materials in the house to natural ones and all of the hygiene products in our home. Our household also became more sustainable and chemical-free. This change was not immediate. It took time, about a year and a half until all of the changes had become part of our life and home. This was not an easy transition for my husband, who was less aware, but I could no longer live as I did when I was sleepwalking.

With time we changed courses and this is why we divorced, but remained great friends. I did not expect him to live in a way that he did not believe in. But I also did not want to live my life in a way that I no longer believed in. So when we divorced, we both became much happier.

I hope that this example from my life did not scare you that becoming more attuned with who you are will lead to divorce, but sometimes it will lead to changes in your life. However, you can trust me that these changes will only make you much happier in the long run.

A small step towards self-care will open you up to be true to yourself and your soul. A much higher quality of life will open up for you because it is based on who you really are, and not the roles that society has placed on you or what other people expect of you.

You start taking control of your life. And when you take more control of your life, although also more responsibility comes with it, you will be happier. Taking on the responsibility for the destiny of your life is a responsibility you want to take on!

So where do you begin?

As always, with awareness.

Think of all the things you love in life but are not giving them space because of all of the many excuses you give yourself, including lack of time, unease, or other responsibilities.

Of course, when you make any change in your life, it will require a reorganization of certain parts of your life to allow this new priority. And this may be uncomfortable at first.

Working with the ambulance service during my medical studies taught me that anyone can die at any moment. You never know what will happen to you. We have one shot at this round, and we should aim to do the best we can be to make the space around us better for everyone else now and in the future.

The second step you can start to do is start saying, "No, I'd rather not."

You cannot do everything. There are things that you must pass on to achieve your full potential. Start saying NO to things that are of less importance, so that you can start saying YES to things that matter.

The third step is to commit to doing something small for yourself daily.

Yes, daily.

Even for a few minutes daily, become more self-loving and think about your needs and desires. Do something for yourself that you may be scared to do or never found the time or courage to do. Exercise, listen to music, sing, play a musical instrument, read, go for a walk in nature, swim, introspect, meditate. Do something just for YOU.

You can be both self-loving and selfless at the same time.

Invest in yourself to have a higher quality of life. You can take care of other people's needs while also caring for your own needs at the same time.

Questions Of The Day

To end off this lesson and help you recognize your own needs and encourage you to become more self-loving, ask yourself:

What can I do for me that will make me feel happier? What do I like and want to do for me that will make me feel happier? What do I need to be happier?

Please answer the questions and then go out and do it!

As usual, I recommend writing your answer in the PDF journal you have received with this book. Then look at your answers and ensure that you are moving your life to fuller awareness.

Affirmation Of The Day

After answering the questions in your journal, and contemplating your answers, sit quietly for a few minutes today and repeat this affirmation:

I AM DOING THE BEST I CAN FOR MYSELF AND OTHERS, AND THAT IS ENOUGH. I AM COMMITTED TO BECOMING MY BEST AND HAPPIEST SELF.

Repeat this affirmation often. With repetition, it has the power to alter your consciousness so you build a better, happier and more purposeful life.

DAY 28 - BECOMING AWARE OF SELF HARMONY

"How you treat others is a direct reflection of how you feel about yourself."~Amber Deckers

How we treat ourselves is how we treat those around us. We often get it backward; we think that how others treat us is how we will treat them. But it all begins with how we treat ourselves. How we treat ourselves is how we will treat those around us, who will, in turn, treat us back as we treat them.

Therefore, the basis to living in harmony in life is, first and foremost, living in peace with yourself. This is such a simple truth.

Most of us are not aware that how we treat others is just mirroring the actual way we feel about and treat ourselves.

In psychology, it is well known that we can only love another in the same measure that we love ourselves. Because we will treat others in the same way we treat ourselves.

Our surroundings will always mirror who we genuinely believe we are and a mirror of our internal self and how we treat ourselves.

You can't be nasty and harsh on yourself and then be kind to another person. You will be harsh on other people as well. You are what you are everywhere you go and with anyone you have contact with.

All change in our environment, therefore, starts with an internal change in ourselves.

This is why you have to take time to care for yourself.

Eat healthy natural foods, exercise daily—even walking daily is excellent for your body and soul. Find time to meditate or be with yourself daily. Also, treat yourself kindly by respecting your time. As mentioned yesterday, saying "no" is an essential step towards self-care, and so is taking the time to be grateful for the simple things you have in your life.

When we find ourselves in the full-fledged rat race of day-to-day life, with all its demands on us, our time, and our well-being, we become demanding and irritable with those around us, which can be harmful to our relationships.

When you treat yourself with patience, kindness, forgiveness, love, and gratitude, you will find yourself in similar relationships, and you will see how the world suddenly has your back. People will be kinder, more helpful, and caring towards you, making your life more harmonious as time goes by.

When you learn to really love yourself, to love and accept all parts of yourself, then people will feel the love radiating from you and will feel uplifted in your presence and will be less critical towards you, if at all.

To feel this self-love, you must get rid of negative emotions towards yourself that may have built up over time. These negative emotions, including guilt, anger, and fear must be removed. We have to forgive ourselves, and accept ourselves as we are, and understand that it is natural to make mistakes sometimes. These mistakes had a purpose in our evolution to help us reach our greatness.

In the Hippocratic Oath that students take before becoming a doctor, they promise to "*first do no harm*".

But how many times are we harmful towards ourselves? This affects all our relationships, including our relationship with ourselves, and the quality of our relationships determines the quality of our life.

I remember being at the lowest point in my life. I was poor and felt significant lack, I thought I had no love, and my family did not support me. I had to care for my two daughters with mental disabilities, which felt at the time as an all-giving with minimal receiving relationship. I hated myself because I blamed myself for their situation. I felt unworthy of good.

And, the way I got out of my mess was, first and foremost, learning to love myself.

Intentionally I decided to change this as soon as I learned the effects loving oneself has on our life. I slowly became aware of my true divine nature, my daughters' true divine nature, and everybody's true divine nature of consciousness, connected in unity and part of a whole.

So how do you do it?

Every day look at yourself in the mirror and say, "I love myself," "I love myself" over and over again. Do this with a forced smile initially, which later will turn into a genuine smile that comes from an awareness of your true divine nature. You will begin to love and appreciate yourself, which automatically will lead you to stop any violence towards yourself.

You can imagine yourself being cradled in loving hands as if you were a baby getting all of the love and attention you ever need.

I recommend you try this compelling visualization. It works and is recommended by top psychologists. Do this daily and see how your relationship with yourself will start to harmonize, as will all your other relationships, making your life happier and fuller.

Questions Of The Day

To end this lesson and help you become aware of your level of self-harmony, please ask yourself:

Where in my life am I not being accepting towards myself, my thoughts, and behaviors? In which area can I be more loving and accepting towards myself? Can I find the true divine nature within me? Can I become more in tune with my true divine nature that is pure love? Can I love and accept myself truly?

Now go out and care for yourself, be kind and loving and accepting to yourself. It could be your health, the foods you eat, your sleep patterns, fun, friends, your job, or physical activity levels. Ask yourself in which area can you be more loving and forgiving to yourself.

As usual, I recommend writing your answers in the PDF.

Affirmation Of The Day

After answering the questions in your journal, and contemplating on your answers, sit quietly for a few minutes today and repeat this affirmation:

I LOVE MYSELF. I ACCEPT MYSELF AS I AM.

Repeat this affirmation often. With repetition, it has the power to alter your consciousness so you build a better, happier and more purposeful life. Have a wonderful day!

DAY 29 - BECOMING AWARE OF SELF REFLECTION

"People who have had little self-reflection live life in a huge reality blind spot." ~ Bryant McGill

Reflection is an active and serious thought process that examines your reason for believing in one thing instead of another through hard evidence.

Reflection is an active and controlled thought process. It means focusing your attention on something and critically thinking about it.

Reflection is crucial to our everyday life because we would live life in the same way without any change or improvement without reflective thought on important subjects and life in general. No new technologies, new ideas, or new projects would come around, and life would be the same without change.

Although this may sound good for some people, it is not suitable for humanity as a whole. When you stop evolving, you are basically dying.

Reflective thought allows you to imagine possibilities and consider new ways for things to happen. This type of thought process must be persistent in focus on one subject at a time. You must stick to one problem or one issue and make sense of it.

Have you ever wondered why you think and believe one thing when you could think or feel another thing just as well?

This is important as it allows you, in the confines of your mind, to see and understand reality as it really is.

Maybe you think something is true, but you would see that it is only an opinion if you reflected upon it. Opinions can be changed, whereas truth cannot.

Self-reflection amplifies self-awareness, and this is a very humbling activity.

When reflecting, you gain personal insight. You examine your perspectives, your choices, your emotions, your actions, and your interactions, and you can understand the motives behind your choices and actions and find the best path for you to move forward.

Reflection is done through curiosity. You must be curious about the matter. When you are curious about yourself and your choices to improve yourself, you become more aware of potential issues that harm you or hinder your progress. And only when you become aware of something can you improve it. Therefore, self-reflection is a necessary process to help you reach your full potential.

Rethink, reexamine and reconsider your behaviors and where they came from. Think about your work environment, relationships, the place you live, friendships, hobbies, lifestyle choices, and how you like to spend your time. Why are you making the choices that you make? Why do you behave in specific patterns? Are you aware of all your preferences and options? Allow yourself to notice if you missed anything before which was not evident to you previously.

The focus of your reflection can be on something that is *not* working well in your life at that moment or something that *is* working out exceptionally well.

When reflecting on something that is not working as you desire, this self-reflection will help you pause any further actions in this field of life and allow you to find out why you are thinking, saying, and doing certain things. Once you understand why you are behaving in a certain way, you can choose to improve your behaviors to benefit you rather than harm you. Ask yourself what could I be doing differently? How can I behave differently in this area of life?

When you reflect on what *is* working, you will also see which behaviors, thoughts, and actions benefit you, and you can use these more often. You may also choose to incorporate some of these behaviors into areas of your life where you have less favorable results. For example, you may find that you are more assertive in a prosperous area of your life, you take more risks, you have a strong reason for doing what you are doing, you are more learned in that area, and so on. If you find behaviors that are not matching the behaviors and habits you follow in areas where you are more successful, then choose to incorporate your beneficial behaviors, habits, and attitudes in those areas where you have less favorable results in your life.

Unfortunately, many people do not follow this vital habit because often they are afraid of the truth they may find through the silence.

Whenever I wake up with a certain unexplainable bad feeling a day after an experience, I reflect on my actions, thoughts, and behaviors from the previous day to see what my intuition is trying to tell me. This is another form of self-reflection. It helps you to understand yourself better.

As you do more self-reflection, you discover more about yourself and then you adjust your behaviors in accordance with how you want to be. You understand yourself better, so you become naturally more assertive. You have more self-love and self-understanding as to why you are doing what you do, and you can choose to continue down this path or change it to what is suitable for you. This is where your power lies.

By self-reflection, you are judging for yourself instead of accepting other people's judgment on a matter.

Self-reflection must come from genuine openness and choosing to pay close attention. This allows you to admit not knowing something, which opens you up to learning or finding new ways of thinking and behaving.

When reflecting, you will notice that most of your beliefs did not come from learning a subject and understanding it thoroughly, but rather through faith in other people's beliefs.

You want to ensure that you take on beliefs from your personal experience and knowledge or credible sources. If they come from credible sources, search for good reasons to accept or reject the expert opinion. For example, when you get a doctor's recommendation, you can search the internet and see if what the doctor suggests is a good, practical idea that makes sense for you.

There are usually alternative ways of doing things. Be open to alternative routes, be curious and get the best information while reflecting on a subject to ensure that you *are* making the best choices for yourself with the knowledge available to you.

Journaling is another practical method for self-reflection. It allows you to explore your ideas and opinions and develop them more thoughtfully and thoroughly.

After every reflection, you should come to your own conclusions regarding what is suitable for you.

I recommend taking time to reflect on every goal you have. Ask yourself why do I have this goal? Why does it matter to me? What will reaching this goal help me do and become? Am I honest with myself? Am I rational? How could I improve? What if I changed my opinion?

These are all excellent questions for self-reflection.

The author Margaret J. Wheatley said, "Without reflection, we go blindly on our way, creating more unintended consequences, and failing to achieve anything useful."

We need to connect with ourselves through introspection, or we will find ourselves living a life that we did not intend to live. We will be living someone else's life with someone else's dreams, a life that is disconnected from our true divine nature. A life that cannot make you happy.

After introspective time alone, you should not feel lonely but instead recharged and ready to cope with life.

Taking time out for yourself must be part of your self-care regimen. It helps you clear your head and focus your mind in the right direction for you. Think about your brain. It needs sleep time to consolidate all of the information it receives throughout the day.

We also need this time to be with ourselves to sort out our emotions, thoughts, and lives.

Introspection also helps you to discover what moves you so profoundly that you forget your egoic self while doing it. You forget your suffering and your sacrifice.

Without this reflective time, we cannot truly connect with our internal desires. We will be distracted from other people's desires, opinions, thoughts, and wishes.

Taking time for yourself shows your subconscious mind that you know that you are important and worthy and deserve care.

All of the greatest minds said that they spent a lot of time alone, contemplating and figuring things out.

Of course, we need to be with other people to live a fulfilled life, and I am not suggesting that you go out and live in the wilderness on your own. I am suggesting that you find the time in your daily life to be with yourself at least once a week, preferably for one to two hours, and on the other days of the week, fifteen minutes of reflective time in the mornings or evenings spent focusing your mind.

We only have so much concentration-time a day, so when you don't give yourself the time to direct your life in the morning, you will find it hard to do it later.

I wake up early every day to have this reflective time before my children wake up and the workday begins, and telephone calls start coming in. This early morning introspection helps me direct my life to where I want it to go. To align my goals with the future I desire and the life I want to live.

Thomas A. Edison said, "The best thinking has been done in solitude. The worst has been done in turmoil."

Introspective time increases creativity and refreshes your mind. It is like when you restart your phone; it suddenly works much better. Contemplative time is like restarting your phone. You need it! It would help if you remembered who you are and where you are going. This is impossible to do when there is so much noise going on from work, colleagues, friends, family, and other obligations.

Regular introspective time allows you to live life on your own terms. And it also allows you to be better in relationships with other people. You become more aware of your thinking patterns and what delays your progress, and then you can be more understanding of other people when they behave offensively.

Introspective time is a beautiful time to enjoy being with yourself. It makes you stronger.

Once you have these solitude blocks in your schedule, you will be laser-focused on achieving the life that will make you happy.

Infinite intelligence is constantly pushing you towards your soul's desire.

When you listen to these urges, your choices will be in line with who you are, with your soul's desire, and will fulfill you.

Now lies the question of whether you can take what you have conjured during your introspective time and take action in the real world with people around you.

Questions Of The Day

To end this lesson and help you take on the habit of self-reflection most effectively, ask yourself:

In critical areas of my life, am I choosing the best option for me? Why am I choosing this option? How would I improve myself if I decided to do things differently? What things could open up for me if I thought differently? Should I believe differently? What would become of my life if I thought differently on this matter? What are the best options for me and the best choice overall? And why should I do this? Is there any knowledge I am missing to make me better equipped to deal with this and advance my life in this field?

These are a few questions to ask yourself about your career, relationships, personal development, and health. These will help you reflect on important matters and open up your mind to new ways of doing things.

Also, ask: How and when can I add introspective time to my daily and weekly schedule? When will I start the practice of giving myself reflective time daily? Can I start today?

As usual, I recommend writing your answers in the PDF journal.

Affirmation Of The Day

After answering the questions in your journal, and examining them, sit quietly for a few minutes today and repeat this affirmation:

I REFLECT ON MY ACTIONS TO PERFORM BETTER THE NEXT TIME. I APPRECIATE MY INTROSPECTION TIME THAT CONNECTS ME WITH TRUTH AND MY SOUL'S DESIRE.

Repeat this affirmation often. With repetition, it has the power to alter your consciousness so you build a better, happier and more purposeful life.

Have a wonderful day!

DAY 30 - BECOMING AWARE OF YOUR PROJECTIONS

"Compliments and criticism are all ultimately based on some form of projection." ~ Billy Corgan

—————————⧜—————————

Our life is based on what we project.

We project to our environment that which we have within us. Our outer behaviors are projections of our inner environment composed of our beliefs, thoughts, and feelings.

Nothing can come to us in our outer world if we don't have it within us. Let's take anger as an example. You won't be angry with someone if you don't have anger within you.

People may trigger something within you, causing you to get angry, but you can only get mad at them when you have anger within you.

The same goes for any quality you find in someone else. If you see selfishness, jealousy, impatience, lying, stealing, rudeness, or any other characteristic, then you often have these qualities within you. Otherwise, you would not be affected by these qualities in someone else, and in most cases, you may not have recognized these characteristics if they were not also part of you. All behavior that triggers an emotion within you may be used as an eye opener to ask yourself why you see *these* qualities in the other person instead of focusing on positive aspects of their nature.

You cannot recognize something that is not within you.

When you find yourself in a situation where you are judging someone for some "awful" behavior, stop and think to yourself where you have this behavior within you? In which situations do you behave similarly?

Every situation that we find ourselves in is mirroring something within us. We attract what we are. And when there are many things that we attract to us that we do not like, these are opportunities to clean up our internal mess.

We aim to become more developed human beings because when we do so, we can enjoy life to the fullest and live in a world surrounded by love and acceptance. But not only this, when we develop ourselves by recognizing our shortcomings, we will also allow more abundance into our life.

Research clearly shows that the most successful people worldwide are always seeking to improve themselves and overcome their shortcomings to get themselves to a higher place.

We constantly get clues about what we can improve through any critical thoughts or emotional outbursts that we have about other people's behaviors. These are indicators for our subsequent efforts to become the best we can be in life.

When we take responsibility for our actions and change what we have within us that brings no value to us, we will improve our lives dramatically and become more fulfilled individuals.

When you find yourself thinking badly about anyone, it is your responsibility to identify the specific behavior that is annoying for you in the other person. Then seek for it within you and improve it.

Spiritual teachings handed from one generation to the next through spiritual teachers all say that whatever you find to be faulty in others is also located within you.

Even the simple but profound act of becoming aware of something, may help it disappear on its own, just through newfound consciousness, Bet even if not, it becomes much easier to deal with and eliminate.

This awareness helps us reach our highest potential—the potential of love. Finding a source of love in everything and everyone around you connects you to your highest potential.

Ralph Waldo Emerson said, "A man is what he thinks about all day long."

We are not what we think we are; we are what we think. The more negative things we think, the more negative we are.

And when we find more sides of positivity in the world around us while slowly removing the negativity within us, research shows that we will also be more successful in life.

A positive attitude was an indicator of success in 85 percent of people who have become successful. Only 15 percent of success is based on ability. The reaming 85 percent is based on having a positive outlook on life. This is why it is of utmost importance to seek and amend negative thoughts in our minds to reach the success we desire.

Even 94 percent of the most successful people on the Forbes 400 list stated that their positive attitude was the most crucial factor for their success and brought them to where they are today. The problem is that to form a positive attitude, you must get rid of the ghosts in your closet, and this is not an easy thing to do. Most people prefer not to know and thus not take care of what needs to be changed within them to become a better version of themselves.

We must confront our fears and become more aware so we can reach our highest potential, and this starts by considering our projections as warning signs.

Once you work on personal development, it becomes easier to look at the most challenging places within us. Releasing these feelings will allow your true divine nature to shine through.

You are already perfect. You just need to remove the negativity within you to allow your perfection to project outwards and shine through. The best way to do this is to observe your outward projections towards others. Follow your projections, and you will get complete clarity as to what you need to improve within yourself to reach your fullest potential.

Questions Of The Day

To end this lesson and help you remove any negative beliefs and attitudes by examining your projections, please ask yourself:

What negative traits do I notice in other people, and where can I find these exact things within me?

Now start to improve these traits one at a time as they come up in your daily life.

As usual, I recommend writing your answers in the PDF journal.

Affirmation Of The Day

After answering the questions in your journal, and contemplating on your answers, sit quietly for a few minutes today and repeat this affirmation:

I AM IMPROVING DAILY BY LOOKING WITHIN MYSELF AT WHAT NEEDS TO BE REMOVED AND DOING WHAT I CAN TO REMOVE IT.

Repeat this affirmation often. With repetition, it has the power to alter your consciousness so you build a better, happier and more purposeful life.

DAY 31 - BECOMING AWARE OF MORAL ISSUES

"Problems are not stop signs, they are guidelines."

~ Robert H. Shuller

When you face some problem in life, something needs to change or you need more awareness. Problems are guidelines for what needs to change or where awareness is lacking to fulfill yourself to the greatest extent.

Often a moral principle could be missing, either within you or within the situation or with the person you interact with. It is always easier to blame someone else for your case, but perhaps you could have avoided the problem if *you* had done something differently. Maybe you crossed one or more of the five common moral principles.

Let's look at the five common moral principles.

1. Independence—where you are the ruler of yourself. You understand that you have freedom of choice and freedom of action. Independence means that you make your own decisions, act through your values, and take responsibility for your choices and actions.

2. No-harm—this means that you are not causing harm to others. "*Above all, do no harm.*" So although you want to make your own choices and choose your actions without being swayed by the opinions of others, you must make sure that you are not inflicting intentional harm on another person through your choices and behaviors.

3. Beneficence—doing the right thing. For example, when you see some wrongdoing, it is your moral duty to do something and not just be a spectator. When George Floyd was lying on the ground under the police officers' leg, the spectators of this horrific scene should have done something to prevent this tragedy. Problems escalate when we are not doing our best to be generous and do what is right.

4. Equality—shows general respect for other people. Treating people as equals, no matter where they come from or what they look like—behaving equally towards anyone who would behave in such a manner no matter their status, skin color, or origin. When we do not act with equality, it leads to corruption. When personal interest gets in the way of our choices and equality is not given to all, this will lead to problems ahead. Indeed most issues in politics stem from unjust behaviors.

5. Faithfulness—being loyal and honoring your commitments.

Note that each one of these five principles is of equal value.

When you encounter a problem in your life, look towards these five moral principles to see which you lacked that escalated this situation to become a problem.

Were you not true to yourself? Did you let other people sway you away from your values? Did your choices or actions harm other people? Were you not preventing harm to others? Were you not generous, or did you lack respect for others? Did you not give an equal chance to others? Were you honoring your commitments? Were you loyal and faithful?

The core of your problem was most likely from a place of not having integrity and not following one or more of these moral principles.

Introspection on the five common moral principles is quite eye-opening, especially when you find out which one you overlooked before the situation escalated into a problem. Where were you untrue to your moral principles? Where did you stray off the path of integrity?

Gain this clarity about your problem. Think about the facts and remove suspicions and assumptions.

Ask yourself, what did I or did I not do?

What am I doing or not doing?

Consider potential consequences of your choices and actions while determining a new course of action. Now how do you know if your new course of action is the right course of action to take now?

Well, you must now check if the new course of action presents new moral issues. Rethink your choices and activities until you find a solution to your problem or find a way to behave that will not exclude moral principles.

When you have figured out what you should do that aligns with all of the moral principles, then do it.

But what if you understand that you have crossed a moral principle that escalated your situation? How can you fix it?

Sometimes taking action to fix the situation is not enough. Sometimes you must explain your mistake, ask for forgiveness and repent.

Becoming more aware of your actions is crucial to not end up in a similar situation again. This will spare you much suffering in the future.

Questions Of The Day

To end this lesson and help you make better choices aligned with your moral principles, ask yourself: When I examine my problem, which of the moral principles was I violating? What could I have done instead that is in line with all of my moral principles?

Can I change the situation for the better right now?

If you can still change the situation, then do so, by all means. Move in the right direction that is in line with all five moral principles. This will ensure you are moving your life to a happier, more fulfilling place for you. Better for you and better for everyone. If the situation has escalated, perhaps you need to ask for forgiveness and repent your actions.

As usual, I recommend writing your answers in the PDF journal.

Affirmation Of The Day

After answering the questions in your journal, and contemplating on your answers, sit quietly for a few minutes today and repeat this affirmation.

I ACCEPT TOTAL RESPONSIBILITY FOR ALL OF MY ACTIONS, AND EVERYTHING I DO IS ALIGNED WITH THE FIVE COMMON MORAL PRINCIPLES.

Repeat this affirmation often. With repetition, it has the power to alter your consciousness so you build a better, happier and more purposeful life. Have a wonderful day!

DAY 32 - BECOMING AWARE OF YOUR REACTIONS

"Life is 10% what happens to you and 90% how you react to it." ~ Charles R. Swindoll

Do you react to situations, or do you respond to them?

Reactions are instinctual. They come from your reptilian brain. A reaction to a situation has no filtering process. When you react, you may say or do things with severe long-term implications that were not considered when reacting to a situation.

On the other hand, responding to a situation means that you think before doing. That there is thought behind the action. You think of the consequences of your actions before you take them.

Most of us tend to react to situations.

Reacting to a situation often involves behaving in a way that is not positive, in a way that we would have preferred not to act.

It is possible to respond to situations from a clear mind without carrying all the weight of previous experiences, justifications, and identification. Responding to a situation involves examining the situation clearly, seeing how we can best handle it, and then responding.

This change from reacting to responding in most situations is spiritual growth.

You can handle any situation; as difficult as it may seem, you can cope, and you can respond.

I know that I do not always respond to situations, and when it comes to something that I perceive as dangerous for my daughters, I often tend to react much more than I respond. Still, this way of behaving usually has negative consequences.

Firstly, and most obviously, there are health consequences. When we react to a situation, our stress hormones flood our bodies and leave us feeling drained and lifeless. But when we respond to situations, we think that we have the situation under our control. We actually do have the situation under our control. We have control over the situation through the power we have over ourselves.

And when we have control over ourselves, we also have power over any situation.

Think of what would happen if you reacted to your child breaking a plate by screaming at them. The child would run away and probably feel hurt, and their self-esteem would also suffer, and they would leave you to clean the mess alone. Now think of what would happen if you responded to the situation instead of reacting to it. You would say, okay, nothing terrible happened, now let's clean this mess up.

Your child would not feel threatened, and they would probably help you clean the mess. Instead of making your child feel small, you made your child feel useful.

The situation has completely changed just by your different response.

All reactions come from the ego, while all responses to a situation come from your soul, our true divine nature of consciousness.

There is always a choice- to react or to respond to every situation.

I completely understand that it may be tough to believe this, especially when your reactions come fast, such as anger or fear.

Your thoughts and beliefs come to the surface through your reactions. Therefore your reactions bring to light what is inside of you in the form of your thoughts and beliefs.

Any time you react to a situation, it is an opportunity to rid yourself of this excess baggage you hold.

Suppose you acknowledge the reaction and understand that this is not how you want to behave in such a situation because it is not for your benefit. In that case, you can change the thoughts and beliefs that caused you to react in such a manner, and thus, you improve your life dramatically.

We all have negativity within us.

The thoughts and beliefs that lead to adverse reactions often come from false beliefs, a lack of understanding, lack of time, or lack of resources, including money.

But your soul knows that there is no lack. Your soul is connected to the infinite intelligence where lack does not exist.

When you react to a situation, you are blocking abundance from entering your life.

When you believe in lack, you are bringing lack to you. As stated in the Zohar, the holy book of the Kabbalah dated back to the 14th century, *"The higher world only gives in accordance to the state of the lower world … if the state of the lower world is one of sadness, then, in response, the flow of blessings is reduced … a person's joy attracts a parallel joy from on high."*

So if you desire to lead a happy and pleasant life, the reactions you have to certain situations are signposts of what you need to change within you to reveal the bliss available for you.

Remember that all beliefs are true only because we believe in them. That's why they are called beliefs. But if you stop believing or start to question them, you will see that they often lose their power.

Become aware of any reactions you have to any given situation. Think about what you took personally. This will bring you evidence of your thoughts on the subject. These thoughts are surfacing so that you can change them and connect with your true essence, your oneness with the all that is.

All that is not true or real will be revealed to you through your reactions, and then you can let go of the thoughts, feelings, and beliefs that lead to a burdened life.

When you release these false feelings and beliefs, you become free.

Can you imagine how much abundance you actually have in your life? Any belief that states otherwise is purely wrong. It comes from the ego, and it is false.

You do have enough! You have enough money, time, love, friends, support, health, beauty, patience, and faith. You have enough of everything. All you need to do to see this abundance is remove the blindfolds that your thoughts and beliefs have created for you. Then you will never again react to anything. You will only respond. But even if you do react and you notice your reaction, then the next time you are in a similar situation, you will be more conscious of it, and you will naturally respond instead of reacting.

Remove all limiting beliefs that don't serve you and start to live your life happily, with feelings of abundance. Review the lesson on removing limiting beliefs if you feel the need. When you stop limiting beliefs, you will stop reacting to situations, and instead, you will start responding to concerns with a clear mind. You will be more mindful and more in control, which will increase your level of happiness.

Whenever you are in a situation that triggers a reaction from you, pause for a second. Thoughts come and go, as do feelings. A reaction to a problem can become a response if you give yourself just a moment. Breathe in. You can quiet your reptilian response. Think for a moment of what you believe is real here. Then think of what you want overall, and respond to the situation in a productive way.

This takes a lot of self-control and awareness, and these take time to build. Go over this lesson a few times until it sinks into your subconscious mind. Practice being responsive instead of reactive as often as you can. With time you will become more patient with other people and the world, and you will respond to situations naturally. This is your genuine soul's desire; to win over the ego and connect with your true identity of consciousness and unity.

Being responsive and not reactive is definitely not an easy task. It takes much practice to reach this state if we can ever achieve it. But you do want to slowly reduce the amount of time you spend being reactive and recover your sanity as quickly as possible.

Viktor E. Frankl said, "Between stimulus and response, there is a space. In that space is our power to choose our response. In our response lies our growth and our freedom."

Questions Of The Day

To end this lesson and help you respond more than you react to situations, ask yourself:

What deep-seated beliefs are being revealed to me through my reactions? Which thoughts and opinions have control over my life and make me feel as though I have some form of lack in my life? Once you uncover the limiting thoughts and beliefs, slowly remove them with truth; that there is no lack. All lack is imagined in your mind and thus should be removed to live your life fully and abundantly. It is in your own hands.

As usual, I recommend writing your answers in the PDF journal.

Affirmation Of The Day

After answering the questions in your journal, and examining them, sit quietly for a few minutes today and repeat this affirmation:

I RELEASE ALL OF MY LIMITING BELIEFS, AND THUS, I AM RESPONDING IN A PRECISE AND CALCULATED WAY TO ANY GIVEN SITUATION NATURALLY.

Repeat this affirmation often. With repetition, it has the power to alter your consciousness so you build a better, happier and more purposeful life.

DAY 33 - BECOMING AWARE OF FEAR

"Feel the fear and do it anyway" ~ Susan Jeffers

There are two classes of fear:

1. Innate fear is all about avoiding physical pain or death. This fear leads us to fear spiders, snakes, heights, flying, or swimming because they have the potential to harm us. However, innate fears do not cripple us concerning our future. They may affect our life, depending on how well we control them, but they often do not block our path to happiness or success.

2. Identity fear. This class of fears happens when we believe that what is happening poses a threat to our standing in society. It comes when we fear we will fail or embarrass ourselves in front of other people. We may fear losing money, staying alone, or being abandoned, or being rejected. This fear is genuine because of our dependence on other people for friendship, support, and survival.

Nowadays, most of our fears are identity fears, and these may block our way to happiness.

The word fear is often used as an acronym where F.E.A.R. stands for Fantasized Evidence Appearing Real. We fantasize about a negative outcome and believe that this will happen to us if we follow through with the action that stirred up the fear.

When you suspect fearful identity consequences, then you are physiologically feeling the fear in your body, just as you would feel when you see a snake. This leads to anxiety and stress way before anything has happened.

Our subconscious mind does not differentiate between actual incidents and imagined incidents; therefore, any negative images we hold in our minds will harm our physiological state and life.

Fear is an essential feeling which helps us be more careful. We should pause before we rush into something that may have negative consequences for us. We should think things over. But we should not overthink things; otherwise, we will not have any forward progress. We tend to freeze or run away from fearful situations instead of confronting our identity fears and improving ourselves as better individuals.

Anyone who has achieved anything worthwhile in life had to overcome fears and take risks to their identity. This is natural and is part of the process towards becoming your best version. Whenever you succeed at something, you overcome the fears along the way. You don't let fear stop you in your tracks; you keep going and take action despite any dangers to your identity or material situation.

A few years ago, my husband and I were planning to buy a plot of land and build a health hotel in Germany. We found the perfect hotel with more land to build in a stunning location in Ruhpolding. Wow, what a sight! After traveling to Germany for many appointments, along with my daughters and a caregiver, I was about to sign the purchase contract when my husband got cold feet. One day he called me from work and said that he was not going through with it. I had no choice but to cancel the purchase. Everyone was in complete shock. It was highly embarrassing.

This is how fear can ruin a person's success. My husband's dream was to move to Germany because of his love of cars. My dream was to open a health center. He ruined his opportunity to create his dream life just because of fear.

A few weeks later, I discovered that I had cancer, and then our lives changed as a result. I understood that life is short and that I still had things I wanted to do in this lifetime, so I began doing them.

But fear does not creep in only for massive life-changing events. Fear is also there when we want to make small lifestyle changes, such as changing our exercise routine or our dietary habits, speaking on stage, or moving neighborhood.

We will often not begin something new because we fear we will fail or embarrass ourselves or fear standing out or how others will perceive us. We fear that our life will become unhappy and that our identity is on the line, which happens before any change is made. This is when our fears lead to our unhappiness and block us from reaching the best version of ourselves.

You cannot be the master of your life if you let your fears run your choices.

The good news is that you don't have to give in to fear and let it run your life. You can proceed despite fear.

So how do you do it?

Here are three introspective thought processes that will help you overcome your identity fears and help you succeed despite being afraid something terrible will happen to you.

1. Connect with your WHY—your reason for doing something. Your "why" or reason for doing something will help you overcome fear. The movie "Into The Wild" is based on a true story. Chris McCandless had a choice of whether to cross the river back to civilization or not. It seemed too difficult for him to do since the tide was up, but had he known that if he didn't cross at that time, then he would surely die, how much effort would he have put into crossing that river? All of his effort! When we have a strong enough reason, we can get over our fears and anything else that is holding us back from taking the steps into our desired future.

2. Acknowledge the worst-case scenario scripts that you have running in the back of your mind. When you notice that these thoughts are running your show, you can aim to take their power away. The best way to remove the power your fears have over you is by replacing these scripts with different ones. Creating other scripts or images in your mind to replace your current identity-fear-scripts will allow you to free yourself from the handcuffs fear has on you.

Write down this script for every identity fear you encounter:

I'd like to do _____, but I am scared of doing it because I think that _____ could happen if I did do it. Instead, I choose to think of me succeeding at _____, and of me handling bravely anything that will come my way.

Once you understand the power that fear has to hold you back from your full potential, you will understand the need to tame it.

3. Understand that doing the right thing always takes courage. Courage is about doing the right thing at the right time, no matter what you are feeling.

We cannot follow our purpose in life if we do not dare to take the right actions no matter what other people say or think and no matter what fears we are feeling.

Aristotle said courage is the first of human qualities because it is the quality that guarantees all others. Without courage, you cannot be true to yourself. You will prefer to be accepted by the group and not take risks of standing out. You will not be willing to leave an unfulfilling job or unfulfilling relationship, or non-beneficial habit if you do not find the courage to do so.

When you are not true to yourself, you are ignoring your soul.

Courage allows you to follow your true essence. This is what being true to yourself is all about. You may not be able to explain things in words, but they are your truths, and if you dare to follow your path no matter what others think or say about you, you are claiming your true essence. Little acts of courage daily will ensure that you are pushing yourself to become a better and fuller awakened version of yourself.

Having courage is the only way to have absolute freedom.

Without having courage over your fears, you will forever stay poor. Poor not only from a financial perspective, but you will block other good fortune. This is the power of fear. It will obstruct all affluence if daily acts of courage do not slay it.

Think of the people you admire. You only know about them and respect them because of the way they lead their lives. They took risks and succeeded more than they failed, sometimes against all odds.

We can all be courageous. Any act of courage first asks you to know what is right and to know your values and be faithful to them.

Fear is like a chain holding you down, and an act of courage is finding the strength of character within you to release yourself from these chains no matter what. The chains of fear may leave you with scars, but once you have left the chains of fear behind, you will be free. Although you may still have the scars as a memory of the bondage that once held you, you have claimed back the strength you have within you and overcome your fears.

No one else can do what you came to this world to do! So it's time to step up into your courage and claim the life that is rightfully yours.

You may always have some self-doubt; you may always be somewhat anxious when you do something that you have not done previously or when the experience is new. Anything new is scary. But staying in your comfort zone because of fear will leave you feeling powerless.

You will never reach your full potential by staying on the sofa. And when you don't march courageously towards your soul's desire and your goals, even the small ones, your internal power will diminish. You will lose your self-respect and become smaller, blander until the light within you will not shine through. Your ego may fight and try to prove the importance of your false identity, but it is incorrect and will not bring you happiness and fulfillment.

Then you are like a living dead. All your dreams slipping further and further away from you.

We will all die at one point. Our physical presence as we are now will pass. This is inevitable. But to be born and choose not to experience life fully is slowly bringing you to your death, even when you are still physically alive. It is like going through life sleepwalking.

Not having the courage to overcome difficulties because of fears running through your head is your own choice.

Find the courage to look at your life and see where you are today. Have the courage to take responsibility for playing a part in bringing yourself to where you are today.

Know that it doesn't matter where you are today if you dare to change what you do not like about yourself and your life. It only matters where you are today if you plan to stay there and do nothing about it.

You matter, and your life matters. Your job is to use your courage to show your true self to the world.

This physical life is short. Claim your life and live it just as you wish it to be. Find your WHY, your reason for doing something, control the script running through your head, and take daily acts of courage to move you closer to your true potential, a part of Source, for this is what you came here for.

Questions Of The Day

To end this lesson and help you overcome identity fears, ask yourself:

What are my dreams? What things do I need to do to advance my goals, and where is identity fear creeping in and scaring me of failure, embarrassment, or rejection? What courageous act can I do today to ensure that I achieve my dreams?

Now write a different script in your mind, one of you succeeding:

I'd like to do _____, but I am scared of doing it because I think _____ could happen if I did. Instead, I choose to think of me succeeding at _____, and of me handling bravely anything that will come my way.

Imagine it over and over in your mind until you have sufficient power to go ahead despite fear.

As usual, I recommend writing your answers in the PDF journal.

Affirmation Of The Day

After answering the questions and filling in the script in your journal, contemplating your answers, and then repeat this affirmation:

I AM CREATING THE LIFE OF MY DREAMS, AND WHENEVER I FEEL FEAR, I BREATHE IN COURAGE AND BREATHE OUT FEAR.

Repeat this affirmation often. With repetition, it has the power to alter your consciousness so you build a better, happier and more purposeful life.

DAY 34 - BECOMING AWARE OF THE IMPORTANCE OF PATIENCE

"To lose patience is to lose the battle." ~ Mahatma Gandhi

We all know that stress, regret, and anger don't help anything. The Bible says, "Hot tempers cause arguments, but patience brings peace."

Success and all things worthwhile in life take time to accomplish and will only be achieved through persistent effort, sacrifice, and patience.

A patient person has time on his side, and time is the most potent force of the universe, and it is there always working for the patient man. Impatience takes into consideration only the here and now and does not look towards the future.

Patience allows you to do your best today and enjoy the moment while still staying on your way to a better tomorrow. Patience provides hope and thus provides a light at the end of the tunnel.

Every farmer knows the power of patience and uses it to their advantage. All hard work in the right direction is rewarded if the person is patient enough to wait to receive the rewards.

Often, we do not entirely understand the meaning of things, but with time we will. In our era, we all want instant gratification and expect to get things without waiting. And although technology has improved so much to allow us to get many things immediately, there are still things that need patience and can never come or last without patience.

Things relating to the body, relationships, goals, and health all take patience, sacrifice, and effort. There is no fast-forward button. In life, time shows us that there is a benefit in everything. We may not see it when the situation is happening, but we will understand the good in everything if we are patient enough.

You get closer to your goals every day that passes if you put in the right focused effort. Effort need not be hard work. But when you have patience, no matter how many days or years it will take, you will get there and win in the end. Everything great that you want to achieve in life will take time, and you have time on your side when you have patience.

When you learn how to delay gratification, your life will be happier. The best way to learn to delay gratification is through practice.

You can practice patience by ordering things through the standard delivery system that takes longer than same-day delivery. Once you get your package, you will be happier than if you got it the same day. A 2012 study published in The Journal of Positive Psychology showed that patience increases well-being and happiness.

You can't make plants grow faster, you can't bake a cake more quickly than it needs to bake. Patience is the key, and the best way to cultivate patience is to get used to waiting for things while releasing the pressure from wanting something immediately. Everything has its time. Put in your best effort today and have patience. Enjoy the moment. Believe that what you desire will reach you at the right time.

When you decide to finish a task before starting another project, you know that you have mastered patience. Many people multitask, and that's nice to do for a varied and exciting life. You may multitask daily between different areas of life, but the key is not to multitask in each specific area of your life.

Let's look at the specific areas of life, including career and work, relationships, health, friends and family, and contribution. To add spark to life, I recommend multitasking between all of these areas of life daily. Make sure you are putting in the effort into each of these areas of life every day. But for each specific area, focus on one goal and make it work with consistent effort, time, and patience.

When you get scattered in any particular area of life, you probably won't achieve greatness in that field. So focus on one career goal at a time until you have achieved it. Focus on one partner, on one sport, on one way to contribute, on one task at home until you complete it, etc.

You can achieve all of your dreams, but probably not all at the same time.

When you find the patience to follow through with something to completion, you will have learned one of the most valuable habits there is to success. Patience.

Patience is the key to success, without which nothing of significant value can come. The longer you put in consistent effort, the better your chances to achieve your goal becomes, simply by the law of averages.

When I was interviewing Dr. Phil and asked him about his view on achieving health goals, he said, "If you want to eat an elephant, you do it one bite at a time," and this is precisely the best way to go when you want to achieve anything that seems too onerous or complicated. With patience, one step at a time, making a small but consistent effort towards your goals.

When you have the patience to do things slowly and allow them to develop in their own time, you will not only achieve much but also be happier.

Often patience is more challenging to apply than hard work. However, anyone can learn to be more patient through practice. All you have to understand is that things take time, and learn to enjoy the process.

Questions Of The Day

To end this lesson and help you be patient, ask yourself:

Where do I need to practice more patience, have more hope, and have a longer-term vision? Can I become relaxed while working towards my goal? If not, then why not?

If you feel you lack enough resources to be patient, then perhaps you could find other ways to achieve these resources while still working towards your goals patiently.

As usual, I recommend writing your answers in the PDF journal.

Affirmation Of The Day

After answering the questions in your journal, and examining them, sit quietly for a few minutes today and repeat this affirmation:

I TRUST THAT EVERYTHING WILL HAPPEN IN ITS OWN PERFECT TIME.

Repeat this affirmation often. With repetition, it has the power to alter your consciousness so you build a better, happier and more purposeful life.

DAY 35 - BECOMING AWARE OF THE NEED FOR OPEN-MINDEDNESS

"A mind is like a parachute. It doesn't work if it is not open." ~ Frank Zappa

There are things that you may like or dislike. But if you keep an open mind and are available to try new possibilities, this can lead you to places you never dreamt possible. Sometimes you may not be open and willing to accept advances in the world. You may prefer to stay in a place familiar to you.

Every day, new technology can improve life dramatically if accepted and appropriately used. All you have to do is be open to change around you. In this way, you open yourself up to a better world. Be open to looking at how innovation can help you achieve your goals in a way you never thought or imagined possible. Open yourself up to something you have never tried before.

It is not easy to try new things and leave your comfort zone. And even if you did try something new previously, did you give this new thing a real chance before deciding that it is not for you? Probably not.

Whenever you feel your options are limited or close your prospects down, you do so only because of lack of information or fear of using what *is* available.

There is so much opportunity available to everyone with an internet connection in the modern world, which is over 60 percent of the global population as of 2021.

We have no more excuses for not making enough money, not being in a good relationship, or not having the health we desire. The only person responsible for our situation is us. When we are not willing to open ourselves to the options available to us, we behave irrationally and block our path to success.

The limits humans have today are so distant from the limitations we had two to three decades ago. We can learn and improve our lives, make more money, meet people, order healthy food, study anything and gain qualifications all from the comfort of our own home. Innovation has also helped people around the world get pregnant and have children at practically any age.

Being open to innovations is vital for any success.

Today life is practically limitless.

Examine where exactly you are in terms of your desires. When you acknowledge where you currently are and take responsibility for your current situation, it doesn't mean that you love where you are right now. But if you do not acknowledge where you currently are, how will you understand what you need in order to open yourself up to new opportunities.

Keeping an open mind is crucial for your livelihood.

It means that you're willing to *consider* different perspectives, different opinions, values, and beliefs from your current ones, even if they contradict your current ones.

When your mind is not open, you cannot see all of the opportunities in front of you.

You are biased. Your mind selects and interprets information in a way that's biased by your current perspectives, opinions, values, and beliefs.

Keeping an open mind allows you not to conform, which most people do. When you conform, you will at best get mediocre results. An open mind leads to more innovation, which will allow you to get extraordinary results.

You do not have all of the answers, but you do have access to all of the answers if you keep an open mind. An open mind will determine whether you take advantage of new opportunities or not.

If you are not open enough, you will not see them as opportunities and fail to take the right actions.

So are you open-minded? Can you entertain a new idea? Are you prepared to throw away any beliefs you have nurtured throughout the years when you learn a truth?

People tend to take on a new idea only when it matches their current beliefs and lifestyle. If there is no match, then they say it's wrong.

Some of the greatest minds all understood the importance of being open-minded.

George Bernard Shaw said, "Those who cannot change their minds cannot change anything."

Henry David Thoreau stated, "It is never too late to give up your prejudices."

And Marcus Aurelius said, "If someone is able to show me that what I think or do is not right, I will happily change, for I seek the truth, by which no one was ever truly harmed. It is the person who continues in his self-deception and ignorance who is harmed."

And the list goes on and on.

Being open-minded predicts how well you will do in life and how well you will feel about your life.

We are all unknowledgeable in one subject or another. Everyone.

And those of us who are most unknowledgeable often don't realize it. Their minds are closed to everything because they think that they already know or should know everything.

Think about your life. What about your diet, should it be changed? Is it leading you to long-lasting health? What about your beliefs? Are they leading you to a happy and prosperous life? What about your habits? Are they beneficial to the way you see your best life?

So how can you become more open-minded?

Here are two good ways to start:

1. Question your thoughts. Ask yourself, *"what if I thought otherwise"? "Could it be true"? "Why or why not"? "What if I am wrong"?* Do this regularly to ensure that your thoughts are based on reality and come from truth. It's essential to question your basics from time to time, even if you do not want to. It's good to rethink your beliefs. Talk to people who think differently from you on a subject and listen to their viewpoint. Why do they think this way? What are their arguments in favor of the issue and against your point of view? Do they have proof? Is this truth or just another opinion?

   Re-evaluate your original thoughts. Are they true or not?

In this way, you become more open-minded.

2. Question your beliefs. Ask yourself how would my beliefs be different if I lived in a different place or had a different background or environment?-would I still think the same way that I am currently thinking? How would I think or what would I do differently?

Meeting new people or visiting new cultures can open your mind to how other people think, behave, what they believe in, and why they believe this.

Questioning your beliefs will help you break free from any primitive thought patterns that are holding you back from your true potential.

Remember that when nothing is certain, everything is open to possibility. Uncertainty is a fact of life, so let's use it to our advantage to help us become open-minded to new thoughts, beliefs, and actions in our life.

Questions Of The Day

To end this lesson and help you become more open-minded, ask yourself:

Have I rethought my beliefs lately? Are my ideas grounded in truth, or are they based on opinions? Is there room for me to review my thoughts and to open my mind to more things in this world so that I can live a better, fuller life?

Suppose you do see that your mind is not open. Try out the two methods I mentioned here in this lesson. Question your thoughts and your beliefs to help you open your mind and allow you to benefit from a vast amount of potential opportunities for joy.

As usual, I recommend writing your answers in the PDF Journal you have received with this book to look over your answers and ensure that you are improving your life and bringing forth your true divine nature.

Affirmation Of The Day

After answering the questions in your journal, and examining them, sit quietly for a few minutes today and repeat this affirmation:

AT THIS MOMENT, I AM OPEN AND KIND.

Repeat this affirmation often. With repetition, it has the power to alter your consciousness so you build a better, happier and more purposeful life.

DAY 36 - BECOMING AWARE OF FLEXIBILITY

"That which yields is not always weak." ~ Jacqueline Carey

Yesterday we spoke of the importance of being open-minded, which is being tolerant to diversity. Today we will talk about flexibility which means that you can bend without breaking under the difficulties of the moment.

Many people are stuck within certain beliefs that make their thoughts rigid. But actually, the strongest trees are the trees that are the most flexible and can withstand strong winds.

We see that after violent winds from cyclones and hurricanes, only the most flexible trees stayed in their place, while all else was either torn down or blown away.

Nowadays, engineers understand this and build tall buildings to be flexible enough to sway and move, although with a solid foundation and center. This flexibility is the secret behind their strength.

When you are **not** flexible, you are not only too rigid to make the necessary changes that will lead to your success; you are also too stiff to see where change is needed.

Flexibility means you are willing to bend out of your comfort zone when necessary.

The comfort zone may feel good, but if you are not where you truly desire to be, this comfort holds you back from your desired future.

Once you have set out goals that you desire to achieve and have made plans to achieve them, and you start following through with your plans, you will see that life may have other thoughts in mind.

Your plans will often need to change, and to do this willingly requires flexibility of character. Without being flexible to change plans, you will stay stuck, frustrated, unhappy, and often fail to achieve your goals. Failure to achieve your goals does not mean your goals need to change, just how they are pursued.

Albert Einstein said, "The measure of intelligence is the ability to change."

A person who thinks they know it all is rigid and inflexible and will have a hard time living a good life because life is dynamic and constantly changing.

Anything that resists change will fall and crumble or get blown away when difficulties arise. When change is unexpected, as is often the case, only those who are flexible enough to understand that change needs to happen fast will succeed in getting out of the situation stronger than they went in.

Being flexible is a necessity for survival.

Think for a moment about humans as a species. My research into the ideal diet for humans taught me that humans were able to survive and thrive and become the most developed species because they had the flexibility to change.

If you find yourself feeling unhappy with something in your life, check if you are too rigid in your outlook on things. Think of how you can become more flexible with new opportunities.

Rigidity is the sure path to a lonely, unhappy, and often unfulfilled life. This is not what you desire. Accept what you can change, which is firstly your perspective. Can you change the meanings you gave things in the past? Can you perhaps give them another chance?

Take a leap of faith going down a new path of innovation even if you may feel quite uncomfortable at first.

The inflexibility of mind is often the result of previous trauma or a child who was not allowed to express their curiosity. When a child is not allowed to make your own choices and take on action and the consequences of their actions, they become inflexible and less aware. Without being allowed to be, a child becomes rigid later in life. The more a child is permitted to experiment with life, the more flexible in mind and aware they become.

Flexibility may seem like a weakness at first, but as with the tree, when you show you can yield, you are showing your strength.

Questions Of The Day

So, to end off this lesson and to help you become aware of where you can become more flexible in life, the questions that you want to ask yourself today are:

Where in my life am I struggling?

Could this struggle be because of rigidity and lack of openness on my part to new options?

Where in my life can I open up and become more flexible to trying something new to help me reach a better place in life?

As usual, I recommend writing your answers in the PDF journal.

Affirmation Of The Day

After answering the questions in your journal, and contemplating on your answers, sit quietly for a few minutes today and repeat this affirmation:

I AM OPEN TO NEW THINGS AND ALLOW MYSELF TO TRY NEW PATHS REGULARLY.

Repeat this affirmation often. With repetition, it has the power to alter your consciousness so you build a better, happier and more purposeful life.

DAY 37 - BECOMING AWARE OF THE BENEFITS OF ADAPTABILITY

"It is not the strongest person who wins in life, but it is the most nimble, flexible, and adaptive person who wins in life." ~ Debasish Mridha

This quote is all about adaptation to uncertainty.

During the COVID-19 pandemic, many people lost their jobs and had significant family difficulties. People survived it by adapting quickly.

Yesterday we spoke of the importance of being flexible. The difference between being flexible and being adaptable is that adaptability indicates long-term changes; whereas being flexible is more about more short-term alterations that are needed to overcome a situation.

Adaptability is the ability to change to fit changing circumstances. Uncertainty is an integral part of life.

About 75,000 years ago, the human population suffered a tremendous blow when the super-volcano at Lake Toba in Sumatra, Indonesia, erupted. The eruption had the highest explosive rating of any known eruption on Earth. This eruption led to what is known as a global "volcanic winter" of six to ten years of lowered temperatures of up to 15 °C lower for each season than before the eruption. This devastated life on earth and led to a significant dwindling of the human population, leaving less than 10,000 pairs of humans on the face of the Earth. Only those able to adapt to the new circumstances fast were able to survive.

Even Charles Darwin said, "It is not the strongest of the species that survives, nor the most intelligent. It is the one that is most adaptable to change."

The adaptability of mind is necessary not only for our survival but also for our success.

We can plan and plan throughout our life, but there will be times when unexpected situations come into our lives and throw most of our plans away. This does not mean that we have to give up on our goals, but it does mean that we have to be flexible enough to find different solutions and rethink our strategies. It requires us to think outside of our usual line of thinking, and definitely to get out of our comfort zone and do things that we are not used to doing.

Adaptability and coping with uncertainty are crucial for living a happy and favorable life. Even in relationships, things change over time. There is never any certainty and this will require adaptability from both partners. Children grow up and their needs change with time. The more adaptable and flexible you are as a person, the easier life will be for you, and the happier you will be. You may lose a few battles along the way, but if you can adapt quickly, and make the necessary changes, you will win the war.

You must understand quickly what you *can* change and what is *not* in your power to change. And when you see what you can change and needs to change, then do it! Have the courage to be adaptable and to make the necessary changes with proper judgment and self-discipline.

The television show Survivor is an example. The person who wins in the end is not the one who wins all the battles during the season and is not even the strongest person in the game. It is the person who is most comfortable with uncertainty and was most adaptable to the complex challenges that happen every day throughout the show.

You must be awake, see what is happening, deal with change and uncertainty and try different directions to keep moving forward. As I said previously, you have all of the resources at the time you need them. Be open to seeing them and adaptable enough to use them.

Uncertainty teaches us adaptability. Coping with uncertainty helps us increase our resiliency and learn to overcome challenges. This makes us grow as individuals, it increases our self-esteem and allows us to become better versions of ourselves.

There are no jobs for life, no guarantees for good health, and there is never any certainty about what a new day will bring. When we search for certainty, we will always suffer disappointment. Trying to prevent uncertainty only leads to excessive worry and anxiety.

When we look back at the most uncertain times you had in our lives, we can see that, in the end, these uncertain times lead to much needed change. When you look back, you will also notice how much you underestimated your abilities to cope and adapt.

When you let go of the need for certainty, you also let go of negative behaviors, you reduce stress and worry, and become overall happier.

Changing our perception about uncertainty is not an easy task since our brains perceive uncertainty as a real threat. But we must overcome this resistance to reach our higher potential.

Nobody likes to be in the unknown, but we are *all* in the unknown at all times whether we understand this or like this, or not. Some people try to remove uncertainty from their lives with numerology, astrology, and tarot cards. Still, the best way to cope with uncertainty is to first of all to accept that uncertainty is an integral part of life.

When we accept, we don't resist what is, which will only prolong discomfort and pain. As the saying goes, what we resist, persists. We can learn to become more adaptable by being more open, more aware, listening more, learning more and accepting that we may sometimes be wrong. Vulnerability and authenticity allow us to work on ourselves and become more adaptable, better skilled, happier and more fulfilled.

Questions Of The Day

To end this lesson and help you become more adaptable, and better deal with uncertainty, ask yourself:

Where in my life do I feel most uncertain and where in my life is this uncertainty of most influence on my life? Can I focus my efforts on making the best I can out of the current situation to bring it to my side? As usual, I recommend writing your answers in the notebook you have received with this book to look over your answers and ensure that you are improving your life and bringing forth your true divine nature.

Affirmation Of The Day

After answering the questions in your journal, and examining them, sit quietly for a few minutes today and repeat this affirmation:

I AM THANKFUL FOR NEW CHALLENGES IN MY LIFE BECAUSE THEY HELP ME GROW AND MAKE ME STRONGER. THINGS ARE UNCERTAIN, BUT I HAVE THE POWER TO HANDLE THEM.

Repeat this affirmation often. With repetition, it has the power to alter your consciousness so you build a better, happier and more purposeful life.

DAY 38 - BECOMING AWARE OF ROUNDING CORNERS

"A shortcut is the longest distance between two points". ~ Charles Issawi

I used to be the queen of shortcuts, always searching for the easiest route to something, but as Beverly Sills, the opera singer, said, "There are no shortcuts to any place worth going."

This awareness has so changed my life that I keep this quote right next to my bed, never to forget.

Not cutting corners is a fundamental lesson that makes all the difference between a mature person and a child. When you do things the right way, you gain so much in the process. For every university degree I finished, there were always courses that I did not particularly like, but I had to do them anyway to complete the degree. Doing them taught me that it is possible to cope with challenges. Not everything in life will always be fun, but instead of seeing something as hard, choose to see it as a challenge.

Now, I know how fun and exhilarating it can be to reach a goal you set for yourself. But most of our lives are not spent touching base with our goals but in the process of achieving them. Therefore, we must learn to enjoy the process just as much as achieving the goal itself. If we savor the process and discover something valuable during the process, then, even if we fail to reach our goal, we never really failed at all. We gained a lot of value and became a better version of ourselves during the achievement of our goals. For this reason, no matter what you choose to do in life, do it with all your heart. You will gain a lot of rewards just from doing that.

There will be difficult times following any path, but if you see these moments as challenges that you *can* overcome, you can gain the awareness and mindset to help you fly through the challenge.

In nature, you can never make the process of growth anything shorter than it needs to be. You can't rush the process. A ripe fruit will fall from the tree right into your hands without much effort when it is ready—the same with everything in life. If we take consistent action in the right direction, we will reach our goal even with minimal but persistent steps. Once you put in constant effort, it will seem as if the goal will fall into our lap at the right time.

When the time is right, if you persist, you will get what you desire.

We often do not persevere because the goal we are after may not be suitable for us, or we believe we may not deserve it.

When you do not enjoy the process needed to reach a particular goal, you will probably never attain it. When you do not fancy something, you will have many competitors. But when you love doing something, you have no competition because you are simply having fun.

For example, in the restaurant business, you will notice that only people who have a great passion for what they are doing will succeed. According to CNBC, sixty percent of restaurants fail within the first year and 80% before their fifth anniversary. The work is so exhausting. But if you enjoy the work, then no matter how hard it will be (and from personal experience as the previous owner of health restaurants, I can tell you that it is hard), you will succeed.

In all fields of life, taking the shortcut will never get you lasting results. As we know, with dieting, you may lose weight fast by following a fad diet, but this can never bring you long-term effects that will come only with a change of eating and lifestyle habits.

Taking the right path, which may also be the longest, most challenging path, and by going through all of the experiences and preparation you need to gain along the way before you reach your goal, you will find that this is usually the easiest path.

When you release attachment to the results because you enjoy the process, then you have already won. You never know; perhaps Infinite intelligence has something better in store for you. For this reason, non-attachment to the results is a vital path towards inner peace. You know that you are doing the right thing and that it is something that you like to do, and then, whatever the result is, which may be far better than you ever imagined, it will be the correct result.

If you don't enjoy the process, you are probably going after the wrong goal, most often for the wrong reasons.

Alan Watts said that when you are dancing, there is no goal, you enjoy the dance itself, and the same is for music. You are not waiting for the music to end to enjoy it; it is during the dance, song or music that you are gaining the most pleasure. If we lived our lives like this, focused but enjoying the process, we would not feel the need to round corners, nor the need for urgency to achieve our goals, and the quality of our life would be much better, happier, and indeed also healthier.

Questions Of The Day

To ensure you are on the right path for you and that you will not desire to round corners, please ask yourself:

Where in my life am I not enjoying the process of reaching my goals?

Where in my life is the process too expensive for me, whether in time or effort?

Where in my life is the process not enjoyable and not worthwhile for me? Where could I put the effort so that the process will be more enjoyable and attractive for me?

As usual, I recommend writing your answers in the PDF journal.

Affirmation Of The Day

After answering the questions in your journal, and contemplating your answers, sit quietly for a few minutes today and repeat this affirmation:

I DO WHAT IS BEST FOR ME! I CHOOSE TO DO THE RIGHT THINGS IN MY LIFE, SO I ALWAYS ENJOY THE PROCESS!

Repeat this affirmation often. With repetition, it has the power to alter your consciousness so you build a better, happier and more purposeful life.

DAY 39 - BECOMING AWARE OF THE IMPORTANCE OF HONESTY

"Being honest may not get you a lot of friends but it'll always get you the right ones."

~ John Lennon

Honesty takes courage and strength. It is not always easy to admit to the truth.

Abraham Lincoln's good name for honesty, and integrity, helped him win four consecutive terms in the legislature. Honesty to him was critical.

In fact, as a lawyer, he stated that there was a widespread belief that lawyers were dishonest. And his advice to potential lawyers was to either resolve to be honest at all events as lawyers or choose another occupation if they feel that they cannot be an honest lawyer.

Because of Abraham Lincoln's honesty, he could devote his energies to solving political issues and winning the war. Abraham Lincoln is often considered the greatest president of the USA.

Never let your actions disgrace your name. It is like a boomerang that will come back to you. Maintain your integrity. Whenever you have the temptation to lie, stop yourself in your tracks. Treat it like a fire that needs to be extinguished immediately because it does.

Being dishonest can ruin your future.

Dishonesty is like an addiction. Once you start and see how easy it is, it can be challenging to stop. A lie may offer a short-term escape from a problem. But this lie may make the situation much *more* cumbersome as time goes by.

Then, more lies are needed to maintain the first lie. This slowly changes your view of reality, which is very destructive to your life.

We face such a dilemma daily. There is, of course, a need for tact when dealing with other people. You don't need to say that a person's shirt is not attractive if you know he just bought it. But a planned lie for personal gain is something to be avoided at all costs. Even with people you do not know.

Being honest builds character. This ensures that you are connected with reality. This makes you stronger and more courageous, making you more able to make things happen in your life.

If you find yourself wanting to lie about something in your life or see yourself doing it repeatedly in one particular area, maybe it's time to do the work to achieve what you are lying about. In this way, you won't feel the need to lie about it anymore. You can become the person you desire to be and have all you wish to have through honesty.

When you lie, you deceive yourself. Deep down, you *know* what is real and what is not, and when you choose to lie, you are sending a message to your subconscious mind that you are not good enough as you are, and you lack something that you think you need to be happy, and this is very destructive for your wellbeing.

You are forming a story that is not connected to reality. It creates a false illusion of what is, and when you live with a false sense of reality, as we said previously, you will suffer.

Second, lying is theft. You are stealing from another person their right to know the truth. You steal another person's view of reality.

Many people take advantage of situations for their personal benefit. Do not be one of those people. It's a small world and lies surface in the end.

All relationships are based on truth and honesty. In the long term, this is the only foundation that a relationship can thrive upon.

All lies start from fear. When you lie, you lack the courage to do what is right and offer what is real. This is cowardliness, and you do not want to leave a legacy of being a coward.

This is the story of an aging king who woke up one day aware of his mortality. He had no son, and in his culture, only a male heir could take his throne. So he decided that he would adopt a son to take his place. The king launched a competition in his kingdom, open to all boys, no matter their background. The winner would become the king's adopted son and heir to his throne.

The competition was long, and out of the hundreds of thousands who applied, ten of the best reached the final round. They were all intelligent, and all were very capable.

The king then said to them, "Since this kingdom depends solely on agriculture for our livelihood, the new king must know how to cultivate plants. He then gave each of the boys seven seeds of grain. He told them to take them home, plant and nurture them for six weeks. At the end of six weeks, we shall see who has done the best job of cultivating the grain. That person will be my son and my heir."

The boys took their seeds and hurried home. Each got a pot, prepared soil, and sowed his seeds. There was much excitement in the kingdom as people waited to see who was destined to be their next king.

In one home, the boy and his parents were almost heartbroken when the days stretched into weeks, and the seeds failed to sprout. The boy did not know what had gone wrong. He had selected the soil carefully. He had applied the correct quantity and type of fertilizer. He had been very dutiful in watering at the proper intervals, and he even prayed over the seeds day and night, yet his seeds had turned out to be unproductive.

Some of his friends advised him to go and buy different seeds from the market and plant them. "After all," they said, "how can anyone tell seeds of grain one from another?" But his parents, who had always taught him the value of honesty and integrity, reminded him that if the king wanted him to plant just any grain, he would have asked them to go for their own seed. "If you take anything different from what the king gave you, that would be dishonest. Maybe you are just not destined for the throne. If so, let it be, but don't be found to have deceived the king," they told him.

The appointed day came, and the boys returned to the palace, each of them proudly exhibiting a pot of healthy seedlings. It was evident that the other nine boys had had great success with their seeds. The king began making his way down the line of eager boys and asked each of them, 'Is this what came out of the seeds I gave you?' And each boy responded, "Yes, your majesty." And the king would nod and move down the line.

The king finally came to the last boy in the line-up. The boy was shaking. He feared that the king might have him thrown into prison for wasting his seeds. "What did you do with the seeds I gave you?" the king asked.

"I planted them and cared for them diligently. Your Majesty, but alas, they failed to sprout," the boy said. He hung his head in shame, and the crowd jeered.

But the king raised his hands and signaled for silence. Then he said, "My people behold your next king." The people were confused. "Why that one?' many asked. "How can he be the right choice?"

The king took his place on his throne with the boy by his side and said, "I gave these boys boiled seeds. This test was not for cultivating grain. It was a test of character, a test of integrity. It was the ultimate test. If a king must have one quality, it must be that he must be above dishonesty. Only this boy passed the test. A boiled seed cannot sprout."

Overcome the temptation to lie, and in the end, you will gain very much from telling the truth. Remember, as Jesus said in the new testament, the truth shall set you free.

Being honest shows that you dare to be who you genuinely are and face all you have done and all that you are not.

A relationship or a job may be at stake, but being honest will always get you to the right place where you want, need, and should be.

Jim Rohn said it best. "Pay whatever price the truth costs because, in the long run, it's a real bargain."

Questions Of The Day

To end this lesson and to help you maintain honesty, ask yourself:

In which area of life do I find myself lying, even small white lies? What do I fear when I tell these lies? Can I put in the time and effort to make my lies become my reality?

If you can, then put in the effort to make your lies a reality for you. But if you can't, then stop the dishonesty and be courageous enough to face reality and be who you really are. You will be happier with yourself, and in the long run, you will have the proper foundation for lasting happiness.

As usual, I recommend writing your answers in the PDF journal.

Affirmation Of The Day

After answering the questions in your journal, and examining them, sit quietly for a few minutes today and repeat this affirmation:

I AM IN CONTROL OF WHAT I SAY, AND MY NATURAL RESPONSE IS HONESTY.

Repeat this affirmation often. With repetition, it has the power to alter your consciousness so you build a better, happier and more purposeful life.

DAY 40 - BECOMING AWARE OF THE IMPORTANCE OF HUMILITY

"Humility is not thinking less of yourself, it's thinking of yourself less." ~ C. S. Lewis

Humility is not about having less self-esteem but rather about understanding that there is still something new to learn every day and that there are others we can learn from, gain, and improve. Humility is understanding that you are not your best yet. There is still much to strive for.

It is also an understanding that we are all in this together.

In relationships, it is not new that nobody likes an arrogant braggart. Humility and vulnerability make us more likable. We know that to reach our fullest potential and be happiest, we have to have good relationships with people.

A lack of humbleness and humility often ruins any relationship. A lack of acceptance and respect for another person is the death of any relationship.

The same is also true with children. Time spent with them makes one more humble. It reminds us of where we came from.

Humility is also crucial for understanding that your children are not extensions of you but are their own beings. They may have different viewpoints and interests than your own, and this is legitimate.

We are all small compared to this wondrous, marvelous world around us. When we understand this, we learn to surrender and release many things. This is good for our mental health and a healthy state of mind.

Humble people attract others because they are more likely to admit their mistakes and don't take credit for other people's accomplishments. These characteristics are not only attractive to others; they are also a factor of success for both the individual and an organization where the individual works.

Being humble also allows one to constantly learn and improve oneself because they do not think they know it all. They are aware that they do not know it all and probably never know it all. They understand that they do not have all the answers. When a person thinks they have all of the answers, curiosity and learning stop, which hinders growth.

When we are humble, we are more open to new ideas and more open to change. And in an always-changing world, this is a valuable gift to have.

Humble people also pay more attention to what is going on around them more than arrogant people. Humble people take advice from people, especially experts. This increases intelligence and success rate and paves the path to their fulfillment.

Being humble is also better for seeing reality as it is. We can determine where we stand in comparison with where we desire to be much more clearly. Knowing ourselves and where we stand is a necessary first step towards progress and improvement.

The coronavirus pandemic led many people to become more humble. Even people of power who were not used to following other people's orders and regulations had to follow them for the sake of others and their community. People saw that they could not be arrogant in the face of a pandemic and that they need to change and follow very uncomfortable rules and regulations at times for the benefit of the community.

Admitting fault when wrong is not easy for anyone, but this is a trait of humbleness. Bosses who know how to give other people credit and take responsibility when they make a mistake are the most loved. This is important since they are seen as better leaders and followed more gladly. They also have strong listening skills. They listen to their workers, making people happier to work for them because they are not constantly giving orders.

Self-esteem is something you want to have and harness for your gain, but having a sense of humbleness, where others can help you and can teach you much and help you move forward, is a trait that will make you more likable and more successful. There is not one or the other. You can be both self-confident and still be humble, and the way to ensure this is by loving and accepting yourself as you are but still understanding that there is progress to be made.

Only a genuinely humble man can be free and can surrender to what life provides. They see themselves through realistic eyes and make improvements through this awareness to reach their ideal self.

Questions Of The Day

To end this lesson and help you develop humbleness, ask yourself:

What can I do to improve myself? Who can I listen to or learn from? Who's advice have I been too arrogant even to consider?

When you ask yourself this question and answer it honestly, you understand that you are not quite where you desire to be. And when you know this, you become more aware and more humble. From this position, you can continue to strive to be better for personal growth.

As usual, I recommend writing your answers in the PDF journal.

Affirmations Of The Day

After answering the questions in your journal, and examining them, sit quietly for a few minutes today and repeat this affirmation:

I SEE THINGS THROUGH REALISTIC EYES AND SEE MYSELF AS I REALLY AM SINCE I AM HUMBLE.

Repeat this affirmation often. With repetition, it has the power to alter your consciousness so you build a better, happier and more purposeful life.

DAY 41 - BECOMING AWARE OF POSITIVE VS. NEGATIVE MOTIVATORS

"In my experience, there is only one motivation, and that is desire. No reasons or principle contain it or stand against it." ~ Jane Smiley

We are not motivated to do something when we do not have a genuine desire.

Whenever our needs are satisfied, we won't have a strong enough reason to pursue a goal that will take much of our time and energy, so we will not be very motivated to do it. Often only unsatisfied needs move us to push forward.

However, some motivators will lead to a life of happiness and others to a life of unhappiness.

Although all motivation comes from unsatisfied needs, two groups of motivators move us to change. Some of those motivators are positive for our psyche, and others are negative for our psyche.

Negative motivators come from a lack of something. Positive motivators come from a choice. Let's talk about negative motivators that come from feelings of lacking.

Lack of money, resources, support, the right environment, health, and a lack of security are all negative motivators. This type of motivation comes from something you feel is missing in your life. You think that your life is not complete without this thing. You feel that you are not whole without it, and therefore cannot be happy without it. Many people find themselves in a mindset of lack. A lack mindset says I cannot be fully alive now because I do not have these things in my life now. I cannot enjoy the present moment and its experiences fully because I have something missing.

Negative motivators will always make you feel bad because you see yourself as broken right now, as incomplete.

Examples of these motivators include:

I need to lose ten pounds

I need to travel more

I need to be fitter

I need a bigger house

I need a better car

I need to heal from this disease

I need a partner

I need a different/better partner

I need a baby

All these state to your subconscious mind that without them, you are not good enough, whole or complete, and therefore you cannot be happy. This type of mindset is actually like a ball rolling downhill, gaining momentum. Because even once you lose the ten pounds and get that better car, new partner, a bigger house, the baby, and have healed from the disease, you will still not be satisfied because the lack never ends; it just grows into another lack.

On the other hand, positive motivators come from a choice, a choice of whether to live to your fullest potential or not. It is an option to make things better **not** because they are not good now, but because you CAN make them better.

Positive motivation comes from an understanding that we have everything within us to allow the love, abundance, and happiness that is already within us to come through. We are complete right now. All we have to do is let this completeness shine through and stop blocking it. We are full of love, we are full of abundant energy, happiness, and power, but we are blocking these from showing themselves to the world.

Positive motivation comes from choosing to improve on what is there because we can. It's that simple! Because we have it within us, we should express it.

This type of motivation reveals what can be, instead of continuing to block the energy, power, love, and abundance that we have within us that wants to show itself to the world. It comes from the natural will for progress, love, serving others, and improving what is to make it better. We all have this will within us, but it is often repressed.

This type of motivation does not come so that we can inflate our ego, bank account, or the way others view us, but rather from a place of giving and serving and showing our true selves to others.

We want to give and serve and love; these are inborn motivators, not because we lack something but because this is our true divine nature.

Some people use drugs or have other addictions that block their light. Other people become depressed because they forgot that they have this light within them; they have gone too long in darkness. Some people are anxious because they have forgotten their power to overcome whatever life throws at them.

Positive motivation comes from an understanding that what we see before us can be improved not because something is lacking but because we can make it better.

Let's take the smartphone invention. Was life good beforehand? Yes? But we could improve it. We could be more connected; we could have a computer in the hands of everyone. It did not come from a state of "I lack a computer in my hand right now" but it came from a thought that "I could have a computer in my hands now."

These inventions came from a motivator of what could be better, not from a viewpoint that we are missing something now.

Let's look at the simple example of weight loss. A negative motivation of lack would be: "I need to lose ten pounds to look and feel good; I am overweight." On the other hand, positive motivation for losing weight would be: "I could be healthier and move myself more easily as I did when I was young and have more energy to go after my dreams."

Now, let's look at money. A negative motivation of lack would be: "I need to make more money; I don't have enough to fulfill my needs." A positive motivation for making more money would be: "I would like to add more value to other people in the world."

Now let's look at relationships. A negative motivation of lack would be: "I need to get married and have children to complete myself."

A positive motivation for being in a great or better relationship would be: "I want an outlet for the love, acceptance, and understanding that I have within me and to enjoy the perfection of life together."

Let's look at healing. A negative motivation of lack would be: "I want my health back; I don't want to die." A positive motivation for healing would be: "I want to live well and long so that I can give back to the world the wonderful gifts I have within me."

In positive motivation, we wish to reach our true potential to be happier and make other people more content in the process. In negative motivation, we want to fix what is broken and not good with us to be okay.

I'm sure you now understand how the results of these two types of motivators will be completely different.

Questions Of The Day

To end this lesson and help you form positive motivation for your dreams, ask yourself:

Why do I want the things that I desire? Is it because I feel I have a lack of some sort, or is it because I want to give off my gifts to an already perfect world to reach a higher potential?

Now write down your dreams and make a list of positive, motivating affirmations to keep you headed in the right direction even when times of difficulty arise.

Aim to keep your motivation positive, so you enrich your life and other's lives and not constantly delve into negativity.

As usual, I recommend writing your answers in the PDF journal.

Affirmation Of The Day

After answering the questions in your journal, and contemplating on your answers, sit quietly for a few minutes today and repeat this affirmation:

I AM COMPLETE AS I AM, BUT I AM MOTIVATED TO UNFOLD MY HIGHER LIFE POTENTIAL EVERY DAY.

Repeat this affirmation often. With repetition, it has the power to alter your consciousness so you build a better, happier and more purposeful life.

DAY 42 - BECOMING AWARE OF THE IMPORTANCE OF SERVICE

"No one is useless in this world who lightens the burdens of another." ~ Charles Dickens

Being of service to others gives meaning and significance to our lives, both of which are foundations for feeling fulfilled.

There is no greater motivator for most people to do anything that seems difficult than doing something for another person. The most powerful motivator for action is when someone else besides you gains if you succeed.

There will be times when we feel as if there is no use for what we are trying to accomplish. We may even feel as if we are wasting our time or that no one will appreciate our work. In such times, the most significant motivating force behind you continuing to go after your dreams are the people who you help and will benefit from your hard work if you succeed.

The thought of people who are dependent on you, and need you to succeed, is a great motivating force to help you go through the hard times.

Ask yourself, who will benefit from my success besides myself?

Who will be helped by my success?

Who will gain from my perseverance?

The bigger your goals, the more you will need other people to become a motivating force. You can't do it on your own. Your will alone is not a strong enough motivator to get you through the difficult times you will encounter on your path towards achieving your goals. And the bigger the goals, the more ongoing motivation is needed.

The promise of personal wealth, fame, or power is not enough to motivate anyone through the difficulties of achieving their goals because these motivators are of the ego, which is not real.

There has to be a strong enough reason to pull you through, to get you to wake up early in the morning and do what needs to be done.

If you are the sole benefactor, one day, you may simply decide to stop.

You can see this in the elementary example of cooking at home. A person who cooks their spouse and children dinner every evening for years and loves cooking will eventually stop cooking or reduce cooking to a minimum when they divorce or when their spouse dies, or their children leave the house, and they have only themselves to cook for.

Deep down within us, we do things for others more than we do things for ourselves, and when we have others as our motivating force behind our dreams, there is nothing that can stop us.

Other people become the real reason for our perseverance, much more than any gain of money, power, or fame, which if they are your only motivators, then when difficulty arises, you will run away, with the understandable thought of "why do I need this?" And you will be correct. If no one else benefits from your actions and success, you will not have the internal energy to pull through all the complexities you will meet on the way.

Doing what you do from a standpoint that what you are doing will also help others will ensure that you reach the finish line. Without this motivation, you pretty much have no chance.

I went into real estate when my lawyer told me that my daughters would be taken away from me if I did not have sufficient income to afford taking care of them with their special needs. They became my motivating force for making money. Before this moment, I did not understand how vital being wealthy was. This completely changed my perspective and my path in life. Until I became financially free, I could not be stopped. I worked so hard the following years after my lawyer spoke those words to me that nothing could stop me from reaching the goal of financial freedom.

Also, when I had cancer, I was told that I would need radiotherapy and that during the treatment, I would not be able to go near my children for a month because I would be radiating, and this would be harmful to them. I decided that I would find a better way to ensure my healing. This fueled my research into the ideal diet for humans. For me, the motivating force was not to leave my daughters motherless and do something that would heal me and others naturally rather than destructively.

Internal motivation to start and continue any task is key to success, but being of service to other people will help ensure we have all the motivation to see things through to the end.

Although helping others may seem as if it is an external motivator, it is actually an internal motivator, meaning that it comes from within. Someone did not tell us to do it, and it does not come from competition, which is an external motivator.

When you have the mindset of being of service to others, you feel the responsibility to succeed, and thus many times, self-sabotage does not creep in and mess up things for you. Because of the belief that you are not doing this only for your benefit.

When we are of service to others, we are also giving to ourselves. It makes us happier, more fulfilled and fills our life with significance, an essential factor for feeling happy and fulfilled.

Questions Of The Day

To end this lesson and help you move into the mindset of being of service to others, ask yourself:

How will the achievement of each of my goals improve the lives of other people in a major way?

As usual, I recommend writing your answers in the PDF journal.

Affirmation Of The Day

After answering the questions in your journal, and examining them, sit quietly for a few minutes today and repeat this affirmation:

I REJOICE IN BEING OF SERVICE.

Repeat this affirmation often. With repetition, it has the power to alter your consciousness so you build a better, happier and more purposeful life.

DAY 43 - BECOMING AWARE OF THE POWER OF GIVING

"To do more for the world than the world does for you – that is success." ~ Henry Ford

Giving is the key to your success. What you give, you will get back. In this lesson, I will talk about why this is so.

We are always in the process of giving something. If you give intentionally, with the mindset of spreading love, abundance, and happiness, then this is what you all get back manifold.

Everything you give out will come back to you. But why?

As Newton stated in his third law of motion, when two objects interact, they apply forces on each other of equal magnitude and opposite direction.

Or, in lay terms, what you give out, you will get it back in equal magnitude.

The energy you feel and the intentions you hold will come back to you in kind. If you are doing things from love, care, and kindness to others, the energy you give out will return to you in equal proportions.

It doesn't matter how much or how little you give, or if what you gave was positive or negative; it is the energy of giving and the energy from the receiver that will come back to you in similar form.

If you help someone heal, you will feel good that you helped him, and since you did it from love and care, these emotions have an energy that will come back to you. But also, the receiver's feelings of happiness, peace, and gratitude will come back to you. If they have a spouse or children who are also grateful for your actions, their feelings of love and appreciation will also return.

Now can you see how whatever you give comes back in multitude?

If you do every action from a place of giving love, kindness, and from a state of abundance, you will only know prosperity, love, and happiness in your life from this moment on.

Therefore, you may give without any expectation from the other person because there is nothing that you give out that will not return to you. This is the law of cause and effect. Fuse your actions with positive emotions, and you will receive back things that will produce the same positive emotions within you.

Give out love and care, and this will come back to you manifold in different ways, such as in the form of money, patience, help, support, health, success, a great relationship, and so on.

It is all about the mindset in which you live your life. If you are with the mindset that you are giving from love, care, and kindness, everything you do will propel even more of these back into your life.

At the beginning of this book, I spoke of the hero's journey. The hero's journey is only fulfilled, and the person only becomes a real hero when they give back to society from what they learned and gained on their journey. Fulfillment of the journey does not mean the journey is entirely over. The tests and trials will always continue; this is life. But the hero no longer has the inner battles, between the ego and their soul's desire, as they had previous to finishing their journey. The act of giving from a place of sharing, unity, and love, is what makes them a real hero.

All the difficulties a person goes through on the hero's journey are only there to bring them to a place of giving from love and care.

In the bible, it says that all things are done *for* you. This does not mean that living through ego or selfishness are the right ways to live life, but rather to see that all the trials you go through in life have their purpose in your evolution towards becoming a hero.

The Golden Rule states to do onto others what you would like them to do unto you. Do what generates good vibes and love within you.

Feel these positive emotions when you are in the act of giving to another. Even when you are writing a message or an email to another person, infuse all your actions with love energy.

Give more than is expected from you, and you will get back much more than you ever expect.

Nothing can make life richer than the act of giving.

Anything you do in life that you do not do only for yourself is an act of giving. If you focus your days on doing for others, you will wake up in the morning energized, happy, and fulfilled even before your day has begun.

If you give from joy and happiness and rouse these feelings when they receive from you, nothing can be better than this for you and the world.

Think of how much love and joy you are spreading. This love and joy that you give one person affects so many others.

But the opposite is also true. When you give out negative energy, you will get negativity tenfold back into your life.

Choose your daily actions wisely! Take conscious actions.

We all can overcome the egoic nature. We just have to make the right choices every moment. We are capable of doing this.

Focus on giving love, health, happiness, inspiration, motivation, education, money, and time. Spreading these energies will transform your life immediately and elevate your soul.

By transforming every action into an act of giving, you are planting positive energy in the soil of your life and the world. This positive energy will blossom into the grandest prosperity and fulfillment for you and the world around you with time.

Wow! What an opportunity every minute of your life holds!

How much joy can come to you, to the receiver, and the world, from a simple act of giving?

Giving from positive emotions, intentions, and a positive state of mind is always more important than what you offer, because whatever you do is infused with the vibration with which you do it.

You will even find that giving can become addictive. This is known as the "helpers high". When you help others, you not only benefit from what will come to you from the energy that you send out, but you will also benefit immediately from the endorphins, those feel-good chemicals that your body produces that fill you with feelings of well-being.

Just like a runner's high, endorphins are released during a run; endorphins are also released when giving, making you feel high!

We were created in such a clever way that when we are doing good things for ourselves and others in line with our soul's desire, they make us feel great and release endorphins.

Other things that are good for us also release endorphins. These include physical contact, eating fruits, nuts, and seeds, and doing exercise. Do you see how we are rewarded in the future and immediately when we do the right things for ourselves and others? People become addicted to these feelings. If only more people knew that giving releases the same well-being chemicals in the body like drugs, alcohol, and cigarettes, the world would be a better place.

This is why so many people who complete rehab choose to help others overcome addictions. They get the helpers-high, making them feel as good as they felt when addicted to the non-beneficial element.

When you forget yourself for the sake of others, you get everything you desire from life and more.

Jim Rohn said, "He who serves the most, reaps the most."

This is your key to success. Give the most with the energy of care, love, and compassion, and you will get fulfillment, joy, and abundance in every field of life in return.

Winston Churchill said, "We make a living by what we get, but we make a life by what we give."

Anne Frank said, "No one has ever become poor by giving."

Spending money is also an act of giving. You are giving back to the person or business that has brought you value in some way. The movement of money from hand to hand keeps this energy moving. This is why it is essential to have sufficient wealth. When you spend, you are giving.

When you spend money with the energy of giving, loving, and caring, the act of spending money will bring you back more. This is why stinginess in any form blocks the life force from you. It is the mindset behind everything you do that will make or break you. When you do everything as an act of giving, as an act of love, appreciation, and kindness, you will bring more of that energy into your life, bringing more love and compassion into the world. You are always giving something anyway, so make sure it is good! Make sure what you give out is really what you would like to get back.

Give everything from a place of love, and love will fill your life in so many ways you can never imagine.

Questions Of The Day

To end this lesson and to help you incorporate giving into your life, ask yourself:

In my day-to-day life, am I spreading the energy that I would like to receive in return? Would I want to get back the energy I am giving out? How can I give more love? Am I stingy from fear that I don't have enough? How can I give more to others? Am I spending my money from love to others?

As usual, I recommend writing your answers in the PDF journal.

Affirmation Of The Day

After answering the questions in your journal, and examining them, sit quietly for a few minutes today and repeat this affirmation:

I AM IN A CONSTANT STATE OF GIVING - FROM LOVE, KINDNESS, AND COMPASSION - TO EVERYONE I MEET. WOW, WHAT AN ABUNDANT LIFE I LEAD!

Repeat this affirmation often as it has the power to alter your consciousness so you build a better, happier and more purposeful life.

DAY 44 - BECOMING AWARE OF UNCONDITIONAL LOVE

"When you start loving unconditionally, you stop judging people" ~ Anonymous

Always judge others favorably if you are to judge them at all. We should understand that we are all part of one big family. We are all the products of consciousness. When we see others in this light, unconditional love becomes natural. When we consider the root of all souls, our connection and union becomes evident.

Unconditional love for others happens naturally when you introspect and learn to have unconditional love for yourself; when you accept yourself as you are, with your gifts and shortcomings.

What we may perceive as negative behaviors often comes from *our* wounded egos. But when we introspect our behaviors and realize that only our ego takes things personally, we will stop taking things personally, and life becomes more joyful. Our true identity can never be wounded.

When you release expectations from any given situation, you will never be disappointed and can only be surprised for the better. This sense of freedom comes from being who you truly are, without trying to change yourself to please others, be someone you are not, or change the situation or other people to please yourself.

When you give unconditional love and acceptance to yourself, love and acceptance will surround you. When you appreciate yourself, you will appreciate all that surrounds you.

Living in unconditional love makes the world a kinder place and makes your experience of the world happier.

Giving unconditional love is up to you. It is a love that doesn't ask for anything in return.

The person who gives unconditional love is the one who benefits most.

Adopt the feeling that you are working only for infinite intelligence. Live your life like this. When you live like this, you will never need to receive anything from the person in front of you. There are no expectations from other people. You receive from your employer, infinite intelligence.

When you come with the attitude that you do not need to get anything in return from the person you are interacting with because you are working in the service of infinite intelligence, you become less judgmental of the behavior of others, and you are naturally more accepting and understanding.

Unconditional love becomes second nature when we know that we are all connected, and that our situation is perfect for our development and the development of the whole.

Know that all problematic situations are there to bring you to a place of understanding that you are one with everything, and part of something much greater than yourself.

It is not always easy to see the connection between all people and all situations, and it is not even necessary. Still, when you understand that all people are doing their best with the level of awareness they have, you can better understand other people's sometimes challenging behaviors.

Love connected to material benefits is not real love. It is conditional. It places a boundary on love. If the material benefit dissipates, so does the love.

Unconditional love is the foundation for a truly deep connection that never ends. Unconditional loves is the basis for our connection with all that is.

The most important thing gained from understanding the foundation of unconditional love is inner peace and a life that is free from expectations—a life of enjoying what is in front of you in the present moment.

If *IT* is there in front of you, it means that *IT* is the perfect experience for you at this moment in time to help you improve yourself, become better and more accepting, and help you show your authentic gifts, and let your light shine through. Every moment holds the space where you can allow yourself to display either the best version of yourself or something less than this. It is always your choice.

Questions Of The Day

To connect you with your true essence of unconditional love, please ask yourself:

Where in my life am I not giving myself and others unconditional love? Can I accept myself and others as a reflection of infinite intelligence? Where do I still need to work on seeing the present moment as a present gift for me and the world?

As usual, I recommend writing your answers in the PDF journal.

Affirmation Of The Day

After answering the questions in your journal, and contemplating on your answers, sit quietly for a few minutes today and repeat this affirmation:

I am whole and complete, and I radiate unconditional love to the entire world around me.

I AM UNCONDITIONAL LOVE!

Repeat this affirmation often. With repetition, it has the power to alter your consciousness so you build a better, happier and more purposeful life.

DAY 45 - BECOMING AWARE OF HOW TO DO YOUR BEST

"Do the best you can, with what you can, while you can, and success is inevitable."

~ Steve Maraboli

If you take a look at nature, you will see that everything always does its best. If you look at the plants, you know that they grow as much as possible and give as many fruit or flowers as possible. If they are not giving enough, there is a reason, but they always do their best in the situation and conditions they have. You will not find lazy plants or lazy ants.

We humans, on the other hand, have free will. We can *choose* not to do our best. We can choose not to make the best choices for ourselves. Therefore it is essential to understand that if you want to be the best you can be, you must decide to do your best in any situation.

Doing your best will change with time as you grow and develop and learn new skills. In effect, you will constantly be changing and improving on what you can do under your circumstances at any given time.

But once you do your best in any given situation, you remove many negative emotions that come when you aren't doing your best, such as regret, self-criticism, and even personal abuse.

When you know that you did your best, you will feel happy no matter the results because you know that you did all you could do under the circumstances.

If you like what you do, it will be much easier for you to do your best. If you are in a job, a relationship, a home, or taking part in an activity you like, it will be much easier for you to do your best. So you want to aim to have most of your day filled with things you like to do.

However, this is not always an option, and there will be times when you will need to do things even when you don't want or like to do them. In such cases, you will still want to do your best because of the person you become. You change and become a better version of yourself when you do things that are not necessarily what you desire to do but still *have* to do. When you become aware of your necessity to do something even though you do not want to do it and do your best, you become a changed individual. You become a better version of yourself.

For example, when studying at school or university, many subjects may not interest you, but you still have to study them to pass your exams and get your degree. And when you do your best even in these subjects, you will understand that you are capable of much more than you think you can do. You will also see that you can do a wide variety of things that you never thought possible for you. I believe this is one of the most important lessons I have learned at university; that I can learn and do things that I am not that interested in, and in a good way if it is necessary to reach my final goal.

Another example is doing the bureaucratic work that needs to be done to reach your goals. Some countries are socialistic where everything done needs to go through a lot of bureaucracy. It takes effort and time to fill out forms to advance anything, and most people hate doing this. But if you go through and complete the procedure step by step, doing your best, and persisting, good things will come from it.

Doing your best results in so many virtues, including:

- Self-control
- Self-discipline
- Diligence.

- Patience.
- Kindness.
- Humility.

You can always at least try to do your best. You will never know if you don't try.

If you have children, you know that each child has their personality, wishes, and desires. If you do your best at raising them to be happy, independent, honest, good people, then you did your best.

Later in life, if you gain satisfaction from your child, this is an extra benefit. But your happiness should not depend on the results you get, but rather only on whether you did your best.

It's better to try and fail than never try. When you fail, you learn something. Failure is not considered a failure if you discovered a vital lesson. However, if you don't try your best, you won't have learned anything and will still be in the same place you were before with no growth, and no lessons learned. You take a risk when you do your best. But if you never take risks, you will have a dull life, indeed a life far from your true potential and a favorable outcome.

Failure is always a possibility. Nevertheless, you want to set high and worthy goals for yourself and do your best to achieve them. You want to try to reach your fullest potential. You must take risks to reach your full potential and do your best to avoid failure whenever you can.

The more involved with something you are, the better you will be at it. Be involved in whatever is essential for you to live your fullest, and do your best as much as possible.

When it comes to health, I help many people understand the ideal diet for humans and incorporate the best lifestyle habits for health into their lives, but what I tell everyone is to do their best one day at a time. With patience and best effort, your health and vitality goals become achievable.

So how do you know if you are doing your best?

Ask yourself these questions:

Have I read as much as I could have today? Have I learned all that I could have today? Did I do as many of my tasks towards my goals as I could have? Have I had time for friends and family as much as I could have today? Have I seen as much as I could have today? Have I earned as much as I could have?

See things through to the end. Finish what you start by doing your best every single day.

Questions Of The Day

To end off this lesson and help you do your best today and every day, ask yourself: In which areas of my life can I do better? And which new skills or knowledge should I gain to do my best in this field? And how or where can I get these skills and knowledge as soon as possible?

As usual, I recommend writing your answers in the PDF journal.

Affirmation Of The Day

After answering the questions in your journal, and examining them, sit quietly for a few minutes today and repeat this affirmation:

I REFUSE TO GIVE UP BECAUSE I HAVEN'T TRIED ALL POSSIBLE WAYS. I WILL DO THE BEST I CAN ALWAYS.

Repeat this affirmation often. With repetition, it has the power to alter your consciousness so you build a better, happier and more purposeful life.

DAY 46 - BECOMING AWARE OF THE IMPORTANCE OF CURIOSITY

"Very few people really see things unless they've had someone in early life who made them look at things." ~ Denise Levertov

Increased awareness of your surroundings is what allows for more opportunities. The more you notice what is going on around you, the higher your perception becomes. And when your perception is high, many opportunities and ideas for improving your day-to-day life and perhaps even other people's lives will come to you.

When you notice things that are happening around you and become more aware, you become more valuable to the world. You will see things more clearly. You will see what other people don't see, and you will recognize more opportunities.

This increased awareness is like the universe opening up and sharing its secrets with you.

All it takes is observation and curiosity to notice opportunities in any field of life. You can notice new foods that others are eating and notice how they are being cooked and served by examining menus of different restaurants.

You will notice different people, and if you smile at them, your opportunity for more relationships opens up, both for business networking and personal relationships.

Business ideas will come to you when you notice what you and other people are doing or not doing or having difficulties with.

Also, ways for implementation, distribution, and marketing will come naturally when you become more aware of your surroundings and how other people behave.

It is a heightened awareness of the things around us that will inspire us to do things we had never done before or even thought possible.

So how can you increase your awareness?

1. Self-knowledge. By educating yourself about yourself, your feelings, behaviors, and motivators, and whatever interests you, you become more aware of yourself and the life around you. You become aware of your choices, perception of life, the people around you, your environment, and new ideas.

   You grow as a person when you implement what you have learned through introspection to make your life better and perhaps even make the world better.

   Jim Rohn said, "Formal education will make you a living, but self-education will make you a fortune.

   The more learned you become, the more understanding you have, and the more opportunities you will notice.

   Self-learning is when you gather knowledge from many sources and then use your thought process to put all the pieces together.

   Knowledge from self-directed study, experience, and awareness will transform your world by changing your perception of the world.

It would be best if you controlled your education; this is the only way to progress in any field of life.

2. Look at things more intensely, with more curiosity. Notice life around you; this triggers your curiosity.

   Once you become curious about something, it sparks your interest, and then you go and learn more about it. No matter what the subject, when you are interested in it, you learn and better retain what you learned.

   Leonardo da Vinci said, "Study without desire spoils the memory, and it retains nothing that it takes in." This is so true. When we are forced to learn things that we have no motivation for, such as learning only for an exam, soon after the exam is over, all of that information is forgotten. Our mind does not find use in it and puts it far away from our consciousness.

   But when we educate ourselves through curiosity that comes from awareness, we can produce original ideas, discover the world and life around us, and move things to make us and others happier while also bringing forth our true divine nature.

   Once you feed your curiosity through knowledge, you see things differently, which will transform your life for the better.

3. Learn from other people's knowledge and experience. You may want to discover how other people overcame specific problems that you are now experiencing. By reading forums, reading biographies, and watching films of people you admire, you tap into their pool of wisdom.

   This will help you comprehend different lessons from other people's lives and implement them into your own life, and then you become more aware of opportunities that can help you reach your goals.

4. Think for yourself and tap into your intuition. Most people do not think for themselves or listen to their gut feelings. Most people are disconnected from themselves. They accept as truth what others tell them. It is like choosing to walk around wearing horse blinkers which prevent the horse from seeing their rear and sides. Most people are unaware of their feelings, emotions, or thoughts, let alone aware of other people's feelings and cues. This forms a limited outlook on life. This is what makes people pessimistic.

If you want to become successful in all fields of life, you must take off the blinkers and become curiously aware of yourself, your surroundings, other people, and nature.

To do this, self-awareness, and alone time is helpful. Introspection and walks in nature help you connect with your values and beliefs.

Observe what is, and then find truths. Sit still and observe. Then understand and use this knowledge to create opportunities for yourself and create a better version of yourself for the world to see.

Isn't it so amazing to know that if you really want something and it is right for you, you *can* most likely achieve it? By increasing your awareness through curiosity and self-learning, by reading books and biographies, watching movies and YouTube videos, and then implementing what you have learned for your own and other people's benefit, you can transform your world.

Many of us have forgotten our curiosity during our school years. Mark Twain said, "I have never let my schooling interfere with my education."

To bring curiosity into your life, you want to have some regular time in solitude, especially in nature, but also in the middle of a bustling city is good. You can sit and observe the people and the things around you and contemplate on them. This curiosity is essential for making better choices for you in the future.

When you become more aware, you will also see more of the wonders that the world has to offer, and you will usually see your situation with brighter eyes. This will make you feel happier and more alive.

Buddha said, "If we could see the miracle of a single flower clearly, our whole life would change."

Now is the time to show more awe of what is happening around you, be more receptive, and intensify your curiosity. Now is the time to walk the path of curiosity and awareness to reach the life you desire.

Questions Of The Day

To end this lesson and help you increase curiosity to raise your awareness, ask yourself:

How can I increase my awe of life? Which movies can I watch, which biographies can I read, and where can I go to sit and observe what is happening around me quietly? Where can I sit in solitude for a few hours and contemplate? Now that you know what and where you can do these things, find the time to do them. It is vital to awaken your senses and open your life up to the bountiful opportunities available but are kept in secret until you are open to these secrets.

As usual, I recommend writing your answers in the PDF journal.

After answering the questions in your journal, and contemplating on your answers, sit quietly for a few minutes today and repeat this affirmation to yourself as you think and dwell upon it:

EVERYDAY OPPORTUNITIES OPEN UP BEFORE ME BECAUSE I AM CURIOUS ABOUT LIFE, AND I AM MORE AWARE OF THE WORLD AROUND ME.

Repeat this affirmation often. With repetition, it has the power to alter your consciousness so you build a better, happier and more purposeful life.

DAY 47 - BECOMING MORE AWARE OF SELF EDUCATION

"Self-education is a continuing source of pleasure to me, for the more I know, the fuller my life is and the better I appreciate my own existence" ~ Isaac Asimov

Self-education is one of the single most important activities a person can do to increase their awareness and opportunity. It opens up the world to you. It allows other people in, people who had something important to say.

The way you spend your days today and how you spend your free time will give you a precise map of where you will be a decade from now. Are you happy with the direction your life is going? If not, then you have to alter the scales of your time spent on entertainment and your time spent on study, learning, and observation.

One of the best ways to tilt these scales is by reading books by great influencers. You never know where great, life-changing ideas will come from.

Leading conversations with intelligent people is also important for influencing your life and widening your point of view, but what if that is not an option available to you because of where you currently are in life?

In that case, one of the best ways to escape an otherwise unhappy and unfulfilling future is by reading books written by strong, influential people, or reading their biographies. This will allow you to tap into their minds and learn from their wisdom, skills, attitudes, and different perspectives that will help you move your life forward to the best place for you.

Another way to self-educate and tap into influential minds is through movies, documentaries, or videos created by or of influential people.

When you tap into such minds by reading books or watching movies, you cannot comprehend how much power they have on your state of mind and life, just as we are influenced in the same powerful way by people who are close to us.

If your family members or close friends do not read books, what are the chances that you will read books? Very low, unless you choose to change and adopt this habit one page at a time.

This is how you can slowly change your circle of influence and make it better than it is by natural circumstances.

When powerful, successful, competent, honest, kind and charitable people fill your circle of influence, your thoughts and habits start to change as a result. When you don't closely watch with a critical eye your circle of influence, you may find yourself in a place that you never desired or dreamed to be ten years from now.

But if you control your circle of influence by reading books and biographies and then taking action following what you have learned, you are ensuring that you *will* reach your goals and your life will be favorable for you now and in the future.

You will believe in yourself and feel competent to follow your soul's desire to a life that will ensure your fulfillment and bliss.

You must pay close attention to the influencers in your life to make sure that your life goes according to *your* plans.

Ask yourself, who am I around? Whose books am I reading? What and who are influencing my life? How am I self-educating?

When you read good books, watch good movies, documentaries or videos, or take courses, your mind develops, your thoughts expand, and your life advances as a result.

By feeding your mind words written by thoughtful people, you expand your thoughts and even your reality, opening doors that you never thought possible to open.

Watching movies based on real stories and documentaries will also introduce you to many concepts that will enrich your life and help you align your life with your dreams.

When you expand your circle of influence through movies, books, and courses you will slowly find yourself behaving differently, observing the world with different, more realistic eyes. You will be spending your time differently, reading more, going to different places, thinking, talking, and even feeling differently. This is the power that self-education has over your mind.

But the same is also true for negative influence. People who are a poor influence will have you thinking, feeling, talking, and behaving differently. This is why it is so important to choose your company well. Surround yourself with likeminded people. Ask yourself who would you like to be like and then self-educate through books or movies that they wrote or were made about them.

Reading is such a powerful self-education tool. It makes your brain more active and engaged. Books also take you on adventures that you could have never otherwise gone on. This opens your life to new opportunities, to more empathy, unity, and love. Books can also keep you company when you are lonely; they help you meet people that you could have never met, even people who may have died many years ago. We can still see reality through their eyes, even for a brief period, by reading their books, or watching movies about them, and this can change everything for us.

The more you read, the better you also become at writing and communicating, which are essential skills to have for success. Because these skills help you become better at persuading and leading others, and the benefits are endless.

When you surround yourself with powerful, good, influential people by self-educating through books or movies, it is as if you are physically surrounding yourself with these people, even if only briefly. And when you surround yourself with such outstanding people, they will help you move your life in the direction you wish to go.

If your associations are not tipping you in the right direction, reading good books and watching documentaries and good movies can help you change this.

How much of life are you leaving uncovered, and unrevealed, because you are not open to reading books?

Think about the wealth of knowledge that is available but not open to you because you choose not to read, learn and investigate.

When you don't read good books, or watch documentaries and nonfiction movies, you don't have an upper hand at things.

Instead, petty things will sway you off course.

Everything we come across, influences our lives so dramatically, and we don't even realize it.

This is why it is so important to take control of your time. Control how you spend your free time and what goes into your mind. Restrict who you associate with. Breakaway or lessen contact with negative influencers. By self-educating through the lessons of influential and mindful people, you can tip any scales in your favor.

This increases the quality of your life because you are putting your time in the right place.

Let's suppose you are not interested in an average, mediocre life, otherwise you would probably not be reading this book. In that case, you must learn to improve yourself through self-education. Reading is a great way to focus your priorities, commitments, and values and help you better understand people, situations, and life.

We have very little spare time with all of the commitments we have today, so it would be wise to spend any free time on something that will improve your life and move you to where you truly desire to be.

When you self-educate regularly, you will secure a positive long-lasting return on your time investment, almost like no other. It will help you secure a better future for yourself starting today.

Self-educate by reading books of substance, about culture, of people of accomplishment and character.

Then create your life plan according to what you learned and connected to from high achievers. Examine their life plans and how they succeeded. What helped them? What moved them? And ask yourself what drives you?

Questions Of The Day

To end off this lesson and help you self-educate, ask yourself:

How can I commit to self-education weekly? How can I better spend my free time? Which subjects interest me? Which people do I admire because of their achievements? Which movies can I watch, which books or biographies can I read?

Now go out and read their books or books written about these people.

It is vital to awaken your senses and open up your life to the bountiful opportunities available to you but are kept in secret until you are open to these secrets.

As usual, I recommend writing your answers in the notebook you have received with this book.

Affirmation Of The Day

After answering the questions in your journal, and examining them, sit quietly for a few minutes today and repeat this affirmation to yourself as you think and dwell upon it:

I LEARN, UNLEARN AND RELEARN DAILY THROUGH THE BOOKS, MOVIES AND COURSES I ATTEND.

Repeat this affirmation often. With repetition, it has the power to alter your consciousness so you build a better, happier and more purposeful life.

DAY 48 - BECOMING AWARE OF YOUR CREATIVITY

"To practice any art, no matter how well or badly, is a way to make your soul grow. So do it."

~ Kurt Vonnegut

On previous days we spoke about how each person has unique gifts and that there is a perfect way for every person to express their talents. We also talked about self-education. To find the perfect expression for your gifts, you must use your creative power.

This creative power is the basis for progress and is the basis for true happiness. This creative power is the essence of life. We are all created in the likeness of Source, a creator. Therefore we are all creators, and to be happy, we must create. In essence, everything created is created two times.

First, it must be created in our imagination, and then it is created a second time physically. This is how any artist works and creates a masterpiece. Everything is first created in mind.

As Kurt Vonnegut said, the creative process makes our soul grow.

Creativity expands what is and makes it better.

We all have this creative force within us. We are always in the process of creating something, whether we are aware of it or not. And when we allow our mind the freedom to create, without boundaries of what is acceptable, what is known, or what is familiar, we can have anything we desire.

But often, we do not use our creative powers consciously and not to their full potential. Either we create without awareness that we are creating or take other people's creations and make them our own.

Sometimes our parents, our community, or our society create a vision for what is acceptable, and we accept this vision as our own.

We may follow a vision that our parents created. Their visions have formed their habits and their habits become our habits. We may eat certain foods, live in certain places, and follow the culture and behaviors that are acceptable in their eyes. But the life that will come out of following someone else's created vision for us will not, in most cases, make us happy.

We often choose how to live by following the habits of our previous generations even though it may not seem this way when observing your children. But they do have similar habits, just different outlets for these habits. For example, a previous generation may come home after work and not want to leave the couch and tv; and in this generation, to relax after a hard day at work or in school, the kids may not want to leave their smartphones. We think as previous generations thought in most cases even though technology makes this more difficult to comprehend. Our health is as theirs, and our love life similar to theirs when we follow their vision that they *created* with their imagination or may have even created unconsciously.

The previous generations may have created their life, and it seemed to work for them.

You have received these creations as a regular part of your life, as habits you accepted, without using your creative abilities to introspect and then create what YOU truly want instead.

The first part of these creations or habits, the thinking and imagining part, is often not done by you but was instead done in someone else's mind. In the person you may have learned this habit from, or perhaps even the person they learned and took this habit from.

Other people may have created their eating habits, their life patterns, their beliefs, their religion, their relationships, etc., and you took on these creations and used them as if you had created them in your imagination yourself.

But what would happen if you changed this? What would happen if you would have made your own creations for your eating habits, for your relationships, for where you would like to work, and for your whole life? What would happen if you chose to create your own habits through your own common sense, and through thoughts of what is really right for you? This introspection can change your whole life trajectory. What would happen if you decided that you do not want to take another person's creations and use them as your own but prefer to create the life of your dreams in every field of life on your own terms and for your own self?

What would happen? Where could your life be now? How happy would you be?

This is true awareness.

We are creative beings, and we should be creating our life though our own common sense even if it is likely to be different from our previous generations' beliefs and choices. This is real evolution.

We are all creators, and we can use this power within us every day. We can create a different and better reality for us; we can create an ideal existence.

The creative process starts in the mind and then moves into the physical plane. Pablo Picasso said, "Everything you can imagine is real."

When you use this creative ability, you can have all that you desire. When you become aware of the creative process, then you can use it for your own benefit.

Pablo Picasso also said, "The chief enemy of creativity is having good sense." When we follow all that we were led to believe is right, we follow good sense, but we will not be living to our fullest potential.

We need to use *OUR* creativity to help us form the vision of *OUR* ideal life in every area and then do the work to make it happen.

Once the vision is formed, it *is* possible. Then do what is required to produce the masterpiece of your life.

Whether you are still clueless about your vision or have a clear picture of what you would like to create, it is still best to use intuition to help you form your ideal vision. There is no need to push or force this creative process, but rather let it come *through* you. Many famous artists and music composers all saw or heard their art before forming it into physical reality. They say it came to their conscious mind through intuition. Michael Jackson said he received the songs from a higher power. So did Beethoven and many other musicians. Michelangelo also stated he received his ideas from higher intelligence. Everything is first created in the imagination, and we can connect to higher consciousness through intuition to perfect the creation. Follow your intuition, create the vision, and then do what needs to be done, one step at a time, to form your creation in reality.

Questions Of The Day

To end this lesson and help you tap into your creative powers ask yourself:

What habits in my life are there because I took on someone else's creation as my own? In which areas of my life am I unhappy with the results of these creations?

Which habits would I like to change in my life?

Now you know which areas of your life were created unconsciously, and you can start with a blank canvas to begin creating anew what you desire to have in that area of life.

As usual, I recommend writing your answers in the PDF journal.

Affirmation Of The Day

After answering the questions in your journal, and contemplating on your answers, sit quietly for a few minutes today and repeat this affirmation to yourself as you think and dwell upon it:

USING MY INTUITION, I AM RECREATING MY LIFE ACCORDING TO MY DREAMS.

Repeat this affirmation often. With repetition, it has the power to alter your consciousness so you build a better, happier and more purposeful life.

DAY 49 - BECOMING AWARE OF YOUR ADDICTIONS

"Though no one can go back and make a brand new start, anyone can start from now and make a brand new ending." ~ Carl Bard

Many people go through life wishing they could have done things differently. Since we can't change the past, we can still choose to make a better life by not letting the past affect our present and ruin our future. Many people have come to addictions because they couldn't cope naturally with what life threw at them. But when you suffer from an addiction, you will never be able to fulfill yourself. Your own habits jail you. Life becomes unbearable.

People may be addicted to different things without realizing they are not free to live their lives as they desire without the addictive element. Any dependence on anything external reduces your connection to infinite intelligence.

In a practical outlook, addictions waste your life, ruin your health, clear out your pockets and leave you feeling worthless.

Addictions are so powerful over us, and the worst part is that when we try out an addictive substance or behavior with the potential to become addictive, we do not realize the power they will have over us. We say, it won't happen to me, I am strong, and all of the other lies we tell ourselves.

Without realizing it, we first use addictive substances to get us out of our physical nature and connect us with the immaterial/spiritual world. Through addictive elements, we feel this connection more strongly. But of course, after using the addictive element or following the addictive behavioral pattern a few times, we forget our connection to the immaterial world and claim a connection to the addictive element or behavior, grounding ourselves deeper in the ego and the material world.

Now the addictive element or behavior becomes a release of tension that builds up when we don't connect to infinite intelligence. We do it or take it again and again only to fall deeper in misery and further from our connection to our true divine nature. We also disconnect from our ability to accommodate feelings without the addictive element or behavior.

As I mentioned, you may even benefit from the addictive element or behavior at the beginning of an addiction. You feel more in control because you may feel that your connection to your divine nature is strengthened. You may also become more creative, better at sports, more relaxed, outgoing, fun, courageous, confidant, and conversational.

At first, the addictive elements may help you overcome challenging behaviors that you feel hold you back from being who you really are and want to be. They allow you to be that perfect version of yourself connected to infinite intelligence that is unlimited, all-powerful, all-knowing, all accepting, and eternal.

But this connective state with your true divine nature is transient.

To reach a certain level of consciousness and integrity, and success, you must go through difficult trials and errors. You must fail at times and must do the hard work to pick yourself up.

These trials change you and connect you to infinite intelligence helping you become the person you desire to be.

Addictions are the shortcut to making you feel this way, but the feeling is transient, and I know of no shortcut worth taking to anything worthy.

Although in the beginning, addictions make you feel as if you are that ideal version of yourself, deep down inside, you know that you are not there yet, and when the high wears off, you are faced with reality as it is, not as you would like it to be. So you take more of the addictive element or do more of the addictive behavior to dull your senses, dull negative feelings, and feel the connection again. But what you are really doing is getting yourself further and further away from your desired destination. And the circle goes around again and again.

Hundreds of thousands of people have their lives lost or ruined due to addictions.

And the craziest thing is that we often do not want to stop.

We know our lives are on hold, we know that we are not doing anything with our life and time except focusing on the addictive element, and we know that our money is also going down the drain even if we owe it to other people.

This is very sad since the people who tend to turn to addictions are usually the most creative, sensitive, and promising people with very high potential. They also know that they have skills and can get very far in life, but they are afraid of doing what it takes. They are scared to take the leap or are fearful of change, or are worried they won't manage to do the work and succeed. They are afraid of failing, but when they succumb to the addiction, they are already failing.

Addictions are slavery.

Some people stay addicted because they are bored. Still, cigarettes, alcohol, drugs, or junk food are not interesting in themselves, so following with the addiction is just burning time.

Without the addictive element, one feels empty. But when we stop the addiction, we slowly fill our lives up again.

Therefore, all addictions must be stopped, or else the cycle is always there. The addictive element enters the body because we crave it, or the addictive feeling is triggered through the craving for the addictive behavior, and then the cravings stop. Slowly the addictive element or feeling leaves our body. Then we need to get some more of the addictive element or do the addictive behavior again to trigger the same feelings, so the cycle goes on forever until we decide to stop it. Cravings go on below the surface of your consciousness, so we are often unaware of these cravings that increase our stress levels compared with someone who isn't addicted to something.

For addictions such as eating disorders and sex, it is hard to stop all at once, especially since you need to keep eating everyday to survive, and usually, if you are married, you need to show up and have sex with your partner if they are not aware of your addiction. So, often you cannot stop doing these altogether. But for other addictions, such as alcohol, drugs, coffee, cigarettes, or sugar, the addictive element is best eliminated or lowered and lowered until we can remove it entirely without too many cravings.

However, there is also a behavioral reason behind every addiction, which makes stopping so tricky.

It is the fear from the emptiness, insecurity, boredom, coping with reality, and fear from the cravings that keep people addicted. After the addiction is removed, suddenly, the feeling of no connection to infinite intelligence is tough to handle.

If you think of it, people who drink coffee, smoke, take drugs, gamble, game, or do anything else that is addictive, usually have the night time and times during the day when they are mostly free from their addiction. They do not smoke, overeat, drink coffee, gamble, take drugs, eat sugar, or play during the night. The cravings for the addictive element are real, but they can be physically coped with when the decision is made. It is the fear that you will have nothing to do or fear dealing with the stress, emptiness, lack of connection, life itself, and other intense feelings that keep a person addicted.

But only when one removes all addictions is one genuinely free and can know actual health, wealth, self-respect, self-esteem, and happiness. When you are addicted, you cannot truly know these.

The addictive element takes away your courage and confidence. It's like being in a relationship with a narcissist. They keep harming you, but you keep them around because they make you believe you need them.

If your addiction harms your health, you know it but are not willing to look at the facts in the face. Remember that you have one body to take your soul through life. It would be best if you cared for it.

To overcome an addiction, begin by stopping the addictive element or behavior abruptly if you can or slowly if you can't, and then get your mind on other things. This is not easy to do due to the unawareness that addictions are based upon, but you can overcome the addiction once you understand this.

Find things that interest you other than your addiction. Write them down.

Become aware that you do not really want the addictive element in your life. Do this by honesty and with awareness looking at the harm, destruction and terrible things this addiction is really doing to your life. People with any addiction see the positive side of the addiction and do not focus at all at the negative side, because when the do, this gets them into emotional turmoil that makes them turn to the addiction again to release the turmoil from their life. This is why it is of major importance to comprehend that the addictive element is doing you more bad than good.

Then look at your list of ideas and keep yourself busy during the withdrawal period. I started writing when I stopped my eating disorder in 2005.

Don't delay stopping your addiction!

Do you really want to live as you live, disconnected from your true divine nature and your true potential, with your addiction for the rest of your life?

No! Of course not!

There is no better time to stop than before you started, but the second-best time is now. Decide now and start today!

Most people use an addiction to overcome the challenging and complex moments of their lives when they feel at their lowest and have forgotten their connection to Source. But these hardships are opportunities to reveal your connection to Source. When you turn to addictions in these times of crisis, you are not learning the lessons, making progress, or making the growth that these hardships offer. You are only drowning in their negativity.

Understand that you *can* cope with stress and hard times. In fact, hard times are what brought humans to where we are today. Hardships led to our evolution, brain growth, and our development as a species. We would not be where we are now if we did not overcome the hardships.

And more recently, in human history, humans lived with much higher stress levels all of their waking hours, which pushed them to grow their foods through agriculture.

Humans had no homes, no regular food supply, no beds, no comforts previous to agriculture. Stress was normal. We are built to cope with stress and hardship.

If we did not cope with our hardships and stress before the addiction, the stress and hardship become bigger and demand more of us to cope, but we are still capable, and the prize at the end will be more glorious.

You are much stronger than you imagine yourself to be. You can overcome any addiction and enjoy life more than you ever can with addiction because you connect back to your true divine nature without it.

Alcohol, drugs, cigarettes, or addictive behaviors do not make you happy. They make you miserable, even if you are not willing to admit it. When you are healthy, strong, and energetic, you can enjoy the fullness of life, the good and the bad times, and benefit from them all.

I promise you will never miss your addiction once you get rid of it! I have personally been addicted to many things; cigarettes, alcohol, and food through an eating disorder for a decade and a half. After you overcome it, you will not miss anything about the addiction if you stop the addiction through awareness that you are only gaining and truly losing nothing, because this is true if you put everything on balance scales. I am now free from all addictions and have never been happier or felt better in my life. I do not drink alcohol, and I was an alcoholic, I do not smoke, and I was a smoker, I do not even drink coffee, and once I was drinking over twenty cups a day, I do not eat processed sugar, take drugs or anything that is addictive. I will never compromise my health, life, and my connection to infinite intelligence again for these fallacies.

Focus on your own life. Do not look around at what other people are doing. When you stop your addiction, you will know that all addicted people are suffering slaves.

That is not you anymore. I wasted fifteen years of my life on my addictions. I am not willing to waste another moment ever again, and neither should you.

Willpower will get you past the physiological cravings if you are addicted to sugar, alcohol, nicotine, caffeine, or drugs.

Talking with yourself, connecting with your true self by walking in nature, exercising, meditation, self-hypnosis, self-forgiveness, and learning unconditional love will get you past the addiction's behavioral part, often the most challenging aspect to get rid of.

Prevent getting into situations, meeting people, or being in places that are triggers for your addiction. Say to yourself, "I am free from this. I am in control of my mind and body. I am connected to infinite intelligence, which is all-powerful, all-present, and all-accepting. The substance has my body addicted, but my brain and behaviors are under my own control.

Reason with yourself. Love and accept yourself as you are, consciousness with a connection to all that is that can never be severed, only temporarily concealed, but can be revealed again at any moment.

Persistently talk with yourself about the benefits of going clean. Talk with yourself about the health, money, energy, and time you spare without the addiction and stick with it.

Holding a masters degree in physiology and in medical science, I have seen and also personally experienced that within two to nine weeks, the physical cravings will be over—no more cravings. The addiction will be physically gone. Then you can move on to care for the behavioral aspect. You must build and persist with new beneficial habits and behaviors for sixty-six days to ensure that you are really free. And then take on new and even better habits to build on these for another sixty-six days, and that's it! After eight months of persistent and sustained daily effort, you are free!

If you fall, you start the count again until you hit the mark.

And never go back to using or doing the addictive behavior ever again.

The only reasons you may relapse are the environment and people around you, especially when you are having a difficult day. But difficult days are a natural part of life, and you must learn to cope with them and benefit from them. They have the potential to make you stronger, better, and happier in the long run because they reveal your true identity.

Talk with yourself. Explain to yourself how the addiction will not make the day better for you but will make the day worse and all the days that follow because you are disconnected from your true self and your powers.

Now beware, automatically your mind starts looking to focus on other addictions to fill the void when you stop an addiction. Don't fall into this trap. Clean out your life and take the reins of control back into your own hands.

What also helps is doing it in a group with other people overcoming the same addiction, or if this is not possible, reading forums of people dealing with your specific addiction and in the process of stopping. You will be shocked by how similar we all are; this will make you stronger.

You can succeed, and you will succeed. You are not giving up anything worthwhile for you. You are regaining your life back and connecting back to your true self, a part of Source.

I also recommend that after eight months of recovery, you never call yourself a recovering drinker, smoker, drug addict, or a person with eating disorders again. I know this contradicts the philosophy of the 12 steps of alcoholics anonymous, but I am absolutely against this. You must create a new image of yourself and then mesh yourself with that new image. It is of no use giving yourself a life sentence for something that belongs to your past. Instead see yourself a healthy, vibrant person who has come out of prison and revealed your true divine identity. Your new life has just begun!

This episode of your life is finished. Your recovery was the last chapter of that book. Now a new book can begin.

You will succeed. Start now, do not waste another precious moment of your life living for the addiction. Instead, it is time to live your life connected to your true self, full of power, potential, love, and understanding.

Questions Of The Day

So, to end off this lesson and to help you overcome any addiction you may have, the questions that you want to ask yourself today are:

Why do I need this? Do I need to continue with this? Do I want to continue with this? How will my life be better if I quit this addiction? Can I decide never to do this again right now? Can I take the necessary steps to move my life forward?

Well, can you?

As usual, I recommend writing your answers in the PDF journal that you have received with this book. Then look over your answers to ensure that you improve your life and bring forth your true divine nature.

Affirmation Of The Day

After answering the questions in your journal, and examining them, sit quietly for a few minutes today and repeat this affirmation to yourself as you think and dwell upon it:

I AM STRONG ENOUGH TO BEAT THIS!

Now tell this affirmation to yourself as many times as you remember to do so today because, with repetition, an affirmation has the power to alter your consciousness so that you think and behave differently for a better, happier life and purposeful life.

DAY 50 - BECOMING AWARE OF THE IMPORTANCE OF HOPE AND FAITH

"The darkest hours are just before dawn" ~ English proverb

It is tough to have hope when it seems that you are in the darkest hours of your existence. To even think for a moment that things can get better may seem far-fetched at certain moments, but things do eventually get better. The dark times are like a wound that heals on the body. At first, when we see the wound, we don't know how to fix or cure it, but we have the internal wisdom that allows our body to take over and heal itself. We stay and fight through difficult situations because deep inside, we hope that things will get better.

This hope motivates us to continue down a path towards a better life for ourselves even though we are not sure where it will lead. Deep inside, we understand that we have internal guidance and that everything is for the best at the end of the day, from a more extensive world perspective.

I heard a story suitable for today's lesson about a young man who met a wise old man. The old man gave the young man a ring and said, "Wear this ring wherever you go, and if one day you will be stuck at the lowest point of your life, then, and only then, open the ring, and it will save you." The young man was delighted with this gift, and he continued to lead his life as usual. Then one day, he traveled to China, and while walking in a street market, he was robbed. His passport and his money were stolen. The young man was so depressed. He did not know what to do, and night was falling. He was exhausted, with no money for food or a hotel, he decided to sleep on a bench on the street. While deep in sleep, he was awoken by the police. Since he did not understand the language they spoke and they did not understand his body language, they felt threatened by him, so they put him in prison. He did not know what to do. Then suddenly he noticed the ring on his finger and remembered what the old man had told him to do. Suddenly he had hope. He *WAS* at his lowest point, and he truly did need the help of the ring now since he saw no other way out of his situation. Slowly he opened the ring, and inside was a small scroll of paper. The young man slowly opened the scroll, and it read, "This too shall pass."

Everything passes. Look at your life in retrospect and see how true this is. I am sure you can think of a time when things seemed impossibly difficult, but somehow you got out of that situation.

When we are in situations that leave us no choice, we tend to have the best ideas and find the best solutions. We become very resourceful and find a way out of our situation. All we need is hope, and this was the point of the ring, to remind the young man that there is always hope, and if he can get his act together, the current situation will become a stepping stone to a better and happier life.

Most of us don't accept change unless we are in a complicated situation that leads us with no choice but to change and become better. Not everyone is willing to work on themselves when everything is going fine, but it is the hope that we have deep within us that comes out in difficult situations. This hope allows us to tap into our inner reserves, and once we open up a new reserve, that resource becomes available for our use forever. It is another tool we have added to our toolbox.

After my first marriage, hope allowed me to remarry even while raising my two disabled daughters. Although I did have doubts that someone will want to marry me in my situation, I had hope deep within me, and this hope allowed me to fulfill that dream.

Having hope also allowed me to earn a decent living when my financial state was a mess, and I could not find work that would accept me with my family situation, divorced with two epileptic and mentally challenged daughters.

So I became an entrepreneur, and I used my gifts to earn a lot of money even with my challenging personal situation.

It was also hope that allowed me not to start chemo and radiotherapy when I had cancer but to go down a natural path to heal my cancer even though this was against my doctor's orders.

Hope brought me to the day when my daughter uttered her first word, Mama, at the age of twenty-one.

Hope gives us the motivation to keep trying even when all odds seem against us, and things look bleak.

Remember, "The darkest hours are just before dawn." I loved this quote so much that I had it written on my kitchen wall many years ago, and I had a painter paint the sunrise. At the time, I needed to see this quote every day to remind me that things will get better.

It did take time, but since beliefs form expectations and what you expect out of life you tend to get, my life slowly transformed for the better.

Hope and faith are closely intertwined. Hope is an optimistic belief that the desire may come to fruition in the future, but faith is unwavering confidence that all is perfect right now because all is for the best.

The truth is that if you do not have faith, you are paralyzed. You cannot even do the simplest of tasks without feeling worried and fearful.

You need faith to cross the street; you need faith to drive a car; you need faith to start any business venture; you need faith to fly an airplane, swim in the sea, or ride a boat. You need faith to raise your children, and you even need to have faith to turn on the light and know that darkness will disappear.

Without faith, we would live in a world full of fear, stress, and anxiety all the time. Anxiety and stress would run our lives leading to disease and unhappiness.

Living with faith is expecting good things to come.

Hope is the foundation for faith. Faith is knowing. A deep belief that what you think will happen is either what will happen or that whatever will happen is best even if it doesn't seem so at that moment. It is knowing that you can achieve your dreams because these dreams were given to you to fulfill. Everybody feels the urge to quit at times. But faith is what will keep you going towards your soul's desire.

Faith is immaterial and comes from the heart and the soul. All hope can be transformed into faith.

Faith is taking the next step when you can't see the entire staircase.

All achievements take time, but having faith in the process and yourself and the movement of things towards progress will prevent you from quitting.

Faith is knowing that you matter in this world.

As you may know, life can change your plans altogether. But faith allows you to know that all will work out perfectly if you keep doing your best daily. And even during bad times, to still believe that better days are coming.

Let your faith be stronger than your fears.

Whatever you believe will happen. It may not happen according to your desired timeline, but if you persist and continue taking focused action, what you believe *will* happen.

Knowledge is limited, but imagination is not. We can all create something from nothing but a thought. What is needed is faith to complete the process. To get back health, become rich, get married, have children, and succeed at anything, we must have faith. Faith will allow us to keep taking the proper steps even when nothing can yet be seen.

Take the leap of faith and believe everything will be all right.

Deep in your heart, you know what kind of seed is really within you. We are all part of Source energy, and when we connect to our true divine nature, anything we desire that is of benefit not only to us, but to the whole, is within our reach with persistent effort and focused attention and action.

Faith can move mountains because where focus goes, energy flows. When you get excited about something and keep your faith high, and take persistent action, it will become real.

Therefore, to lead a satisfying, fulfilling, abundant and happy life, faith becomes just as important as the air you breathe. Faith nourishes the heart and soul. Faith is essential for one not just to stay alive but to be alive.

Everyone encounters dark times, and in these times, it is our faith that will carry us through.

Miracles exist everywhere in our lives, and it is faith that helps us see them. Faith allows us to see the abundance that is found everywhere around us. We can tap into this abundance through faith.

We can also see what faith brings through the story of Job in the bible when all of his possessions were taken away from him, Job held his faith, and when he did, he was granted back all that was taken away from him and much more.

Questions Of The Day

To spark the light of hope in your life, ask yourself:

Where in my life do I currently feel my darkest hour? What baby steps *CAN* I take today to help me transform my situation to be slightly better than yesterday? Do I believe in my ability to create the life of my dreams? Do I have faith in myself and my abilities as a creator of my destiny? Do I know my connection to Source energy? Can I consider the option that I am in the right place for me and that all difficulty is there to move me to the best place for me in life in the long run?

Answer these questions, and they will help you transform your mindset to focus on faith, solutions, and understanding that all is right.

Keep your faith high through prayer, meditation, and visualization.

As usual, I recommend writing your answers in the PDF journal.

Affirmation Of The Day

After answering the questions in your journal, and contemplating on your answers, sit quietly for a few minutes today and repeat this affirmation to yourself as you think and dwell upon it:

GOOD THINGS ARE HAPPENING TO ME AS I ACKNOWLEDGE MY CONNECTION WITH INFINITE INTELLIGENCE.

Now tell this to yourself as many times as you remember to do so today because, with repetition, this affirmation raises your level of consciousness and supports the revelation of your connection to Source.

DAY 51 - BECOMING AWARE OF THE PATH TO SELF-ACTUALIZATION

"It's very simple; just look at your life to see where you're heading. You're always in a momentum of something." ~ Maria Erving

We are always in the process of moving towards something. If you are interested in moving your life to a better place, you must consider the path you are currently on and your direction.

Let's say that you are at a crossroads in life. There are many paths you can take. And let's say that these paths are unidirectional, meaning that they will lead you to one particular outcome. You can always get off the path and change to a different path, but so long as you are doing the same things, you will be stuck on the path you are on with the results destined for this path. You understand this and want to change paths to one of a better destination. How do you know what to do and what you need to do next? How do you build up momentum in the new direction?

Let's use Abraham Maslow's hierarchy of needs pyramid as a tool. Abraham Maslow was a psychologist and researcher who suggested the hierarchy of human needs pyramid. It's divided into five levels, each layer representing a different type of human need.

The pyramid suggests the conditions of the first level must be met so that one can move on to the second level, which must then be completed to move on to the third level, and so on. The hierarchy triangle has a broad base that becomes smaller as one goes up the needs ladder.

Here is a picture of Abraham Maslow Hierarchy of Needs Pyramid:

Self-actualization
desire to become the most that one can be

Esteem
respect, self-esteem, status, recognition, strength, freedom

Love and belonging
friendship, intimacy, family, sense of connection

Safety needs
personal security, employment, resources, health, property

Physiological needs
air, water, food, shelter, sleep, clothing, reproduction

All the levels below the very topmost level are known as deficiency needs, meaning that you won't be able to focus on pretty much anything else until these needs are first met, each at their own time, one after another.

The deficiency needs are divided into physiological and psychological needs. The physiological needs include the base level of survival needs—sufficient food, water, a place to live, and clothing. And the second level from the bottom—safety, security, health, and basic financial needs.

The following two levels represent psychological needs. The third level of the triangle is the need for belonging and love - to connect with other people in meaningful ways.

The fourth level is about the second psychological need and the last of the deficiency needs and includes the desire to feel accomplished, successful, and respected.

Once all these needs are met, you can finally focus on realizing your full potential, the self-actualization level at the top of the pyramid. Self-actualization is not a deficiency need but rather an abundance need. Meaning that the more it is met, the more you will want to continue to do more of it.

The self-actualization level leads to you accomplishing your highest potential and being the best and happiest version of yourself. This happens when you reach the final stages of the hero's journey, "The Return" phase.

The desire to achieve self-actualization is inside every one of us, and for every person, self-actualization means something different. But before you reach this level, you must first focus on addressing your deficiency needs which will help you become happier, self-assured, and ready to take the leap towards self-actualization.

So how do you use this tool? You want to examine where you currently stand at the moment in the pyramid.

When I wanted to show one of my clients why he was feeling so bad, I showed him that none of his deficiency needs were currently being met, and that's why he could not be happy. Although he did have shelter, he lived with his mother, who did not want him there, and he was miserable. This client also did not have health because he was addicted to medication, and he did not have good relationships because he lacked the love and support of his mother. He also had no job, so he was not feeling accomplished. How could he be happy when none of his needs were met?

Now, I want to point out that when you are not happy with a particular area of your life, even if you *DO* have it, then it is still considered an unfulfilled need. For example, if you are living in a house that you hate, or if you are in a job or a marriage that makes you unhappy, then this need is not considered satisfied, and you will not feel ready to move on to the next level in the hierarchy of needs pyramid.

When you see for yourself where you are in terms of your needs, you know where you currently need to place your focus to reach self-actualization. Without going through the process of making yourself better, you cannot realize your full human potential

Once you embrace personal development in your life, you become more aware of your potential and your connection to Source. Then you can improve your life in ways that will lead you towards living the best life for you.

Questions Of The Day

To end this lesson and help you determine which needs you need to work on, ask yourself:

Where am I on the Hierarchy of needs pyramid, and what can I start to do today to move myself up each level towards self-actualization?

As usual, I recommend writing your answers in the PDF journal.

Affirmation Of The Day

After answering the questions in your journal, and contemplating on your answers, sit quietly for a few minutes today and repeat this affirmation.

I AM BECOMING MORE AWARE OF MYSELF AND AM MOVING TOWARDS THE BEST VERSION OF MYSELF!

Repeat this affirmation often. With repetition, it has the power to alter your consciousness so you build a better, happier and more purposeful life.

DAY 52 - BECOMING AWARE OF A FAVORABLE OUTCOME TO YOUR LIFE

"Successful people do what unsuccessful people are not willing to do. Don't wish it were easier; wish you were better." ~ Jim Rohn

Success is not something you reach; it is how you live your life. You can live successfully, and then be a success, or you can live it unsuccessfully, and then your life will be considered by you as unsuccessful.

Success is defined as, "the accomplishment of an aim or a purpose". But it is also described as "a favorable outcome" and I like this description best, especially if we are the ones to judge the outcome, and we are the ones who ought to be happy with our outcomes. Usually, we are the hardest on ourselves, more than anyone else.

An outcome is not necessarily something that will happen in the future. An outcome is a result you also have in the present moment. It is the outcome of your past decisions and choices. This is the outcome I want you to contemplate.

So what would make a favorable outcome for you in your life? For each person, the answer is slightly different, but what is considered a favorable outcome is similar for most of us. mIt is essential to recognize what a favorable outcome is in order to be able to ensure that you are living this favorable outcome every day, and if not, then to make better choices that will lead you in the right direction.

Although we spoke about the hierarchy of needs pyramid yesterday, to grasp the concept of a favorable outcome to life in simpler terms, we must fulfill all six components of a favorable outcome to life.

Let's look into each of these components:

1. The first component is having peace of mind, meaning that you are free from the chains of fear, guilt, anger, and other negative feelings. This means that you have mastered your mind enough to overcome these feelings when they arise within you. It means that you have a healthy mindset. Although you *can* feel feelings of guilt, fear, and anger once in a while, you are free from the chains they may have on you. Fear will no longer freeze or disable you, guilt will not bring you down and make you please others but not yourself, and anger will not come out of you in an uncontrolled manner. You feel overall happy and in control of yourself. You understand that you are separate from your mind and know that you are not your feelings or emotions. Feelings are external to you. This is peace of mind. There is no more war between the ego and who you really are. There is peace, acceptance, calmness, and a loss of attachment to specific results. It is a knowing that what you are doing is right, and what you are doing is what you should be doing.

2. The next component for having a favorable outcome in your life is having health and energy and lacking any addictions, or in other words, a healthy mind living in a healthy body. Without health of body and mind, you cannot enjoy the fruits of your efforts, and you will

also not have the energy to do much other than care for yourself. You cannot be happy and fulfilled if you are not healthy. You cannot be satisfied and fulfilled when you suffer from pain, disease, or addiction. Furthermore, the more at peace you are, the healthier you will also be in your body because of the mind-body connection and the direct connection between the hormones the body produces and the overall health state of the body.

3. After you have a healthy mindset and a healthy body, you will feel ready to enter into a healthy, supportive relationship, one that accepts you as you are, and one where both partners are seen as equals and push each other towards becoming a better version of themselves. In this type of relationship, no one needs to do things just to please the other. Each is mature enough to understand their differences and are even happy and accepting about these differences. There is an understanding and a balance in the relationship. In their free time, the partners like to spend time with each other. Being in a healthy relationship is an essential part of an overall healthy personality, and it is a crucial component of a successful and favorable life. However, one can fulfill this part of a favorable outcome through a relationship with one's children or with Source. This is common with people from different religions or on full spiritual paths and provides them with the same feelings and advantages that a formal physical relationship does.

4. We usually turn to the next component once we are in a secure relationship, but it may also happen before that. The next element is having a healthy bank account. This is a vital part of happiness and, since without it, one cannot be of much use to society or themselves. Debt puts a constant strain on what you can do and leads to a lack of contribution to society or becoming a burden on society. This lack of contribution will not make you very happy. You will be too busy with your survival to focus on anything else. It would be best if you had enough income to support your needs and desires. How much is enough money to be considered financially independent? There is no definite number because financial freedom means different things to people.

5. The fifth component is having a worthy purpose and meaning behind what we do. Without having meaning and purpose behind what you do, the results you achieve will never make you happy. And to be successful in your own eyes and consider yourself as having a favorable outcome in your life, you need to be satisfied and fulfilled. Having meaning and purpose behind what you do is the greatest driver towards progress.

6. The last component of success is to strive for self-actualization, as we spoke of yesterday. This allows you to aim towards achieving your fullest personal potential and becoming your best. It is the highest level of psychological development. It is the stage when you are doing and being all you are capable of doing and being. In Maslow's book, he explains: "[A] musician must make music, an artist must paint, a poet must write if he is to be ultimately happy." We must find and share our gifts with the world to be successful, fulfilled, happy and self-actualized. We must realize and shine our talents and potentialities to the world if our lives are to be considered favorable and successful in our own eyes. This does not mean that we are in any sense perfect, just that we have accepted ourselves as we are, with all of our flaws, and we fully accept others as they are too; however, our imperfections do not hinder us on our path of doing what we feel we need and are moved to do.

Even in our era with so much abundance, globally, people still:

- Live in clinical depression (5% of the global population, according to the CDC/National

Center for Health Statistics),

- Live in poverty with barely with enough money to make ends meet (22% of the global population, CDC).
- Stay in faulty relationships (19% globally, according to TIME), are overweight (40% of the global population according to WHO),
- Suffer from health issues (67% globally, according to the CDC),
- Smoke (8.5% globally, according to the CDC) or drink too much (26% globally, according to the 2019 NSDUH), I
- Live a life without meaning or purpose (30% according to the Cato 2019 Welfare, Work, and Wealth National Survey.

Most people reach retirement age practically broke, needing to depend on others for their livelihood. According to The Motley Fool, less that 50% of people over 60 feel that their retirement savings are on track.

Some of us do not have parents who set good examples of how to live a successful and favorable life, so we do not know how to make the best choices for ourselves. Then we spend half of our lives figuring out the basics of how to make the most of ourselves. The more interested you are in your personal development, the sooner you will get there. This is why I have created this book to help you self-actualize and reach a state of bliss as quickly as possible.

If you currently lack one or a few factors for a favorable life, you must change something within yourself, not your circumstances. All these lessons will lead you in the right direction.

You must examine your life and see which limiting beliefs, habits, actions, or thoughts you are holding onto that stop you from achieving any of these components of a favorable life. If you do not know what is stopping you from becoming your best, you must do some more introspective work to figure this out. Talking to someone who does not know you at all and releasing your thoughts randomly while they ask questions is an excellent way to reveal what may be hidden from your conscious mind. Without changing something within you, you will not see different results.

And the most important thing to remember is that once you *have* reached a favorable place where you can call yourself successful, you have earned it by entertaining specific thoughts, habits, beliefs, and actions which have brought you to your success. And now that you are there, you must keep up with these habits and everything else that led up to your success.

Once you reach favorable results, do not go back to your comfort zone in any field of life. Stick to the new path that got you to favorable outcomes and continue on it till the end. This is the only way to lead a genuinely favorable and worthwhile life.

It is not easy to do. We figure that once we have reached the money, family, relationship, health, peace of mind, and our purpose in life, we can relax and release some of the habits and actions that got us there. This is not true if you want your achievements to last and to maintain self-actualization.

I see this every day in my clinic. People who stick to the Guerrilla Diet Lifestyle plan heal from difficult health conditions and diseases, lose all excess weight, and are delighted with their results. Still, some go back to their former lifestyles after they reach success and with time lose their health again, also their happiness. The habits that get you favorable results in life must become part of your lifestyle for good. You must persist with practices such as patience, honesty, loyalty, no harm, a good work ethic, respect for others, a healthy lifestyle, and a positive mindset.

Only then will you have a favorable outcome that lasts. This is truly a life worth living, a life of bliss, joy, and health.

Questions Of The Day

To end this lesson and to help you reach and maintain a favorable outcome for your life and view yourself as a winner, ask yourself:

Which areas of my life have I not yet reached the desired state of success? Which habits, beliefs, actions, or behaviors am I holding on to that block me from reaching my fullest potential?

As usual, I recommend writing your answers in the PDF journal that you have received with this book. Then look over your answers to ensure that you improve your life and bring forth your true divine nature.

Affirmation Of The Day

After answering the questions in your journal, and examining them, sit quietly for a few minutes today and repeat this affirmation to yourself as you think and dwell upon it:

I AM STRIVING TO LIVE LIFE TO MY FULLEST POTENTIAL, AND I CAN NEVER FAIL BECAUSE EVERYTHING THAT HAPPENS IN MY LIFE CONTRIBUTES TO ME BEING MY BEST.

Repeat this affirmation often. With repetition, it has the power to alter your consciousness so you build a better, happier and more purposeful life.

DAY 53 - BECOMING AWARE OF YOUR DIRECTION

"The future depends on what you do today."

~ Mahatma Gandhi

This quote says that we must take action to make the future as we want it to be and that there are no limits to what we can achieve except the limitations we have in our minds.

So how do you create the life that you've always wanted and dreamed of? You must define what you want and be proactive about it. And the best way to start is with a plan of the end picture.

This may seem a little crazy. People may say, you could die tomorrow; what are you doing planning for a decade or two in advance? Most people live past the age of eighty, so if you want to succeed, no matter your age, you must plan.

Even if you are young and you work daily towards the goals you think you want now, you may miss the whole point and create a life for yourself that you do not wish for.

For example, I have a friend who was very career-oriented. She was not at all interested in a love life or a family. She made it to the top of her career at forty-five. But then she suddenly was so sad that she never got around to creating a family and building a relationship. She became very anxious because her biological clock was ticking. Today she is fifty, without children. She doesn't want to adopt, but at least she is now in a happy, supportive relationship.

This is what happens when we live our lives based on short-term goals without having the bigger end picture in mind. Time may go by without us thinking about how we see our life in the future and where we really want to be. For this reason, it is essential to sit quietly in introspection and think about where you want to be ten years from now and, if you are young enough, also twenty years from now.

How would you like your life to turn out?

Build a plan just as you would build an outline of your dream home. You don't go about building it with weekly goals. No. You have to have an end picture in mind. It is great when you know your end result because you understand which actions you need to take to bring you to where you want to be.

Then you have your answers for many daily choices you will need to make. This way of thinking makes life much easier for you. You know where you are going. All you need to do is to stay on the right path to secure the future you desire.

Your past doesn't matter. You can create the life of your dreams in all areas of your life no matter where you came from, what your background is, and where you are today.

These facts are not necessary. Only what you do from this moment on is essential.

Once you have your vision carefully planned out, you know exactly what you need to study to get there. As Malcolm X said, "Education is our passport to the future, for tomorrow belongs to the people who prepare for it today."

You also know which type of person you want to marry. And which type of house you desire and where this home is located in the world. You also know what your perfect job is, and even the ideal workout schedule that will be right for you, as well as the ideal lifestyle that will support your health in the long run.

All of your questions become answered when you know the outcome you desire in the long run. All difficulties that arise from making choices disappear.

Furthermore, when you look towards the future of how you wish to see yourself, I am sure you see yourself as healthy. And of course, when you see the vision of you being healthy in the future, you take the proper steps now to reach this vision of future health.

Also, when you envision your future self, you understand that all things take time, and this awareness takes off most of the pressure and allows you to do the right things for you today that will lead you to your dream life in the future.

So now go ahead, find yourself a quiet spot and start to visualize the perfect you in ten and twenty years. But what if you see that you do not like the path that your life is headed based on your previous choices? Know that it is never too late to follow your dreams and to change your direction in life.

There may be many reasons to change direction in life. You may have had a passion for something but never pursued the path because of different obligations and responsibilities. Or you may be free now because technology may have replaced you in your job, and you may need to start afresh. Or maybe your values or priorities changed throughout the years and are different from when you first started your career, and you are looking for something that is more in line with the improved version of yourself.

There are many reasons to start something new in later years. Research shows that 80 percent of people want to make a career change after forty-five, but only 6 percent of people follow through.

If you are one of the few who are willing to follow through with something new in later years, know that you are not alone. **J. R. R. Tolkien** published his book *The Hobbit* when he was forty-five years old. This book has now sold over **100 million** copies and has been translated into over fifty languages. He completed The Lord of the Rings when he was fifty-six.

John Warnock founded Adobe when he was forty-two years old and developed the PDF at age fifty.

Charles Darwin was fifty years old when he wrote: *On the Origin of Species.*

Julia Child, the famous chef, wrote her first cookbook when she was fifty, which started her successful career.

Joseph A. Campbell from the Campbell Soup Company only started his canned food company when he was fifty-two years old, and the company only sold their first soup when he was seventy-eight.

Leo Goodwin was fifty years old when he started his own insurance company GEICO.

Ray Kroc was a milkshake-machine salesman before he bought McDonald's when he was fifty-two.

My mother started her laundry company that now has 100 laundromats all over Mongolia at fifty-four.

And these are only a few examples.

You have a lot going for you when you start later. Maybe your kids have grown and left the house, leaving you with more free time. Perhaps you recently divorced and have more time, and you also want to do something that your relationship may have prevented you from doing. You may also be a late bloomer or someone who has suffered from low self-esteem, and this has changed with the years giving you more self-awareness and higher self-esteem to go after your dreams.

It is good to know that your chance of success has nothing to do with your age. Your chances of success have to do with your willingness to try persistently until you reach a breakthrough.

It's never too late to change direction or to decide to invest more of yourself in something you may have kept as a hobby or on a small flame throughout your previous years.

You can learn something new so long as you are alive. You can learn from your mistakes or from other people, and you can always learn a new skill. It is never too late so long as you decide and follow through with it and keep going. Never give up.

Suppose you have passion for your ideas and a lot of curiosity. You have learned from your previous years how to remain persistent in a particular field, and you generally have a positive attitude. In that case, there is nothing that can stop you from achieving your goals.

The amazing story of the author **Harry Bernstein** who believed in himself as a writer but only really came down to doing exquisite work after his wife died. His memoir "The Invisible Wall: A Love Story That Broke Barriers" became an immediate success when published in 2007. Harry was ninety-six at the time.

The key to success when you are starting late is not to be afraid of failure. People become more cautious as the years go by, so only 6 percent take the leap and create something new at a later age. Often people become too comfortable to take required risks.

But you *can* reinvent yourself at any age, and you *can* succeed. Others have done it before you, and you can do it too. All you need is the willingness to go after your dreams and the health and energy to give it your all with persistence and determination to persevere.

If you keep learning and stay curious, you will remain young at heart and mind. The only thing that could be limiting you is you. There are endless opportunities, and all things are possible if you believe them to be. Go after your dreams. Study, learn, make the change, take action, and if you fail, it just means that you are one step closer to success. Do not give up at any age.

Life is a gift, so why waste this precious opportunity? Do what you believe in. Put in the effort. You will only regret what you never tried. How much more exciting can life be if you bet on yourself and do what you have been dreaming of doing. Wow, think about this.

So let's begin planning the life of your dreams, and yes, it is never too late to do this.

Questions Of The Day

Begin by asking yourself:

Where do I want to be in life? What is holding me from getting there? Will these goals will make me happy and help me fulfill my purpose in life? Do this for both your ten and twenty-year visions.

Think of all of your answers to these questions before coming to conclusions.

As usual, I recommend writing your answers in the PDF journal.

Since you can't control anything except for your thoughts, feelings, and actions, you will never know if life will turn out exactly as you planned. Still, at least you are going in the right direction. And even if hardships come your way, you will know what needs to be done and which choices need to be made to get yourself back on the right path for you to be happy no matter what happens that is outside of your control.

Affirmation Of The Day

After answering the questions in your journal, and contemplating on your answers, sit quietly for a few minutes today and repeat this affirmation to yourself:

WHATEVER I AM DOING TODAY IS GETTING ME CLOSER TO WHERE I WANT TO BE IN THE FUTURE. I AM ALIVE, SO I CAN CHANGE MY LIFE AND CIRCUMSTANCES! IT'S NEVER TOO LATE TO START!

Repeat this affirmation often. With repetition, it has the power to alter your consciousness so you build a better, happier and more purposeful life.

DAY 54 - BECOMING AWARE OF SMART GOALS AND PLANS

"Only three percent of adults have written goals, and everyone else works for them."

~ Brian Tracy

Staying in your comfort zone will not get you to where you want and deserve to be. It just belittles you. If you want to be happy, you have to make progress in your life. To make progress, you have to make goals that you can follow. Most types of goals involve increasing something, reducing something, producing something, improving something, or saving something.

You will never get more done than what you plan to get done, so you might as well plan for big goals and aim to reach them. As we mentioned earlier, your goals should be long-term with the end picture in mind. It's never too late to follow the path to your bliss, so let's begin right now.

Write down what you desire to accomplish in all of the critical areas of your life. Start in the work field and ask yourself what would you like to accomplish in this area in the next five to twenty years, depending on your age. What do you want to do for work, where would you like to do it, how would you like to do it, and what is the level of income you desire to achieve?

Next, write down your goals regarding your home life. Where you would like to live, what standard of living is vital for you? In what type of home would you like to live in? What is crucial for you to have in your home, and where would you like to go on vacations and with whom?

Then write about your relationships; how many children would you like to have? What is crucial for you in a partner, and what is essential for you to in your friendships? Which social groups would you like to join? What would you like to do for your community, and which worthwhile organizations would you like to donate your time or money to?

Now write about your health. Which dietary preferences are aligned with your values? Which sports are you happy to participate in? How many hours are you sleeping daily? When are you waking up, and when do you go to sleep daily? What are you doing to ensure that you are following the best regime for you?

All areas are interconnected, you cannot build the life of your dreams for each area separately, and therefore you have to write down your short-and-long-term goals for ALL of these areas in your life.

Also, you cannot reach any goal if it is too vague. The goal has to be precise. Therefore, the best criteria for making goals is known as the S-M-A-R-T (SMART) criteria.

Specific. What exactly do you want to accomplish?

Measurable. A goal must be measurable so you know when you've achieved it.

Achievable. You must be able to follow through with your goal.

Relevant. Your goal must be aligned with who you are and what is important to you.

Time-Bound. You have to have a specific timeframe for reaching your goals.

For every relationship, work, home, family, and health goal, set a time frame to take the right actions that will lead you to its accomplishment. There will often be setbacks along the way, and perhaps you will not achieve your goals at the exact time you specified, but you WILL be headed in the right direction and WILL be closer and closer to achieving your goals as time goes by.

All you need is:

1. The desire to advance yourself
2. Belief in yourself
3. To ignore the naysayers
4. Take daily action that is usually out of your comfort zone because it is something new.
5. To persist.

We often destroy our dreams by not believing in our abilities and not thinking that we can do whatever it takes to achieve our goals. We may also be too scared to leave our comfort zone. We may also have a non-supportive environment full of naysayers, who may be our parents, friends, or even partners who feel like rocks on our shoulders. We must release ourselves from these shackles, increase our self-esteem, and move out of our comfort zone to do what is required to move us forwards.

A Plan For Success:

The 34th president of the United States, Dwight D. Eisenhower, said, "In preparing for battle I have always found that plans are useless, but planning is indispensable."

You must have plans to reach your goals. Still, even if our plans are useless and Infinite intelligence has better plans for us to get to our desired destination, we must take what we currently see as the proper steps to advance ourselves in the right direction towards our soul's desire.

The following action may not always be clear to us, but don't let this freeze you from doing anything. Most people do not take any action because they don't know the following steps and don't have the whole path mapped out. But even if we could have the entire path mapped out, it often would turn out wrong. There are surprises and delays and inconveniences and new responsibilities and new people that enter our lives on the way that can completely change our path.

Knowing the whole path towards your success is not necessary nor relevant.

It's okay to start without having a complete plan in place!

Taking any possible step from the place you currently stand and then seeing how far that step takes you is a great way to begin to gain momentum. New opportunities will show up only when you are in the game. Not when you are looking in from the outside.

You need to commit to taking the next best step that can move you forward, but you don't need to know the whole way, just your direction.

Now, although a vague goal is not optimal, a vague plan is better than no plan.

For example, a person moving to a new location for their career cannot plan everything to the finest details before they move. This will often be scary and may delay their departure, leading them to miss many opportunities and perhaps even decide that it's too hard to go.

You may have vague plans such as which neighborhood you plan to live in, which schools the children will go to, and your overall goal, but without physically making a move, you cannot anticipate everything in advance. You must have faith that the proper way will reveal itself for you.

When you are already in the water, a different perspective and different opportunities will show up for you. Since your dream is not something you have ever accomplished before, there will be grey areas in your plan. You will be in uncharted territory. It would help if you *tried* to fill in the blanks with a mentor, books, or programs, but you can never really entirely do this. Your personal path will be carved out by you step by step by treading down the path into the unknown at times.

It is okay to feel fear, but it should not stop you. Be courageous to keep moving along the path no matter what other people say to you or think about you. This is *your* life journey, not theirs. They cannot understand your choices or path because it is not theirs; it is yours. Everybody has a different perspective on life. Follow yours so that you will be the one who will feel fulfilled in the end.

The famous science writer and inventor Arthur C. Clarke wrote, "All human plans [are] subject to ruthless revision by Nature, or Fate, or whatever one preferred to call the powers behind the Universe."

All you have to know is where you desire to go and course correct your plans on the way to getting there with better and better plans.

For example, in my online Guerrilla Diet Health program, every week, a new plan is laid out to follow. Then one follows through with it and builds on it the following week. Just as in life, things build on each other. Past experiences gave you the knowledge, experience, and self-esteem to take on new and improved projects and so on. A person doesn't make it to the finish line of meaning, delight, and success without going through the whole run.

Writing Your Goals:

One critical way to keep you focused on your soul work is to write your goals and plans on paper, even though they might change. Why? Because writing your goals and your plans to achieve them on paper brings you clarity during the writing process. And when you have clarity, you know where you are going. When you spend a few minutes in the morning reviewing or rewriting your goals and plans, then your actions will focus you in the right direction for your soul's desire.

Writing your goals and plans leads to focused action, which removes many of the distractions we face daily. With focus, you will be spending your time on meaningful activities for you that move your life in the right direction.

When you write down or edit your goals in the morning, you narrow your field of focus for that day, which is good, especially in our era when there are so many options available for us. These options are basically distractions that will leave you scattered and may lead you to stray away from your life vision and soul's desire. Writing your goals and plans on paper helps you become clear on what exactly you would like for your future and what you need to do to get there. You home in on your destination and the way to get you there. By writing your goals, you can also put your mind on what you need to remove from your life and what you need to add to your life to be where you want to be.

During writing, your brain is free to think and create the vision of your desired future. Writing your goals is also a form of commitment, like signing a contract between you and higher intelligence. You make a statement when you write your goals down. You are stating that you are serious about accomplishing the goals that you have written.

Writing down your goals makes you more productive, and the wheels of advancement start moving you in the right direction. When you write, your memory records things better. Your goals and plans stay longer in the forefront of your mind. And this allows for more focused action without you even realizing it.

The action of taking the time to write your goals and plans out, and go over them in the morning before you start your day, shows that you are not only committed but also motivated towards the achievement of your goals. Motivation breeds excitement, and excitement breeds action. Motivation is the spark that lights the fire that moves you to action.

Brian Tracy said, "A goal that is not in writing is like cigarette smoke: It drifts away and disappears. It is vague and insubstantial. It has no force, effect, or power. But a written goal becomes something that you can see, touch, read, and modify if necessary."

When you start writing down your goals and plans on paper or in notes on your smartphone, your life will transform for the better. I cannot explain it, but only when my goals and the plans I made to reach them were written down with timelines, and I reread them daily and modified them when necessary did I gain a success level much higher than I could have ever imagined.

And when you have your goals and plans written, you will also notice the progress you make.

Questions Of The Day

So, to end off this lesson and to help you build a life plan through goals, the questions that you want to ask yourself today are:

What are my five, ten and fifteen-year goals? What are my specific goals for my relationships, career, family, living conditions, health plan, and life in general? Where would I like to live? With whom? How many children would I want to have? What work will I do? How will my days look like? Where do I want to be in my life? What is now stopping me from getting there? How can I remove this hurdle? What do I need to have, get, or accomplish to achieve them? Do I really believe I can accomplish these goals? Are they relevant to my more extensive long-term picture? What are my next steps to fulfilling my goals? What is my plan of action to ensure I head in the right direction? By when will I take these actions? Do I have my most important goals and plans written on a sheet of paper on a pad that I can carry around with me or on my phone? Can I look at my goals and plans daily and modify them when need be? And can I schedule into my daily morning ritual a few minutes a day when I read over my goals and plans and focus on the feelings that I would feel had I already achieved them? By when do I plan on achieving each goal?

Remember that writing down your goals and plans is like committing to achieving them, and when you commit, you are very likely to succeed because your subconscious mind helps you with all of the efforts.

As usual, I recommend writing your answers in the PDF journal.

Affirmation Of The Day

After answering the questions in your journal, and contemplating on your answers, sit quietly for a few minutes today and repeat this affirmation to yourself as you think and dwell upon it:

I AM SUCCESSFULLY MOVING TOWARDS ALL OF MY GOALS CONSISTENTLY AND DAILY. MY LIFE IS AN EXCITING ADVENTURE THAT LEADS ME TO MY GOALS. MY GOALS AND PLANS ARE WRITTEN ON PAPER, AND I REVIEW THEM DAILY, WHICH IS HOW I KEEP A LASER FOCUS ON ACHIEVING MY DREAMS.

Repeat this affirmation often. With repetition, it has the power to alter your consciousness so you build a better, happier and more purposeful life.

DAY 55 - BECOMING AWARE OF YOUR FOCUS

"Where Attention goes Energy flows." ~ James Redfield

I have a question for you. Where is your attention right now? Are you awake? Have you planned your day? Where is your focus now?

We all know the power of focus, and we can see it in the experiment where the magnifying glass focuses the sun's energy until we have a fire. This is the same power of focused thoughts and habits.

Are your thoughts scattered, or are they focused on living a life of purpose?

And what exactly does it mean to live a life of purpose? Although we want to focus our attention on reaching our goals, we will only see results if we focus on the changes we need to make while reaching our destination, especially the changes within ourselves. Thomas Jefferson said, "If you want something you've never had, you must be willing to do something you've never done," and we can add to that, "*and think in ways you never thought.*"

You can't achieve anything new if you remain the same person with the same mindset, habits, and actions that brought you to where you are today. You want to focus your thoughts on the **actions** that will produce the results that you desire.

And the great thing is that the more you focus on the action steps that bring you closer to your desires, the more these actions become your habits. And when something becomes a habit, especially a positive habit, it changes your character for the better. And if your goals are aligned with your soul's desire, then focusing will change you to become the person you need to evolve into to reach your desires.

Habits are things that we do daily. This means that when an action becomes a new habit, you are moving towards attaining your goals daily by taking habitual action steps. There is no procrastination. There is here and now.

The speed of reaching a goal should not be significant. Everything happens at the right time and the right stage in life. When you move in the direction of your dreams through daily actions, and your goals align with your purpose, you will attain your goals no matter what the speed. Just as with the turtle during its race with the rabbit. We see that it is the consistent focus on *the activities* that need to be done that gets us to our goals.

Focusing on what seems urgent and what catches our attention is not the right way to achieve our goals. This actually moves us away from their attainment. Only by placing your focus on the action steps that are important to reaching your goals will you get closer to achieving your dreams.

Today, in the information age, we have endless distractions. It is almost impossible for us to focus if we do not have the discipline to stop these distractions. We have many different ringtones for various messages that come into our phone, usually placed at arm's reach.

We *do* have the option of blocking out these disturbances to do what is essential for *us to do* to move our life forward to where we desire and need to be to fulfill ourselves.

People who know me well know that I may go into my WhatsApp many times a day for necessary things, but I will only answer other people's requests at night after I have finished my daily tasks.

We only have a certain amount of hours in a day when we are at peak focus, and there are often many things to achieve during this time; therefore, distractions need taming.

We do not need to be like Pavlov's dogs that every ring we hear, we need to pick up and check our phone. But because this quickly becomes a habitual behavior, it is best to put the phone in silent or do-not-disturb mode when concentrating on essential tasks.

Focus on finding solutions to your problems and acting upon them. Focus on creativity; focus on the proper action steps to move you forwards.

Often we try multi-tasking, but this is not the best way to move forward. An hour of focused action is worth more than a few hours of partially concentrated effort. Quiet focus is the most crucial thing for producing quality work.

Do one thing to completion and then do another, and you will move forward much faster than when you try to do everything all at once. This is the basis for doing your best in everything you do.

Focus is a behavioral pattern that is similar to a muscle.

We are not necessarily born with the ability to focus, but the more we focus, the better at it we become.

Questions Of The Day

To end this lesson and help you focus your attention on the right tasks to do to move your life forwards, please ask yourself:

What are my dreams? (Write them down in your notebook), and when can I start to dedicate a quiet, focused effort to achieve each goal in its own time? Write down a time of day that you will commit solely to focus on the actions needed for achieving each dream. You may need an hour, a day, or even several months or years of intervals of focus, depending on the size of your vision and the time you will need to dedicate to it. Now begin following your plan.

As usual, I recommend writing your answers in the PDF journal.

Affirmation Of The Day

After answering the questions in your journal, and contemplating on your answers, sit quietly for a few minutes today and repeat this affirmation to yourself as you think and dwell upon it:

I EASILY FOCUS MY ATTENTION DAILY ON THE RIGHT ACTIONS THAT MOVE ME TOWARDS ACHIEVING MY DREAMS.

Repeat this affirmation often. With repetition, it has the power to alter your consciousness so you build a better, happier and more purposeful life.

DAY 56 - BECOMING AWARE OF MEANING AND PURPOSE

"Life is never made unbearable by circumstances, but only by lack of meaning and purpose." ~ Viktor Frankl

Viktor Frankl said this after suffering in the concentration camps during the holocaust of World War II. The same message was stated slightly differently by Friedrich Nietzsche when he said, "If you know the why, you can endure anyhow."

Viktor Frankl wanted to survive for his wife. He found meaning and purpose in his survival so that he could be of service to be there to care for his wife after the war ended. This meaning helped him survive the perhaps most challenging reality of our era.

When we choose to do something, it must have a deeper meaning and make us content and fulfilled. Without meaning and purpose behind everything we do, the results we achieve will never be great and will not make us happy.

When you do not have passion, you lack energy, enthusiasm, and ideas, and may not be very sensitive to other people. These are the reasons that a person lacking passion will often fail.

When you have passion for something, it means that you love that something, and it is vital for you. When you follow your passion, you spread the love further to other people who can enjoy your gifts. Then your life will be full of meaning and purpose and will bring you all the satisfaction and abundance you desire.

Many marketing books state that you should listen to what the customer wants and then create it for them. This may be good for some people to form the wealth they desire, but if you are not doing something that gives you a sense of meaning and purpose, you will not be happy.

In relationships, we sometimes have an imbalance when one side gives and gives, and the other is always on the receiving end. When you are doing anything, for it to be successful, it must be in alignment with your soul's desire. It must have meaning and purpose for you.

We are happiest when we share our gifts. And isn't this what we all seek? Continuous ongoing happiness? And this can only be achieved when we are involved in something that gives us meaning; sharing our gifts. When we share our gifts, we are sharing love. And love connects us to all other beings in unity, which is our soul's desire.

Your gifts may be many, but not all gifts will you enjoy sharing. The ones you enjoy sharing are the ones that will bring you the abundance you desire.

Sometimes the hardships and the lessons you learned, as a result, have become your gifts. You are more sensitive to the feelings of others through your past difficulties.

When you share your gifts with the world, you directly connect to your higher self. You received your gifts (and your hardships that may often transform into gifts) from Infinite intelligence, and when you share these gifts with the world, you are spreading true divine nature.

We each have brilliance within us. It is of significance that you find your brilliance and share it with the world. This will fill your life with meaning and purpose, which leads to a life of bliss.

Your first job is to be authentic and let your light shine through with love.

Your second job is to surround yourself with people who appreciate you as you are and love you unconditionally.

Your third job is to find your brilliance.

Your fourth job is to find a way to share it with the world in a way that gives you pleasure and profit of any sort.

Once you show your authentic self and find your brilliance, you will have meaning and purpose behind how and with whom you spend most of your waking hours, and this will fill your heart and your life with bliss, keeping you fulfilled and content.

When you are in touch with your inner truth, you will touch the inner truth of others as well.

The happier you are, the more your heart is open, and the more you will share your gifts lovingly to all the people around you, improving your life and the lives of others and the world at large.

It is as if infinite intelligence is telling you, "I *was just checking you out; you did a good job, here, are more gifts for a job well done.*"

We all have gifts to share. Being your authentic self is the most basic and most significant gift you have to share. And when you share your gifts, you allow all of those close to you to share *their* gifts as well. You permit them to be who they really are without judgment or fear.

When you are in the right place for yourself, you gladly permit others you care about to be in the right place for them and let their light shine through.

In the book of Genesis, God asks Adam, "Where are you?" Wise people have understood that this question "Where are you?" is a question of our purpose and path in life. We must each ask ourselves this question to contemplate our path and ensure we are headed in the right direction for our soul's desire.

Questions Of The Day

To end this lesson ask yourself:

How can I add more meaning and purpose to my life? How can I be of more service to others? What are the gifts that I can share with the people around me and the world? What do I love doing? Can I connect with my authenticity to lead me to a life of meaning and purpose? Who can I share my gifts with? Can I share my gifts with more people? Where am I?

If you don't have clear answers about your gifts, ask yourself:

What are the substantial hardships I went through? What lessons did I learn as a result of these hardships? What exactly did I do to get myself out of the difficulties? What changes did I make in my life? How did I sustain these changes? Can I teach others to do the same? In what ways will I enjoy doing this?

As usual, I recommend writing your answers in the PDF journal.

Affirmation Of The Day

After answering the questions in your journal, and examining them, sit quietly for a few minutes today and repeat this affirmation to yourself:

I AM LIVING MY LIFE WITH MEANING AND PURPOSE. ABUNDANCE FILLS MY LIFE AS I SHARE MY GIFTS WITH THE PEOPLE AROUND ME AND THE WORLD.

Repeat this affirmation often. With repetition, it has the power to alter your consciousness so you build a better, happier and more purposeful life.

DAY 57 - BECOMING AWARE OF YOUR LIFE VISION

"The only thing worse than being blind is having sight but no vision." ~ Helen Keller

Steve Jobs, the founder of Apple computers, made his famous Apple ad campaign in 1997 before he even had a new product. He made his vision into a reality by taking the first step before producing the product to sell. Once completing the ad, he could not turn back. This is the power of having a vision and taking risks to share your vision with the world so that you can move it forward.

This sharing forms a commitment to either make a fool of yourself or hold through and as long as it takes and work towards making your vision a reality. When you have the vision of how things should be in your mind, even when they aren't there in front of you or even in existence yet, you already have the foundation for transforming that vision into reality.

When you commit to your vision, providence moves in to help you create it.

You don't have to figure out all of the steps of how to get there, as we mentioned before. You can never do that even if you try (especially if your vision is big, which it should be).

If your vision is something new, even if only for you, you have not been there yet, and you are not aware of all the steps needed to get you there.

Although you cannot foresee all the steps, you *can* start, and you *can* take the first step, and the next and the next after that, and so on, until your vision becomes a reality.

Even the most complex achievements that seem impossible to achieve, such as Bill Gates and Microsoft, Jeff Bezos and Amazon, Steve Jobs and Apple, and now Elon Musk and Tesla and Space X, when you examine these cases carefully, you can see that all is a series of steps beginning with the first logical step and then the next logical step and then the next one, and so on. But you have to be in the game to know what is the next logical step. Most often, you cannot foresee it in advance.

Your vision may seem so complex that you do not know where even to start. All you need to do is find the first logical step you *can* take from where you are right now and do it. And then make a new plan every day. And when you are in a situation that you cannot follow through with your plan, change it but do not compromise your dream. Find a different way to go about it, an out-of-the-box way, that will keep pushing you forward.

When you have a vision, that vision produces passion for the results you see in the future, and this passion is the fire that fuels your engines.

You never need to worry because you will always know the next step to take once you complete the previous step. And you will always have what you need to take the next right step. Nothing is impossible. You have to believe this. A way will always show up if *you* show up! It is like running in the dark with a flashlight on your head. You can only see the next step. You can't see it one moment before you are ready to take it, but when you are prepared to take that step, it will show up in front of you.

Every step, no matter how small, moves you one step closer towards your vision.

Every complex achievement was made by taking small, simple actions. As Jim Rohn said, "These actions are just as easy to do as they are easy not to do."

So choose to do them.

The limiting factor is never any external situation. No. It is only you. Your choices, beliefs, and actions are the only things limiting factors on your way towards realizing your vision.

They say that you will be living in the past if you do not have a vision for your life. It is the vision that pushes you forward. Your vision inspires you to move forward and take action.

Your vision is the sight, in your mind, of how things should be and how you can help them become that way.

The vision of what should be is not only seen but is also felt in your bones. It generates energy that fuels you to action. This is your inner guidance system.

When you know your vision, and it is clear to you, you will only choose relationships that support your dreams and vision. You will spend your time mainly on your vision, and your habits will be well-chosen to help you align yourself and your life with your vision.

Your vision must be clear and specific and detailed always to point you toward a particular future.

So what do you do if you don't have a vision, or if you feel you want to change your vision?

You can't find your vision through the normal thought processes. Your vision has to come from your soul which is consciousness connected to all.

It would be best if you spent time in nature contemplating, meditating, daydreaming, and letting your creativeness flow through you when you are not held by the constraints of time, so that your mind can wander freely and imagine things as you would like them to be.

Think of your SMART goals and review the lesson on meaning and purpose.

I suggest asking for help from a higher power. Dream big, and use your creativity, and allow your imagination to run a little wild. Your vision comes from your soul; you will know it when you feel it. Your vision is the way you want and think things should be. A life vision is always positive and supportive for many more people than only yourself. A vision improves the world in some way or manner.

Connect with what you desire on the deepest level. Think to yourself what you would like to be remembered for at the end of your life. For which exceptional accomplishments? And ask yourself what you are incredibly passionate about and how you visualize the world as a better place?

Think about what you would like to have in each area of your life.

Think about your ideal relationships, ideal health, ideal financial state, ideal career, ideal ways of enjoyment, and what fills you on the deepest level, your soul's desire.

You want to be clear on the life you want to live. You want a crystal clear vision of your soul's desire in motion in each arena of life so that you can put all of the pieces together as one. As your ideal life.

Think of each of these areas of your life in introspection and solitude. See a vision for each of these areas as if you already have exactly what you desire.

Think of what success in each area means to you and envision it in your mind.

All your power comes from seeing what you want in your life first in your mind. This is the first step of the creative process.

See the exact outcome you desire in your imagination.

Now, although knowing your vision clearly and playing it out in your mind constantly is a powerful technique to move you towards your dreams in the best and most secure way, you may need some encouragement, and there is no better way of encouragement than creating a vision board to become a GPS for you.

When you know where you are headed, and the picture remains in front of you constantly, then you will be led by infinite intelligence to take the right actions that will take you to your soul's desire.

Vision Board:

A vision board is a board that has images of your dreams on it. The vision board helps you see your specific goals right in front of you in their completed form daily. You may also add some critical affirmations printed onto your vision board.

By having a vision board, you ensure your actions move you forward. It may seem at times that you are failing to reach your desires, or you are not making sufficient progress. Relax and do not lose hope.

Never, never, never give up on your vision. There is no such thing as failure, just a recalibration of the way to reach your vision. So long as you are doing something productive, no matter how small, you are making progress. Only when you do nothing will you also have nothing.

All failure is there to help you learn and improve yourself to get on track in a better way towards reaching your highest vision for yourself.

When you have your vision stuck on a board in front of you many hours a day, you know that your actions will move you in the right direction. You will gain momentum, and you will be making progress.

When you show that you treat your soul's desire seriously by working and preparing a vision board and placing it in a central location for you, your actions will move you towards the growth you desire. You will be of the small percentage of people who dare to go after their dreams.

When you dare to take your dreams seriously, nothing can stop you from achieving them.

Creating a vision board should be a fun activity. The vision board itself will serve to motivate you in hard times and inspire you that you *can* reach your dreams.

Your soul's desire was given to you because you have the potential to achieve it. You definitely can succeed if you are willing to take the daily steps in the right direction.

Your vision board should be a detailed visual portfolio of where you want to be, what you want to do, what you want to have in your life, and with who. The vision board should stir up positive feelings within you as if you have already accomplished your dreams.

It is essential to state that when you have a vision, you do not need to know the details of how to get to your soul's potential.

You just need to know where you are headed and the next logical step to take.

You can then take focused action when you know where you are going.

Have this vision board in front of you, and whenever you have the time to sit and allow your thoughts to roll out, these visions will subject themselves onto your subconscious mind, and slowly you will get impulses to act. Then when you take action, despite any fear, you will see that you are moving closer to your vision and your ideal life. Your efforts will keep you right on target when you have the vision right there in front of you, day in, day out.

By seeing your goals as complete every day through the pictures on your vision board, a state of internal conflict will form in your subconscious mind between what you see on the board and what you now have in your life. Your subconscious mind will move you to resolve this void by turning your current reality into the ideal vision you have created for yourself on the board. The more you look at the board, the more internal conflict is formed through this void, and then you must fill it. You'll feel motivated to move forward.

Your mind will search for solutions to fill this void, and infinite intelligence will support you by sending you information to go ahead and take right focused action to solve this void. This is why having a vision board with your vision is extremely powerful!

Creating a vision board helps you not only create through your eyes but having affirmations and saying them to yourself aloud when you see them enables you to use your ears to create. And if you can also get yourself to smell the smells of having your goals met inside your mind, and also if you can feel as if you are touching what you desire to have on your vision board or taste what is there if this is relevant, then you are imprinting even more firmly onto your subconscious mind your new reality. According to your vision board, these will help you bridge the gap between what is and what should be.

So how to create your vision board? Buy a board or an A3-sized thick drawing paper. Meditate in a quiet place about what you would like to achieve in the seven critical areas of life, including relationships, health, finances, career, fun, personal fulfillment, and your legacy.

Write down both your long and short-term goals. Gather inspiration for your vision board online. Choose the best pictures that resemble what you desire. Find quotes that resonate with your desire. Send everything to a printing shop. Print out affirmations as reminders.

Collect them when they are ready and find a place to sit comfortably and quietly. Get a tube of glue, scissors, and markers. Once you have all of the pieces ready, cut them into the shapes you desire and spread them out on a table, or better yet, on the floor. Look at them and then place them in the order you wish on your large poster board. Glue them and use colorful markers to make your vision perfect. Use your creativity to make the vision board a true reflection of your vision for your life.

Find a central place to hang your vision board. Maybe where you work, or near your kitchen or in your bedroom. This will become your daily reminder of where you want to go in life, no matter what the daily distractions. Now you are ready to continue your journey to the life of your dreams. And please do not forget to celebrate your success whenever you notice progression towards your goals.

Questions Of The Day

To end this lesson and to help you follow your life vision, ask yourself:

What is my vision for my life? If you don't have one, spend the free time in introspection until you discover it. Ask yourself, what would I like to be remembered for? What would I want to be written on my tombstone? What would I like people to think and say about me after I am gone?

If you know what your vision is, ask yourself, what am I doing daily to live out my vision? Then ask yourself: when can I set out two to three hours to create a vision board, and where will I hang it so I can see it as often as possible every day? As usual, I recommend writing your answers in the PDF journal.

Affirmation Of The Day

After answering the questions in your journal, and examining them, sit quietly for a few minutes today and repeat this affirmation to yourself as you think and dwell upon it:

I AM BREATHING LIFE INTO MY LIFE VISION DAILY BY TAKING THE RIGHT ACTIONS AND CHOICES. I SEE THE EXACT OUTCOME OF MY DESIRES ON MY VISION BOARD, AND ALL MY ACTIONS ADVANCE ME TOWARDS THE LIFE OF MY DREAMS.

Repeat this affirmation often. With repetition, it has the power to alter your consciousness so you build a better, happier and more purposeful life.

DAY 58 - BECOMING AWARE OF THE POWER OF DISSOCIATION

"At times I seek dissociation to associate with myself." ~ Booma Balan

Previously we spoke about how associating with something is the best way to move you closer to the life of your dreams through visualization. But what happens when previous trauma follows you through life, preventing you from reaching your goals.

When we want to create a vision of our perfect life, we must associate ourselves with this future vision. We must see ourselves and feel ourselves experiencing the life that we wish to have in the present.

Since association with something or an event is so powerful, just as it can take us down a positive path, it can also carry us down a negative path. Associating with something also can hinder our progress and prevent us from reaching our goals, mainly if we associate ourselves with the adverse event.

This is what happens in the case of post-traumatic stress disorder (PTSD). We see ourselves as part of the traumatic event in the past and the present, and this association makes us feel the adverse event in each cell of our body. It is as if the event keeps happening to us over and over again. We keep re-living the event. Now the traumatic event need not even be so traumatic. For example, if we keep finding ourselves in the same kind of relationships, this is the exact mechanism working against us.

Associating ourselves with a negative situation will hinder our progress and suppress our life in many areas. So how can we heal from such situations and move our life in the direction we want it to go?

Just as visualizing the ideal life situation by associating ourselves with it moves our lives to the place we want to be, withdrawing ourselves from negative situations in the past or future through dissociation will help us remove these negative thought patterns from our lives and allow us to form the life of our dreams more effectively.

Instead of seeing yourself as taking part in a negative event, distance yourself from the event in your mind. See yourself as an observer of the situation instead of an active partaker of the situation. When we are observers, we do not feel the situation through our senses, and we do not feel the feelings associated with the situation. We are disconnected from the situation. As if we are observing two people fight near us, we are not involved in their feelings or their pain. We are more like bystanders watching the situation without involvement.

We can transform association to a situation into dissociation and withdrawal from the situation. To do this, we must imagine ourselves as being only observers of the situation and slowly moving physically away from the situation.

We can make this transformation inside our minds.

Please try this short meditation now. Think of something that happened to you that still has a grip on your life. An event keeps coming up in your mind or keeps showing up in your life, and you feel you have no control over it. Now sit quietly and focus on your breathing for a few moments, close your eyes, and relax your body parts one by one. Then loosen the muscles in your face.

Now imagine yourself taking part in the traumatic situation that you chose. Look at yourself. What are you wearing?

Watch yourself move. Look at yourself as if you are not you. Hear the sounds of the situation but hear them as if they are off in the distance, not as the person in the situation would hear them. You can see what you are doing, but you can't feel the sensations or feelings you feel. It is you, but you are not experiencing this version of yourself. You can't feel the heat or the cold, you can't smell the smells, you can't feel the clothes on your body, and you can't hear the sounds clearly. You notice the actions that you are doing, but you see them from a distance, as an observer, as if someone else is doing them. Now look around at the situation from a distance. Look at the other people there. See them from a distance. Now turn around and slowly move further and further away from the other people in your vision. Then look back at where you were in that situation, and you notice that that version of you has left and is no longer there. Now change your vision into a bird's eye view from above. See yourself walking off into the distance away from the situation. There are no feelings associated with that version of you. You are observing that version of you until that version of you disappears into the horizon.

You now come slowly back from the hypnotic state to your present. You will perhaps not be aware of any change that has just happened within you, but there IS a change within you.

If you continue to practice this meditation a few more times for the same situation, you will see that the grip that the negative situation had on your life will soon be gone entirely.

One day I was on my usual early morning run. A small dog that was not on a leash came running towards me. I slowed down and thought he would smell me and continue. But instead, he attacked me. He bit my leg four times. I was hysterical, bleeding from my muscle. I managed to walk back home and went to the hospital to get vaccinated and bandaged. I could not walk for a few days afterward since the dog had bitten my muscle. I was so traumatized by the event that the next time I was running, I saw a huge dog that came towards me. I started to scream. I couldn't control myself. I was so scared. I was still wounded and in pain. I understood that I must do something about my emotional state, so I used this withdrawal method, as I call it, to withdraw myself from the original negative situation. This was so powerful that even a day later, I was no longer completely debilitated when meeting dogs.

Go ahead and try this powerful withdrawal method and see how you can remove any negativity you are holding on to from previous events and clear the effect they have on you immediately.

Questions Of The Day

To end this lesson and help you dissociate from negative emotional states, please ask yourself:

Where did I have trauma? Use this withdrawal method to remove the effects the past event has on your current life. As usual, I recommend writing your answers in the PDF journal.

Affirmation Of The Day

After answering the questions in your journal, and contemplating on your answers, sit quietly for a few minutes today and repeat this affirmation:

I SLOWLY WITHDRAW MYSELF FROM ANY PAST ADVERSE EVENTS AND ASSOCIATE MYSELF MORE AND MORE WITH THE BEST VERSION OF MYSELF.

Repeat this affirmation often. With repetition, it has the power to alter your consciousness so you build a better, happier and more purposeful life.

DAY 59 - BECOMING AWARE OF YOUR CORE VALUES

"Efforts and courage are not enough without purpose and direction." ~ John F. Kennedy

Without feeling that you have a real purpose in life, you will feel lost. You need to know what you are aiming for. We talked recently about directing your life in the perfect direction for you. Although you may have prepared a vision for your ideal lie, you must know that what you are aiming for is really right for you.

You want to ensure that you are happy and fulfilled now and in the future. You want to ensure that your dreams and goals are aligned with your true purpose, one that comes from your soul.

So how can you know?

To identify whether you are on the right track, first examine your core values.

Your core values are your guiding principles that dictate your behavior. They may have come from your early experiences and influences in your life, but nonetheless, you have chosen them unconsciously, and they guide your life.

Below is a list of core values. Which five do you resonate with most?

- Adventure
- Autonomy
- Beauty
- Compassion
- Challenge
- Community
- Contribution
- Creativity
- Faith
- Fame
- Friendships
- Fun
- Growth
- Happiness
- Honesty
- Humor
- Influence
- Inner Harmony
- Justice
- Kindness
- Knowledge
- Leadership
- Learning
- Love
- Loyalty
- Meaningful Work
- Openness
- Peace
- Pleasure
- Recognition
- Responsibility
- Security
- Service
- Spirituality
- Stability
- Success
- Wealth

Find your five most important core values. Not necessarily those that have to do with your duties, for example, as being a parent. Examine which core values really resonate with who you are!

Once you find your five core values, you may wish to go into more detail about some of them and explain how you see them come about in your life. For example, one of my core values is contribution. So when I go into more detail about this core value, it is all about my contribution to the world and my family by teaching from my experience and knowledge, giving my time and effort to helping others.

Now take a moment and choose your five most important core values and then detail each one explaining how you see each core value appearing in your life.

Wonderful! Now that you found your core values and went into a bit of detail go back to your life vision you prepared for yourself on day #57 and see if your vision is aligned with your core values.

Now, take a moment and rewrite down your five most important life goals by refining what you wrote on day #57 to match your core values.

Your two lists of your core values and your life goals must come together so that you can genuinely feel fulfilled once you achieve your goals.

For example, one of my core values is influence. I must be influencing to be happy. And a few of my goals allow me to influence others, like my writing and social media. My entrepreneurial work enables me to be of service, another of my core values.

Aim to have all of your goals involve all of your core values together. If you can find a few passions that are in line with all of your five main core values, then you have hit the jackpot. These will make you happiest and most fulfilled.

For me, lecturing, being on television, my clinic, my social media content, and my family life allow me to combine all of my core values to feel happy and fulfilled.

When your values are fulfilled through your goals, then you will feel a deep sense of fulfillment and joy in your life.

Take some time for introspection. Go over your two lists of core values and life goals, and see how you can connect them into one big goal or two to five smaller goals that will make you happy and fulfilled once achieved.

Then create the vision of you living the life with your goals achieved and make all of your choices from this point of view from this moment on.

Questions Of The Day

To ensure you are headed in the right direction backed by your core values, please ask yourself:

What are my five core values, and what are my five goals to achieve this lifetime? Now go and find the connections between the two to ensure that your goals are expressions of your core values and authentic self.

As usual, I recommend writing your answers in the PDF journal.

Affirmation Of The Day

After answering the questions in your journal, and contemplating on your answers, sit quietly for a few minutes today and repeat this affirmation:

BY LOOKING WITHIN MY OWN HEART, I FIND AND FOLLOW MY CORE VALUES ALLOWING MY LIFE TO BE FILLED WITH MEANING AND PURPOSE.

Repeat this affirmation often. With repetition, it has the power to alter your consciousness so you build a better, happier and more purposeful life.

DAY 60 - BECOMING AWARE OF STRESS FOR MOTIVATION

"It's not the load that breaks you down, it's the way you carry it." ~ Lou Holtz

—————————⬿⬿⬿—————————

The only way you can have no stress in your life is when you are dead. The graveyard is indeed very peaceful, but is this where you want to be now?

Stress is something that happens to us regularly throughout life. Once you set goals for yourself, not small and easy-to-attain goals, but big long-term goals, you add more stress to your life.

When you become overstressed by something, you will suffer the physical consequences over a while, which will move you away from reaching your goals.

If you handle stress inappropriately, you will suffer from the physical consequences and have trouble concentrating and other mental and emotional repercussions. You will feel overwhelmed and lose your creativity. All of these move you further away from your dreams.

Stress is a part of life, and being goal-oriented may increase it. So what is the best way to handle this stress, and how can you still do what is required of you to move forward on the path towards achieving your goals even if they inspire high-stress levels?

There is a path to help you manage your stress levels most effectively. Firstly you want to change your perspective about the situation. When a situation feels very intimidating, and it is very stressful to cope with. It would be best to change your perspective on the situation to make it seem less intimidating for you. To do this, you must think all the way through to the worst-case scenario that could happen. What is the worst-case scenario that could happen? Ask yourself is you can learn to cope with this situation in your mind. Think about all of the negative things that could result from this worst-case scenario, and think about whether you could cope with these situations. You will see that you probably can. Also ask yourself, what is the most likely scenario that will happen and the best case scenario.

After you finish following through with these scenarios, now is the time to do your best to prevent the worst-case scenario from happening, not through fear driven actions, but through decisive, proactive, focused, and positive steps that will lead you to where you desire to be naturally.

This helps significantly reduce the power that the situation has over you, and as a result, your levels of stress will decrease.

We spoke about transforming obstacles into opportunities previously. When you can see all stressful situations as opportunities for your personal growth rather than frightening, you will allow this stress to push, encourage, challenge, and energize you to move forward towards your dreams.

When you change your perception of any situation, you feel more in control over the situation, even though it only controls your response to the situation, but this naturally lowers stress levels.

And when you take action through the stress, instead of freezing because you are too overwhelmed from the stress, you will also feel more at ease because you are doing something about it instead of just sitting and accepting your difficult situation.

Taking a stressful situation and transforming it into a personal challenge will make the stressful situation become something that moves you towards a better life instead of moving away. Any difficulty becomes a challenge that you wish to take on.

Of course, life situations can feel very overwhelming at times. But it is good to understand that it is not the situations themselves that are necessarily overwhelming; it is your perspective. They are overwhelming to you now because of your attitude about them. You are giving the situation too much energy. No matter how extreme the difficulty, you can tone down your attitude towards it and find a way to mentally cope with it.

You are strong enough to cope with everything, and if you changed your perspective on the situation and see it as less threatening for you, then now is the time to improve your outlook on yourself. You CAN handle all that comes your way if you take a baby-step attitude. Taking small baby steps to get yourself out of a stressful situation is the best way to move forward in high-stress situations. If you are overwhelmed and do nothing, you will become even more stressed. It becomes a downward spiral. The key is to do something small continually. The continual actions you take will reduce the stress load because you will feel more in control. You will feel that you can influence your situation when you take the right actions.

You are responsible for your response, and your response will be based on how you view the situation and how you view yourself.

View the situation as something that you *can* overcome, and see yourself as being strong enough to do what it takes to overcome the situation. The stress will not be as destructive and have less negative influence over your life. In this way, stress can even take a positive role in your life to energize, push and move you forward.

Stress becomes a motivator to move you forward rather than something scary that keeps you from taking action because of fear that you can't handle or cope with the situation. You can always respond to a situation. You don't have to react to the problem or sit there and do nothing and accept it as it is. You can always choose to take lawful action with courage. It is up to you.

Any assertive response to a situation will bring you feelings of control. When you view the stressful situation as a challenge that can be coped with one step at a time, you will not only reduce your stress levels; you will also be more in control of your life and happier overall.

Questions Of The Day

To end this lesson and help you transform stress into motivation, ask yourself:

Where am I giving my power away in acceptance of a situation when I can choose to respond to the problem and influence it by taking action? Have I thought of the worst-case scenario all the way through and found that I can cope with whatever happens? Which actions can I take to motivate myself to get to where I want to be instead of where I do not want to be?

As usual, I recommend writing your answers in the PDF. Then look over your answers to ensure that you improve your life and bring forth your true divine nature.

Affirmation Of The Day

After answering the questions in your journal, and contemplating on your answers, sit quietly for a few minutes today and repeat this affirmation:

I AM IN CONTROL OF MY RESPONSE TO EVERY STRESSFUL SITUATION. I USE STRESSFUL SITUATIONS AS MOTIVATORS FOR ACTION AND CHANGE! I AM PATIENT AND TAKE SMALL DAILY LAWFUL ACTIONS TO MAKE MY LIFE BETTER.

Repeat this affirmation often. With repetition, it has the power to alter your consciousness so you build a better, happier and more purposeful life.

DAY 61 - BECOMING AWARE OF PROGRESS AND MOMENTUM

"Successful people keep moving. They make mistakes, but they don't quit." ~ Conrad Hilton

We seek progress in our lives. In fact, without feeling that we are making some form of progress, we will not be pleased.

This progress takes different forms throughout different stages of our life. At youth, progress is about physical growth, learning, creativity, and understanding.

In adulthood, progress is about doing, creating, working, building a family, healing, and building wealth. In later years, progress can come through grandchildren, or see our previous projects take on a life of their own, or by making new friends and enjoying different and unique activities or visiting new places than we previously had the time to enjoy.

You want to have progress in all stages of your life for you to feel fulfilled, happy and prosperous.

We all have this innate intelligence within us. We seek to express it more fully all the time. This is what progress is. It is a fuller expression of our true essence all of the time.

Progress is necessary to make us feel that our life is worthwhile, to make us fulfilled and happy.

We see progress everywhere in nature. We see it with the growth of the trees, with the spread of plant life, and with the coming of new generations that are better equipped than previous generations.

People are always seeking more of something, which is good because we are contributing our gifts to the progression of the whole through our personal progress.

When you cease to progress, at any age, you cease to live; Benjamin Franklin said it best. "Some people die at 25 and aren't buried until 75."

When we have no form of progress, no more learning, no more growth, no more new adventures, no more new people in our lives, or no new communication, or no more love, then we are dying. We instinctively know this, and for this reason, we are always seeking more life in one form or another. That is why we always have a constant desire for more. We shouldn't hinder or banish these growing desires. We should embrace this will within us for more life, for when we act upon this will of ours, we lead to progress not only for ourselves but also for everyone.

Do not fear that your desires are too big. The bigger they are, the more life they will bring to the world, which is a blessing. Big desires may seem harder to attain but through small, dedicated, and focused daily action and much faith in the work, progress is achieved for everyone.

Therefore, you should cherish constant change, constant development, constant growth, learning, and advancement of life. This will keep you young at heart and energetic to live a fuller and happier life. So please do not be scared of constant change; embrace it for it leads to progress; fear it not.

No change is easy. It may cause shock to your system, but this shock will not weaken you; it will make you stronger. And the stronger you are, the more self-esteem you have to do whatever you can do on any given day, leading to progress.

More progress in life leads to a life lived more abundantly, more fully.

Do not be shy or timid about your will to live more fully than you are currently living; remember that most people do not dare to live fully. They do not go after their dreams in all fields of life. They block themselves from progress in one or a few areas of life because of fear of what may happen in the future, fear of what may change, and wish to know all of the details every step of the way before committing to something. Of course, we cannot know everything that may happen until we walk the path, so someone who does not do, will have no progress in life and live, as Benjamin Franklin said, like a living dead.

Accept change and welcome all opportunities for progress in your life. Do not be afraid to try new things, live in different places, meet new people, and aim for growth in your job or business. Aim to become greater than you currently are.

Allow the thought of progress to fill your actions. When you become happier, you are also making others more content; when you become healthier, you will be making others healthier. When you become more prosperous, you will make others more prosperous, and when you become more loving, you are making other people more caring.

So when you make progress, you allow for the advancement of all of those who surround you.

When you become too big for the place you are currently occupying, you are making progress. Do not move on from one thing to another until you have mastered what you have desired to achieve in one place. Then you can progress further towards another job, relationship, study, or life. Make progress and keep making progress throughout your life, and you will indeed have lived a life that will be honored by many people, and you will leave your mark in the world in the hearts of all who know you.

You can become what you desire to be. So aim to advance your life. Learn a new language, see a new place, communicate with new people, share ideas, share knowledge, beauty, and share life.

Opportunities will always come to you if you are making constant progress, even with little steps.

Barack Obama said, "If you're walking down the right path and you're willing to keep walking, eventually you'll make progress." Notice how he said "the right path" because change will happen whether we like it or not, but progress will happen only if we go in the right direction for ourselves while positively influencing others' lives in the process.

One key to making progress is building momentum. But what does this mean exactly? It means that you want to keep making strides towards your goals no matter what is happening in your daily life. It would be best if you still took the time daily to make small strides towards your dreams. You need to maintain some form of momentum.

Most of the daily work you do towards your goals will be mundane and perhaps dull. But this **is** the momentum that you **need** to ensure that you achieve your goals. All the way to the top will not always be exciting. Most of the work will be dull, boring and some of it may be challenging. But this is the foundation that you need to build your dreams upon.

Once you stop taking even the most minor steps, you will need to rebuild momentum again.

As an example, let's look at addictions. If you don't keep away from the addictive substance or activity and go completely clean, you will often find yourself addicted again. You must keep up the momentum of staying clean, or you will have to start all over again. It would be best if you sustained momentum even at the minor level to keep the energy going to keep up with your goals.

Speed is never a function when you are looking at long-term goals. But the steadiness of action is what will ensure momentum and progress so that you reach the desired outcome.

It is important to note that it is just as easy to keep up the momentum as it is to stop it. The key is dedication, and this is always your choice. You need small steps in the right direction to keep up the momentum.

Sometimes overthinking can also destroy your momentum.

Now taking one day off your regimen will not have any immediate negative effect. Still, when you do not move towards your goal for even one day, you are doing the opposite and moving away from your goals. And this, compounded over time, will have a detrimental effect on the outcome of your life.

Even when you are on holiday, commit to reading a book that will advance you somehow. This is also considered keeping up the momentum. When you are in the car, listen to a video or book regarding personal development to keep up the momentum.

Choose one task that you must do either to achieve your goals or that helps you become a better version of yourself, and you do it. It is best to focus on one task at a time. However, some tasks do not take up all of your time and are spread over several months or years, like a university degree or a business plan. If you feel that you have more time available for you, you can take on more actions that you know will move you to your ideal life. It is crucial to complete the tasks that you have planned for each day/week/month/year on the best side possible.

When you leave things open or incomplete, they block momentum. They will pull you back to complete them, and generally, until you finish them, they will eat away at your self-esteem and make you feel unworthy.

You can't rush things, but you still must maintain some form of momentum and keep making some progress. There are times when you can do more, and there are times in your life when you won't be able to do very much. But believe me, even the most minor action adds up. Trees cannot accelerate their growth, but they keep growing steadily nonetheless.

The most remarkable thing about maintaining momentum is that it becomes part of your daily routine. These everyday actions become habits. And good habits help ensure a favorable outcome in any field.

Questions Of The Day

To end this lesson and to help you continue toward your goal, please ask yourself:

Am I continuously striving for growth? Am I making improvements regularly in all areas of my life, including more experiences with friends and family, more adventures, more creativity, better health, sufficient money and love? What may be stopping me from my growth and progress? Which tasks have I started that need completing? And which small steps can I take daily that will move me forward towards my soul's desire?

As usual, I recommend writing your answers in the PDF journal.

Affirmation Of The Day

After answering the questions in your journal, and contemplating on your answers, sit quietly for a few minutes today and repeat this affirmation:

I AM ALWAYS MOVING FORWARD WITH UNSTOPPABLE MOMENTUM TO MY DREAM LIFE, AND I CELEBRATE MY PROGRESS DAILY.

Repeat this affirmation often. With repetition, it has the power to alter your consciousness so you build a better, happier and more purposeful life.

DAY 62 - BECOMING AWARE OF COMPOUNDING EFFORT

"When the going gets tough, put one foot in front of the other and just keep going. Don't give up." ~ Roy T. Bennett

When you are consistent with your efforts, you will see that things become easier with time. This is called compounding. To explain the effect of compounding interest better, here is a small example:

A man was offered a thirty-day job, and he got to choose his salary.

- **Either**, every day he would be paid $100 more than the day before. For example, he would get $100 for the first day, $200 for the second day, $300 for the third day, etc.,

- **Or**, his salary would start with 1 cent, and every day he would be paid double what he was paid the day before. He would start with 1 cent on the first day, 2 cents on the second day, 4 cents on the third day, etc.

Most people would choose the first option, and they would be right if the time period would be for only three weeks, but if you look at the numbers after 23 days, you will see that for the second example, the numbers start to explode. That's the power of compounding interest. Although only in the third week would he start to see any money, the fourth week would be the game changer, because with compounding interest, time makes all the difference.

Almost the same is valid with goals. When you work towards a goal, the compounding effect of the effort you put in will make reaching your goal easier with time.

When you push a car that has no more petrol to the nearest gas station located a few miles away, in the beginning, it is tough to move the vehicle. It barely moves and takes a lot of physical effort. But slowly, as you consistently push, momentum kicks in, making the pushing much easier.

When you are doing whatever needs to be and can be done daily to move towards your dreams, even on days when you do not feel like doing anything, and there will be many such days, you will benefit from the process of compounding effort.

There will be days when you will prefer to rest and not do what needs to be done. But due to the process of compounding effort, when you continue to do some work and remain consistent, momentum kicks in, compounding your results.

Our habits are the consistent actions that move us towards or away from our goals. It is never one single dramatic action, just as it is never one single push that gets the car to the petrol station. It is a consistent effort over time, and you can do this only by forming the proper habits that will lead you towards your dreams. It is the mundane habits that will help you reach the life of your dreams. Deep down inside, we know this to be accurate; therefore, people who have had some form of immediate success or fame have a hard time with it and tend to sabotage their success.

Some people have success come more easily, but nothing ever comes without consistent effort, or it will be lost just as fast as they gained it.

It is all about your daily habits. Do you procrastinate during the workday? Do you watch too much Netflix? Do you spend too much time with negative people? Do you eat unhealthy foods? Do you spend too much sedentary time? Do you read the wrong things? These small daily choices will either move you towards or away from your goals. It is all in the little things. When you make the right decisions in the little things, compounding interest in your effort is formed, and momentum is gained, making it much easier for you to do the right things also for the bigger things.

Basically, in this way, you put time on your side. You are using your time effectively to move forward towards your dreams.

Back to the car example, when you first moved the car towards the petrol station, it was hard and stiff, and it was tough and uncomfortable to move it. If you didn't need the petrol so much, you would have probably never done the hard and uncomfortable work necessary to move the car there. This is why only five people in one hundred will ever succeed in reaching their long-term goals and dreams. It is not easy to be consistent, especially in the beginning when you see no return on your investment of time, effort, energy, and money. Most people prefer to live easy, and while they do not reach their goals, they fancy an easy life, which is fine if they are okay with the outcome.

To reach your dreams, you must do the work while maintaining the belief that you will succeed even when nothing is currently in sight. I It is like a plant growing underground before we can see it above ground.

Keep moving forward towards your dreams by taking small planned actions daily even when you cannot see any results. When you work towards something and take the correct daily steps, then, eventually, you will see great results.

You have to believe that what you are doing is right, and you have to keep at it even when you do not see any advancement for a while. It would be best if you continued to put in the effort, which takes an actual act of courage.

For my real estate business to form valid results and bring me passive income, it took six years. For the Guerrilla Diet™ to reach over 1 million people, it took three years. It will usually take two to six years to see significant results for your efforts on big goals, but this doesn't matter if you enjoy the process.

You can learn to enjoy the process, even the most difficult parts of the process, by understanding that your efforts will lead you to where you desire to be. It is your attitude that counts. Your attitude is your choice. If you know that you are headed towards a better life for yourself, you may also enjoy the process if you check a particular activity off your list. As we all know, the process of reaching your goals is what takes up most of your life. This is what living in the moment is all about. You enjoy the moment but still seek progress towards a vision you have created for yourself. How exciting!

Your choices in every moment count through their compounding effect.

Your habits are your choices, and those small choices that you make daily, compounded over time, will have a significant effect on your life. Jim Rohn said that if you were to eat an apple every day and another person would eat a Snickers bar every day, and all else was the same, your outcome would be very different a few years later.

Consistently put yourself in conditions that will help encourage better habits. Make situations and engagements as incompatible with your old ways as possible and keep yourself busy on your new path. Make your new habits known to others as this will form a public commitment to your new way, and it will help other people ensure you remain on track.

I tell my weight loss clients to view change as a marathon, not a sprint. Just make sure that when you are running, or taking action, you are headed in the right direction, choice after choice, step after step. Make it easy to go running or to take the right actions, and make it difficult to do the wrong things. Set yourself up for success, not failure.

Just as with the car on the way to the petrol station, you want to make sure you are pushing the car in the right direction. The right choices, compounded over time, will bring you the life of your dreams.

Questions Of The Day

To end this lesson and help you reap the benefits of compounded effort, ask yourself:

Which habits do I have now that are not taking me in the direction that I desire to be, and what can I do today to change them and form better habits for me?

Research shows that to form a new habit, it takes sixty-six days of persistent repetition of the new habit. After that, it becomes embedded into your life. So think about it. Only sixty-six days of repetitive challenge, and after that, you have formed the proper habits that will steer you to your success.

As usual, I recommend writing your answers in the PDF journal.

Affirmation Of The Day

After answering the questions in your journal, and contemplating your answers, sit quietly and repeat this affirmation:

I TAKE ACTION EVERY DAY AND DO WHATEVER IT TAKES TO REACH MY HIGHEST POTENTIAL AND MY DREAMS.

Repeat this affirmation often. With repetition, it has the power to alter your consciousness so you build a better, happier and more purposeful life.

DAY 63 - BECOMING AWARE OF THE POWER OF PERSISTENCE

"The big talent is persistence." ~ Octavia E. Butler

Persistence is true dedication. No talent is strong enough to lead to a favorable outcome to your life without persistent effort.

By sheerly examining a person's level of commitment and persistence towards a goal, you can determine who will reach their goal and who will not, just as the turtle won the race against the much faster rabbit due to its persistent effort towards a focused destination.

Persistence is one of the most essential qualities that differentiates a person with a favorable life from a person with an unfavorable life.

Most people do not persist.

People get sidetracked and forget where they were headed. They forget their ideas, or they prefer the easy and comfortable way, without the emotional challenges. When the going gets tough, most people bail out.

But the people who do reach favorable outcomes in life persist even though they are, just as anyone else, confronted with failures, challenges, difficulties, and setbacks.

Everyone meets hardships when they leave their comfort zone, and so will you, but you can't reach different results than you currently have if you remain in your comfort zone. All favorable outcomes require persistence.

Hardships are inevitable, and the bigger your goals, as stated before, the more complex the challenges along the way tend to be.

You have to be different to succeed. Les brown said it perfectly: "To be successful, you must be willing to do the things today others won't do in order to have the things tomorrow others won't have." Only 2 percent of Americans have reached the stage of financial freedom for life. From this you can conclude that many people are not willing to do what successful people are willing to do. So what are people not willing to do?

Many people are not willing to suffer now for long-term results.

Many people want to get their pleasure or paycheck now even though they will eventually have to pay the price and often suffer later on.

Many people are not willing to do the work if they don't see immediate results.

Many people are afraid of doing things differently than everyone else.

Many people fear being different.

Many people prefer stability rather than taking risks.

Many people prefer comfortable and secure to scary, adventurous, and demanding.

This is why only 2 percent are financially free.

And if you look at marriage, you will see that only 11 percent of happily married couples see themselves as being in the best relationship for them. When looking at the entire population, that number is under 4 percent.

When looking at health statistics, the death rate from non-communicable diseases such as stroke, heart disease, cancers, diabetes, chronic kidney disease, osteoarthritis, osteoporosis, and Alzheimer's disease, is 71 percent (according to the WHO - World Health Organization).

That means that over 7 of 10 people will die from a disease that most often can be healed naturally or prevented since non-communicable diseases are considered preventable as they are caused by modifiable risk factors.

People who are healthy, wealthy, and in good long-lasting relationships are doing things differently than people who are not. They have different habits that allow them to be healthy, wealthy and in good relationships. So if your goals are in one of these fields of life, you must form habits that allow you to be persistent, to focus deeply, to put in the effort even when it is uncomfortable, to take necessary risks, and to do it over a long period. Then success will be yours to reap.

When people are willing to do things differently and follow their instincts and do what they know is right to do, they will reach exceptional results in all fields of life.

You cannot stay the same person and fulfill big dreams. You must change. And the path to change is the path of persisting towards a specific goal, no matter what the odds are, no matter what the feat, and no matter the amount of time and effort it will take to get there so long as you understand the price of your dreams and are willing to pay them, and even better, enjoy them.

It is good to know that you do not need to persist and be stubborn about a specific plan. You only need to be persistent about achieving your soul's desire and what your soul's desire will bring for you and other people. Your persistence is about the big picture, not the way to reach it.

Therefore, the big picture must be one that you are very passionate about and find as a worthy cause with a price that you are willing to pay because you will suffer at times on the way.

When you perform something that you are not passionate about, even though you find it worthy of your time and effort, you will stop.

To persist on your big picture goal, you must be passionate about the subject and enjoy the process as well.

Taking risks is not easy, and the results are never known beforehand; taking calculated risks involves doing sufficient research beforehand and determining that the chance of success is higher than the chances of failing. Calculated risk has much forethought and is unlikely to lead to failure, although it still could.

Because you are trying to reach a goal that you have never reached before, there will be a learning curve before getting things right. You will have setbacks and disappointments, but if you learn the lessons and improve yourself and your plan, and you persist on the path towards your success, with time and consistent effort, you will, without doubt, reach them.

Quitting is losing. Persevering is succeeding.

Even if your goal has to do with relationships, you will succeed if you believe in the possibility and persist with the same partner. If you stay in the game, you will find a way to get things right. It may need some creativity, but you will find the way if you desire.

It may get shameful at times (think of Steve Jobs getting fired from Apple, the company he founded, only later to come back and help it become one of the most successful, innovative companies).

It may get painful at times (think of Nelson Mandela, who was confined to different prison cells for twenty-seven years where he experienced much physical and mental torture only to come out and help end apartheid peacefully and become elected by parliament as the first president of a democratic South Africa.

And it also will be hard (think of Mahatma Gandhi embarking on a fast to protest in a nonviolent way against the British government, which, in the end, led to India's independence from British rule).

And it will be long (think of Henry Ford, Thomas Edison, and Walt Disney, and their failures, trials, bankruptcies, and hardships before they became what they became and did what they did).

Think of what you could achieve if you persisted with your goals with consistent effort, not giving up on your dreams and aspirations.

It took me many years to complete my university degrees. But I did complete them. It took years before my real estate company made me sufficient funds to retire.

It took many years before my research into the ideal diet for humans, which I called The Guerrilla Diet™, became a household name.

As the saying goes, the best way to predict the future is to create it.

We are constantly creating our future, sometimes unconsciously. It is pretty much predictable to those watching from the side when they see your level of persistence and determination. When you have goals, it is your level of persistence and dedication that will determine where you will be in five or ten years from now with regard to these goals.

The control is really in your own hands. There will be setbacks that you cannot foresee, but if you persist beyond them, the rewards are yours for the taking.

Persistence with better habits will help you embed them in your mind for your long-term benefit.

The ability to persist is very powerful indeed, and we all can endure. The question lies in whether we choose to use this ability in our favor or not.

As a side note, it is essential to note that persistence is a choice. Only persist when it is right to do so, where it belongs. Persistence should not be used as a default behavior for all situations. Persistence, when you are not in the right place, will only delay your happiness and fulfillment.

Questions Of The Day

To end this lesson and to help you take on the habit of persistence for a worthy goal, ask yourself:

In which areas of life do I seem to prefer comfort over success? Which habits will I need to form to succeed with my big goals? What can I persistently do every day to make sure that I move forward towards my goals, even in small increments?

As usual, I recommend writing your answers in the PDF journal.

Affirmation Of The Day

After answering the questions in your journal, and examining them, sit quietly for a few minutes today and repeat this affirmation to yourself as you think and dwell upon it:

I WILL PERSIST UNTIL I REACH THE GOALS THAT I KNOW ARE WORTHY OF MY TIME AND ENERGY.

Repeat this affirmation often. With repetition, it has the power to alter your consciousness so you build a better, happier and more purposeful life.

DAY 64 - BECOMING AWARE OF THE NEED TO DELAY GRATIFICATION

"Don't give up what you want most for what you want now." ~ Richard G. Scott

Delaying gratification means that you are resisting a smaller but more immediate reward for a larger or better and longer-lasting reward later.

Now that you have a plan in place for your future and you have some momentum going by taking the right actions, it is time to understand there is a price to pay for what you desire.

With long-term goals, the full price does not need to be paid upfront. You can pay it in installations, but you must pay it before you reach your goals.

Whatever you desire to have in your life comes with a price tag. For everything good that you want, there is something that you will have to give up or leave behind to get it. If your goals are in the health field, you will have to give up or change your choices to reach your ideal health.

If your goals are in the relationship field, you will have to either give up on the specific partner if you cannot have your needs met or give more time and effort to the relationship. You may have to give up some space by considering another person's feelings before you go ahead and do something. You may also need to give up the need to always be in control or even to allow yourself to be rejected. These are some of the price tags that you may need to pay to reach your relationship goals.

If your goals are in the work field, you may have to give up some family time and delay certain expenses so that you can start to fuel your business, especially in the beginning. It is like Earl Nightingale said in "Strangest Secret", "You first have to put the wood into the fireplace before you get the heat."

Payment needs to be paid daily or on a steady and regular basis.

The one thing you have to decide upon is whether the price you need to pay to get to where you desire to be in life is worth it for you.

Sometimes, what you are not willing to pay for your dreams, may come back to you with a different price tag. For example, the hefty price that we may pay if we are not willing to pay the cost of discipline, hard work, discomfort, overcoming fears, and giving up on a few things, may include regret, poor health, pain (both emotional and physical), and failure.

I can tell you from my personal experience that the pain of regret is much greater than the pain of delayed gratification.

If you choose not to take care of your health today, you may live with medications or pain in the future that may take away your livelihood, your sex life, and your happiness.

If you choose not to do what it takes to form the relationship of your dreams today, then in the future, you may find yourself living alone without the support and compassion of someone close.

If you choose not to do what it takes to form the wealth of your dreams today, you will have to live with hardship or be dependent on the goodwill of others in the future. You will not be living the life you truly deserve and desire, full of enjoyment and opportunities.

And the list goes on.

M. Scott Peck said, "Delaying gratification is a process of scheduling the pain and pleasure of life in such a way that you are meeting and experiencing the pain first and getting it over with. It is the only decent way to live."

Now, of course, you may find that you are not willing to pay the price for a particular goal because when you put it on the scales, you see that the price is too high for you and not worthwhile. For example, to become extremely wealthy, you do need to sacrifice many things in your life. Your values and ideals may not allow you to do this. This is when you should go back to ensure that your goals are aligned with your core values, or else the price to pay for achieving them will always be too high for you to pay.

Question Of The Day

To help you ensure that the price paid for your goals is worthwhile for you, please ask yourself:

What price do I need to pay to get to my dream? Please go over this question for each goal on your list. Am I genuinely willing and committed to paying these prices? If your answer is YES, then start to pay the fee every single day. You cannot have debt. You must pay the price daily.

If you found that you are not willing to pay the price, check your core values list that you wrote on day 58 and see where your goal is misaligned with your core values. At this stage, you may notice that you have other core values that went unnoticed before.

As usual, I recommend writing your answers in the PDF journal.

Affirmation Of The Day

After answering the questions in your journal, and contemplating your answers, sit quietly for a few minutes and repeat this affirmation:

I HAVE POWER OVER MYSELF AND WILL REACH MY DREAMS THANKS TO MY ABILITY TO DELAY GRATIFICATION AND DO WHATEVER IS NEEDED FROM ME TODAY.

Repeat this affirmation often. With repetition, it has the power to alter your consciousness so you build a better, happier and more purposeful life.

DAY 65 - BECOMING AWARE OF THE FEEDBACK YOU ARE RECEIVING

"There is no failure. Only feedback." ~ Robert Allen

We can never know if we are doing things right without getting feedback from others. You need honest feedback to advance in the right direction of your dreams.

You will make mistakes along the way, but as the quote says, "There is no failure. There is only feedback." Making mistakes is not failure, it is feedback about your path, choices, mindset, beliefs, and actions towards your goals.

You cannot know how things will work out in advance since you have never been where you are trying to reach. You must do something you have not done before and take calculated risks and see where they lead you. You must examine if they are the proper steps for you to take at that moment in your current situation, and the best way to this is to seek out feedback.

As Bill Gates said, "We all need people who will give us feedback. That's how we improve."

This is so simple yet so profound.

Feedback can come from any person. It is crucial to consider the feedback you get rather than its source. Anybody can give you valuable insight. You just need to be open and humble enough to understand the feedback and incorporate it into your life if it is valuable and useful.

Feedback is not always comfortable to receive, but it is vital for you to have a major impact or wish to improve yourself. Feedback may even be painful. But just as pain in the body points our attention to what needs to be healed, the same goes for feedback; it guides our attention to what needs to be healed, changed, or improved.

Feedback is always given to us, but we are not always aware that we are receiving it.

The way people behave around us is a measure of feedback regarding our behavior. Suppose we notice consistency in people's responses around us regarding an aspect of our behavior that may be negative somehow. In that case, this is the feedback that we need to change our communication method regarding that subject or situation.

Feedback is also given to us through results.

A lack of money, poor grades when studying, regular complaints, criticism, and suffering of all sorts is feedback through results.

Feedback through results also shows us where our actions are or are not reaping the rewards we desire, so we should be open to change in that area of life. Our current situation in every field of life is feedback regarding our thoughts and actions in that field of life.

All mistakes are growth opportunities. If we made a mistake, this in itself is feedback that is there to help us grow and evolve as human beings and put us on a better path for our progress.

The bigger the goals you are after, the more likely you will be criticized. Do not see this as judgment towards you personally, but as something you may need to correct.

Not all the steps you take will be proper, but so long as you are taking the actions that you believe are the best next steps in the direction of your dreams, and you are open to getting feedback about whether these are indeed the best steps for you to take, then you will improve yourself favorably.

You will understand which steps or behaviors should be continued and which actions or behaviors are not in your best interest and should be changed. Even minor changes will help you improve.

The important thing is never to give in or give up. Make the changes, even if they are uncomfortable.

Do not ignore the feedback.

Listen and see what you can take from the feedback and what you can do to improve yourself. If the feedback is negative, don't be angry with the person. You should thank them!

In most nations around the world today, people can demonstrate against their governments if they believe they have been wronged.

But can you imagine how the world would be like if the leaders of nations would thank their people for this feedback and seek ways to improve their choices and decisions?

How do you think people would view these leaders?

Yes, these are different times, and the leaders of today are bound to make many mistakes. But, in democratic countries if they are open to accepting the feedback from their people and listening, they will be loved, cherished, and re-elected, which is most often their wish.

This is how feedback is win-win for everyone. The person giving the feedback thinks things should and can be done differently, and the person doing, can improve to become better in ways that they perhaps never thought of. In the end, everyone is happier with the results.

Do not take feedback personally. It is not about you, so it should not threaten you.

Feedback is about your choice of actions, behaviors, or thoughts. It is never about your core, but only about your choices, so there is no need or advantage in taking the feedback personally. Focus on your goals and your desire to reach them. Seek and welcome feedback, all types of input.

There are three types of feedback

1. Positive, appreciative feedback

2. Coaching feedback explaining a different way to do things

3. Evaluative feedback regarding where you currently are compared to where you desire to be.

All types of feedback are equally important.

Positive feedback shows you where you should continue doing the things that you are currently doing. Coaching, evaluative and negative feedback in general, shows you where you can change and improve.

Don't just wait for feedback to come along. Then you are wasting valuable time.

When you are going after your dreams, you want time to work for you, not against you. Therefore, you want to explicitly ask for feedback from people whose opinions you respect. Ensure that you are trying to improve yourself and that their views won't hurt you, but that you will learn to become better at whatever you are asking the feedback about.

Once you get truthful feedback from one person, this does not mean you must make the change immediately or stay where you are. This is only one person's opinion. It means that it is time to seek other people's views and see patterns emerging regarding their feedback.

Then, by examining the patterns that show up in the various feedback you receive, you can ensure that you make the right moves or make the right changes where needed for you and everyone around you.

Remember, to reach your highest calling you must be open to change, growth, and progress. You do not need to achieve perfection, but you must continue to improve yourself and your actions to become your highest self and produce what you consider to be a favorable outcome to your life.

Question Of The Day

To end this lesson and help you ask for feedback, ask yourself:

In which field/s of life do I need some feedback to improve myself, but I am too afraid to ask?

Now go ahead and ask for this feedback about how you can improve, where they think you may be limiting yourself, and what needs to be done to get to where you desire to be.

As usual, I recommend writing your answers in the PDF journal that you have received with this book. Then look over your answers to ensure that you improve your life and bring forth your true divine nature.

Affirmation Of The Day

After answering the questions in your journal, and examining them, sit quietly for a few minutes and repeat this affirmation:

I TAKE ACTION ON THE FEEDBACK I RECEIVE AND AM IMPROVING MY LIFE DAILY!

Repeat this affirmation often. With repetition, it has the power to alter your consciousness so you build a better, happier and more purposeful life.

DAY 66 - BECOMING AWARE OF OUT-OF-THE-BOX THINKING

"The difficult is what takes a little time; the impossible is what takes a little longer."

~ Fritjof Nansen

The impossible takes a little longer because it requires some out-of-the-box thinking. This means using your creativity and intuition to find different solutions to problems or create new ideas. Out-of-the-box thinking is different thinking, altering how you interpret information.

It is using the brain differently to come up with different conclusions than the norm. It allows you to approach the problem or situation in a new innovative way.

We usually function with default thought patterns that show a distinct approach to how we face problems. We typically follow our natural line of thinking and produce the same or similar results. When we want to innovate our lives or work to have different results, we need to think differently.

Thinking out-of-the-box comes naturally to some people, but it needs a little development and practice for others. All people using out-of-the-box thinking must make an effort to push their thinking beyond its limits.

When we think inside the box, we assume certain things about a given situation and follow these assumptions to form our behavior around them. But what if you put those assumptions aside and make different assumptions that could just as well be true?

What if you steered your thinking to new avenues that could also provide viable solutions that you never thought possible?

Thinking differently means being open-minded and pushing your thoughts to non-conventional solutions for any given situation.

When you reject the accepted paradigm and come up with new ideas through creative thinking, you may seem odd to other people at first, but you will be true to yourself and your soul. And when you are true to your soul, you will be happiest and most fulfilled, and so will the people around you.

Your ideas may seem wild to some people; think of Elon Musk and his SpaceX mission of colonizing Mars. Still, if your thoughts seem to be the right path for you, and you have the passion and energy to follow through with your ideas, you will probably reach great heights since most people are unwilling to even try to think outside the box.

Examining things from a new perspective, through "different eyes" and unconventional, creative thinking, is a more complex way of thinking. It will take more effort from you.

George Bernard Shaw said, "The reasonable man adapts himself to the world; the unreasonable man persists in trying to adapt the world to himself. Therefore all progress depends on the unreasonable man."

The unreasonable man is the one who thinks outside the box and strives to create a better world as he sees it in his imagination.

If you want to think outside the box and create opportunities for yourself, you must also get comfortable with feeling foolish at times. Not everyone will "get" you, but this doesn't matter if you are making progress in the right direction for your soul. Allowing yourself to feel foolish also helps unlock your fears which is the main obstacle for creative thinking.

In the poem by Robert Frost, "*The Road Not Taken*," he writes, "*I took the road less traveled by, and that has made all the difference.*"

So how can you encourage yourself to think outside of the box?

The best way to do this is to contemplate your situation in a very focused manner when you are in solitude without disturbances. One place could be when you are in the shower, or during a walk in nature, or when you know you will not be disturbed at home. Meditate on your situation. When you are alone, you can contemplate in a very focused manner on one situation. Your creativity can take leaps to help you find different solutions or ideas, providing you an advantage over normative thinking patterns.

In this way, you can foster your creativity to tackle enormous problems.

Also, try examining the situation from a different perspective. Think of how a child views this situation. How would a person from a diverse cultural background or another part of the world view this situation? What viable solutions could they come up with?

Ask yourself, what if I saw this problem from a more optimistic viewpoint, and what if I saw this problem from a more pessimistic viewpoint?

You may also ask yourself, what is the truth behind this and not just an opinion? What can I take from that?

Also, try to think from the end vision in mind back to where you are now. How could this backward vision produce the best next step for you to take to move you towards your dream?

You could also change your thinking perspective about a problem by removing yourself from the equation. Ask yourself, what if the problem had nothing to do with me, or what if the situation did not affect me? What would I do then? These questions help you bring in a different perspective and move you closer to reality.

The key is to shift your thinking from solely the logical left brain to the more creative right brain and then to form a bridge between them. Logic must be present for an idea to be accepted by the mind, but creativity must also be present to allow innovation. Both must be present for out-of-the-box thinking.

Brainstorming with other people is another way to form out-of-the-box ideas. The mind is forced to produce or accept new ideas when there are also rules to follow or a specific outcome needed.

You may also read biographies of people who have thought outside the box. Their life stories will show you how thinking patterns can change by pure will.

Learning a new skill can also help change the way you think.

When I went to study mediation after my whole career revolved around health, this opened me up to new things that I never thought about previously.

It is great to be an expert in your field, but sometimes learning something different in a different domain than your specialty can be helpful even to advance you in your area of expertise.

New insights lead to mental flexibility. Other fields may have faced similar challenges that you are encountering in your area of expertise and may have developed compelling solutions for dealing with them that could be used in your field as well with slight changes.

We are hardwired to do things automatically and unconsciously when they are repetitive. We do not have to rethink them every time we do them, so we don't have to waste energy on the small details repeatedly. This makes our thinking efficient but does not make it innovative.

Overcoming our fear of looking foolish or different will encourage more spontaneous thoughts. When we free ourselves from the constraints of rejection and fear of seeming silly, then we can open our minds to new ways of solving issues and advancing our lives.

No one needs to be exceptionally smart to develop innovative ideas. Anyone can do it if they allow creative effort in, and at the same time push their mind to become more open.

It does take effort to think out-of-the-box, but it is worth it. With practice, you will use this line of thinking more often, and your ideas and actions will take you on a more innovative path in life, enriching your life and the lives of those around you, and connecting you with your soul essence. Conformity will be a thing of the past.

Questions Of The Day

So, to end this lesson and help you think out of the box, ask yourself:

How can I view my situation from a new and more creative perspective? What if I was an outside observer of my problem instead of being an active participant? What could I do differently? What if I were the other gender? How would I think about this? What if I were from a different cultural background? How would I feel about this? What if I were more positive or more negative? How would I think of my problem? Think where you can get inspiration from. Some people get inspiration from quotes, some people get inspiration from art, others from brainstorming in a mastermind, and others get inspiration while in solitude, letting the mind wander.

Think about what works best for you and follow through to develop out-of-the-box thinking.

As usual, I recommend writing your answers in the PDF journal.

Affirmation Of The Day

After answering the questions in your journal, and examining them, sit quietly and repeat this affirmation:

I LOOK AT ALL SIDES OF THINGS, I DAYDREAM AND ALLOW MY THOUGHTS TO WANDER TO NEW CREATIVE HEIGHTS.

Repeat this affirmation often. With repetition, it has the power to alter your consciousness so you build a better, happier and more purposeful life.

DAY 67 - BECOMING AWARE OF YOUR EFFORTS

"The only place success comes before work is in the dictionary." ~ Vince Lombardi

———————⚬⚭⚬———————

It's not easy to accept, but you can't achieve your dreams without putting in time and effort, or in other words, hard work.

Once you have your goals written down and you are happy with your list of goals that you have created for the future, now is the time to put in the effort to get to the life of your dreams. You will not reach your goals if you do not put in the work. And this is true for every field of life.

Everything worthwhile takes effort. Relationships won't fulfill your needs if you do not put in the time and energy to create intimacy and keep this intimacy going for a lifetime; this certainly takes effort.

Your job will not make you a decent living or make you "rich" if you don't take your work seriously and put in the effort. The same goes for health. If you do not care for your diet, exercise, and rest sufficiently, you will not have the health you desire.

Your children will not give you peace if you do not provide them with their physical and emotional needs.

Everything worth having takes effort.

Ask yourself what kind of results you will get if you do not put effort into every field of life? Where will you be in five years if you don't put any effort into improving where you are today?

I think you will not be happy with what comes up in your mind.

To achieve any goal in any field, an effort is crucial, and no one will put it in for you. You have to put in the effort because you will be the one who enjoys the results in the end.

It is so important to understand that when you put in the effort consistently towards any one of your goals, then what you are doing is slowly becoming a different person.

You become an improved version of yourself.

You become more disciplined; you believe more in the process and yourself, which increases your self-esteem. You become more humble and happier with yourself. You also become more courageous. These are qualities that not all people share in equal amounts because not all people are willing to put in the effort. The more you have of these qualities, the more successful you will be.

The more courage you have, the more calculated risks you are willing to take, which will often increase your net worth. Also, your outlook on failure will change, and your perspective on learning new skills will change. Success requires a change within you. You evolve into someone better. The *You* that set the goals cannot be the same person as the *You* who achieves them. Some metamorphosis is necessary.

You cannot have anything different than what you have today unless *you* change.

A change from within is necessary to have an outer change in your life. Effort can take many different forms. Creating new habits to form a better life for yourself is arduous, as most of us know. The work and effort you put in need not be physical, but it does need to be consistent.

The most important thing that I have learned about hard work is that it is never something you will regret. It is never effort wasted. Even if you did not achieve that thing you set out to achieve, the effort you put in, even if it was a failure, has changed you for the better.

You learned new skills; you became better at something as a result, and the better you become as a person, the more you have to give away. You are more valuable to the marketplace and the world. And the more valuable you become for the market, the more money you can earn if you use your skills properly.

The only real magic that makes dreams come true is persistent effort towards a worthwhile cause.

Thomas Jefferson, the former President of the United States, said, "I'm a great believer in luck, and I find the harder I work, the more I have of it."

Of course, the effort we put into our goals must be the right effort and the best effort to move us forward. You will know which action you need to take when you are crystal clear on your goals. Ask yourself, what is the prize I desire and what price is necessary to get me there?

When you know precisely what you want to achieve, you will understand the first logical step you need to take to set you in the right direction. The rest of the path will unveil itself as time goes by and as you slowly change in the process and move forward.

You change due to new skills, new lessons learned, and new behavior patterns necessary to move you forward to where you desire to be.

Questions Of The Day

To end this lesson and help you determine the effort you need to put into your goals and to do these actions persistently, please ask yourself:

What things am I spending too much time on that is actually moving me further away from my dreams? And which actions do I need to take today, this week, this month, and this year to get the ball rolling towards the manifestation of my dreams?

As usual, I recommend writing your answers in the PDF journal.

Affirmation Of The Day

After answering the questions in your journal, and contemplating on your answers, sit quietly and repeat this affirmation:

I AM CRYSTAL CLEAR ON MY GOALS AND TAKE THE RIGHT ACTIONS DAILY TO MOVE ME TOWARDS THE LIFE OF MY DREAMS.

Repeat this affirmation often. With repetition, it has the power to alter your consciousness so you build a better, happier and more purposeful life.

DAY 68 - BECOMING AWARE OF YOUR EXCUSES

"Ninety-nine percent of all failures come from people who have the habit of making excuses." ~ George Washington Carver

Making excuses for anything in your life means that you are not taking full responsibility for your situation. When you take full responsibility for the conditions in your life, you are on the path to creating a favorable outcome in life. When you do not take responsibility for the situations in your life, you are ensuring failure. Why? Because when you blame others or the government, or the weather or anything else for your life situation, you are giving away your power and will not be able to transform your life and reach your dreams. You will continue to suffer in some form.

Even if you were born into a broken family with parents who were addicts and you received nothing of what another child receives typically, this is only your starting point. It never has to be your endpoint. When you take responsibility for what you can change, which is you, your thoughts, your behaviors, and your actions in any given situation and stop blaming and complaining, but rather take focused action to change your place in life, then you are headed for greatness.

You are 100 percent responsible for how happy and fulfilled you are. There are no excuses. It's all up to you. What I am saying may not be easy to accept, especially for someone in a challenging situation, but taking personal responsibility is the most important step towards maturity and success.

Once you take responsibility for your situation, you understand that where you are and how you feel is in your own hands, and where you want to be and how you want to think is also in your own hands.

Other people can do things that annoy you, but if you get annoyed or distracted, it is up to you. Your reactions are within your own responsibility, always. And as your responses, so is the world around you.

When we take full responsibility for our life and the direction it is going, our self-esteem will automatically rise because we are taking back our creative powers, our true essence.

We create our experience of life through our thoughts and choices. You are always responsible for your responses to any given situation, and you are always accountable for handling every problem you encounter in life.

You can take things to your advantage by improving yourself and becoming a stronger, more refined version of yourself as a result, or you can feel offended or feel that things aren't fair and remove all the power that you have within you. Taking full responsibility means owning your power. You have this power always. Why would you want to give this power away to someone else?

When you learn this vital truth and take responsibility for your situation in life, everything will change for you. You unlock your potential. You have the power to improve any situation. You can change your thoughts, communication skills, behaviors, feelings, and actions.

My future second husband had a tough time coping with the difficulties of my two elder daughters. One daughter wouldn't sleep well at night and woke up at 3 a.m. almost every day. The house was hectic, practically twenty-four hours a day. Although my future husband loved my daughters, he also liked his peace and quiet. So I thought outside the box and decided to physically separate my home into two living quarters with a connecting door between them. That way, my soon-to-be husband would have his peace, and I would still have my daughters with me under one roof. It was perfect. This also allowed my elder daughters' father to come over to their part of the house to be with them whenever he wanted without causing any disturbance.

This was a perfect solution that could have only come about when I took full responsibility for my situation and searched for a good, win-win solution instead of weeping over my misfortune.

A willingness to be accountable for every part of your life is the foundation for happiness in life. Then you have reached maturity.

As babies, we are totally dependent on our parents. As teenagers, we find our independence and think only of ourselves and our own needs and desires. When we reach maturity, we can finally be depended upon by those close to us. Unfortunately, not all people mature fully by eighteen. In fact, some people have not reached this level of maturity even at the age of sixty. You don't want to live your life like this because you cannot be satisfied in this way.

When you do not take responsibility for your situation in an area of life, you cannot depend upon yourself in this area of life. When you take responsibility for your situation in any area of life, you lead yourself, and then you can also teach others in that field.

When you accept responsibility for your thoughts, feelings, and actions in any situation, then you are in a position to transform your life into something extraordinary by making better choices for your future.

When I learned to take responsibility for everything in my life, I never wanted to give this power to anyone ever again. This was the foundation for my success.

When I divorced my second husband, we decided on joint custody but, due to his work, he requested that the children live with me, and only once a fortnight would they come to sleep at his home. Although he speaks to them daily and in this way he is involved in their lives, almost 100 percent of the responsibility of the children's care is on me. I love being in this situation because it allows me to take full responsibility for my daughters. I know that whatever happens to them is on me, good or bad. I am happy because I have more control over what they are exposed to and how they live their lives. Although it is not easy to raise them practically alone, I am truly happy about this. When you take responsibility, you have more control. And when you feel more control, this immediately increases your level of happiness.

You are definitely in control of many things in your life, not all things, but enough things to determine the outcome of your life.

Take responsibility for things in your life that you *can* control, and take responsibility for your perspective on the things in life that you can't control.

Every situation you experience in your life is a result of your previous choices. If you don't like where you currently stand in life, do not blame other people or the situation, instead take responsibility for your situation and change your thoughts, beliefs, behaviors, and actions so that they will lead you to where you do desire to be rather than where you do not desire to be.

Listen to your inner dialogue, become aware of what is happening inside your head and what you are saying to yourself.

If you complain or blame others, it is often that you are not willing to do what it takes to make the necessary changes. You are not taking responsibility for your situation when you complain.

Take responsibility and change this inner dialogue if it is not getting you to where you want to be.

Nobody can hurt your feelings if you don't allow them to. And when you take full responsibility for your feelings and thoughts, only then can you regain your power to make the necessary changes in your life that will move you towards the life of your dreams.

Questions Of The Day

To end this lesson and help you take full responsibility for your thoughts, beliefs, behaviors, and actions, please ask yourself:

Which difficult situation/s am I now forming or allowing to happen through my chosen thoughts, beliefs, and actions, and which behaviors can I immediately change to prevent disaster from happening?

As usual, I recommend writing your answers in the PDF journal.

Affirmation Of The Day

After answering the questions in your journal, and contemplating your answers, sit quietly for a few minutes and repeat this affirmation:

I TAKE RESPONSIBILITY FOR EVERYTHING IN MY LIFE, AND I TAKE FULL RESPONSIBILITY FOR ACHIEVING MY DREAMS.

Repeat this affirmation often. With repetition, it has the power to alter your consciousness so you build a better, happier and more purposeful life.

DAY 69 - BECOMING AWARE OF DEDICATION

"If you do not change direction, you may end up where you were heading." ~ Lao Tzu

———————————⊂∞∞∞⊃———————————

We may take this quote in a few directions to improve our lives.

The first direction is obvious: if we do not change direction for the better, there's no telling where we'll end up. Through the law of cause and effect, our previous actions became seeds that grew into the lives that we are currently living. If we sow the same seeds, nothing will change in our lives.

If we sow seeds of fear, hesitation, unhappiness, and pessimism, we will have a life where our worries and different forms of despair and pessimism will rule. If we do not change our direction and become more aware of our thoughts and choices, then our non-beneficial habits will lead us to where we would prefer not to be headed.

However, you can also take this quote in an opposite understanding, a more positive version: if you do not change direction all the time (and continue on the path you started), then you may end up where you wanted to be heading in the first place.

This way it becomes a quote about consistency and dedication.

Nowadays, most people in the world have so many options available to them. It's very common to skip from one new shiny thing to the next without trying our best to go in one direction until the end in a dedicated and focused manner and reap the rewards that come from sticking on the path. Before giving up with any direction, we must give a real chance to the current way, which is true of course for every field of life, including relationships, health, and building a fortune.

If you focus on one path and do not change direction from this path to another, perhaps easier path, and you dedicate yourself to something you believe is right for you, you will get the results that the path offers.

Dedication to a specific goal or path that you believe in from the depths of your heart will lead you to a favorable outcome.

It takes a bamboo tree five years to grow; the only problem is that the tree does not seem to be growing during the first four years. Only during the fifth year does it shoot up from the soil to reach its full height. Would you keep tending to a seed for five years before you saw any growth?

The test of dedication and commitment comes from the level of belief in something.

If you believed that the tree would grow from the seed, you would stay dedicated and committed to watering it even if you saw nothing in the meantime. You would know how the tree behaves and would persist. Therefore, knowledge is crucial for commitment. If you know and understand how things work in this world, then you can be dedicated and committed to something even when in the beginning you do not yet see any results.

We all know that nothing in nature grows in a way that is only visible to the naked eye. Everything takes time, and some growth happens underneath the surface. Farmers know this, and due to their knowledge, they keep tending to their seeds to reap the rewards in the future.

Dedication is directly connected to the level of belief you have in something. If you genuinely believe in something, then you will seize the opportunity and persist even if there are no visible results in the beginning. Underneath the surface, what you planted is growing. And if you persist, you will reach success.

Now you only need to decide whether the direction you are taking is right for you, or in other words if the seed you are planting is the best seed for you to commit yourself to and to focus upon for the life you desire.

Questions Of The Day

If you choose to take a particular direction in life, you should start by asking yourself these three questions to raise your awareness and determine whether this path will lead you to the results that you desire in life. If there is one "no" answer among any of these three questions below, then the direction is wrong for you. So let's begin the questions:

1. Has this direction or behavioral pattern helped others before you in reaching the results you desire?

2. Will this choice lead you closer to your overall goal and purpose in life?

3. Is your belief based on something true?

4. Are your answers coming from a growing awareness within you?

This will bring you to the core of the situation. If something is true, it will lead you to a particular result. But if something is not true, then it will lead to pain and suffering. Now, it is also good to ask yourself, "What if the opposite of what I think is true?" Ask yourself this question to make sure you can deal with the failure of not reaching your goal. By asking yourself if the opposite were true, you can choose what you would do if you really couldn't get the results you were hoping for. Would you still follow this path because it seems right for you or not?

This method is there to spare you some suffering through the gaining of awareness. When you ask yourself these questions, you become more aware of how you make your choices and decisions and what may be standing behind your choices.

Since today I have supplied you with four questions to ask yourself for every direction you choose, go through your current choices in life and checking the areas you are less happy with and determining if your current direction is right for you following the four questions.

I recommend writing your answers in the PDF journal that comes with this book.

Affirmation Of The Day

After answering the questions in your journal, and contemplating your answers, sit quietly and repeat this affirmation:

I AM MAKING GREAT CHOICES FOR MYSELF.

Repeat this affirmation often. With repetition, it has the power to alter your consciousness so you build a better, happier and more purposeful life.

DAY 70 - BECOMING AWARE OF THE PEOPLE AROUND YOU

"The ones who say you can't are too afraid you will." ~ Nike, Inc.

We are social beings, and we want to have people around us. Some people may say they want the best for us, but usually, they are also caring for their own needs. People around you may not favor change for you and would like to keep you in the same space that you currently occupy in their life. They may be afraid of change for themselves, and any change for you will also often mean a change for them. This is why the people you surround yourself with are crucial for your livelihood.

If you spend time, even weekly, with people who are not aligned with your life goals and do not see the future as you see it, their mindset will tend to become your mindset. You will find yourself complaining about your current situation just as they do about theirs instead of taking the lead and producing change.

I understand how hard it can be to change your social environment, and even impossible at times, but you have to watch the day-to-day influences for your peace of mind, happiness, and mental health.

Are your day-to-day influences pulling you down or pushing you up? Are the people in your life afraid of your success?

If this is the case, then change is a must.

Some people preach that you must sever bad relationships completely and immediately. I agree that you should not work on the relationship or give it another chance if the relationship is abusive in some way. But if the relationship is adding some value to your life, then this can mean that you have not yet outgrown it. In the meantime, there are other actions that you can take to ensure that you are still headed in the direction of your soul's desire and that you are happy.

Here are three action steps that you should take daily to support your path to a life of inner fulfillment for you.

1. Have some solitude time, or, even better, a daily walk in nature. This allows you to connect with your true self, your highest nature. Remember that you are like a small rock taken off the mountain. You are still part of the mountain even when you are separate. We are all part of infinite intelligence, and solitude time or taking a walk in nature will allow you to connect to this. The truth will appear before you. You will become more aware of yourself, and you will be stronger in mind because you have this solitude time to contemplate essential issues for yourself and get intuition from your inner being.

2. Listen to the words of people who had similar dreams. Listen to their lectures, talks, and videos. Read their books, blogs, and articles. Watch movies about them, read their biographies and how they overcame difficulties, and read their quotes. Do this daily. By doing this, you allow them to form part of your environment. They become your influencers. It would be best to choose these people wisely since they will affect your choices and the way you move through life when they start to fill the bulk of your time.

3. Watch your thoughts. Notice the bulk of your thoughts and their nature. Are these positive thoughts or self-limiting beliefs? Are they pulling you down, or are your thoughts uplifting and moving you forward? We are constantly having these conversations inside our heads. We

are often not even aware of this internal conversation, but it is happening, and these thoughts are influencing us and our behaviors.

There are still times when I catch my thoughts harming my life. Especially when I think of how I make other people feel, even when I state my needs. At these times, I may have this internal conversation going on in my mind: Perhaps I shouldn't have said this or that. Maybe I didn't think of their feelings, and so on. This internal dialogue is not helpful for me and brings me down. So, when I become aware of it, I stop it and let go of what I did and how it may have affected others. You will become stronger when you become more aware of your emotions, thoughts, and beliefs. Your thoughts, feelings, and beliefs are not who you are and can be changed with a moments' awareness. This is called mastering your mind instead of letting it push you to places you don't want to go.

Our conscious minds direct our subconscious. Our conscious minds are influenced by our surroundings and the people around us. It's vital to ensure we have optimistic people around us. Naysayers can have a significant influence on our choices. Only a few people have the capacity to use the naysayers in their lives to increase their motivation and prove them wrong. But for most people, naysayers have a negative, self-degrading influence.

Removing the influence of negative people around you by becoming aware of our true self and allowing your true divinity influence you instead is crucial to living a life that is truly worthwhile for you.

No two people are alike. Everyone has different dreams and desires; therefore, relationships should allow each person's individuality to shine through. This is a must for the relationship to be happy and fulfilling, and long-lasting.

The quote of the day says, "The ones who say you can't are too afraid you will." Don't give in to other people's fears. Life is short. It is your responsibility to make it worthwhile for you. Do not waste your time staying in a place that does not move you forward in life towards your goals.

Even if someone says to you that you can't or shouldn't do something, understand that it is your life, and you have a choice to do whatever you want with your life, time, and resources. You did not come to this world to play it safe. You came to have fun, to enjoy your life, to fulfill your purpose, and to make a difference in the world. Ensure you have people around you who will help you on this path and not take you off of it.

Questions Of The Day

To end this lesson and help you stay committed to yourself, ask yourself:

Who in my life has a negative impact on my thoughts and beliefs? How many hours a day or a week do I spend with them? Can I reduce it? Can I increase time spent with people I admire?

How can I have more contact with people I admire daily? Have they written books that I can read? How can I learn life lessons from them? Find ways to fill free time with input from people you admire.

As usual, I recommend writing your answers in the PDF journal.

Affirmation Of The Day

After answering the questions in your journal, and contemplating on your answers, sit quietly for a few minutes today and repeat this affirmation to yourself as you think and dwell upon it:

I AM FOCUSED ON MY PURPOSE, AND I AM SUPPORTED BY POSITIVE PEOPLE.

Repeat this affirmation often. With repetition, it has the power to alter your consciousness so you build a better, happier and more purposeful life.

DAY 71 - BECOMING AWARE OF YOUR ENVIRONMENT AND ECOSYSTEM

"You are a product of your environment. So choose the environment that will best develop you toward your objective." ~ W. Clement Stone

———————— ⬯⬯⬯ ————————

Clement Stone also said, "Analyze your life in terms of its environment." Are the things around you helping you toward success—or are they holding you back?

This is something we need to consider seriously. Our environment has a primary effect on how our lives turn out. There are many environments that we encounter daily that we should consider.

There is your home environment, your neighborhood, your city, your country, your group of friends, your close relationships, your schools. There are many factors to consider when asking yourself whether you are in the best environment to make your dreams come true. Environment refers to our surroundings, where we live, and all that we have in our surroundings.

Another factor of our surroundings is our ecosystem. An ecosystem is the interaction between the environment and the living organisms living within it. The ecosystem is a community or group of living organisms that live and interact with each other in a specific environment."

Both our environment and our ecosystem are fundamental to our success or failure.

We will cover both of these in our lesson today.

Environment:

In the case of your environment, you want first to get your largest environment right. You must *first* examine your physical location. Are you living in the best place to support your dreams?

If you are interested in surfing and your dream is to have a surfing beach or surf as much as possible, but you live in Switzerland in the mountains, this environment cannot support your goals.

A good friend of mine loves motorsports and car racing. Israel is not the best country for this, so after much thought, he's moving to Germany where he can live his motor dream life near the Nürburgring.

Your talents can only really grow and serve you and others when you have access to the right resources that will allow you to use your abilities.

If you are adamant about realizing your potential, dreams, and soul's desire, you must make sure that your environment supports your potential. The more there is for you to develop upon, the greater you can develop.

Think about how one product can be a massive success in one place but may be useless in another. For example, if your dream is in the home pool business, but you live in an urban crowded area with high-rise buildings or in a place where people cannot afford swimming pools, you will not succeed with your dream in this location. The same is true with personal gifts.

Think of Arnold Schwarzenegger, who left his hometown in Austria to live in the US to make his dream of becoming Mr. Olympia and a famous Hollywood actor come true.

Think of Elon Musk leaving South Africa to Canada and then the US to build his businesses in California. Think of Steve Jobs being adopted by a family that lived in Silicon Valley, the best place for him to develop his business and computer innovation skills.

If your dream is important enough for you, then you need to do what it takes and take the necessary steps, as hard as they may be, to get yourself into the best environment to allow your talents and gifts to flourish. This way, you utilize what already exists somewhere to realize your gifts and interests. We all have the right to contribute to the evolution of life. In fact, it is our duty.

Listen to your intuition.

If funding and visa permits were not something holding you back, where would you live to fulfill your soul's desire and make your dreams a reality? What can you do about it if these are holding you back? How can you overcome these obstacles? Are there any other places you can live that do not need special permits or much funding but still support you to achieving your goals?

Make yourself available in the place where you can contribute the most and where your dreams can become a reality.

We each have our unique gifts and skillsets, and there is inspiration somewhere in the world for you to fulfill yourself, so find that place and live there.

The best location for you could be right under your nose, such as was the case for Steve Jobs, or it could be on the other side of the world or the country, as it was for Jeff Bezos. Today we can move relatively easily to a new location; all we need is boldness and courage.

And if you have no choice and cannot move your life somewhere else because of commitments, then it is good to know that you are exactly where you should be, even if it is hard to comprehend.

Once you find your place in the world, it is essential to consider your smaller environments.

Is your city the best city for your gifts? And if not, which city is best?

Is your school the best school to improve and develop your gifts? If not, which school is better, and what can you do to move there or get into that school? It needn't be the best school in your field but it must be good enough to help get you closer to your dreams.

What about your neighborhood? Is it the right one to develop your gifts and to network with the right people?

Is your home right for you? Some people garden for their happiness, so a ground house would be best, while others fear insects, so they may thrive better in a high-rise building. Which home is most conducive to your health and peace of mind to allow your creativity or gifts to flourish? Your house creates an atmosphere that influences your mindset.

What about your group of friends and your close relationships? Are they believers in you and in general? Are they making the most of *their* lives or just waiting for government support or help from others? Your life will be transformed, shaped, and moved by the kind of people you come in contact with daily, as we spoke about previously. You know, and you decide.

It is essential to understand that your environment is crucial to your success. So make sure that you are where you can make the most of your life and fulfill your soul's desire.

Remember that what you have and see around you every day is what you will become. Your environment rubs off on you whether you are aware of this or not. Your environment also dictates which options are available to you.

A move to a different location and all the things that accompanied that move and were learned due to it may be part of your journey to success. Deep inside, only you are the one who knows this.

Now let's dive into your ecosystem.

We have all been programmed by our family and environment to behave in certain ways that are acceptable in our family and the ecosystem that we belong to.

As an example, where I now live, in Israel, it is acceptable to have no less than two or three children. So, people who do not have any children will tend to feel as if they do not belong.

On the other hand, when I lived in Germany, having one child and perhaps a dog is considered the norm, and if you have more than this, you feel different.

It is all about what is acceptable in your ecosystem. What is acceptable in your ecosystem forms your sense of belonging and your boundaries. And these boundaries feel very real.

For example, if you have much more money than the average person in your community and you are much more successful than most of the people there, you may not feel as if you belong; you will feel different. And these feelings of belonging are critical to us since belonging to a group, and sensing acceptance by our family and society is what allowed and secured our survival in the past. We feel very uncomfortable when we feel as if we do not belong.

Suppose you live in a place where wealthy people will stand out from the crowd, and your dream is to become very rich. In that case, you may be self-sabotaging this success to feel a sense of belonging to your ecosystem and feel a part of your tribe.

This is a fundamental awareness to have since your ecosystem subtly forms the boundaries of what you feel you can or can't achieve in your life.

Becoming aware of competing factors in your ecosystem that may be holding you back can be a real eye-opener.

Many of us behave in ways that sabotage our path to the life of our dreams only because our ecosystem may have a competing element with our desires.

Think what is the experience you think you will have once you achieve your goal, and why do you think you may self-sabotage your success once you have achieved or are close to achieving your goal? This is most often due only to competing values between your desires and the acceptable norm in your ecosystem.

What is the experience that you want to have, and what is your current experience? Why do you think you are not where you would like to be?

What is it about *not* having this achievement that is keeping you feeling safe?

Get curious about your situation.

Once you understand the reasons behind your underlying behaviors, you are in a better position to control these feelings and allow yourself to reach your true desires.

Here are the steps to remove yourself from an ecosystem that competes with your desires:

Well, the first step is to acknowledge what it is that you are scared of losing. We feel secure in the life that we currently have. We have the support of our ecosystem, or else we would not have what we have. We would lose it fast; just as many lottery winners lose all of their money within a few years of winning. Their new wealth does not match their ecosystem.

If your life is not the way you want it to be, these feelings of security and belonging to your ecosystem may be holding you back from reaching those dreams.

Think to yourself what exactly are the beliefs and ecologically acceptable behaviors of your current ecosystem.

Then think of what you would want to have different than the norm in your ecosystem.

Then find the beliefs, behaviors, or mindset in your ecosystem that are holding you back from achieving the life of your dreams.

Honor your commitment to these behaviors in the past while slowly making a conscious commitment to move away from your ecosystem that is limiting your beliefs, actions, and progress.

You must get your desired experience to align with feelings of safety for you to reach them.

Find a way to view what you desire to have in a way that is aligned with your ecosystem's belief pattern. If there is no way to make it match your current ecosystem, you must move to somewhere with an ecosystem where you will have a sense of belonging and feel accepted.

Questions Of The Day

Ask yourself the following questions:

Is my environment pulling me in the right direction? Think about your answer thoroughly. If your environment is not conducive to your success, ask yourself: What will I do about this?

Now ask yourself: Is there something in my ecosystem belief system that is blocking me from becoming the ideal version of myself? If your ecosystem does match the opportunity of achievement of your desires, ask yourself: What do I need to change about my thoughts so that my desires align with my ecosystem?

Remember that if your behaviors do not align with what is acceptable in your ecosystem, you will most often self-sabotage any chance of your success. So either find a way to align your actions with the beliefs of your ecosystem or move to a place where your actions and beliefs align better together.

As usual, I recommend writing your answers in the PDF journal.

Affirmation Of The Day

After answering the questions in your journal, and examining them, sit quietly for a few minutes today and repeat this affirmation:

I CAN REACH MY FULL POTENTIAL SINCE MY ECOSYSTEM IS ALIGNED WITH MY SUCCESS AND SUPPORTS ME. I AM IN THE PERFECT PLACE FOR ME TO BRING FORTH MY GIFTS.

Repeat this affirmation often. With repetition, it has the power to alter your consciousness so you build a better, happier and more purposeful life.

DAY 72 - BECOMING AWARE OF SELF SABOTAGE

"The only reason I can't jump in and engage life is that I've told myself I can't. Yet I can't help wondering would happen if I told myself I could?"

~ Craig D. Lounsbrough

Many people have self-sabotaging behaviors rooted deep within their subconscious mind. Self-sabotaging behaviors create problems in daily life and interfere with goal achievement. We may fear success or failure, or have other limiting beliefs that underestimate our capabilities, suppress our feelings ,or we may have feelings that we are not worthy of a better life for ourselves.

Even when things are going our way and everything seems fine, those of us who have these self-sabotaging tendencies, tend to feel anxious about succeeding, about being the center of attention, about feeling good and feeling fulfilled and happy.

It takes real courage to overcome self-sabotage and to allow yourself to step into your greatness. Not only to start believing in yourself, but also to start allowing yourself to reap the fruits of your actions instead of trampling all over them.

Feeling inadequate oftentimes prevents us from even taking the first step.

We *CAN* achieve our wildest dreams. We deserve not only to go after our dreams, but also to achieve them! This is why we are alive. We are creators. We have the powers to create what we desire in our life through our connection to the immaterial world. But we must believe in our abilities before we can even start.

It is crazy that even when we put in so many hours, days, months and even years honing our craft and becoming great at something, a self-sabotaging person still does not feel they deserve their success, so they either hide their work, keep it to themselves, or pass it onto to the wrong people who do not appreciate it. Think of Vincent van Gogh. Only after he died, and stopped self-sabotaging his own success, did he reach the great fame he was so deserving of.

Self-sabotaging behavior often comes from having deep rooted guilt.

Having feelings of guilt ingrained within us leads to loss of self-esteem. These negative feelings lead to the destruction of our relationships and even to destruction of our life.

Guilt is destructive to the psyche. Guilt usually comes from early childhood, from parents or caregivers who used guilt to manipulate and control our feelings and behaviors to suit their needs.

Our caregivers learned this method of raising controlled children from their own caregivers, and stuck to this method because it works so effectively.

Children who have experienced destructive criticism or lack of love during childhood will often have guilt about their actions and will self-sabotage their own success in the future in different areas.

They will have a tendency to believe that even if they do have some level of success, it must be transient and they expect that something will go wrong soon. As I mentioned before, what you expect, you will get, because of the functioning of the levels of consciousness of our mind.

Self-sabotage comes from deep seated beliefs in our subconscious mind that we are not good enough to get what we want and that we cannot reach greatness and do not deserve greatness. We believe that we are inadequate. Even if something is good, people with self-sabotaging beliefs see it as being only temporary.

There is no reason why our lives cannot and should not be filled with a series of great, lucky, and prosperous events. Why should we hold the beliefs that we are unworthy of good and deserve to have bad luck. Why should we hold the belief that we do not deserve the very best for ourselves when other people do have what we desire?

People with guilt feelings tend to be overly critical of themselves, and are always excusing their behavior in the face of others. People with guilt feelings also tend to be very critical of other people's behaviors, and this leads to difficulties in their personal relationships.

As you become more aware of your negative emotions it will become clear how you may actually be creating a negative reality for yourself from these emotions.

Negative emotions disrupt good relationships, and lead you to expect bad things to happen to you. So you don't put in the effort or don't even take the first step towards your goals and desires.

Everything always begins with a belief you hold, a limiting belief, that leads to your actions. In turn, your actions lead to a self-fulfilling manifestation of your negative beliefs.

People who self-sabotage are always saying, "I wish I could do this or I wish I had the power to do that" with a notion deep within them that they can't.

Since positive results are just as much a manifestation of positive thoughts as negative ones are, how can you get rid of any guilt feelings and stop sabotaging your success?

1. Never criticize your own behaviors in a destructive way. If you do, your subconscious mind, which is constantly absorbing information about you and your environment, will assume that these criticisms are true, since your <u>conscious</u> mind accepted them as being true and allowed them to seep into your subconscious mind. The subconscious mind is always listening, always awake, and like a sponge, accepts whatever beliefs reach it as being true. Your self-talk should only represent what you want to be true and real in your life, and nothing else.

2. Don't allow others to talk negatively about you, not even as a joke.

3. Stop blaming others for your failures, and take responsibility for your own choices and actions.

4. Forgive others. There is a future lesson about this very important subject.

5. Learn the art of allowing what wants to enter into your life to enter. Remove the blockages that are stopping good energy and good things to enter your life.

6. And lastly, ponder this question: What if all of your dreams ARE already happening in your life but are just beneath the surface? Just like a growing seed beneath the grounds' surface just before it comes through the soil. All you need to do is allow for sufficient personal development to allow the new you become the current you. What you want is already yours in the making. All you have to do is allow it to happen by becoming the person that you

need to be in the reality where your dreams have materialized.

Accept that good things are meant to happen to you. You are good at your core as everyone is. You deserve good because you are doing your best persistently daily.

You are meant to bring your gifts to the world and get gifts back from the world in return. It's like any transaction in the supermarket. You pay and get stuff in return. When you share your gifts with the world, the world pays you back. The better you become at sharing your gifts, the more you will get back.

Think about you being a supermarket owner and giving your merchandise away for free, without getting paid for anything in return. People take and take and give nothing in return. You still have to pay the bills and to maintain the stock and the store. Very soon you will be out of business and you won't continue to sell your merchandise. Who do you think loses most in this situation?

Actually the people who want your products lose more than you lose, because they don't have access to your unique merchandise any more. You also definitely lose, but your clients lose even more.

The same goes for relationships. You must honor and respect yourself first. If you don't, then you ruin your relationships, and both sides lose. You deserve great relationships with the people in your life. Let others enjoy your gifts and allow yourself to get love and respect back in return, not criticism.

So think about this every time you are self-sabotaging your success. Not only will you lose greatly, but many more people will lose as a result of your self-sabotaging behaviors.

Do not be like Vincent van Gogh. Allow yourself to win while you are physically alive. Allow yourself to reap the rewards and keep giving back. You deserve a good life, and other people deserve your gifts. Make the move into the parallel reality where all your dreams are your reality by connecting yourself to your true divine nature as part of infinite intelligence.

Questions Of The Day

To end this lesson and help you stop any self-sabotaging behaviors, ask yourself:

Where in my life am I self-sabotaging my success? Where in my life do I feel that I am still not good enough to gain the rewards I deserve for my efforts? In which areas do I feel I do not deserve the best?

Slowly learn to allow yourself to reap the rewards of your efforts, for the good you bring, for who you are and for the people who need your gifts!

As usual, I recommend writing your answers in the PDF journal that you have received with this book. Then look over your answers to ensure that you improve your life and bring forth your true divine nature.

Affirmation Of The Day

After answering the questions in your journal, and examining them, sit quietly for a few minutes and repeat this affirmation:

I DESERVE THE BEST, BECAUSE I AM DOING MY BEST TO SHARE MY GIFTS WITH THE WORLD.

Repeat this affirmation often. With repetition, it has the power to alter your consciousness so you build a better, happier and more purposeful life.

DAY 73 - BECOMING AWARE OF YOUR EXPECTATIONS

"Expect the best and get it." ~ Norman Vincent Peale

Did you know that your attitude comes from your expectations? And as I said previously, your attitude is the determinant for your level of life satisfaction and the amount of love, income, reputation, and status you achieve.

Only 15 percent of your success in life is attributed to your abilities, 85 percent comes from your attitude. And since your expectations for yourself form your attitude, your expectations are crucially important.

Suppose you hold positive, optimistic expectations that you will succeed in a given task. In that case, you have a positive attitude which will lead you to make the right choices and actions, eventually leading to your success.

But suppose you are full of doubts and concerns about the consequences of your actions in a specific field. In that case, your tendency is toward a negative attitude, which will often sabotage your opportunity for success.

The difference between successful and unsuccessful people is successful people develop positive expectations before an event happens. They expect the best to happen as a result of their efforts. Successful people have learned to develop their own expectations even when they have no information to support a positive expectation. They still hold, deep within them, a positive expectation for their efforts. They learned how to develop a positive and enthusiastic attitude that influences other people to respond positively.

If you can learn and sustain the habit of having positive expectations for your actions, you have developed one of the founding keys to your success.

The expectations you currently hold come from your deepest beliefs about yourself and the world.

And these beliefs about yourself are based on your *view* of yourself. You will never be able to act in a way that differs from how you view yourself. How you view yourself is the key to whether you achieve your potential or not.

It's all about your mental story. Suppose this story says that you don't have what it takes to succeed in a specific field of life like relationships, making money, or even losing weight. In that case, you will, unfortunately, self-sabotage your success in that field every time. You can never go against your inner story.

When your expectations are low in a particular field of life, you won't even start the path to reach this goal, or you may begin halfheartedly, only to stop shortly after.

Such a negative inner dialogue limits your potential. You will not even start, let alone put in the long hard hours of work necessary to make any venture succeed, because you hold the belief that you have no chance to begin with. This is why your belief in yourself must be high so that you will start, expect the best for yourself regarding your achievements, and put in the effort, and finally reap the rewards.

Your day-to-day actions result from your beliefs, and if you hold a negative attitude, with negative expectations and beliefs that you cannot succeed, this becomes a self-fulfilling prophecy.

You will not do what you need to do to succeed because you do not believe that you have a chance of success, and then, because you do not do the work, you will surely not reach the success you desire.

We will always behave in alignment with the way we view ourselves, with our self-identity, and with our story. You cannot reach anything outside of your deepest beliefs. So how can you change your beliefs, and improve the story you have running in your mind and start expecting the best for yourself?

The best way to do this is through affirmations, and this is why I introduce a new affirmation at the end of every lesson for you to use because I know the power of affirmations.

When you reaffirm an ability, over and over again, in confidence, through a positive statement, with complete faith in the process, then it penetrates your subconscious mind. And when your conscious mind allows a thought or a belief to penetrate your subconscious mind, then the subconscious mind accepts it as accurate. Then the subconscious mind takes over and supports the actions that will make it into your reality. The subconscious obeys and executes the instructions it gets from the conscious mind.

There is so much power in your subconscious mind, not only in your life but also in the people around you. Your most profound thoughts have a magnetic pull that can even change the behavior and thoughts of the people around you. This power that comes from your subconscious mind is unlimited. All you have to do is reinforce what you desire, the expectations that you wish to have, into your subconscious mind, clearly, confidently, repetitively, and with complete faith.

The keys towards stating your affirmations in a way that will affect your subconscious mind quickly and most powerfully are that:

1. The affirmation is personal, meaning that you must use "I" and not "you".
2. The affirmation must be positive, meaning that it focuses on what you want and not what you don't want.
3. The affirmation must be in the present tense as if you are affirming what has already happened.

These keys will change your attitude, changing your expectations, which will change what you can get in your life.

Questions Of The Day

To end this lesson and help you form great expectations from your efforts, the questions that you want to ask yourself today are:

Where in my life do I expect less than the best for myself? Where do I see a less-than-perfect outcome for myself? Why do I think this way? Is this belief the truth, or is this something I may have picked up during my childhood?

Now that you know where you expect less than the best for yourself, affirm what you **do** want instead so that your subconscious mind will accept your new story as reality and will begin to bring it to fruition. As usual, I recommend writing your answers in the PDF journal.

Affirmation Of The Day

After answering the questions in your journal, sit quietly for a few minutes and repeat this affirmation:

I EXPECT THE BEST FOR MYSELF IN EVERY SITUATION.

Repeat this affirmation often. With repetition, it has the power to alter your consciousness so you build a better, happier and more purposeful life.

DAY 74 - BECOMING AWARE OF ASSERTIVENESS

"Nobody can make you feel inferior without your consent." ~ Eleanor Roosevelt

Today we will talk about being assertive. To live the life of your dreams, you cannot expect it to be handed over to you. You will need to go out and get it.

To be successful, you must be assertive. You have to say no at times to people who want your time, help, support, or attention. You will have to know how to communicate what you want clearly, honestly, and respectfully. Assertive communication is neither aggressive nor passive.

To receive other people's respect takes courage, which means that we have to stand up for ourselves. Almost every day, we may confront people who may be selfish and inconsiderate of ours or other people's needs. When we allow for these behaviors without responding when necessary, we will lose self-esteem and self-respect.

You are not invisible, so you should not behave as if you were. You have feelings, goals, ideas, and desires. You must go out and do what needs to be done to get them.

On the other hand, you should also not be aggressive. Assertive behavior is right in the middle. It is not submissive nor aggressive behavior. It is between these two extremes.

Humor in certain situations is often the best route to go to express your feelings and desires. For those people who know how to use humor, that's great. But even if you think that you are not funny, you can still find an assertive way to get your message across and get your needs met.

Assertive people are the most trusted people because those around them know what they are thinking and feeling. Assertive people do not hide from others. They also choose their fights accurately.

An assertive person will understand that they do not need to react to everything that does not suit them. They will be more focused on the bigger picture and respond only if an issue is worthy of their reaction. They will also be conscious and aware of their emotions when they are reacting.

So how do you become aware of whether something is worthy enough of your reaction or not?

Ask yourself, "Will this matter to me a month from now, or a year from now?

If your answer is yes, then you must respond. But if the answer is no, try not to turn a minor issue into a more significant concern than it is by spending too much emotional and mental effort on it.

Say what you want and what you feel from awareness of what is going on outside of you and within you. Listen to the other person's response. Once you hear their response decide whether the battle is worth fighting or not, and consciously decide what to do.

It is not always comfortable not to be nice and to be more assertive. This is especially true for people pleasers. But you cannot always be nice to everyone and achieve the life of your dreams. Learn to feel comfortable showing other sides of yourself courageously and assertively. When you practice not always being nice and learning to say no to other people's requests when you have other things that are more important for you, you will become better at being assertive.

Taking focused action on your dreams takes time. Since our time on Earth is limited, you will not always be free to meet other people's demands and desires. When you practice being assertive and saying no when you feel it is right for you, you will see that you can still be loved even when you are true to yourself.

You will see that people will accept this behavior from you and even respect you for it when you come from a place of love. It would be best if you experimented with being assertive because you will never find the time to do what needs to be done to reach your dreams without assertiveness.

Instead of saying yes to everyone immediately, say you want to think about it and have an answer for them by tomorrow. Think about whether you want to or can commit to doing what is requested of you.

You owe it to yourself to be true to you, and the only way to make sure that you get what you want and need in life is to express your needs assertively.

Questions Of The Day

To end this lesson and to help you become more assertive, please ask yourself:

Where in my life am I too generous with my time and resources? Can I afford to spend this time, or should I be doing other things to forward my life and dreams? There will be things that come up that will be more important to your soul at that moment, so you will want to commit to them but always search within for the correct answers for you.

As usual, I recommend writing your answers in the PDF journal.

Affirmation Of The Day

After answering the questions in your journal, sit quietly and repeat this affirmation:

I AM DOING MY BEST EVEN IF I DON'T DO ALL THE THINGS OTHER PEOPLE WANT.

Repeat this affirmation often. With repetition, it has the power to alter your consciousness so you build a better, happier and more purposeful life.

DAY 75 - BECOMING AWARE OF YOUR COMMUNICATION

"If there was any great lesson in life it was this: No battle was ever won with silence."

~ Shannon L. Alder

This quote is all about communication. Communication is a crucial skill and the basis of a favorable outcome and happiness in life. This is because communication skills will determine the level of satisfaction from your relationships, job, and life.

Effective communication builds trust. People will trust you and believe in your integrity and will feel safe with you. What could be better for relationships in the personal and work fields than trust?

It's good to know that communicating effectively is a skill that can be learned and improved if you choose to work at it.

Communication is done with words and body language and tone of voice, and eye contact.

These can be learned and improved to allow you to form better relationships with the people around you.

So how can you improve your communication skills?

The first step is vulnerability. To be an effective communicator, you must become more vulnerable.

There is a close link between how we physically and mentally feel and how we communicate with others because communication is an external expression of our inner energy. Miscommunication between people is at the heart of most difficulties in relationships, and the reason often stems from not allowing yourself to be vulnerable.

Communication begins by communicating your true feelings with yourself first. Just as we must first love ourselves before we can love another, we must first know how to communicate effectively with ourselves before communicating with others.

Miscommunication or lack of understanding of what is going on inside us is the root cause of tension and discomfort in relationships with other people. The reason for this miscommunication with ourselves comes from the way we process our feelings.

Expressing feelings in words is difficult. We often don't even understand our feelings and forget the real reason we decided to communicate. Then we may find ourselves expressing something that may be completely different from what we planned to communicate. This leads to confusion in the other person. However, in truth, it is we who are confused about what *we* are trying to convey. We are not aware of what we are feeling, and we are also not aware that we are not aware.

We need to bridge the gap between what we are feeling and how we are expressing ourselves. The gap is usually based on fear. As we grew up, we may have learned that showing our feelings was not always acceptable, and since being accepted is one of the most profound human needs, we learned to filter our emotions and sometimes even feel guilty that we have certain feelings. We stop connecting to what we feel inside and stop ourselves from acting on what we feel.

We did this to protect ourselves from criticism and disapproval of others so that we would feel accepted. We stopped being our authentic selves. Now, as adults, through habit, we deny our true feelings. This leads us to become distant from ourselves and distant from others as this affects our communication skills.

To stop this downward spiral of communication from occurring, we must let go of our fear of rejection and self-rejection and allow ourselves to become more vulnerable. We must learn to accept our feelings as they are and acknowledge that they are natural human responses.

Of course, we do not need to express all of our emotions, but we need to be aware of them and see how they are driving our behaviors, and we do need to express what is important to us without fearing the consequences.

So how can you learn to communicate more effectively?

1. Release your fear of rejection and let your true self shine through.

    Be authentic to yourself and others.

    You will only gain if you are honest with yourself and others since those who respect and appreciate you as you are will stay, and those who don't will slowly drift away. Although this may seem scary at first, it is what will make you much happier in the long run.

    You also want to become more aware of your emotions. Understanding your and other people's emotions is known as Emotional Intelligence (EQ). Emotional intelligence means that you are aware of and understand your feelings and master them, so you also understand other people's emotions and can work well with them.

    Emotional intelligence is far more critical for your success in life than intellectual intelligence (IQ).

2. Decode non-verbal communications such as tone and pitch of voice, body movements, posture, facial expressions, eye movement, eye contact, and even physiological changes such as sweating. You can be sure that your message is conveyed more clearly when your words and body language are consistent. When you understand other peoples' non-verbal cues, by hearing what is and isn't said, you can understand their point of view more effectively, and so you will understand them better. This takes practice and also takes adequate listening skills, which is the next step towards communicating effectively.

3. Practice good listening skills. Communication is a two-way process. We are not in a monologue with ourselves, where we just broadcast our message and do not listen to the response. How many times in a conversation, instead of listening, are you planning what to say next? **You can decide to stop doing this.**

It takes practice to listen correctly. Listening properly involves paying attention to the words being spoken and *how* the words are being said, and the non-verbal cues. But this can be learned and used to your advantage.

Everybody likes to be heard, so when you listen attentively, you get to know the other person by giving your full attention and genuinely concentrating on what they are saying and not saying. When you get to know another person, you understand them better, which is the basis of a good relationship. To avoid any confusion, ask questions if you did not precisely understand them. This is called active listening and makes the other person feel important, creating a better bond between the both of you.

To summarize good communication skills, you want to:

1. Show vulnerability and understand your emotions

2. Understand your and other people's non-verbal communication cues

3. Have good listening skills

These three actions will improve your life and allow you to be happier and more successful.

Questions Of The Day

To end this lesson and help you improve your communication skills, please ask yourself:

Which of these three steps for communicating effectively are most needed by me now, and how will I improve these communication skills?

As I mentioned, practice makes perfect. Practice effective communication with your family and close relationships where you naturally feel more open, and then you will be ready to use the essential new skills with other people.

As usual, I recommend writing your answers in the PDF journal.

Affirmation Of The Day

After answering the questions in your journal and contemplating your answers, sit quietly and repeat this affirmation:

I COMMUNICATE MY NEEDS EFFECTIVELY AND LISTEN ATTENTIVELY TO OTHER PEOPLE'S NEEDS TO BETTER UNDERSTAND THE PEOPLE IN MY LIFE.

Repeat this affirmation often. With repetition, it has the power to alter your consciousness so you build a better, happier and more purposeful life.

DAY 76 - BECOMING AWARE OF THE SKILL OF ACTIVE LISTENING

"To say that a person feels listened to means a lot more than just their ideas get heard. It's a sign of respect. It makes people feel valued."

~ Deborah Tannen

Active listening is a vital life skill that improves communication and helps us reach our goals and full potential. We are connected, and we need other people and their skills and abilities to help us reach our goals and potential. We need people, and to bring people closer to us, we must show them respect. We need to show them that they matter and that they are heard while also have them respect us. And one of the best ways to do this is through active listening.

I studied conflict mediation as part of my personal development, and the program taught me many essential skills. One of the most important skills I learned was how to listen actively. Active listening is a significant part of conflict resolution and equally important for coaching. Giving people a place to be heard without judgment is sometimes all that is needed to move the person to a place that they feel listened to, understood, and respected. When you listen to someone actively, you are also helping them understand themselves and their behaviors better. Active listening opens the hearts of both the listener and the speaker. It allows for a safe environment for emotional expression.

Active listening also helps you understand what drives people, what is important, and their needs. This helps avoid misunderstandings and encourages connection and sometimes even collaboration between people. As I mentioned, a person's version of reality may differ from yours. We see life differently because we interpret situations differently. Active listening opens us to the reality of the person talking.

We are open and not defensive, always ready to negate the other person's words.

Also, when we listen actively, we are fully present in the moment, not planning our next steps, or our following words, or our next anything. We are there, present and listening, absorbing everything that is being said and not being said and how things are being told. Active listening involves noticing more than just the words being spoken.

So how do we listen actively?

1. You cannot truly listen to anyone while doing anything else at the same time. You must be completely present. You must be quiet and listen to them.

2. When you listen, express interest through direct eye contact and face the other person. You may want to nod when you empathize with what they are saying. In other words, your body movements also show an interest in what the other person is communicating. If you are sitting near the other person, try to copy their body movements to align your emotions.

3. After listening quietly and attentively, you may have questions. This is fine so long as the questions asked do not come from a place of judgment but rather from a place of curiosity. You ask questions because you genuinely want to understand them better. For example, you could ask, "Why do you think you did it?" rather than asking, "Why did you do it?"

4. Asking why do you think you did it? is asking from curiosity, while asking why did you do it? is

judgmental. The questions you ask should also be open questions, meaning that you ask questions that they cannot answer with a short yes or no answer. Open questions can only be answered with a free-form response. An example of an open question is "What did you enjoy or not enjoy about the show?" rather than a closed question such as, "Did you enjoy the show?"

5. This way of communicating is definitely more challenging and takes more effort from the listener, and this is why it is known as active listening. The listener is actively thinking, reviewing, and acknowledging what is being said. The rewards from the effort of active listening are also many times more significant. You learn about the other person in more depth. You know why they do what they do; you understand what moves them. You can see their grander picture.

6. The last stage of active listening is a confirmation of understanding. In this part, you want to summarize the facts they said to make sure that you got everything right. You don't add any of your own judgments or interpretations about what was told. You repeat everything that they said. You basically summarize their words without adding anything.

7. This helps them feel that you emotionally understood them.

8. I genuinely recommend that you listen actively as often as possible. It is a vital skill, and you will get better at it the more you practice.

An imperative facet of Nelson Mandela's leadership was his willingness to listen and learn, which he said he got from his father. This skill allowed him to become South Africa's first black head of state elected in a fully representative democratic election.

Whenever you are having a conversation with a business partner, friend, colleague or a lover, try to put active listening to the test. You will see how it can make your relationships much more fulfilling, and it will undoubtedly help you reach your goals faster, because as Hemingway wrote, "*A man alone ain't got no bloody chance.*"

You need other people around you to succeed. Understanding a person's needs will help you bond with anyone.

Questions Of The Day

To end this lesson and help you develop the skill of active listening, ask yourself:

With whom would I like to improve my communication skills so I can understand them better?

Can I try the steps of active listening in my following conversation with them, including:

1. Giving full attention to the conversation. Being present
2. Showing my interest in them through copying their body language
3. Asking questions to get a better understanding of what they mean
4. Summarizing what they said for clarity.

As usual, I recommend writing your answers in the PDF journal.

Affirmation Of The Day

After answering the questions, sit quietly and repeat this affirmation:

I AM AN ACTIVE LISTENER, MAKING OUTSTANDING BONDS WITH THE PEOPLE AROUND ME.

Repeat this affirmation often. With repetition, it has the power to alter your consciousness so you build a better, happier and more purposeful life.

DAY 77 - BECOMING AWARE OF YOUR RELATIONSHIPS

"The most important thing in life is to learn how to give out love, and to let it come in."

~ Morrie Schwartz

From an immaterial perspective, we are whole the way we are without the need for anyone apart from us to complete us. We are whole. But that does not mean that we should not accept and let love come into our lives and give it out to others.

Much evidence from research shows that a close-knit relationship makes most people happier overall. We need to give out love and accept love from someone special to be at our best.

When in a healthy relationship, we find it easier to venture out into the world, do things that we genuinely desire to do, and fulfill our purpose completely. We may not feel the courage to do this if we do not have a steady base that supports us and provides us with a secure foundation to venture out. This close-knit relationship needs not to be a partner, but a partner is the best in most cases. So why are there so many people today who are running away from commitment and feel they do not want the confines of a relationship? The human species became dominant and strong due to our ability to work cooperatively with one another. We shared commitments and helped each other when our survival was threatened. The need to be in close-knit relationships is in our genes and has been passed down from generation to generation to ensure our survival.

So how is it that there are many people today who seem to steer away from relationships and fear their independence being suppressed when they get into a close-knit relationship? Well, this has come from a different survival mechanism that is more recent.

In the modern era, when wars became more common, a person without the burden of a family or someone dependent on them increased their chances of survival. This led to lone wolf behavior. This behavior makes a person fear a close-knit relationship because of the burden and lack of freedom to do what is necessary to survive when the need comes.

One more mouth to feed and care for, one more person to be responsible for in times of war and uncertainty, would reduce the chances of survival.

These people also like to hoard stuff and constantly search for faults with their partner, as if screening them for a situation where they are stuck with them in a war zone. During wartime, in such highly adverse circumstances, a close relationship could have harmed a person's chances of survival.

According to PSYCALIVE, at least a third of the current population is living their life like this. Unfortunately, it not only makes them unhappy but also leads to the unhappiness of many people around them. But, for most of us, this is not the case anymore. Nowadays, a relationship has gone back to its natural role and the natural benefits that the relationship can provide. Nowadays, a close-knit relationship has the potential to be much more gratifying than being alone.

These commitment-phobes miss out on a loving, supportive relationship, and this is very unfortunate. It does take some getting used to for a person with genetics from a family that was previously in a problematic survival situation.

A commitment-phobe tends not to care so much for their partner's emotional and intimate needs or even ridicules their partner for having such emotional needs because having these needs is something that would have hindered their chances of survival in the past. They block out such emotions. This, in turn, reduces their partners' level of happiness, which comes back to reduce their level of unhappiness. This makes them sure that they were right from the beginning and should not have entered the relationship in the first place. It's a downward spiral from here.

We are emotionally dependent on our partners, and this is natural. It was meant to be like this to ensure that we stay together through the rough times. If your partner does not understand this, your level of bonding will be reduced, which may give a good feeling in the short term to the commitment-phobe, but in the long term, it will negatively impact the commitment-phobe and their relationship.

If you or your partner are commitment-phobes, the only way to change this is through a genuine wish to change due to the awareness of where this behavior came from and its benefits in the past, and the adverse effects in the present. Then and only then can real and lasting change begin.

A healthy relationship can bring you immense pleasure.

It is healthy and natural to want intimacy with someone. No one should feel bad for having the desire to bond deeply with someone. It is normal to desire intimacy in a relationship. There is nothing wrong with a person who desires this. They are showing the other person that they trust them to fulfill their needs for closeness and support. It is not a weakness to need help and to request it. No person has ever succeeded in a big way without the aid of someone close to them. It is a false belief that you can do it all on your own. You can't. You need a support system, and nothing could be better than having it in your own home, someone to go with you on the path to success, happiness, and fulfillment for both of you.

In a relationship with a commitment-phobe, you may feel that there is a constant wall between you. You may not understand their behaviors at times. They will not want closeness with you and may always walk ahead of you instead of walking beside you. They also tend to do this with their children, as if no one is good enough for them.

They will put their own needs and desires before yours, and some may even ignore your needs. They look for negative behaviors in their partners instead of focusing on what the relationship can give them.

Love is not a feeling that they are comfortable with. They may push you away when you want a show of affection. But don't blame yourself for this. Fighting about this with your partner will not solve the problem and will only confirm to the commitment-phobe that their idea of closeness in a relationship was a bad idea. They will always withdraw from closeness no matter who they are with unless they decide to change one day through awareness of their behaviors and what pushes them to behave in this way. This change is not easy, but really worthwhile for them and anyone around them.

A healthy relationship is when none of the partners feels threatened by their partner's happiness and success. Both partners see their partner's happiness as their responsibility; even if a change in their partner could affect them negatively in the short term, they are still accepting and loving towards their partner. They don't interfere with their partner's work or other endeavors.

A healthy relationship is when both partners are available for each other and say what's on their minds in a courageous, encouraging, and loving way. Both partners are honest with each other in a healthy relationship and do not fear telling their truth and being authentic. And when a problem arises, they focus on finding a win-win solution. Yes, this is the relationship you definitely want and deserve to be in.

If you understand the value of having a close-knit relationship with someone, you will feel less threatened to be in such a relationship. You may feel threatened that your autonomy will be taken away from you if you are with someone. Still, in a healthy relationship where both partners are supportive, everyone wins, and the perceived threat will slowly dissipate.

This type of relationship is possible when a person is secure within himself or when a commitment-phobe understands where their behavior comes from and the benefits of making a change to being engaged in a healthier relationship structure.

Relationships should be comfortable, supportive, encouraging, fun, and close for both partners. Suppose you fear your partner will leave you, or you fear your independence is being threatened. In that case, you must change your relational pattern, or else relationships will seem more like addictions for you, with roller coaster emotional rides.

A healthy relationship will make your life richer and happier in all senses; you will be peaceful, relaxed, and blissful. A healthy relationship will make you less rigid and your life more fulfilled.

My relationship with my two mentally challenged daughters helped me become better and more understanding about relationships. They needed me to be understanding and loving towards them no matter what they did. This is how a healthy relationship should be.

My daughters never did anything on purpose to hurt me, even when they ruined the furniture, flooded the house, or slapped me in the back. I never held any grudges towards them, even if they woke me up at two in the morning or made a serious mess all over the place. I would have to stick by them and be helpful no matter what I felt or how hard my day was. I understood that it was never their fault, and I accepted them as they are. With this attitude, any relationship can thrive. Of course, you want to avoid any physical and emotionally abusive relationship at all costs and get out. Still, although there will never be perfection in any relationship, it will be immensely gratifying.

Accept another person's shortcomings, and give the support, encouragement, and honesty in your communications and leave the games out of the relationship while he does the same for you. Then you will know the power of a healthy relationship for every field of your life.

When both partners accept the other just as they are and understand that sometimes people do not behave from their true self, but from their ego, the partners can wake each other up to awareness.

Loving relationships may take time until they balance out and reach calm waters, but this will happen more quickly if you are willing to make some changes in your point of view about relationships and make healthy bonding become part of your makeup.

Questions Of The Day

To end this lesson and help you pursue a healthy relationship, please ask yourself:

Can I commit to being in a healthy, honest, encouraging, loving, and accepting relationship? Am I also willing to accept this type of love in return? Perhaps this love may be boring compared to having the emotional roller coaster relationship with a commitment-phobe. You'll enjoy the benefits of a happy and fulfilling relationship that you deserve.

As usual, I recommend writing your answers in the PDF journal.

Affirmation Of The Day

After answering the questions in your journal repeat this affirmation:

I AM IN A SECURE AND LOVING RELATIONSHIP WHERE WE LOVINGLY COMMUNICATE OUR NEEDS AND FEELINGS, AND WE RESPECT AND APPRECIATE EACH OTHER.

Repeat this affirmation often. With repetition, it has the power to alter your consciousness so you build a better, happier and more purposeful life.

DAY 78 - BECOMING AWARE OF THE NEED TO ASK

"Asking for help isn't a sign of weakness, it's a sign of strength. It shows you have the courage to admit when you don't know something, and to learn something new." ~ Barack Obama

How many of us are one request away from what we really want? Well, you will never know until you ask… Many of us have a problem asking for what we need from those who can give us what we need.

Most people do not like to ask for help because they feel that asking either lowers them in another person's eyes or puts them in debt to him. It makes them look too needy and incapable. But as I mentioned so many times, no one has reached greatness without the help. Those people who ask for what they need are often the only ones who get it.

You must learn how to ask for what you want and overcome feeling timid, and overcome any fear of rejection. It is natural to fear rejection. As a species, as I mentioned before, it was best for our survival to be in a group from an evolutionary standpoint. Therefore we always want to be part of the group, and as I mentioned previously, this is the first phase of life that we go through. We learn from a young age how to best belong to our group.

Being rejected by someone is not easy for anyone. But if you do not take risks, you will not be in any better place than you are now. Do something different, and often the other thing that you did not do beforehand, is to ask for what you need from someone who can give it to you or help you get it.

If you fear rejection so much that you choose not to ask, then you will never maximize your life. You must overcome this intense fear of rejection and ask for what you need. And I tell you that the more you ask, the better you will become and the easier it will become for you to do. You will start asking for the things you need much more easily. This will increase your self-esteem and drastically increase your chances of success.

I remember when I first asked for a loan from a family member. I needed some help in buying a property I found that was a great deal. I needed to buy it fast, and I needed a small loan for a few months until I would sell a smaller property that I had on sale. I never asked anyone for money before this. I had previously only requested from the bank, but never from someone I knew. In this case, taking out a bank loan for a few months would be too tedious, expensive, and too lengthy of a process to secure the deal.

I sat with that person for lunch, and then someone came into the restaurant wearing a Nike t-shirt with the logo "*Just do it*". This motto gave me the courage to blurt out what I needed. To my utter surprise, not only was I given the money a day later but part of it was given to me as a present. I could not believe it!

I did not even want or suggest something like that, but I received it only because I found the courage to ask. You will never know until you ask for what you need. And if you don't ask, you are rejecting yourself before you've given the other person a chance to say what they want to do. Successful people ask confidently. They ask without fear. If the answer is yes, then fantastic; if the answer is no, then they are in the same position they were before they asked, but at least they tried.

There is one thing that is of utmost importance when asking for something you need from someone. You have to know and ask for exactly what you want. Be specific. If you ask someone out, don't just ask if they want to go out with you. Instead, ask if they want to go out for lunch on Sunday at 2 p.m. If you ask for money, don't just say you need some help, ask for a specific sum, when you need it, for what, and when you intend to pay back. Be specific. Give details.

Sometimes when you can't get what you want or need from one person, you should try someone else, or even try the same person again later.

In the meanwhile, you may try to think of a better way to get what you want by thinking out-of-the-box, but often you have no other way to get what you need than by asking. In such circumstances, don't hesitate to ask again and again. Don't give up on your dreams. You see this all the time with children. They never give up on what they want. They become more adamant the more they ask. And what usually happens? They usually get what they want! Right?

Sometimes when you ask for something, the timing may not be correct, or the other person cannot do it this time. However, they may be open to your request at a different time if you ask again.

Things can change. Your relationship with that person can change and become more trusting. Even a person's mood may vary, and that may be enough. Asking can undoubtedly be very uncomfortable. But the more you do it, the more comfortable and confident you become with yourself and others' replies. You improve yourself every time you ask for something important for you.

If you have a strong enough reason to achieve any specific goal, this can be a powerful motivator to stir up your courage to ask for what you need.

Persevere on the path to your goals, and at times you will need to ask other people for something. Do it in a friendly manner, with a smile, and you will never regret trying.

If you persevere, the chances are that you will get a "*yes*" from someone some time! Statistically, if you keep trying, you will eventually get a "*yes*."

Now, as a side note: Asking doesn't necessarily mean asking for something physical. Sometimes you may want to know something. Then you may request to understand better. Instead of making assumptions, you can ask questions and get answers. Asking will always get you one step closer to where you desire to be.

Questions Of The Day

To end this lesson and help you stir up the courage to ask for what you need, please ask yourself:

Is there something that I need to ask from someone to get me closer to my dreams? Why have I not asked until now? What can happen if I do get what I ask for? What will happen if I get rejected? If I get "no" as an answer, can I live with rejection?

There is an equal and opposite reaction for every action, so think to yourself, what price will I have to pay for not asking?

As usual, I recommend writing your answers in the PDF journal.

Affirmation Of The Day

After answering the questions in your journal, repeat this affirmation.

I DARE TO ASK FOR WHAT I WANT AND NEED WHENEVER I NEED IT.

Repeat this affirmation often. With repetition, it has the power to alter your consciousness so you build a better, happier and more purposeful life.

DAY 79 - BECOMING AWARE OF THE NECESSITY TO IGNORE

"Weak people revenge, strong people forgive, intelligent people ignore." ~ Albert Einstein

—————————⬡⬡⬡—————————

If you want a favorable outcome, there are things you must learn to ignore. And to do this, I want to talk about what you should ignore to make your decisions the best they can be so that you can move your life forward to what you dream it to be.

Two types of minds work simultaneously within every one of us. Some people use one type of mind more than the other type. Of course, our mind is one unit, but people use different thought patterns more often. It is best to use both minds equally to create a balanced state of mind from which you can make intelligent decisions.

Let's begin by talking about these two minds. The first is the emotional mind, and the second is the analytical mind. Most people make their choices from only one of these minds. Still, if you genuinely want to have a good life, the best option is if you use your intelligent mind, which takes some of the information from the analytical mind and some of the data from the emotional mind and balances them out by ignoring some of the information from both minds.

I think that this is what Albert Einstein had in mind when he stated that intelligent people ignore.

This is such a profound understanding.

So let's understand what each mind brings to the table:

The analytical mind examines everything. It looks at all of the numbers and fine details. It overthinks everything. This mind gathers a lot of data and details, but there is no action when there is too much reasoning. This mind usually stops people from taking action. It checks all of the possible scenarios, and often there are many, so it becomes paralyzed from indecision. This mind also tends to focus on negative scenarios. This mind often asks what if this happens, and what if that could happen? All of the petty details drive the person to fear, and they do not move into action. They are paralyzed with details. When this mind is in control, it will lead to analysis paralysis and no action. The person often stays in his comfort zone.

On the other hand, we have the emotional mind, which acts from the gut. It is the reactive mind that goes in the direction that the feelings drive the person to go. If it feels good, the emotional mind jumps right on in without considering the consequences of their actions first. When something does not feel good, the emotional mind runs away from it. There is no rational thinking whether it is suitable or proper to run away or whether it is some limiting belief that is causing fear for the emotional mind. In the emotional mind, feelings govern actions without real rationalization of the consequences. Details aren't checked, but rather everything goes according to an emotional reaction. This mind, when followed, leads to making choices without thinking them through and can lead to disaster for the person.

An intelligent mind is different. It is uses both of the other minds; the analytical mind and the emotional mind.

The intelligent mind gathers information from both minds and forms a balanced decision.

The intelligent mind is the balanced mind that can help you make the best decisions for yourself.

It considers both your emotions and gut feelings, as well as the numbers and fine details before making a decision. The intelligent mind is conscious of the environment and is mindful of the feelings you have about something and the numbers. The intelligent mind helps you to make responsible choices and not just whims of the moment. The intelligent mind thinks clearly and looks for the truth, not just what we feel we wish to be the truth or what the numbers show. It looks at the bigger picture.

On the other hand, the intelligent mind also ignores the stories we tell ourselves that stop us from taking action. The intelligent mind also puts aside the extreme emotions that may not be based on reality but on our own thoughts, beliefs, and the meanings we give things. The intelligent mind questions everything in search of the truth. It looks for the truth based on objective evidence and not biased stories.

When we make choices from our intelligent mind, we will move forward, grow and expand our thinking, become more aware, and expand our lives to new and better dimensions.

The intelligent mind is the mind that allows fundamental change to occur because it encourages awareness.

I read about a group of people who were asked what they would do if they were stranded on an island without a lot of food and saw that not too far away was what looked like land to them, but it could have also been another bigger island. About 50 percent said they would check the details, and the number of sharks in the water, the temperature, the winds, and the exact distance before they would think about leaving. Another 40 percent said they would jump in the water and swim towards the other island. The last 10 percent said they would build a raft and set off for the land.

The scientists checked what happened to these people later in life. They found that only the small group had become successful in life and had reached their ultimate goals.

Using the intelligent mind to help you make decisions is also essential in relationships. You can learn to ignore the irrelevant details in relationships, such as some minor faults, and continue to explore the person's friendly, good, and fun aspects.

The same goes for health decisions. You want to examine a food's ingredients before you buy it and listen to expert opinions while ignoring less learned individuals' opinions on what you should or shouldn't be doing in your relationships, with your finances, or for your health. This is the only way to make good long-term choices.

Questions Of The Day

To end this lesson and help you make better decisions and know what to ignore, please ask yourself:

Which mind is controlling my actions? The analytical, emotional, or intelligent mind? How can I ensure that my intelligent mind takes over my decision-making process?

Look back at your recent decisions and examine which mind you most often used for decision-making. This awareness is crucial for a good life based on wise decisions. As usual, I recommend writing your answers in the PDF journal.

Affirmation Of The Day

After answering the questions in your journal, repeat this affirmation:

I ALWAYS CONSIDER BOTH MY EMOTIONS AND THE LOGICAL SIDE OF ANY SITUATION BEFORE MAKING A DECISION.

Repeat this affirmation often. With repetition, it has the power to alter your consciousness so you build a better, happier and more purposeful life.

DAY 80 - BECOMING AWARE OF THE BENEFITS OF FAILURE

"People who avoid failure also avoid success." ~ Robert T. Kiyosaki

The reason for this is that you may not get it right the first, fifth, or tenth time, but if you persist and continue to experiment, you will find a way to achieve your goals. As we said before, you can gain something from every delay or difficulty.

When you encounter difficulty on your path towards your goals, you must understand what caused the setback. Failure is valuable if you learn from it. If you can determine the reason, you can correct it and navigate yourself to a better path. Sometimes, you have no control over situations, but if you take responsibility for your failures and any devastation in your life, you can find a way to grow from them, as difficult as it may seem.

Try to see yourself or the situation from an observer's eyes. Eyes that are not emotionally attached. Perhaps you have a weakness that you haven't noticed before. If you have become aware of a weakness, be willing to take action to correct it.

If you can find the courage to face your shortcomings and change what needs changing to become the person worthy of the outcomes you desire, then everything that happened was not a failure. If you can ask yourself why you lost this battle and how you can improve yourself, then you are becoming more aware. This allows for positive change, making you stronger and more capable.

You gain much from introspection, checking yourself, finding your shortcomings, and working to improve them.

There is no need to be good at everything, but there is a need to be good at the things that help you become the best version of yourself.

For example, if you're not good at basketball, that's fine. Don't focus on improving your ball skills, but if you're not so good at relationships, earning a living or maintaining good health, then you definitely want to make sure you are always working at improving and learning more about these critical life skills.

From every failure, there is a lot to gain. Improve your weaknesses when they are in areas that are necessary for your self-actualization. We do not need to be good at everything, but we need to be good at what is essential to become our best version. View mistakes as stepping stones towards becoming more aware and better skilled at life.

Avoid the attitude of whatever will be will be. Take action, and when you make mistakes, learn from them, experiment some more, use good judgment. Stay with your goals, but if desired results don't come your way, change your approach.

My goal in life is to help people live better, healthier, and happier lives. The health center I opened was a dream come true. But as it happened, I opened the center just a few months before the coronavirus outbreak. I invested a lot of money in this project but was forced to close when the pandemic hit. Due to the recent opening, I lacked more resources to reopen after the pandemic. I understood that the health center was only one way to achieve my goal, and there were many other ways that I can accomplish this goal as well. I was wounded financially but had the grit to continue. There is no need to persist on a path that is not giving you the results and happiness you desire. Stick with your goals if they are getting you closer to your soul's desire, but find better ways to achieve them if one way has failed. The first time you try something, you will probably fail at it, just like riding a bike. It doesn't mean you should quit and decide not to ride a bike. You have two choices: continue on the same path until you become better, or find another way to learn.

There is always a good way to handle a problem. This belief, even following failure, is the key to achieving anything. If one way hasn't solved the problem, there are other ways. When you believe there is a way, then you will find the way. But don't give up on your goals just because one way has failed you.

Take a step back; this will give you a different perspective.

We are all familiar with the story of Thomas Edison trying thousands of different designs before developing the light bulb that would last over 1,200 hours and was affordable to the masses. He didn't give up on his goal after failing; he just tried different ways to get there.

Even if getting to your goals takes you through many trials and errors until you find the right way, if you persist and keep experimenting, then all of a sudden, you will see how lucky you are.

Questions Of The Day

To end this lesson and to help you overcome a fear of failure, ask yourself:

Am I self-aware enough to acknowledge my weaknesses and failures? What can I learn from each failure? And how can I change my approach or direction towards achieving my goals after this awareness?

As usual, I recommend writing your answers in the PDF journal.

Affirmation Of The Day

After answering the questions in your journal, repeat this affirmation to yourself as you think and dwell upon it:

I USE MY FAILURES TO LEARN, IMPROVE, BETTER MYSELF, AND GROW STRONGER EVERY DAY!

Repeat this affirmation often. With repetition, it has the power to alter your consciousness so you build a better, happier and more purposeful life.

DAY 81 - BECOMING AWARE OF THE BENEFITS OF DISAPPOINTMENT

"We must accept finite disappointment, but never lose infinite hope."

~ Martin Luther King, Jr.

Disappointment and hardship are finite. They have a beginning and will have an end if your hope is infinite.

Hard times happen to all of us, and the more we take risks, the more complex the hard times tend to be on the path to success.

If the goal is worthwhile for you, the only difference between one who succeeds and one who doesn't succeed is a person's ability to navigate the hard times and come out alive enough to let in good times that will follow.

I know that at times it is hard to believe that you can ever come out of your situation, but I assure you that you can. And when you do and will have learned the lessons that accompany the hard times, then the success you reap as a result of learning the lessons will be yours to keep.

When you have taken risk and then hard times come along, when you have no other choice but to weather them out, you will discover how strong, powerful and innovative you are.

Being strong during hard times is not enough. You will also need to use your imagination. In fact, you will need to use your creative faculties most; you will need to think out of the box and use your money wisely to get you ahead in such times.

There is nothing better for creativity than to be cornered. At such times, only your imagination can get you out of the mess that you are in. This is not a time to listen to people who do not believe in you because they will only block your path and your creativity. They will also tell you to stop because they could not cope with your situation.

You cannot expect another person to believe in your dreams as much as you do, so don't expect them to. It is you who needs to continue believing in your goals and yourself, and it is you who needs to keep pulling through.

So what can you do in such hard times to get through?

I've known some challenging times in my life, and there were a few things that helped keep me going:

1. Knowing everything is always in flux. Nothing ever stays the same. Even if we don't do anything, times will change. The darkest hour is right before dawn. One moment we are down, and then the next moment we can be up, and then down again. When you understand that things constantly change around you, and you accept this change, you can choose to have faith that things will turn out for the best for you if you stick around long enough. Weather the tide, even if it's a really long tide. If you have faith and the reason you entered this situation in the first place is worthwhile for you, then when you remind yourself

of your reasons, you will tend to keep moving forward. Hard times do not last forever. But the strength and self-esteem that you will gain from the hard times *will* last you forever.

2. Checking your viewpoint on your situation. Is it really so bad? Are there things that *are* going well for you, even in this low place? Are there some patches of light? Is there perhaps a light that you can see, even faintly, at the end of the tunnel? A quote says that "if you change the way you look at things, the things you look at change". Perhaps it is only your perspective that needs to change. Maybe you *can* see things in a more positive light. It's good at such times to remember what Henry Ford said. "The airplane takes off against the wind, not with it." It's the trying times that will eventually lift you.

3. Asking yourself, which creative things can I do to help me move forward with the least harm done? Where can I find funding or produce more money? How can I use what I do have to push my ideas forward? If the hardship is in a relationship, ask yourself, could this be in my favor? Do I want to change things? What do I want to change? Are there any people I can consult who have gone through similar experiences and have come out favorably?

4. Taking action. As hard as it may seem for you to do now, you must do something and not freeze or get into depression. Move forward. The steps you take do not need to be extreme or significant. They can be subtle, but you must do something. It is like getting back into the car after being in an accident. Will you take the uncomfortable step of getting into the car and driving again, or will you give in to your fears? Do not lose hope. Do what you can in your current situation. Do your very best, and that will be enough.

5. Sometimes, there is nothing that you can do. So don't overthink, instead just breathe and maintain the faith that things will work out. But keep your eyes open for opportunities. I am not saying to close down and go into hibernation. I *am* saying to go into power-saving mode. Become more efficient, and slow down but remain aware of what is going on around you. When you release the pressure, you can sometimes see opportunities that were right before you but never noticed before because of all the stress you were going through. Taking a break can open you up to intuition that is always available for you but not always tapped into due to stress. When connecting to your intuition, you are tapping into unlimited resources available to immensely help you.

There are lessons to learn to make you better. Don't give up following disappointment before you can use the lessons you learned. The best days for you are yet to come if you fight this battle and find reasonable solutions for your challenges.

I believe that every problem is handleable. Sometimes ways to handle the situation are more challenging to identify, but you can still find them if you are willing to seek them. In the sermon on the mount, Jesus preached to his disciples:

"Ask, and it shall be given to you; seek, and you shall find; knock, and it shall be opened to you."

Everyone who asks receives, and he who seeks finds, and to him who knocks, it will be opened.

We must first ask to get our questions answered. Then we must seek how to handle our situation, and then we should physically take action and do what is necessary to move forward.

We should attempt to find, obtain and do by searching for or discovering means that will help us.

Do your best to try to acquire or gain the knowledge behind the hardship.

When you feel that the best choice is to sleep and wake up when all of the difficulty is over, it may be a good idea to relax and let the time do its magic, but it may also be the wrong thing to do. In hard times, you may need to wake up earlier than ever, work harder than ever and become more focused than at any other time. Then you will succeed not only at passing the trying times but passing them and becoming much more capable after them.

You may decide to reinvent the path to your dreams, or you may choose to stick with your current approach if the results are decent. Whatever you choose to do should come from deep contemplation on your future and the steps you should take today to realize your goals in the future.

They say that infinite intelligence gives the most challenging battles to the best soldiers, the ones who can win them, and that is you, my dear! The hardship is there for you to improve, grow and reach a better version of yourself, and you can do it!

See all suffering and hardships as stepping stones to a better you. There is nothing you have in your life that you cannot handle or overcome. Nothing! All was intended for you and should be seen in this light.

Questions Of The Day

To help you change your perspective on disappointments and become stronger than before, please ask yourself:

What can I learn today? Who can I speak to today? Which actions can I take to move me forward through these trying times? What can come from this disappointment that will make me and my life better in the future?

As usual, I recommend writing your answers in the PDF journal.

Affirmation Of The Day

After answering the questions in your journal, repeat this affirmation:

CHALLENGES ARE MY OPPORTUNITIES FOR LEARNING AND GROWTH. I CAN GET THROUGH ANY CHALLENGE BECAUSE I AM THE SOLDIER WHO WILL WIN THE BATTLE.

Repeat this affirmation often. With repetition, it has the power to alter your consciousness so you build a better, happier and more purposeful life.

DAY 82 - BECOMING AWARE OF THE POWER OF YOUR HARDSHIPS

"I have had dreams and I have had nightmares, but I have conquered my nightmares because of my dreams." ~ Jonas Salk

Every challenging situation or person you have encountered was perfectly aligned for you to become a better version of yourself, to reach your true potential, and to find your gifts that were always there within you. Once you discover these gifts, the trials in your life will help make you better so you can go ahead and make your life the blessing it was meant to be.

You are exactly where you need to be, even if it doesn't feel that way. There are stages in life that we must pass to reach our potential and our life path. The more we have to endure, the more potential we release if we bear the hardships and become stronger through our challenges.

Obstacles will always be in the way of our dreams. Jim Rohn said, "Don't wish it were easier, wish you were better."

Many people live mediocre lives. 72% of the population are middle class and poor. People give up on their dreams because it is hard to reach them. But who said that hard was bad? Someone made this up. Imagine how your life would look if you believed the opposite was true. That hard was a positive thing. That the harder it was, the larger the prize at the end. How would your life be different with this small change of perspective?

How much happier would you be if you were doing what was right for you? If you knew deep in your heart that you made the full effort to make this the best life for you?

Your dreams make you come out stronger from every downfall. Do not surrender to the difficulty. There will always be difficulty. The difficulty is part of the perfection. There is perfection in all of the imperfections.

Your dreams will pull you out of the hardships stronger than when you went into them.

If you become more powerful and more intelligent, you are one step closer to fulfilling your destiny. All you have to do is learn something from every challenge. Improve something about yourself. Increase your self-love and self-esteem. Become a better person. You see, difficulties and hardships that cross your path make you more relatable, authentic, empathetic, and better understanding of others in more profound ways. Your fears will have less control over you, and you will be more courageous to handle even harder things after overcoming hardships.

When you understand that all difficulties you meet in life only make you a better version of yourself and more able to overcome challenges with steadiness, faith, boldness, and inner hardiness, you will always live in gratitude, no matter what happens to you. You know that you are learning something new and conquering something within you that has held you back when confronting all that scares you. Confront all that you think you don't have within you to overcome because you do.

As I am writing these words to you, I am sitting with my ninety-nine-year-old grandmother in the hospital after breaking her thigh bone. One of my elder daughters has Coronavirus; one of my properties burned down yesterday because my renter left a candle lit in her bedroom which lit the curtains and burned the house. People owe me money but can't pay me because they have lost their jobs, while I also lost my health center and restaurants due to the Coronavirus.

But what do I do? I do the best I can every day to improve my situation. I make a plan and make sure it is still good the next day, and I put in the hours to improve my current situation. But most importantly, I do not complain. If there is one thing I learned from my grandmother, it is this. In the hospital, her roommate asked me how a person can live so long? I said that my grandmother never complains and likes to live even when it is not always easy. My grandmother did not have an easy life, but her attitude is what keeps her young, and I hope that she will overcome this fall as well.

At times life is hard, and at such times we have an opportunity to reinvent or improve ourselves where necessary. If you are aware, you will know what needs to be done. Hardships are a time for introspection. Hardships are there *for* you, not against you. Do not pity yourself. Instead, thank infinite intelligence that it has bigger plans for you. Prove that you are up to it. Just as the army will not send you to battle before practice and training, think of your hardships as your practice and training. These hardships are there to improve you and make you more resilient.

Hardships make you more humble and a better person and leader. Hardships are a time to break the chains of conformity and become the extraordinary person you were meant to be.

I have heard from many of my friends that it just wasn't meant to be if a relationship starts complicated and full of hardships. But on the other hand, my studies in Kabbalah, the profound lessons of the bible, taught me that precisely the opposite is true. If something is hard in the beginning, and the hardships are overcome through persistent effort and love, then you have found the right place to be. If things are too easy, then it is often not suitable for you because it will not move you towards change and progress, something that we all strive for throughout most of our lives.

Change your attitude to accept hardships with love and gratitude because they make you better than you ever dreamed you could be. They come to reveal your true powers to you.

Self-examination of any problem helps to change your perspective on it. It enables you to find the reasons behind the hardship. Then formalize a plan to get you out of your situation and follow through with it.

Questions Of The Day

To end this lesson and help you change your attitude regarding hardships in life, the questions that you want to ask yourself today are:

Where in my life am I stuck in being ordinary? Where am I suppressing the revelation of my true self because of fear and insecurity? Why am I in this situation?

When you overcome these difficulties and come out better than you were before, you are free.

As usual, I recommend writing your answers in the PDF journal.

Affirmation Of The Day

After answering the questions in your journal, repeat this affirmation:

I ACCEPT ALL THAT COMES TO ME WITH LOVE AND GRATITUDE, FOR EVERYTHING I ENDURE MAKES ME BETTER AND MORE CAPABLE.

Repeat this affirmation often. With repetition, it has the power to alter your consciousness so you build a better, happier and more purposeful life.

DAY 83 - BECOMING AWARE OF YOUR RESOURCES

"Fear and anxiety many times indicates that we are moving in a positive direction, out of the safe confines of our comfort zone, and in the direction of our true purpose."

~Charles F. Glassman

We must become more resourceful in times of stress, hardship, worry, anxiety, and fear.

When we train our "resourcefulness muscle", it will help us in every field. Being resourceful will help you find more creative ways to achieve your goals if one route fails. If you are not used to using your resourcefulness muscle, you may be misled to believe you do not have the resources you need to succeed.

When we are placed in a situation where we have no other alternative, suddenly we see how resourceful we can be. Life or death situations certainly bring this out of us, but not only these extreme circumstances can help us become more resourceful. My doctoral research study into the ideal diet for humans has proven to me many times that being resourceful is a trait that is part of our DNA and has allowed our species to survive and thrive for so many millennia.

We can all be resourceful when we need to be. We just need to come out of our comfort zone. It is much easier to blame the government or anybody else apart from ourselves and not be resourceful, but what do we gain from doing this? The answer, we all know, is nothing at all. When we choose to become resourceful, take action, and change our situation, we grow, improve, and become better.

Even if you are not to blame for your situation, it is your responsibility to get you out of it. For example, I could have blamed the government or the Coronavirus or other more creative things for the closing of my businesses. Instead, I took responsibility and became resourceful, and took action. I recycled one of my mortgages to get the money to pay back my debts plus a little extra. I then decided to move back to the big city to open a clinic in one room of my house while bringing in more clients. I talked to people about my business and advertised it on the radio and social media. This succeeded, and my business in its new location immediately thrived thanks to resourcefulness. Tony Robbins says that our only limitation is in how resourceful we are. And I am telling you that we are all resourceful; we just have to agree to move out of our comfort zone and let our resourcefulness take off, leading us to a better, happier, and healthier life.

Questions Of The Day

To end this lesson and help you become more resourceful, ask yourself:

In which areas do I feel fear and anxiety? What tools do I need to come out of my situation? Which innovative, creative, and out-of-the-box, yet legal ways can I get the resources I need right now? Which steps can I take to transform my situation into a better one for me in the long run? As usual, I recommend writing your answers in the PDF journal.

Affirmation Of The Day

After answering the questions in your journal, repeat this affirmation to yourself:

I AM HIGHLY RESOURCEFUL AND ALWAYS KNOW WHERE TO FIND HELP AND THE TOOLS I NEED.

Repeat this affirmation often. With repetition, it has the power to alter your consciousness so you build a better, happier and more purposeful life.

DAY 84 - BECOMING AWARE OF ANGER

"Holding onto anger is like grasping a hot coal with the intent of throwing it at someone else; you are the one who gets burned." ~ Buddha

Yoda, from Star Wars, put it best when he said, "Fear leads to anger. Anger leads to hate. Hate leads to suffering." This is such a profound understanding. All negative emotions we hold will lead us to suffer.

To be angry is not our natural state. Think of how much addiction, health issues, and misery would be spared from the world if more people understood that they could be free from their anger.

There are many examples of negative emotions, but when you sum them up, most of them come down to one specific negative emotion: anger, directed inward or outward. Anger directed outward takes the form of jealousy, disgust, annoyance, and hatred. Anger directed inward takes the form of guilt feelings, depression, or sadness. These are just a few examples.

Anger is not a good feeling; even though, at times, it can move us to action. There are better ways to push ourselves to action than through anger. Anger is a destructive negative emotion. We function poorly when we are angry. All of our organs become stressed, and disease states often result from a chronic condition of anger. Even our ability to think is impaired. We do not communicate well, and we do not treat people as they should be treated when we are angry. We have trouble sleeping, and when we do sleep, we clench our teeth and do not sleep peacefully.

Anger affects our bodies so much because it comes from within us. Anger causes the body to release adrenaline, and heart rate and blood pressure rise and energy goes to muscles and the brain, Your senses become more acute..Anger never comes from outside of us. Any situation outside of us is not the cause of our anger. We are the cause of our anger. Anger comes from *perceived* threats. This perception is something that we hold inside us. The threat is perceived. It is an illusion within us that leads us to this destructive emotion.

Since anger is not a natural feeling for us, we *can* remove it from our lives. There are two things that we must do to stop the emotion of anger from arising within us.

The first step we need to take to remove anger is to stop justifying it. When we are mad and believe we have a good enough reason to be angry, we justify our behavior. If we cannot convince ourselves or others that we have the right and deserve to behave in this way, then anger will have no place in our lives.

The second step is to stop identifying ourselves with the situation that made us angry and stop taking it personally. When we don't take something personally, it will not affect us.

A big disaster can happen and not affect us in any way when we do not identify with it. On the other hand, someone who cuts us off on the street can make us angry for a whole day when we take it personally and when we justify our anger. People who protest about something that made them angry are identifying with the problem.

Once we justify being angry and take the situation personally, then we will be angry. With the example of the car cutting us on the street, we justify that the driver must have been an idiot; they don't know how to drive, so we have the right to get angry. Then we identify with the situation by thinking that they must have seen us on the street and did it on purpose, so we take their behavior personally.

But if we choose that we never have a right to get angry and that nothing done by another person has to do with us personally, then we become free of anger. This is the basis of peace of mind.

Even in a relationship, if your partner says something to you and you feel that you have the right to get angry, then you will dwell in anger. But you can change your perspective. Instead tell yourself that it's best never to justify getting angry. Perhaps your spouse behaved like this because they had a bad day at work or were hungry or tired. When you stop justifying your reason for getting angry, you will not get angry. This will spare you a lot of suffering and ensure that you are healthier for longer and have peace of mind, an essential component of a favorable and prosperous life. You can say that you feel that you were wronged, but say it assertively and not with anger, which will immediately turn the other person against you in defense of themselves.

Keep in mind that you cannot be angry at anything that you cannot justify in your mind or identify with. You will stop justifying and identifying with a situation when you stop blaming other people or things for the conditions in your life. Stopping the blame is the easiest way to hold anger in its tracks. This does take some practice and a lot of awareness, but with time, you will be able to notice your reactions and the blame when it is happening in real-time, and you can stop them before they get out of control.

So how do you stop blaming others? By taking responsibility for whatever happens to you.

I have mentioned previously that you can only entertain one thought in your mind at a time. Instead of holding an assumption of blame (that someone or something is to blame for your situation), change your thought to one of "I am in charge."

When you are feeling in charge, and in control, it is practically impossible for negative emotions to grow in your mind. When you take full responsibility, and feel in control, most negative feelings tend to disappear from your life.

In that moment of anger, right before you burst out, stop if you can and say to yourself, "I am in charge." This can prevent the explosion from happening. As with anything, the more you practice saying this right before an outburst, the better at it you will become. It will become second nature for you.

You *are* in charge of your emotions. When you justify them, identify with the situation, and blame others for the problem, you will have negative feelings. Still, when you feel in charge and take responsibility for yourself, you can remove anger from your life.

Smiling more often can also help, but it is not enough. There is mental work to be done to get rid of negative emotions.

As we grow older, we collect more negative emotions and more and more reasons to be angry. We carry these reasons for being angry with us wherever we go. But we will never fully control our destiny if we keep holding onto these negative emotions and the reasons that we justify getting angry.

It is as if we are holding a massive stone on our shoulders. Can you imagine how difficult it is to go through life holding such a stone on your shoulders and taking it with you wherever you go? We must release our anger and the thoughts that justify our anger, and we *can* do it.

Our ego will interfere with this initially and will not want us to remove anger from our lives. But when we do replace angry and blaming thoughts with positive thoughts that we are in charge and responsible, we will become free from the chains of anger and slowly become more in control, which will make us happier and fulfilled.

The third step we need to take to remove anger is to understand that we are not in control of everything. Understanding that if something happens to you that you have no control over, getting angry about it is useless. Acceptance is the only way to peace of mind. Of course, if you can do something, then definitely do your best, but acceptance is a must when there is nothing to do. Although moving from emotional to logical thinking is not easy, maintaining a balance between these two minds, as we mentioned before, is crucial for lasting peace of mind and overcoming feelings of anger.

The fourth step we need to take to remove anger is to believe that not all that appears to be bad is bad. Try to pause your reaction for a moment during the annoying situation. Contemplate that all is good and right and even perfect to bring you to a higher level of awareness. Take what you can from the situation and immediately turn the situation from a negative one to a positive one of growth, self-achievement, and love.

The fifth step we need to take to remove anger is to try and anticipate it beforehand and then handle it before the event happens. For example, suppose you are late for work, and someone is driving very slowly in front of you on a one-lane street. You can control yourself better by talking to yourself out loud about the situation, and the consequences of being late, as well as the consequences of being stressed. Then once you get to work, you will be in more awareness and can handle the consequences better. You can also anticipate the situation that can make you angry and prevent it from happening. For example instead of getting angry for being late almost every day, set an alarm clock for 10 minutes earlier than previously so that you won't be late in the future.

Questions Of The Day

To end this lesson and help you stop anger or overcome it, ask yourself:

In which field of my life or with whom do I find myself getting angry often? How am I justifying getting angry? How can I change my perception and see that I do not need to personally take other people's behavior?

Remember that no one is to blame for your anger. You have the full capacity to remove anger and bitterness from your life entirely through focused practiced action. Think about how removing anger could improve your life, your career, and your relationships. Now ask: how can I get angry by such trivial events?

As usual, I recommend writing your answers in the PDF journal.

Affirmation Of The Day

After answering the questions in your journal, repeat this affirmation to yourself as you think and dwell upon it:

I AM IN CHARGE. I AM RESPONSIBLE FOR MY STATE OF MIND AND MY FEELINGS, ALWAYS.

Repeat this affirmation often. With repetition, it has the power to alter your consciousness so you build a better, happier and more purposeful life.

DAY 85 - BECOMING AWARE OF DEATH AND ETERNITY

"There is a magical dream that fills the gap between birth and death; we call it life."

~ Debasish Mridha

Every day that we have in our physical form is a privilege because it was given to us.

So, what are you going to do with this day?

Don't postpone your mission and the revelation of your gifts for another time. Start today if you haven't already done so. Show your brilliance.

Also, never delay a show of love to those who are important in your life.

Would you be doing what you are currently doing if you now remembered that your time was limited? Would you waste your days fighting with those close to you, or would you show them love and respect?

But what if your days weren't limited? What if you considered your soul to be eternal? Would you do what you are currently doing if you knew that your soul would live eternally? Would you behave in the same way with other people who are also immortal souls? Would you make the same choices, or would your choices be more sustainable?

We all have the dimension of the finite with our physical bodies that will die someday, and the dimension of infinite with our souls that are eternal. Therefore, you want to make sure your choices are good for the future as well as the present. You want to make sure that you do take risks and take actions to ensure that you use this lifetime in a way that pushes the human race forwards.

If you look at your life from this broader perspective, how would you live differently? Would you stay in your current line of work? In your job? In your environment and home? In your current relationship? What would you do if you knew your time was limited, yet also unlimited?

You only have a few more summers to live in your current physical form. Maybe eighty, maybe twenty, or only perhaps five more summers. We do not know. However many, they are always limited in your physical form.

Therefore, it is just as necessary to care for your health so that you can have more days alive, full of energy, in absolute freedom, to care for your soul's desire for meaning and connection with consciousness.

Put your energy into your life's purpose. Share your gifts with the world today, not tomorrow. This way, you ensure your days alive will have been worthwhile and will leave a positive dent in the world.

But since the soul is eternal, ask yourself if it will be proud of your actions and choices today.

Put your energy into your family and friends, and those close to you, and those whom you love. Don't delay telling everyone you love how you feel about them and what value they bring to your life. Do this every day so that you will never regret not telling this enough.

Spend your days wisely on worthy causes and with worthy people.

Also, enjoy your days. It is just a decision to enjoy rather than to suffer through life. Accept what can't be changed and change what can and needs to be changed.

Don't put off enjoyment. Don't wait for the perfect partner, for wealth, or for things to happen to start enjoying your life. Most of the most enjoyable things in life are free if you are free in mind to enjoy them.

You were given the gift of life, so today, do what you can and do what you feel the urge to do. Of course, you should never harm others in the pursuit of your joy. When you harm another, you also harm yourself in another dimension. We are all interconnected and in this together.

When taking any risks, use common sense but constantly keep in the back of your mind that you were given this opportunity, so make the most of it. Please don't waste it.

You have all you need and all it takes to make your life truly magical. Put in the effort where it will bring you the most joy. Let the things that make you happy be your guiding light as to where you should focus.

With this line of personal conduct, you will ensure that you make the most of your life. Leave all excuses behind.

Be productive, creative, loving, and giving today. Don't wait for tomorrow. Leave fear, anger, guilt feelings, and frustration aside.

Yes, these are a part of life. Still, as we spoke in previous lessons, these hardships, disappointments, difficulties, and frustrations are there to help you see your strength, perceive your power, and help move towards the progress you desire if you have the right attitude. Difficulty is part of everyone's life. Without difficulty, we would not appreciate what good we also have in our lives.

Steve Jobs, the co-founder of Apple, said that the single best invention of life was death. He said, "No one wants to die. Even people who want to go to heaven don't want to die to get there. And yet, death is the destination we all share. No one has ever escaped it. It's life's change agent."

We all share this fate in the physical dimension, so we should make the most out of every minute of our stay while still acknowledging that our decisions and choices will last for eternity and impact the future of life on earth, so we should make wise choices.

Do what you want to do, what comes from your heart and soul. Your heart knows best for you. Put in the effort, do what you can, and know that it will always be enough when you do your best.

The world-renown speaker, Les Brown, said, "The graveyard is the richest place on earth because it is here that you will find all the hopes and dreams that were never fulfilled, the books that were never written, the songs that were never sung, the inventions that were never shared, the cures that were never discovered, all because someone was too afraid to take that first step, too afraid to keep with the problem, or not determined enough to carry out their dream."

Don't miss making the most out the life you were given, just as you wouldn't miss making the most of your vacation time. Allow life to touch you. Absorb all that life has to offer and give back as much as you can to leave a legacy worthwhile for future generations and incarnations.

Leave the world a little bit better than you got it when you arrived. This is your contribution to human evolution and your legacy.

Acknowledging death of the physical realm should not come from fear but rather as a push to succeed at doing the best and most you can do now. When you live your best, and maximize your potential, you will not fear death.

If you are coping with the death of a loved one, this is a challenging situation indeed. Apart from the emptiness, the lack that you feel, and the loneliness, another reason why this situation is taken so hard is that you were not ready for it and consider it final.

But what if it isn't?

What if everything is going perfectly according to a karmic plan for the lost one's soul and your soul as well?

What if they came here to do exactly as they did and in their departure, the way that it was chosen was perfectly planned to move all those close to them to specific action or change following their loss?

What if this was like a barter that you had planned between you before you came to this world for the benefit of both of your souls? Would it be bad to believe something like this?

My mother is suffering from Alzheimer's disease, and being open to this perspective, that we "planned" this together to heal our souls made all the difference for all of us.

What if you knew that all is perfect just as it is, even if it does not seem so in our limited perspective. Would you not live better, more happily, more at peace? Is this not always your choice? You can't change what can't be changed, but you can change your perspective no matter how difficult it may seem.

What if you knew that you cannot ever lose anyone? That your souls are intertwined for eternity?

If you connect to your true divine nature, of consciousness and unity with all creations for eternity, how would you experience all situations in life?

You would most often see them as planned gifts that your soul needs and even requested to move you to a better life and help evolution because the progress of one means progress for all.

Questions Of The Day

To end this lesson and help you live life to the fullest while you are here and leave the most and best you can for the future, ask yourself:

Am I living my life in a worthwhile manner? If I knew I'd soon die, would I be doing the same things? Would I spend my time with the people I am currently in contact with? Or would I do things differently? If I knew that my soul is here forever, would I still make the same choices? If I knew that all was pre-planned by me for my benefit and those around me, would I still react the way I do to external circumstances?

Once you have your answers and are not happy in all fields, ask yourself, what would I be doing if I could do only the things that matter long term for me?

Now find a way to spend most of your waking hours focused on the things that matter. Be true to your soul and follow through with your soul's desire.

As usual, I recommend writing your answers in the PDF journal.

Affirmation Of The Day

After answering the questions in your journal, repeat this affirmation:

I KNOW THAT MY DAYS ARE NUMBERED, SO I AM DOING MY BEST, BEING MY BEST, AND LOVING MY BEST EVERY DAY.

Repeat this affirmation often. With repetition, it has the power to alter your consciousness so you build a better, happier and more purposeful life.

DAY 86 - BECOMING AWARE OF FORGIVENESS

"Lack of forgiveness causes almost all of our self-sabotaging behavior."

~ Mark Victor Hansen

———————⦿⦿⦿⦿———————

I find that this quote is equally correct for forgiveness as well as self-forgiveness. Both cause almost all self-sabotaging behavior.

When we did things in the past that we cannot forgive ourselves for, we form a victim mentality which is the worst it gets for our self-esteem. A victim mentality leads to a lot of suffering. The first step to stopping this suffering is to learn to eventually forgive ourselves for anything that we feel we may have done wrong or bad.

We deserve this forgiveness since, more often than not, we are hardest on ourselves. While others may have long forgotten or forgiven us for our behaviors, we may still find it hard to forgive ourselves for past behaviors and move on with our lives. It does us no good to keep treating ourselves in a harmful way because of something we did or failed to do in the past. In effect, when we do not forgive ourselves, we are punishing ourselves repeatedly for that one mistake we made. This is not even done in the criminal justice system. There you are tried for your mistake only once and given one penalty. But when we hold a victim mentality, we are punishing ourselves for the same mistake over and over.

We need to forgive ourselves for anything that was not as we or others think it should have been.

Even if you did do something that is not acceptable by society, if you understand that your actions were wrongful and should not have been done, you must forgive yourself and move on as best you can.

Sometimes an unwanted result happens in our life. We may have taken responsibility for it out of the belief that we supposedly could have predicted the outcome or by thinking if only we would have acted differently, the result would have been different. We cannot truly know what would have happened if we had done things differently. We have to deal with the present reality, not what could have happened.

In all these situations, we forget the simple truth: we are always doing our best from the wisdom and awareness that we have at that moment. From my personal experience and listening to countless people in my clinic, although life doesn't always bring us what we desire, life always brings us what we need.

I have made many mistakes. I married my first cousin because I was scared of rejection and being left alone and wanted security. Even though I did love him, it was certainly not a wise decision. The result of our marriage was the birth of our two mentally challenged daughters. I carried the blame on my shoulders for many years and held a victim mentality that caused me so much suffering. In effect, I felt that I ruined my daughters' chances for a good life even before they were born. But with time, I forgave myself for my bad decisions and understood that if my daughters came to this world, they were meant to come, and I am happy that they came to me. I have become a great mother to them, and from them I have learned the true meaning of unconditional love. So, maybe the result was not as I desired or expected, but the result has made me who I am today and brought me to the place where I am today; a peaceful place for me mentally, emotionally, physically, and spiritually. My daughters are also truly very happy, which is something that many people cannot comprehend due to their situation, but is true nonetheless. Isn't this all what we desire?

After we forgive ourselves, we can forgive others for any wrongdoing we feel they did to us. This is a very spiritually powerful place to be. This is awareness. Forgiveness allows you, the forgiver, to be free from the negative feelings you may be carrying on your shoulders, such as anger, hatred, disappointment, and frustration.

Human behavior research points out that every person does their best with the wisdom and awareness available to them at any given moment. So when someone does anything that hurts you, you must remember that their behavior was not necessarily from a place of hurting you, but rather from a place of supporting themselves in some way. We can only cause harm to others and ourselves when there is no awareness.

When someone hurts you, it is only because you believe that they were not supposed to behave the way they did. If you wouldn't hold this belief and be more aware that a person's behavior has nothing to do with you but rather with their own inner dialogue, you wouldn't be hurt by their behavior.

In a sense, nobody can mentally hurt you but you alone. Only your beliefs, expectations, or lack of awareness cause you to feel hurt and wounded by another person. Of course, your beliefs may be backed by socially acceptable behavior. Still, it is always your choice.

When the level of your awareness rises, you are ready to welcome a better life for yourself.

It is essential to state that when you forgive someone that wronged you, this does not justify their behavior in any way. Of course, you can still take action against their behavior if there is a need. But for your mental health, releasing the blame is crucial, which can only be done by authentic and deep forgiveness.

Questions Of The Day

To end this lesson and to help you forgive yourself and others, ask yourself:

In what areas of my life am I holding a grudge on myself for making a wrong decision?

And am I ready to forgive myself for this and move on in life? Remember that you have probably already paid your dues for this mistake, maybe even more than once, so it's time to move on.

The following questions to ask yourself are: Who do I feel have wronged me in the past that still make me feel bad when I think of them?

Am I ready to forgive them and release myself from this self-made prison?

As usual, I recommend writing your answers in the PDF journal.

Affirmation Of The Day

After answering the questions in your workbook, repeat this affirmation:

I ACKNOWLEDGE MY FAULTS AND FORGIVE MYSELF COMPLETELY FOR THEM. AND AS I FORGIVE MYSELF, IT BECOMES EASIER FOR ME TO FORGIVE OTHERS.

Repeat this affirmation often. With repetition, it has the power to alter your consciousness so you build a better, happier and more purposeful life.

DAY 87 - BECOMING AWARE OF PARENTING AND LEADERSHIP SKILLS

"The thing about parenting rules is there aren't any. That's what makes it so difficult."

~ Ewan McGregor

There is much to learn from today's lesson, even if you are not a parent. This lesson is all about becoming a leader. To be happy in life, you must be a leader. You must know the keys to leadership, and these are the same keys as the keys to proper parenting.

Since many of you are parents, and parenting takes a big chunk of your life, it is crucial to have the skills to raise your children well since this will impact all parts of your life.

There aren't any rules for parenting or leading, just for communicating.

I have learned so much from raising my four daughters. I have learned so much from them about myself and personally changed so much thanks to them. Raising children has never been easy thing for me. I have learned three crucial keys from my daughters that have made me happy and more successful in life.

1. Acceptance. The only way to raise a child to become the best they can be is to first accept them as an individual who is different from you. Your child is not a smaller version of you. You do not have control over them. You only have control over yourself. And when you control your thoughts and emotions, and when you consistently behave with integrity, self-love, and self-esteem, you will not only automatically accept their uniqueness, but you are an example for your child to learn to act in a way that is acceptable and good.

   Your children do not need to be like you, and they do not need to do things to please you. You do not want them to become people pleasers. This is very destructive behavior, as I mentioned before. You also do not want them to live without empathy. They can learn how to behave by following your example. Accepting them the way they are and loving them the way they are, as different from you, is the first step towards good parenting.

   If you love your children unconditionally, you accept them for who they are without trying to change them.

   Our children do not need fixing. We are the ones who need first to fix ourselves before we go and harm our child's self-esteem in a way that will follow them throughout their entire life. Of course, children will still need to learn and grow to become better versions of themselves. Still, learning and growth can only happen on a foundation of acceptance rather than changing them to become miniature versions of you forcefully.

   Of course, you do not have to suffer because of your child's behavior. If your children exhibit problematic behaviors harmful to you or others, you must help them understand the consequences of their actions. They will not have respect for you if you do not have respect for yourself. It's best not to accept problematic behaviors from your children that you would never accept from anyone else.

   Although you love your children unconditionally, you must have boundaries regarding what is acceptable for you. Kids will feel more secure when they have clear set boundaries. If you were seated on a chair, you would be much more likely to get off the chair and discover your surroundings if you had walls surrounding your chair rather than having your chair in a place with no walls around but just vast space around you. You feel more secure when you have boundaries. Children must know what is acceptable to you and what is not. They can often see this for themselves through your behaviors, but things are best stated in advance to prevent any negative emotions on either side.

The best way to follow through with disciplining your children is first and foremost to discipline yourself. Do not ask from your children to do things you don't ask from yourself. Work on your self-esteem. Be willing to treat your child the same way you would another adult whom you respect and love, who would behave in this way.

You may hold different points of view than your children, but if you show them understanding, and acceptance, rather than insulting them, then they will feel seen and heard. Imagine another adult that you admire behaving in such a way as your child behaves. How would you react to them?

Would you insult, chastise, or lecture the adult you admire if they behaved similarly to how your child behaves?

Probably not.

2. Effective communication. There are many ways in which you may communicate with your children. Some of these ways may be harmful to their self-esteem, the foundation for enjoying a good life. For this reason, communicating must be a conscious and aware process.

   Communication starts by listening to what your children are saying while also acknowledging their thoughts and feelings. After improving your listening skills which we covered on a previous day, you also want to know how to talk with your child effectively. When they do something that is not to your liking, the best approach is to DESCRIBE what they did, then to DESCRIBE how this makes you or anyone involved feel about their action, and lastly to DESCRIBE what they need to do, if anything.

   Describing is the keyword for effective communication. Make the shift from blame, insulting, chastising, or lecturing, towards a show of understanding and acceptance by describing the situation, your feelings, and what needs to be done. Then they will feel seen and heard.

   If you show respect to your children through courtesy and listening and acknowledging their feelings and thoughts, then they will be more respectful to you, to themselves, and others.

   Now, what about praise? Well, there is appropriate praise and praise that is not helpful or even confusing. Appropriate praise states what exactly we like and appreciate in children's actions. We describe what the children have accomplished and explain why it is considered good by you. Children then feel recognized and understands what was good about their behavior. This type of praise increases their self-esteem.

   But when praise is vague, like you are a good boy, they will feel confused and feel a sense of loss of control. They do not understand why they are praised, and instead of increasing their self-esteem, this type of praise just eats away at it.

3. Surrender! And this was the hardest for me to learn. The ego should not be allowed to enter the equation of parenthood. For good parenting, you must leave the ego out. Power struggles are not a part of good parenting. You did not receive children to become their boss, but rather bring a unique being into the world. Your children are also not a reflection of you. They are their own individual beings, and you cannot change who they are. Through

effective communication (listening, describing, and being your best version), you can lead them to a good place.

They are not your toys. They are unique beings that need the freedom to go out and find their purpose and gifts in life. Surrendering what you think is suitable for your children and accepting and supporting them for who they are is the only way to allow them to grow into the best version of themselves. You cannot force your will on your children without having a very negative effect on their emotional state.

Of course, you may not be delighted with every act of self-expression. There may not be agreement on everything, but acceptance allows self-esteem to develop. Stop fighting with your children. Let go of your expectations of how they should behave and how they should be.

Let go of your fantasies for your children.

When I realized that my eldest daughter would never be like other children, my fantasy of having a happy, typical family just flew out the window. It was as if my child died that day for me. None of my dreams for her could come true. But when I released my attachment to my expectation of how my life and her life should look like and what it should be, I became free, and I also freed my eldest and then later my second daughter to be who they are. This was a very liberating moment.

You can never change other people, and it is not your responsibility as a parent to make your children happy. It is not your job as a parent to make your children the way you think they should be because this is how society or the neighbors think it should be. Your children are here to experience and engage in life, and all that life provides uniquely.

And this also includes hardships.

You cannot and should not remove all hardships from their life.

In retrospect, some of the most incredible things that happened to me in my life came from my hardships. They made me who I am. I learned to overcome problems and improve my character because I had no choice. It was through the hardships that made me become a greater and better version of myself.

Children need to experience difficulties, and if we as parents take away these opportunities from our children, then we are not good parents. I know that this may be controversial wisdom, but this is true. I allow my daughters to experience the consequences of their choices. I definitely give them my opinion, and warn them of the consequences before they do something they may regret, but I also provide them with the freedom to make their own choices once they have all of the details. We can never really control another person, we can only educate, and support with physical means and emotionally, giving our children the best foundation to make the right decisions for themselves.

I am also open with them about all sides of my life: the hardships and the good times. This way they see that they are not alone with their experiences, and that other people go through similar situations.

And when *they* have difficulties, they must learn to deal with them. They must also learn to accept *no* as an answer at times, not only from us as parents, but from others as well. I am there to support them but not to remove their hardships from them. For example, I brought my daughters to the hospital to see their grandmother on her death bed. I also say no to them when there are other responsibilities we must do.

By allowing them to deal with hardships, they learn the lessons from these hardships, and you are allowing them to become better, more compassionate people.

Hardships are real, and they point out our attachments, which we learn to release through our hardships. Releasing attachment to results is one of the greatest lessons of life.

Our attachment to results and our expectations always lead to our suffering. When we release what we think a result should be and surrender to what is, we gain the skills to go through life in a better, more fulfilling way, no matter what life throws at us. This is a fundamental lesson for your children. When you allow your child to go through the struggles of life, you prevent them from continuing to suffer for the rest of their lives. When you learn to give up control but still do your best, what will come is what needs to come.

Moreover, when you give your children the freedom to experiment, they know you trust them, so they try to live up to your trust.

Parenting is physically and financially hard for many people, but emotionally, it is hard when we make it hard. We make it hard by trying to teach all we have learned through our lifetime, and through hardships to a child who may not be ready. We make it hard by resisting that our child is a person different and separate from us. We make it hard by seeking power and control over our children. But power and control over our children may only mask our true feelings of unworthiness, and this is not ideal for any of the sides.

If you set aside all the reasons you had children, and understand that having children does not give you power over them, but it is a relationship to help you and them learn about life from a different perspective, with someone different from you so that you learn to accept other people with unconditional love while learning to surrender what you are not in power to control.

From parenting, you have the opportunity to learn effective communication and listening skills and to learn how to release all attachments. This is what bringing up children is all about. It is a process of removing the ego and becoming a better version of yourself through the often difficult path of raising children.

Questions Of The Day

To end this lesson and help you become a better parent, leader, and communicator, ask yourself:

Where can I improve myself as a parent and leader? How can I become better at communicating? Can I describe my feelings and what I think my child is doing to understand their mistakes instead of blaming and chastising them?

How can I show more love? Can I release control and attachment to results?

As usual, I recommend writing your answers in the PDF journal.

Affirmation Of The Day

After answering the questions in your journal, repeat this affirmation:

I AM A GREAT PARENT. I LOVE AND ACCEPT MY CHILDREN UNCONDITIONALLY WHILE ALSO GIVING THEM BOUNDARIES THROUGH EFFECTIVE COMMUNICATION AND SURRENDER FROM THE RESULTS.

Repeat this affirmation often. With repetition, it has the power to alter your consciousness so you build a better, happier and more purposeful life.

DAY 88 - BECOMING AWARE OF THE IMPORTANCE OF LAUGHTER

"Trouble knocked at the door, but, hearing laughter, hurried away." ~ Benjamin Franklin

Laughing is one of the best things we can do for our health, both mentally and physically.

Laughing helps us cope with all of the craziness that we sometimes encounter in life. Laughing makes us feel better by releasing endorphins, just as we release after a good workout. Laughing helps reduce the pain threshold, lowers blood pressure, increases circulation, increases confidence and social bonding. Laughter is the best medicine.

And when we dare to laugh at ourselves, we show that we love and accept ourselves just the way we are. It shows that we are resilient and comfortable in our skin. It shows awareness of our shortcomings which is the only way to start change and self-improvement.

When you have the courage to laugh at yourself and your mistakes, no one else can make a fool of you because you are aware of your actions and your mistakes.

Laughing at yourself shows humility, a paramount virtue.

I live my life simply, do not drink alcohol, or eat meat. Some people think I am missing out. But in fact, I enjoy my life so much because of the many opportunities I find to laugh. Although I am serious about my work, when I go out with friends, I do not need anything but a great deep conversation and a good laugh. A girlfriend and I go to the park with our children. While they play, we sit on the bench and spend hours just laughing, mostly at ourselves and our needs and sometimes at our kids' behaviors. This is one of the greatest entertainments for me.

Nothing could be better for anyone, no matter their condition or situation, than to have a good laugh.

Life is not always easy. Choose to see the funny side of the circumstances and problems. This will help you form a positive attitude about life and to go through life more enjoyably. If we honestly examine our lives with awareness, we can see how ridiculous most of our actions are.

If you do not have any friends that elicit laughter in you, you can go online and watch hilarious videos.

We all know that no one is perfect, and if you can find the courage to laugh at your shortcomings, this shows a real strength of character.

I know it is not easy, especially when going through something difficult in life. But if you do, the benefits to your mental and physical health will be immense. Laughing at your situation shows that you are becoming more aware, and the more aware you are, the more enjoyable and peaceful life will be.

Laughing boosts the immune system and also helps you relax, and it is great for relationships. Because when you laugh with someone, this leads to closer bonding and more intimacy.

Laughter is the best investment you can make for every field of your life because it is free, fun, and creates intimacy. Laughter even helps you with your finances because it builds good relationships with people. Laughter also helps in personal relationships because it is easier to laugh at a problem that to fight over it. And laughter helps with your health. It can even help you achieve your goals by recognizing how funny your behaviors are at times and how they can lead you in the wrong direction.

Laughter helps you put things into perspective. And when you choose to laugh at yourself with someone close to you, it enables you to forget your troubles and move on more quickly. This is why Patch Adams, the clown doctor, was so successful, and to this day, we still have clowns in hospital wards following his vision of the importance of laughter for healing. Laughing helps heal the body and soul.

Even Barack Obama said that you should never take yourself too seriously.

So today, go out and have fun the simple way, with pure laughter. Either with a close friend or a family member or by watching some funny videos or a comedy movie.

Questions Of The Day

To end this lesson and help you increase the amount of laughter in your life, please ask yourself:

Where do I know I have done something absurd in my life, and can I find the courage to laugh at myself about it? Can I find something in my current situation to laugh about?

Can I become more aware of what pushes me to action and see that it may be funny?

As usual, I recommend writing your answers in the PDF journal.

Affirmation Of The Day

After answering the questions in your journal, repeat this affirmation:

LAUGHTER AND HAPPINESS COME EFFORTLESSLY AND NATURALLY TO ME, AND EVERY TIME I LAUGH OR SMILE, I CREATE POSITIVE HEALING ENERGY FOR MYSELF AND THOSE WHO LAUGH WITH ME.

Repeat this affirmation often. With repetition, it has the power to alter your consciousness so you build a better, happier and more purposeful life.

DAY 89 - BECOMING AWARE OF TIME

"Lack of direction, not lack of time, is the problem. We all have twenty-four hour days."

~ Zig Ziglar

This quote is about how well we manage our time and control our workload.

Today we have the option to take our work everywhere we go thanks to smartphones and technology. To take a break and ensure some work-life balance is achieved, we need to decide when not to work. We have to choose whether to spend time with our children, family, friends or work even when we are at home.

These choices are great to have, and we are indeed a fortunate generation to have such options available to us, but most people don't make a conscious decision about what is right and when it is right for them.

We often go after the easiest choice. But everything is a tradeoff. Whatever you choose is your responsibility. This places a lot of stress on everyday decisions. Primarily since everything we do is judged by other people. There is an intense pressure to succeed and to do what is right.

It is up to you to make the right choices for yourself and your time. Don't let other people choose your options for you. Make your own choices from your own internal wisdom.

Make the right personal management choices. Choose to put your phone on flight mode during your most creative moments of the day. Turn off phone notifications or have them silenced.

By managing your creative time, you will manage all other aspects of your life much more efficiently. Use the first two hours after waking for sport, breakfast, getting the kids ready for school, travel to work, and thinking and making plans. Then use the next two to three hours on the job for your most creative jobs. Use your creative time to work on your most important projects. Then eat lunch, nap if you need, and do other things that still need to be cared for. After work, you have plenty of time for your children, free time to be with them and listen to them and read books or play games with them. You also have time for friends, family, and hobbies after this. If you are working 9:00am-5:00pm in an uncreative job, I recommend waking at 5 in the morning, exercising if your job does not involve physical work, and then doing some creative work to forward your goals before caring for the needs of your children before school and before getting to work.

All you need to do is do the right things at the right time of day, and you will see how productive you can be in much less time than you think while also caring for your health and spending time with family and friends.

You can have it all if you manage your time well. Arnold Schwarzenegger said, if you need more than six hours of sleep, just sleep faster. I personally think that we *can* sleep more than six hours and still have sufficient time for everything we need if we follow the natural rhythm of our bodies through a carefully structured plan.

Instead of choosing what is easy to do, decide to do what is right to do at the moment, even if it is not easy. Thema Davis, the once American Psychological Association representative to the United Nations, explains, "Say no to distraction so you can say yes to your destiny."

It would be best if you focused on achieving your goals, and in today's world, this is not easy to do. The phone is constantly ringing, not always from people you know or want in your life. There is constant ringing noise from notifications from our phones and computers. There are family responsibilities, and the body sends signals of hunger, so you need to stop and eat, and there are constantly things you need to take care of. It is not easy to maintain focus in such away.

So how can you place focus on achieving your goals with so many distractions? You have to control the distractions in your life and take control of your schedule so that you have the time to do the productive work in your most productive hours.

We often spend our day overeating, drinking too much, shopping too much, socializing too much, and then sleeping too much at night or even during the day.

We try to multitask with many things, but we end up doing much less than an ideal job at anything. We can't be focused when we are doing more than one thing at a time. And when we multitask, we usually lose focus on one or all of the things that we were trying to do simultaneously.

You can't talk to everybody, accept all calls as they come, and always be available for anyone and stay productive. You must learn to say no and to focus on your primary goals.

When we don't achieve our goals, we blame others or other external factors for our situation, but it is often our fault. *We* gave in to the distractions. And often, we not only allow distractions to enter our lives, we actually search for them in a desire to run away from our fears and our what-ifs. We are just as afraid to succeed as we are to fail.

Most often, whenever you genuinely have a good idea that you know you can follow through with, and when you start to work on your vision, fear enters your mind. Then you seek some form of distraction so that you don't have to follow through with what you intended to do. The result is failure or no improvement. You stay in the same place and allow your fears to rule over you. You become bored and boring. You lose the vitality, curiosity, and enthusiasm that you had for life.

You cannot be happy when you dim your light. You cannot be satisfied when you willingly choose distractions over productivity.

We all need time for introspection to reach our greatness and to ensure that we are sticking to the right path for us. When you spend a few productive hours a day on distractions instead of focusing on your goals, you will not fulfill your destiny, you will not enjoy life, and you will not have progress.

When I was addicted to food and suffered from bulimia, this took up all of my free time. It was my distraction before the smartphone era. I wanted to distract myself so that I wouldn't have to cope with life and I wouldn't have to show my gifts to the world. I never felt good or worthy enough to be all I could be. I did not believe I deserved to reach my full potential.

As Marianne Williamson said, "Our deepest fear is not that we are inadequate. Our deepest fear is that we are powerful beyond measure. It is our light, not our darkness, that most frightens us."

This is so perfectly stated. When we start to achieve things and move forwards in the right direction for us, fear seems to creep in, and then we search for distractions to halt our progression, which scares us. It is scary to come out of your comfort zone and do things you never did before.

We must become bigger to allow bigger things to enter our lives, and the way to become bigger is through focused, productive time without distractions.

If we don't do what is necessary to block out distractions, we will never reach anything great. We will become more and more unhappy with our lives and conform like almost everyone else.

We are all unique, and we all have greatness within us in some form. But if we, like many others, choose not to follow the path of bringing our gifts to the world out of fear, we will be left with unhappiness and frustration.

Chuck Palahniuk said, "People don't want their lives fixed. Nobody wants their problems solved. Their dramas. Their distractions. Their stories resolved, and their messes cleaned up. Because what would they have left? Just the big scary unknown."

We are all afraid of the unknown. This is built into our nature as it helped us to survive in the wild. But today, fear of the unknown is something that hinders our growth, hides our talents, and surpasses our abilities and our progress. We must actually fear the *fear* of the unknown rather than fear the unknown.

There are also many emotional distractions. Anybody in a poor relationship will admit how much negative thoughts take of their time. Any bad relationship is a distraction. Any bad and negative feelings towards another person are distractions. Think of how long feelings of anger linger after an annoying event. Victimhood also lingers. How much of your time is spent thinking of how you should have or could have done things differently. Gossiping is also a distraction; focusing on another person's world instead of your world is a pure waste of time. It is not only a distraction, but it also affects your mood. All negative emotions are distractions.

When you become aware of these distractions throughout the day and how time-sucking they are and that your time is limited, you will learn to stop them. You can eliminate all physical and emotional distractions once they are noticed. The key is to catch them on time.

To ensure that you maximize your time, I suggest having a plan for the day and following it through. When you wake up at a set time every day, your health will benefit immensely. Go to sleep so that you will have enough time to rest and wake up at the same time daily.

It is crucial to work with a plan. It need not be strict, but you have to have a daily plan that works for you to make the most of your life.

If you do not know where your time is going, you will need to figure this out first. Just as I do with my health clients, I ask them to fill out a food journal of whatever they eat for three whole days so I can analyze it. If you do not know where your time is going, write a time journal of everything you do throughout the day for the next three days. Every half hour set the alarm and write down as a list what you are doing and what you did in the past thirty minutes. Then analyze your list and see where your time is going. At what times of the day are you wasting most of your time?

You will find this exercise very revealing! You may see how much of your time goes to waste consumed by distractions that you didn't control, such as phone calls, time spent on social media, or time spent watching television. Instead, take control of your time, and use it to move your life and your projects in the direction that will make your dreams a reality.

Ensure that other people are not in control of your time with their agendas. Make your own plan and stick with it. Put into your daily planner time for creative work as well as time for appointments. Make this creative work time sacred and put out your best during these hours of the day.

As I mentioned, it is also vital to put into your schedule time to care for obstacles that arise almost every day. Squeeze in one hour to take care of disruptions after creative time.

Taking control over your time will give you a sense of control over your life that will raise your self-esteem and make you even more productive and motivated for action.

Questions Of The Day

To end this lesson and help you take better control over your time, and remove distractions as much as possible from your life, ask yourself:

Am I in control of my time and my day? Do I have enough creative time, family and friend time, and enough self-time? Do I accept phone calls all day? Do I find myself in front of the television or on social media following other people's agendas every day instead of caring for my agendas?

If you are not in control of your time, start a time journal for the next three days to see when you are less focused and least productive. Create a plan for your time to work for you instead of working against you.

As usual, I recommend writing your answers in the PDF journal.

Affirmation Of The Day

After answering the questions in your journal, repeat this affirmation.

I APPRECIATE THAT TIME IS A VALUABLE ASSET, SO I MAKE WISE USE OF MY TIME.

Repeat this affirmation often. With repetition, it has the power to alter your consciousness so you build a better, happier and more purposeful life.

DAY 90 - BECOMING AWARE OF COMPETITION AND OBSESSION

"Competition whose motive is merely to compete, to drive some other fellow out, never carries very far. The competitor to be feared is one who never bothers about you at all, but goes on making his own business better all the time." ~ Henry Ford

Is competition a good thing? Depends on who you ask. Competition is only good when you are competing with a previous version of yourself. Otherwise, competition is a mindset not beneficial to you.

Doing things to be better than others is a motivator that doesn't hold sand long-term.

Competition is not what leads us to do our best. It's an internal drive to become better than we currently are. When you are in a competitive state, your creativity becomes suppressed. However, when you are doing something to improve yourself because of an internal drive to become better than you currently are, your imagination soars, leading you to much higher chances of success.

The mindset of competition is that only one person can win. However, there are many ways to win. There are many ways to gain from every situation. Competition means that there is only one winner and everyone else loses.

Only a winner mindset will ensure you overcome the difficulties you meet on the path towards your goals, not a mindset that you must be better than another. A mindset that focuses on what you can do to improve because you want to be better than *you* currently are because you want to be your best is a winner mindset which will lead to great success.

Competition is not a powerful enough motivator. Only a mindset of self-improvement and inner drive will and can last as a motivator in the long term to push you towards your goals in a way that can overcome the hardships you will inevitably encounter along the way.

Confucius said. "The will to win, the desire to succeed, the urge to reach your full potential … these are the keys that will unlock the door to personal excellence."

It is never about the competition. It is always about you. Making your goals a personal obsession that doesn't involve anyone but yourself is an excellent way to achieve them.

Obsession is a deep-seated, intense dedication to a purpose. A passion that is intensified. Obsession breeds curiosity, engagement, excitement, and a will to learn and focus on the obsessed object or subject.

Being obsessed with something is a powerful internal driver that will help you reach your goals faster. This is very different from focusing on your competition. An obsession with beating someone is less potent of a motivator because it is an external motivator when compared to being obsessed about becoming better than you currently are, which is an internal motivator.

People see obsessiveness as a negative characteristic, but when you look at the people who have achieved a lot in life, they will tell you that they were obsessed with what they were doing.

Having an interest in something is not enough to move you forward. There must be some form of internal motivation or obsession to succeed.

An obsession will naturally lead you to increase your level of competence in that area and to become better at it every day. It is a state that you are willing to do, try, learn and get anything that will help you move towards your goal. And when you maintain your integrity even though you have an obsession with something, you will reach great heights.

When you are improving yourself daily, and setting goals that you can physically reach, you slowly grow and become a person who can handle more internal stress. Internal stress is always there when you go after goals that need you to grow to achieve them. Although competition does provide internal stress, it is short-term, whereas obsession provides long-term internal stress.

Having a powerful internal motivation for something is definiteness of purpose that can move mountains, much more than competitiveness can, and usually, there will be some mountains on the way to your goals.

The most important thing about having this strong internal drive is that you remain loyal to your values as a person. You will not give up your values to pursue your goal no matter what. This cannot be said when competition is driving you.

There is no need to take risks to be better than your competitors. It would be best if you took risks to become the best you can be. If you take risks to be better than your competitors, there is more chance of making the wrong decisions.

The more informed and educated you are, the more self-awareness you have, and the higher your willingness to improve and persist with consistent effort. These are the factors that will help you succeed, whether or not there are any competitors.

You can learn from competitors in your field. You may not have all the answers, and there is much to learn from others, so long as you don't place all of your focus on becoming better than they are, but instead on slowly becoming better than you currently are and continuing to do this daily.

You may even want to co-operate with competitors to both of your advantages. This is how Bill Gates started. He found a way to work together with companies selling to his target audience, which made him hugely successful.

Have the satisfaction that you put in the effort to become the best that you are capable of being. Not that you put in the effort because you want to be better than anyone else. When you focus on the other, you may lose sight of yourself and what is important.

When you don't make the most of yourself, you do make others more comfortable in your presence because they know that you are no competition for them. But what is really important for you? That you make others feel comfortable, or that you make the most of yourself?

Focus on becoming the best you can be. Enjoy the process and do not focus on other people's achievements unless you learn from them. A competitive mindset means that someone will always lose, but this is never so because there are many things to gain from any situation, even if you don't come in first.

Furthermore, a competitive mindset is less enjoyable in the present moment, so it will be less of a motivating force to move you to success. Focus on becoming a better version of yourself without comparing yourself to others. Have you improved? This is the only competition your mind should be focused on. Be happy with what you are doing and do your best in all fields of life because you have one life to live right now, and you want to make it your best.

Questions Of The Day

To end this lesson and help you focus inwardly on your achievements and forget any competition, ask yourself:

Where am I focusing on things that are external to me? Am I focusing on my competitors rather than on my own self-improvement? Can I focus on my own self-improvement instead of what others are doing? Do I have an internal drive to succeed? Do I love the process and not only the result?

Now that you know in which areas of life you tend to focus externally, decide to focus inwardly on how you can improve yourself in these areas to become better.

As usual, I recommend writing your answers in the PDF journal.

Affirmation Of The Day

After answering the questions in your journal, repeat this affirmation:

SELF-IMPROVEMENT IS MY GREATEST MOTIVATOR.

Repeat this affirmation often. With repetition, it has the power to alter your consciousness so you build a better, happier and more purposeful life.

DAY 91 - BECOMING AWARE OF GRATITUDE

"This a wonderful day. I've never seen this one before." ~ Maya Angelou

This is an excellent quote about gratitude. It is about being happy for what comes and seeing what *is* as a blessing.

Living from a place of gratitude is a choice. You have an option to either see the cup half full or half empty. This is a conscious choice that you make every moment of your life. When you live in gratitude for what you *do* have, you will feel lucky, abundant, and joyful. When you see yourself through these eyes, you see yourself as fortunate. Repetition of your belief in your cup being full leads you to act differently on many different levels. You start to take different actions than previously. Your new set of actions will deliver different results and inspire you to believe that you are lucky on a deep level.

You will get more things that represent the same level of gratitude that you are feeling back to you through your changed attitude and different actions.

The more you choose to live in gratitude for what you DO have, the more your brain will get used to this line of thinking and the happier you will be overall. And the more abundance you will bring into your life through a different set of behaviors you have adopted due to feeling grateful.

The most influential people worldwide all understand that when you live from a place of gratitude, you will bring in more things to be grateful for in your life because you are repetitively doing the right things.

So how can you practice more gratitude?

You can choose to take all that comes to you that is not under your control and decide that it is good for you even if you do not know this to be true right now. When you believe that something can be good for you, you will search for the goodness in it, and you will usually find it, if not now, then indeed in the future.

A gratitude mindset understands that even what may seem to be bad today will have some benefit to you in the long run. With this frame of mind, you feel as though everything around you is there to support you on your path, including the hardships, as we mentioned before. You understand that nothing is a hindrance. All things that happen to or around you can have a beneficial meaning in your life somehow.

This is the frame of mind of gratitude. All that comes to you can be in your favor. You may not understand what this favor is quite yet, but you know that it exists, and you can figure it out later.

When you can live your life in this way, you live in the moment a happy and fulfilled life.

It is always a matter of choice.

You can live your life thinking, "Oh, why did this happen to me..." Or you can live your life thinking, "Oh, there is surely something good for me in this, and I will find it...."

The only thing that changed about the situation is the perspective on the situation, nothing else.

A perspective of gratitude will make you feel better about any situation, no matter how difficult it is. You will find something to appreciate, grow, or help others, no matter how difficult the situation may be.

It is all about where you choose to place your focus. If you focus on the half-full cup, you tackle any problem from having what you need and from a place of possibility and potential.

If you focus on the half-empty cup, you attempt to tackle the situation from lack, disability, loss, incompetence, or weakness.

From these two opposite frames of mind, which results do you think will be better for you?

Living life from gratitude will be more substantial, happy, and more fun for you. This frame of mind will reward you much since your behavior will follow this belief.

It is only your choice. You can change your mindset right now. Life is about how you feel because how you are feeling shows how connected you are to your true divine nature, which is the purpose of life. Gratitude will make you feel good.

Stop worrying about what you currently lack, and instead focus on the abundance that you *do* have. This may not be easy to do in certain extreme circumstances, but it is still possible, and if you ever want to get yourself out of this situation, it is actually a must.

By focusing on what you *do* have, you connect to your inner guidance system, which will undoubtedly show you how to get rid of all you *lack* in your life when you are open to it.

Of course, there are many difficult situations when it is hard to find what good there is. Still, when you start to focus on finding the good, this small gesture already helps you connect with your inner guidance system, which in time will free you from misery and connect you to endless bliss.

It is all about where you place your focus. Will you focus on the lack in your life or on what you *do* have available for you.

It is your choice.

The focus on being grateful for what you have opens many doors of opportunity that you can only tap into through connection with your inner guidance system. All you need is right there for you. But you can only see it when you focus on gratitude.

When you live from the gratitude of what you DO have instead of what you lack, you will suddenly see that you have a lot! Rejoice in what you do have!

This will also affect your health positively because positive feelings reduce inflammation in the body and allow you to function and sleep better. Gratitude also reduces feelings of pain and increases feelings of pleasure and self-esteem.

You also want to show your gratitude to others, not just to feel it within you. People's most profound need is to feel appreciated. The more appreciation you tend to show others, the more people will want to be around you. You will have more friends and a happier social life. Also, your one-on-one relationships will be better. Showing appreciation for others is essential. When you say, "thank you" and mean it, people will feel your gratitude.

You can say some kind words to people who have helped you. You can call or write a message of thanks to someone who has given their time and effort for you. Show your appreciation gladly. It doesn't take much effort or time, but it gives the other person such a good feeling, which is priceless.

The author John E. Southard said, "The only people with whom you should try to get even are those who have helped you."

Acknowledge that no one has ever made it alone. There are always other people who have helped. We are all born with specific gifts. We should show appreciation for these gifts, feel the joy of having these gifts, share these gifts with the world, and thank our parents for them.

Living from gratitude does not allow you to take things for granted.

Everyone who is born and is alive has something to be grateful for. Nobody has any excuse for this.

The most I have ever learned about gratitude is from my daughters. They were my best teachers in life. My second daughter, who is now twenty-two years old, is such a happy girl. She appreciates and enjoys everything in her life. Whatever she gets, she makes it fun and enjoys it. This is such a gift to live like this. All the people who come in contact with her love her because she is grateful for everything and shows all people her gratitude for what they provide for her. She lives her life happily all of the time, no matter what she goes through. The people around her live more happily, too, thanks to her joyful attitude. It's a win-win situation. I don't think she will ever understand what she has done for the people around her and me and how much I have learned and gained from her.

To increase your sense of gratitude throughout the day, focus on things that you are grateful for at set periods at least twice a day. The moment you wake up, snooze your wake-up alarm, and during this time, focus on what you have going for you. Do not allow negative thoughts to enter into this gratitude time. This is also the time when it is easiest to insert positive thoughts into your subconscious mind because the conscious mind is still half asleep and does not guard what goes into the subconscious mind as much as it does during the day. Think of all of the things you have to be grateful for during these few minutes, and this will make your days so much happier.

Then also, before sleep, take a moment of gratitude. List in your head, or better yet on paper, all that was good for you during the day and the things you have in life that support you.

It should take no more than two minutes, but this will shift your focus completely before the brain starts consolidating the information of the day at night and will allow you to live much happier overall.

Of course, you can feel gratitude at any time during the day, but it's easiest to remember and do this consistently as a habit during these two times each day when you have no distractions.

Questions Of The Day

To end this lesson and to help you appreciate the gifts of life, ask yourself.

What can I be happy about today? What are the gifts that I am thankful for, and what do I have in my life that makes me feel lucky and happy and appreciative? Is there any situation in my life that I can change my focus from seeing it negatively to finding even a slight benefit that I have in my life due to it? (usually, this will come many months or even years after the situation has passed when you can understand its benefit.

As usual, I recommend writing your answers in the PDF journal.

Affirmation Of The Day

After answering the questions in your journal, repeat this affirmation to yourself:

I AM LUCKY, AND I HAVE MUCH TO BE GRATEFUL FOR.

Repeat this affirmation often. With repetition, it has the power to alter your consciousness so you build a better, happier and more purposeful life.

DAY 92 - BECOMING AWARE OF LUCK

"Being deeply learned and skilled, being well trained and using well spoken words: this is good luck." ~ Buddha

Do you believe in luck and chance, or do you believe that life is in your own hands?

This is a critical factor that will determine how well you live your life.

I believe that luck is just like our genes. We get our DNA from our parents, and it is set and cannot be changed. This may be how you view luck; one person may be born luckier than another.

However, a relatively new science known as epigenetics shows that your lifestyle habits can influence your genes. I talk about this in my book, *The Guerrilla Diet & Lifestyle Program*.

We can't change our genes, but we can certainly influence which genes will be expressed and which not, depending on our lifestyle choices. I believe that the same goes for luck. We may influence our fate and our "luck" through the choices we make.

There is no doubt that some people were born with more of an advantage than others. But what they did with this advantage is up to them and their choices. Your family and environment can only take you so far or hinder you so much. The rest is up to you.

The most extraordinary people who have reached the highest achievements and great heights in their careers and lives did believe in some form of luck; however, they understood that luck was not enough. Jeff Bezos said that for Amazon to have become a success, all the stars aligned up perfectly. Bill Gates said that he was fortunate enough to be born to his family and to have the good genes he was given, but the rest of their good fortune was up to them, it was not only in their stars or their genes, but it was also in their good choices and decisions.

These highly successful people understood that life is not a lottery ticket and that they must do what it takes to succeed. Bill Gates is not the smartest man alive; he is unquestionably intelligent with an IQ of 160, but not the *most* intelligent. Many other people have come from similar backgrounds and have similar intelligence levels but did not get as far as he did because they did not do what he was willing to do.

While he and other great achievers may have had some advantage, they had to do the work to get to where they are today.

In fact, it is often people that have had less of an ideal upbringing who have built big brands or companies that became so large and powerful because of the lessons these people learned early in life. They most often learned to take responsibility for their actions and learned independence very early on.

You hear them say that they felt that it was up to them and that no one will come and save them.

Eliyahu Goldratt, the business management guru, said, "Good luck is when opportunity meets preparation, while bad luck is when lack of preparation meets reality."

When you are ill-prepared, you suffer the consequences of reality.

If luck is considered a chance occurrence how can it be made you may ask? Well, those who have succeeded and are considered the luckiest often say that the harder they worked, the luckier they became. Whether there is or isn't chance occurrence we will never know. We will never understand why certain people were found in a specific place at a specific time. But you can do our best to make yourself more likely to be lucky through intense effort on a focused goal that you believe has the potential to help you and many others lead happier lives. We can all transform misfortune into good fortune by determination, skill, and will to learn and overcome it or become stronger as a result of it.

Even if you examine outward circumstances and conclude that they were bad luck, you can still choose to believe that some form of benefit came to you. Furthermore, the situation could have been worse. You can also choose to view any misfortune to prepare you to become a better version of yourself.

If you understand that your future is not a matter of chance but that you can shape it through your choices, you know that your efforts are not wasted. It is all about your attitude. Whether you believe in your power or not, or you believe that the stars or some other random fate hold the key to your future for you, it is your attitude about this that will determine your actions.

There are four basic attitudes of people:

1. A pessimistic attitude that believes in creation.

2. A pessimistic attitude that believes in chance

3. An optimistic attitude that believes in chance

4. An optimistic attitude that believes in creation

Let's look at each of these:

- A pessimistic attitude from a person who believes in the human ability to create believes in building a future by copying what other successful people did. This allows them to create on ideas of others without a large risk for anything adverse happening to them.

- A pessimistic attitude from a person who believes in chance will be self-fulfilling. It will create a glum life outcome for that person as they expect the worst to happen and do not take any action or take the wrong measures to ensure that the worst does happen.

- An optimistic attitude from a person who believes in chance believes that the future lies in the hands of a higher power, so they will not produce much value even though they are optimistic. They are naive in their optimism as they do not take action. No one can ensure progress without planning and effort. People with this attitude will find themselves adapting to their environment and confronting an ever-changing environment daily. They are optimistic, but they do not create anything new. They go with what is and perhaps improve on it. Often they will suffer when reality hits them in the face.

- An optimistic attitude from a person who believes in the human ability to create builds the future they envision. In their business, they tell their customers what they need before their customers know that they need it. They have definite long-term plans and execute these plans slowly but surely. These people create the future.

Suppose you are a pessimist who believes that the world is drifting to some unknown future, you will have no motivation to do anything to change the situation. You will be more inclined to go for cover and do the things that go unnoticed, not to make any ripples that will get noticed.

You will more likely live your life and hope for the best but often expect the worst.

On the other hand, if you are an optimist, who believes in creation and in the opportunity people have to make a dent in the world, then you believe that through the law of cause and effect, you are responsible for the results in your life. The circumstances in your life are not responsible for the results in your life.

Only a person who is both optimistic and believes in the human ability to create can live a good life and make this world a better place. A person less inclined to understand the law of cause and effect but rather attributes things to chance is more likely to copy what worked in the past to work for them in the future. They may try to improve things but will not use their imagination to envision the world as it can be and work to create this reality.

The law of cause and effect, as we covered in a previous lesson, states that everything that happens first starts with something, most often thoughts, that are creative by nature. This leads the way to make long-term action plans for a better future following this creative thought. This is the state of mind that understands that the best future is created and not just allowed to happen as the wind blows.

You may be pessimistic and believe in your ability to shape the future, but you will not want or tend to do this since you think things will generally turn out badly. And when you don't put in the effort to make things better because of the pessimistic outlook you hold, your pessimistic visions will tend to fulfill your predictions.

Or you may be an optimist who believes in chance and not in cause and effect. You believe that you don't have any influence on things, although you do believe that things *will* be good in the end. You will tend to go for less innovative jobs because you do not know *how* the world can improve, just that it *will* overall be better. You don't think you can design the future, but only perhaps rearrange the present and improve on it slightly. You like to keep your options open because you do not know what the future will hold for you. You tend to go less after focused attention on one thing and have a general focus on many things.

This way of living is how most people live nowadays. Most people *are* optimistic by nature but do not believe that they hold the reins to do what is necessary to make real change for the better happen.

Although you feel entitled to good and therefore believe that good things should be yours, you expect to receive the good things easily and on a platter rather than go out and get or create them.

But if you want to think big and leave a legacy for many generations to come, you must take the optimistic approach and believe in your ability to create your future.

This is the best state of mind for success. It means that the future will be better because it will be made better through your effort and other people doing good things to change the world for the better.

Some luck may be helpful, but it is nothing more than helpful. A creative life is not based on luck. A pessimist born into harsh conditions may play on their situation and leave no place for significant improvement because they believe that since those were the cards they were dealt, they cannot change their position.

An optimist will see that things will get better and know that they deserve things to get better. But an optimist who doesn't believe in their creative power to form their destiny and design their future will live a life that lacks creativity and purpose and will be much less happy than someone who believes in their ability to shape their future to make them happy.

There is nothing more important than a vision with a plan to determine your future. A plan, even a bad plan, is better than no plan. When you have a plan, you know where you should go and what you should do to influence your future for the better.

Jim Rohn said that if you don't design your own life **plan**, chances are you'll fall into someone else's **plan**. And guess what they have planned for you? Not much.

Jim Rohn also said, "If you don't like how things are, change it! You're not a tree."

People with no plan will try to make the best of what is available to them now. There is no vision for the future, neither a positive nor a negative future.

So there is only perhaps renovation, but no innovation.

A commitment to one path that you believe in, and enjoy, and are willing to put in the effort, pay the price, and implement a plan, is what will take you the farthest.

This, when backed with an optimistic nature and a belief in the law of cause and effect, will ensure you reach your dreams.

You are not in the audience of your life; you are a player on the field. And when your play is planned for success, and you improve on your skills daily and put in the effort to succeed and believe that you can do it, then nothing can stop you.

Yes, there may be luck, but that will only maybe get you onto first base. It will not lead you to a home run and will not lead you to the life of your dreams. Don't sit on the sidelines.

When you believe that you design your future, and you are optimistic by nature, the gold is yours for the taking.

Questions Of The Day

To end this lesson and help you be optimistic and creative, ask yourself:

Do I believe in my abilities to change my future? Do I believe in my abilities to create my future? Do I believe that for every action, there is an equal reaction? Do I believe in my abilities? Am I optimistic?

See what you answered for each question. If you answered yes, then you are headed down the right track for the future of your dreams. If you answered no to any of these questions, then read this book daily to help you form an optimistic life view and help you understand the law of cause and effect, whether you believe it or not. It is best to change your thought patterns so that you learn to take responsibility for your choices because your choices form your destiny. Life is not about chance and luck but about planning and creating.

As usual, I recommend writing your answers in the PDF journal.

Affirmation Of The Day

After answering the questions in your journal, repeat this affirmation:

I AM THE CREATOR OF MY LIFE. I CAN MAKE MY DREAMS AND MY VISION FOR THE WORLD COME TRUE THROUGH CONSISTENT EFFORT, HARD WORK, AND PATIENCE.

Repeat this affirmation often. With repetition, it has the power to alter your consciousness so you build a better, happier and more purposeful life.

DAY 93 - BECOMING AWARE OF THE IMPORTANCE OF RELAXATION

"Sometimes the most productive thing you can do is relax." ~ Mark Black

We all know the significant physiological changes that occur with meditation and relaxation, including a reduction in blood pressure and heart rate, dilation of peripheral blood vessels in the body to increase blood flow to all tissues allowing the supply of nutrients and oxygen to more cells of the body, and increased activity of alpha waves in the brain.

These all occur when the body is in a state of rest.

Meditation is the most well-known method to reach this state of deep relaxation. However, another less well-known method for relaxation is *autogenic training* or auto-suggestion to your subconscious mind. It is a form of meditation.

If you are not yet meditating regularly, you'll want to incorporate this technique. When you reach a state of deep relaxation, as this training and meditation will help you enter, you can achieve your goals much more readily.

This is because when you are in a state of deep relaxation, as our quote of the day suggests, you become overall more productive.

In a relaxed state, your subconscious mind is most receptive to suggestions. When your subconscious mind is open to suggestions, you can completely transform the way you behave in day-to-day situations. Behaviors that are hindering your path towards achieving your goals can be replaced with more productive behaviors. The limiting beliefs that you hold, which may be self-sabotaging your success, can be eliminated when you regularly use auto-suggestion in a state of deep relaxation.

Autogenic training was developed by Johann Schultz and was found to be the best way to bring about rapid behavioral change through auto-suggestion. This method was used in sports, especially by communist countries. This allowed them to win the most gold medals in the Olympics. This was not because the athletes were necessarily better, but because they had better mind control.

Autogenic training means self-training. You are training your mind to relax so that you can plant the best beliefs and thoughts into your subconscious mind. Beliefs and thoughts that will help you attain your goals and live the life that *you* desire. This allows your subconscious mind, which is responsible for your default thought patterns and behaviors, to work for you instead of against you. Once you are in a deep state of relaxation, you can easily imprint what you want on your subconscious mind, and these suggestions will be accepted as truths quickly.

For example, suppose you know that you have certain destructive behaviors for relationships essential for your personal and business life. In that case, you can remove these negative behaviors when you are in a state of deep relaxation by imprinting on your subconscious mind what you *do* want to have and how you do want to behave instead of what you don't want to have or how you don't want to behave.

When you are completely calm, your mind is running at slower brain waves. Alpha waves are the dominant brain waves at the beginning of deep relaxation and meditation with a frequency range of 8-12 Hz. These brain waves calm the nervous system, helping you detach, relax, lower anxiety levels, and be more at peace. But not only that, alpha brain waves also help reinforce new behaviors by forming new beliefs.

Inside the brain during deep relaxation, the frontal lobe, responsible for planning and reasoning, slows to an almost complete standstill. The thalamus, which transmits motor and sensory signals to the brain, slows down as well. The parietal lobe, which gives a sense of time, also slows down. And the reticular formation in the brainstem involved in consciousness and regulation of breathing also slows down.

This sets the stage for feelings of harmony and well-being, which are perfect conditions for auto-suggestion.

So how is autogenic training done?

- First, make sure you are wearing comfortable loose clothing.

- Find a quiet, comfortable place to relax where you will have no distractions for 15-20 minutes. It is preferred that you use the same spot for your relaxation techniques regularly.

- Sit or lie down in a comfortable position.

- Close your eyes.

- Breath slow, and even breaths, while repeating to yourself, "I am completely calm."

- Every 30-60 seconds or so, while continuing to breathe slowly, deeply, and controlled, focus your attention on one body part.

- Start for example with your right hand, and repeat six times the statement: "My right hand is completely relaxed, I am completely calm," Do this again with your other hand, and then go through the same process with your arms, legs, shoulders, belly, chest, back and forehead. Repeat the statement *"My (body part) is completely relaxed"* for each body part, and then add, "I am completely calm."

- Lastly, move on to your heartbeat and say six times, "My heartbeat is calm and regular; I am completely relaxed."

Now you are in a state of deep relaxation. This state of deep relaxation is the perfect time to envision the goal you want to achieve, the ability you want to gain, or the behavior you want to change or improve and auto-suggest these new situations, behaviors, and habits until they become part of your being. Auto-suggestion in this state of consciousness is the fastest way to help make these changes become part of your reality.

Form a clear picture of you having these qualities that you want to nurture within you and living with the goals you strive for. Opposite of what we most often believe, when you are in a completely relaxed state and putting in the least effort, you can assimilate things into your reality fastest. This is the best time to imprint your subconscious mind with what you truly desire to have and who you truly desire to be.

If you do not meditate regularly, give this method a try, as it provides all the benefits of meditation. Yet, it is straightforward to implement into your life for people with no meditation background or experience.

Questions Of The Day

To end this lesson and help you make the most of your relaxation time and add autogenic training into your life daily, ask yourself:

Which traits, abilities, and mindset are most vital for me to accommodate my future goals and achieve success in all fields of life?

Now follow through with autogenic training and autosuggest to your subconscious mind that you have these traits, abilities, and mindset already as part of you.

I recommend writing your answers in your PDF journal.

Affirmation Of The Day

After answering the questions in your journal, repeat this affirmation:

I REACH DEEP RELAXATION DAILY, REPROGRAMMING MY SUBCONSCIOUS MIND TO HELP ME ACHIEVE A WORTHWHILE LIFE.

Repeat this affirmation often. With repetition, it has the power to alter your consciousness so you build a better, happier and more purposeful life.

DAY 94 - BECOMING AWARE OF REGRETS

"Forget regret, or life is yours to miss." ~ Jonathan Larson

We all have things we regret either doing or not doing.

Regret is hard to live with.

And worst of all, regret may elicit guilt, the most destructive of all negative emotions for a person's self-esteem.

Our regrets may involve:

- Not being there enough for our children.
- Not giving enough care to our parents before they got some disease.
- Not spending enough time with our partner.
- Not going after our dreams.
- Not doing what we felt was right to do.
- Not expressing our true feelings.

We get into situations that may not be right for us because we knew no better. We all make mistakes. The question is, what do you do about your regrets and mistakes.

Some things and situations can't be reversed or changed. You may have made wrong choices or plain bad choices, and their results may hang around forever. Now the only question is, what do you do from this day forward?

Is it going to be a new beginning? Did you learn the lessons from the mistakes you made? Have your mistakes made you into a better, more humane person?

If yes, then these mistakes were not in vain.

The lessons were learned, and there was growth through hardship, perhaps more than could have ever been if all things went according to plan and if all of your choices were perfect, and if life would have gone as you desired. But it did not, and you can learn the lesson or notice some form of behavior that you have that is not in your best interest.

Yes, regrets are the hardest lessons to learn because they affect so much of your life in the future. Most often, we live our regrets over and over again, so we pay a very high price for any regrets we hold.

Bad judgment may have led you down a difficult path in life, but the more complex the path you went down, the even better path you can go up from there after learning the lessons and developing and progressing as a human.

Life is not easy all the time for anyone, and we all have bad judgment at times. For some lucky few, bad decisions did not leave heavy scars; for others, they did. You have these scars to remind you of how far you have come regarding your choices, behaviors, and beliefs. You have come a long way, and not only do you have the scars to prove it, but if you learn the lessons, you gained the wisdom.

Regret can only be removed when you understand that the lessons you received were exactly what you needed at the time to drive you to the progress that YOU desire deep within. Steve Jobs said it best: "You can't connect the dots looking forward; you can only connect them looking backward. So you have to trust that the dots will somehow connect in your future. You have to trust in something—your gut, destiny, life, karma, whatever. This approach has never let me down, and it has made all the difference in my life."

In his essay Compensation, Ralph Waldo Emerson believed that every hardship you go through carries the seed of an equivalent benefit. Nothing is in vain, so there is no need for regret. Eventually, you will reach the place you desire to be if you learn the lessons, keep your belief high, and take the following best logical action to move you in the right direction.

Write down your regrets. Write down the worst choices you made in your lifetime. Then write down the lessons you have learned due to your past faulty judgment. What could you have done better? How *have* you become better as a result? What changed in you? Have your behaviors, thoughts, or beliefs changed as a result? Can you see how much you have changed?

Now forgive yourself and remember that this was one of the most important lessons you had in life, and then make sure that you will never have to relearn this lesson with another, different situation in your life again.

You may even want to write this lesson down on a post-it note and have it near you until this lesson has become so ingrained within your being and are sure this lesson is part of you from now on.

There may also be some regrets that you can still change, perhaps situations where you still have an opportunity to turn things around. Do this immediately once you have recognized these situations not to suffer regret from these issues in the future. Improve yourself and change your behavior until you are happy with "who" you are now.

But even if the situation is non-reversible. Harness the lesson. Make sure you understand the lesson so well that any feelings of regret will naturally subside.

Was the lesson never to give away your power? Was the lesson to believe in yourself or to love yourself more? Was the lesson to become more educated on a subject? Was the lesson to help another person or to be more caring and more loving? Was the lesson of accepting another or accepting yourself and your feelings as they are and sharing them?

Whatever the lesson, embrace it. You did the best you could with the capacity and abilities you had at the time. Forgive yourself and move on to be the better person you have become due to making these mistakes. Never mind the past. All will usually forget once you change and become the better version of yourself.

And once you learn the lesson, the most important thing you can do is to pass your lesson onto others. Pay it forward. If you learned a lesson that brought you great value, pass it on so that others can learn from your mistakes and wisdom and spare themselves the same suffering you went through to learn this lesson.

Remember, we do not live forever as the physical beings that we are. We sometimes behave as if we will live forever, but we won't. Our physical body will die, and how we lived our lives and what we left for future generations is our legacy. Even if you made mistakes on the way, what did you do with the lessons learned?

Every moment you are alive, you are creating your legacy. How will you like to be remembered after you are gone? A person who improved the world even slightly is better than anyone who gave nothing back to the world and only took during their time spent here.

There are countless stories of how people rose from the worst possible places into a life of greatness. So can you!

Speak your truth, and tell others what you feel in an empathetic way. When you hide your feelings because of fear of rejection, you will regret it because you are hiding who you truly are. You are the one who will lose the most from not sharing your true feelings, but so will others around you. We often regret what we did not do or say rather than what we did or say.

I know that it is not easy to forgive your past mistakes, flaws, and imperfections. Let go of the time that you wasted on self-pity, anger, and regret so you can live to your highest capacity.

You can't get there if you are constantly putting yourself down.

As I have said before, do your very best in all situations, and you will avoid regret. Even if you did not live like this before, it's never too late to start.

Questions Of The Day

To end this lesson and to help you release any regrets, ask yourself:

What were the worst choices I have made? What things do I regret doing or not doing, saying or not saying? And what lessons should I have learned from these mistakes? What could I have done better? How *have* I become better as a result? How have my behaviors, thoughts, or beliefs changed as a result? In which fields of life have I made the most progress as a result?

Now keep these lessons close to your heart so when the time comes, and it will, you can react differently and do things as you wished you would have done them the first time.

As usual, I recommend writing your answers in the PDF journal.

Affirmation Of The Day

After answering the questions in your journal, and examining them, sit quietly for a few minutes today and repeat this affirmation to yourself as you think and dwell upon it:

I CAN MOVE BEYOND MY MISTAKES AND HEAL FROM THE HURT AND PAIN I HAVE CAUSED MYSELF AND OTHERS.

Repeat this affirmation often. With repetition, it has the power to alter your consciousness so you build a better, happier and more purposeful life.

DAY 95 - BECOMING AWARE OF YOUR WAKE AND REST TIMES

"The first step to win yourself is wake up early" ~ Sukant Ratnakar

———————⟨∞∞⟩———————

"No day is so bad it can't be fixed with a nap." ~ Snow.

Waking up early and napping when needed are two habits that form an integral part of a healthy, productive, and energy-filled life.

If you wake up early to seize the day and reach your highest potential, you know that napping is an integral part of maintaining a healthy body and mind.

Research shows that napping has a direct effect on mental health. It improves memory, cognition, alertness, performance, and overall feelings of well-being and mood. Napping also reduces body inflammation and improves blood sugar level control and cortisol levels. Overall, napping helps ensures healthy body and brain function.

Of course, when you wake up late, there is no need to nap. However, when you take on the wonderful habit of waking up early, between 5 and 6 a.m., exercising regularly in the morning, meditating even shortly, and then starting your day, you will be amazingly more productive. You will feel better and be more satisfied with yourself and with your life.

Waking early is not an easy habit to secure, but once you master waking early, you will gain many physical, emotional, and productive rewards from it.

Waking early is a commitment that has the potential to completely transform your life and rid you of many of your problems.

When you wake up early, you have solitude time to reflect on your life and choices, allowing you to make better choices for your life whenever needed.

Waking early toughens you up and shows you that you *can* do things differently from most other people. You can be stronger, more persistent, and more determined than others.

Yes, of course, the cost is always there, but the highest price is only in the beginning when forming the habit. It is like the business term "economies of scale", which is about the advantages reaped by companies when production becomes efficient. The cost to you *will* be high in the beginning. There will be discomfort, maybe even fear of waking up when it is still dark outside. And there is the discomfort of going to sleep early while your friends stay out late. But as you become accustomed to waking early and your body adjusts to it, you will see the great rewards. Once your body and mind adjust, there will be no more cost because this will have become your new norm, but the benefits will be massive.

There are no telephone calls, the kids are still asleep, no disturbances in the early morning hours if you keep your phone on flight mode from the night, and no businesses are open, so you are not expected to be available to whoever may need you. Your pets are also still asleep during the very early hours of the morning.

You have quiet. You have peace. Your cares seem to fly away when you wake at this time. You feel as if you are alone in the world and can do anything.

I love going on a run before dawn because when I run in the dark, and there are no people or cars around, I don't lose focus. The air is cleaner, and there are no distractions, so I can meditate while running. It's easy to get into theta brain waves when there are no disturbances, and I run on the same path at the same time every day.

Getting into this meditative brain state is not only a very healing practice for the body and mind. It also allows deep and profound learning and a sense of inner peace that follows you for the next six hours of the day.

I genuinely recommend implementing this early wake-up schedule for its life-transforming effects. I personally need these early quiet hours to exercise, read, and write for you in the morning. Otherwise, I get wound up in the days' responsibilities and my business and family duties.

I am much happier since I took on this habit a few years ago.

When I changed my wake-up time, at first, it was hard, and I did, at times, get off track, but I got back on track the following day. Even if you do get off track and stop the early wake up for one day, don't worry about it; get back on track the next day. In this way, even if you do get off track every other day but get back on track the next day, you will still be in the good habit at least 50 percent of the time.

Another main advantage of waking early is that your actions become evidence for your subconscious mind about who you are. When you wake up so early every day and exercise and meditate, and in a state of peace of mind, you are telling your subconscious mind that you are strong, powerful, persistent, determined, under control, calm, and can achieve anything.

When the subconscious mind regularly gets this feedback, it will ensure that you become that person you wish to be. When you start a new action and adhere to it long enough, you actually change who you are. You are changing your identity as a result of your new habit. You are becoming a more developed person—the person who you truly desire to be.

You become stronger, fitter, healthier, both emotionally and physically, and a more powerful person just because of this one new habit.

Wow, can you imagine the effects on your life when your subconscious mind accepts these attributes to be confirmed for you?

Can you imagine how powerful you can become because of this?

You can achieve anything you set your mind to attain!

It usually takes 66 days to build a new habit, or rather 66 consecutive repetitions of the habit. But it may take up to three months of consecutive repetitions of the action to fully incorporate the new habit into your life as a norm. Devote three months to trying out this powerful habit of waking up at 5:30 a.m. at least six times every week. If you find that you do not connect with it and do not feel the benefits, stop, but do not choose before trying it out for three months and are open to experiencing the massive benefits.

Now I understand that there are night owls and do not like to wake early in the day. But I still suggest you give it a try because the most regenerative sleep happens if you fall asleep before 11:00 p.m. This is why you should be in bed, ready for sleep maximum by 10:30 p.m.

The reason is that when you are asleep, there is no surge of stress hormones that usually happens if you stay awake after 10:40 - 11:00 p.m. This surge of stress hormones will further prevent you from falling asleep for the next few hours. With time, this ruins your body's rhythm and affects learning, concentration, and calmness.

People with insomnia have been cured by waking up early and slowly going to sleep early.

When you do something new, you become someone new.

If the richest man in the world (currently Jeff Bezos) says, "Go to bed early and wake up early. The morning hours are good," then I think it's safe to say that this is a good habit to adopt.

The best way to get into the habit of waking up early is by being consistent with bedtime and wake-up hours. If I delay my bedtime to after 10:15 pm, it also disturbs my wake-up time, making it much harder for me to get out of bed in the morning.

I also recommend permanently turning off the blue light on your smartphone and computer screen by moving them to night shift to not mess with your sleep rhythm.

Now, since you can't turn off the blue light on your TV, try not to watch TV for at least 30 minutes before you go to sleep, and spend the last half hour of the day for reflection, reading, meditation, or spending quality time with your partner or children.

An unknown source said, "Successful people wake up early, talk less, stay laser-focused, don't waste time, live healthily, and ignore nonsense."

The habit of waking early helps put your whole body back into its natural, peaceful rhythm. Back into sync with the day and night cycles that our bodies lived by for millions of years before the modern era began.

Melatonin, the hormone that regulates our sleep-wake cycle, is released about an hour after sunset and reaches its peak at midnight. If you are not sleeping an hour earlier, then you miss out on the night's best restorative sleep when the body is healing itself, and the brain is reorganizing all of the data it received throughout the day.

Remember that it is your choice when to wake up and what life you want to live. Set up your day to be the best possible day for you, and stick with your plan. Start your day early to reap the most benefits of life!

When you wake early, you will often notice that you may reach the peak of daytime tiredness by mid-afternoon. This usually happens after lunch, when the digestive system uses up most of your energy, and the brain desires a rest.

If you aim to stay productive and control your emotions, then a nap is the best thing to do.

Albert Einstein, Aristotle, John F. Kennedy, Leonardo da Vinci, Margaret Thatcher, Napoleon Bonaparte, Thomas Edison, and Winston Churchill all woke up early and understood the power to nap after using their brains to a great degree. They believed it helped them get twice as much done.

Churchill said that you should not think that you will be doing less work because you sleep during the day. You will be able to accomplish more.

Salvador Dali and Einstein recognized the importance of napping but not reaching deep sleep. They called it "micro napping" and said that it increases imagination and creativity. They both fell asleep holding a metal object so that when it fell from their hands when they entered deep sleep, it would make a noise and wake them. They would reach a state that they were half asleep and half awake, which is a state great for inspiration, creativity, and genius.

Research says that if you wake by 6 a.m., the best time to nap is between 1 and 4 p.m., and the nap should last between twenty and maximum forty minutes to avoid deep sleep. Take your nap in a quiet place. Sitting on a comfortable chair or lying on your back are the best positions to incorporate a micro-nap into your day. If you are at work, and wish to nap, you may do so during your lunch break. You can go to your car if you have one, push the seat back and take a short nap. At university you may find an unused classroom and take a short nap on some chairs. If you get creative, you can use this habit anywhere to increase your daily productivity.

Napping is also great for students since napping helps support learning. You learn faster and will maintain more of what you learn after taking a rest. Napping also reduces hyperactive, inattentive, and impulsive behaviors.

People who were known to be very self-controlled may lose that during the later hours of the day if they don't rest. A lack of napping and resting of the mind has sometimes ruined whole careers due to a lack of self-control.

Weight loss is also a lot easier when you regularly nap since napping affects hormone levels. The immune system also relies on rest to function best throughout the long hours of the day.

A regular habit of napping is also associated with a longer lifespan. When examining blue zones, where people generally live healthier and much longer lives than average, it seems that all blue zones incorporate the habit of midday naps.

Napping helps people get along better. There are fewer feelings of anger, fewer mood swings, less impulsiveness, less anxiety, and increased motivation and emotional stability.

What could be better?

Also, when you care for your needs by napping when you feel tired, this sends the message to your subconscious mind that you love and respect yourself, a crucial message since you act from your subconscious mind most hours of the day.

For you to reach the best version of yourself, I truly recommend taking on the habit of waking up early to seize the day while taking a nap in the afternoon to restore and revitalize your body and mind.

Questions Of The Day

To end this lesson and to help you incorporate the habits of waking early and napping when necessary, ask yourself:

Am I willing to try to incorporate the habit of waking up before dawn every day for the next three months? Am I currently sleeping enough? When should I go to sleep if I need 7.5-8 hours in bed to sufficiently rest my body and mind? Do I find that I often need an extra boost of creativity or more self-control or calmness later in the day? Where can I find a quiet place to nap during the day? Perhaps in your car parked in a calm area where any chance of disturbance is rare?

As usual, I recommend writing your answers in the PDF journal.

Affirmation Of The Day

After answering the questions in your journal, say the following affirmation every morning as you wake up.

I AM AN EARLY WAKER. I AM A POWERFUL PERSON. I AM STRONG, COMMITTED, AND ENERGETIC. I AM PERSISTENT AND DETERMINED, AND BECAUSE OF THESE QUALITIES, I WILL REACH ALL OF MY GOALS AND DREAMS!!!

You may also add another affirmation at midday:

I HAVE PERMISSION TO SLEEP SO I CAN REFRESH, RESTORE AND REVITALIZE MY MIND.

Commit to speaking these affirmations daily because, with repetition, affirmations have the power to alter your consciousness so that you think and behave differently for a better, happier life.

DAY 96 - BECOMING AWARE OF YOUR HEALTH HABITS

"There's nothing more important than our good health - that's our principal capital asset."

~ Arlen Specter

———————⦚⦚⦚———————

Without health, you cannot reach your fullest potential. Preservation of the body is fundamental to your success and satisfaction from life.

The keys to success all require you to be healthy, both in body and mind.

Without health, you cannot work hard, nor can you focus for long. You cannot motivate yourself when you are unhealthy because your concentration will be on your dis-ease state. When you are not in good health, you cannot follow all of your passions because you will not have the energy or the focus to do so, and you will not be able to do or be your best. The primary keys to success will lack when you lack health.

Self-awareness is another critical element for success and is usually lacking when you are not caring for your health properly.

Even if you do achieve some form of success, you will not fully enjoy it if you are not healthy.

Certain handicaps or disease states may not be under your control. But you can control how you treat your body from this moment on. You can control the foods you allow into your body, and the amount of exercise you do, and your hours of sleep and rest. Managing these is possible for most people.

It is your responsibility to do the best you can for your health.

When you are not feeling well, this is not a sign to take medication to cover your symptoms. It is a time to introspect which habits got you to your current situation and what you can do to change the source of the problem and not waste your time by dealing with the symptoms of your condition.

The Apostle Paul wrote, "Your body is a temple." When you take good care of your body as if you were caring for a temple, you also take good care of your mind. The body and mind work together and lead to your behaviors, and your behaviors and choices will eventually lead to your destiny.

Health is your true wealth.

You cannot reach your desired destination if what is carrying you there is not in good shape. When you are in good health, your body will support all your endeavors. Any state of ill health is a warning sign that something you are doing is not suitable for you. It is a wake-up call to make a change. Therefore, all sickness and disease can be viewed as gifts to push you back on track for your benefit. Sickness, disease, or poor health often occur after many nudges that we have gone astray with our choices and habits.

The disease often gives us a break from the perhaps frantic day-to-day life we are leading.

When I broke my knee bone during a run and was put into a cast from thigh to ankle, I was forced to rest. This was the time I was introduced to the Master Key System by Charles Haanel which I would have never read otherwise. I healed my knee through the power of my mind and the right physical exercises in such a way that the doctor who I returned to after ten days of my accident, had to recheck my X-ray exam to ensure there really was a broken bone beforehand.

This wake-up call transformed my life completely.

When you care for your health, mental and physical, you will feel good, and when you feel good, you can do your best, and when you don't feel good, you cannot do your best.

Your health is your responsibility.

Mental health is a significant cause of suffering in our era. This book is here to help you with this aspect of your health.

Physical ailments must be cared for through diet, sufficient sleep, fasting, sunlight, physical activity, good hygiene, stopping bad habits such as excessive drinking of alcohol, smoking, drugs, and other stimulants. We have talked about addictions in a previous lesson. The benefits of fresh air, nature, and sleep have also been covered. The whole subject of the ideal diet for humans is covered in my book *The Guerrilla Diet & Lifestyle Program*, following my research into the ideal diet for humans.

These simple changes in habits hold significant benefits for the physical and emotional state of an individual.

The body can heal itself in a relatively short period once the proper habits are adopted.

Only one-third of Americans participate in regular physical activity.

To reach your highest potential, you must feel good. You must find the time to exercise daily if your health permits. It doesn't need to be a lot of exercise, but it does need to be something that you can commit to doing daily.

When you do exercise daily, even for 30 minutes, you will find that you have more energy than when you do not exercise.

Exercise makes you feel good by releasing the feel-good chemicals, endorphins. Exercise decreases stress and anxiety and is closely related to higher levels of success. Physical activity will make any day better.

You can find a long list of benefits from exercise in my book, *The Guerrilla Diet & Lifestyle Program*.

Unfortunately, two-thirds of the population is overweight, and only 0.1 percent of the American population is considered to follow a healthy diet, with 8.2 percent of the population considered to follow a *somewhat* healthy diet. This is very unfortunate since our dietary choices are in our own hands.

When you are living in a healthy body, you can take yourself anywhere you wish to go.

Maybe buying cheap food now seems like a good bargain, but it is not because you will have to pay the price one day. And the price will always concern health which will not allow you to work and will not allow you to earn a decent living for yourself and your family. Medications are much more expensive than buying healthy food in the long run. Furthermore, whole grains and lentils are the cheapest foods and will make you full, strong, and healthy. If you add a few vegetables, some nuts and seeds, and one to two fruits a day to these basic foods, then you have all you need to be healthy. All of these foods are not expensive for your pocket nor your health, in comparison to a cheap hamburger which may be cheap today but has a very hefty price in the future.

Naval Ravikant said, "The modern mind is overstimulated, and the modern body is under-stimulated and overfed." It is your responsibility to take care of yourself.

So, how well are you taking care of yourself?

We are holistic by nature, so if you don't care for your physical body, this will influence every other aspect of your life.

When one field of your life is out of alignment, then all other areas of life suffer as well due to imbalance.

You must take control of what enters your body just as you want to control what thoughts enter your mind. You must be proactive about this.

Think thoughts with the end in mind. Eat foods with the end in mind. Live your life with your preferred end in mind.

It's the small bad choices that add up. In the end, everything adds up.

If you want to be a leader in your field, you must live a long and healthy life. Few people have become legends and led short lives, but their lives were fuller than most people's lives. Most people need time to mature. So it takes more time to learn and incorporate the proper habits, behaviors, and skills required for success. Most people only start to achieve greatness in later years. It is never too late to start, but you must be healthy to start. If you are healthy, you will tend to live longer, and if you live longer, you have more of a shot at living what you consider a favorable life.

Your physical health affects everything. When you change your diet for the better, you change everything for the better.

Healthy foods will change your brain and change your life. You will sleep better, feel better, have more energy, and will be able to focus and function better. What could be more beneficial to your life and to your success than that?

So how can you become healthier?

Well, the absolute first step is to stop the habits that are not benefiting you. Stop smoking, stop drinking alcohol, sugary beverages, and drinking more than two cups of coffee a day. Stop taking tranquilizers or other pills that are not must-haves. Stop sleeping late, stop wasting time on social media, and stop watching too much news. Stop overeating meat and dairy or anything else that is harmful to your health. If you are thinking a low carb diet is the way to health, please read my research into the ideal diet for humans on my website: theGuerrillaDiet.com. When you change your current health condition, then you are open to improvement.

Only after you stop doing what is harmful to your health can you start doing what will improve your health.

You want your health habits to reflect your highest ideals.

You may encounter some withdrawal symptoms initially after stopping some harmful habits, but in the long term, you will gain much more than you ever lost, I assure you.

Think about how your body and life can be a year from now if you stopped your bad habits.

Just imagine how your health would improve as a result.

After you stop negative health habits, you can start with health-promoting habits such as eating healthy whole plant-based foods, taking on a daily exercise routine, waking up early, flossing your teeth, and using natural hygiene and cleaning products.

Any new habits will take time, effort, repetition, and persistence to embed into your life. When you know and understand this, you won't betray your true potential for everyday comforts, and you will commit to making the change.

It will take approximately 66 days of consecutive repetitions of the new habit to embed it into your life. Sixty-six days of persistent, repetitive effort. But after that, the new habit will become your default automatic behavior.

This is well worth the effort. Your whole life will change as a result. You will be happier, more fulfilled, and with the same amount of persistent effort, you will also become much more successful in life.

Once you take control of your habits, you reduce your fear of pain and disease. It is well documented that the more a person fears pain, suffering, and poor health, the less likely they are to succeed in life and the less happy they will be. Mastery of the body shows that one has mastered their mind to make the right choices for themselves and mastered their thoughts crucial for any progress in life.

Questions Of The Day

To end this lesson and help you improve your health, ask yourself:

Do the foods I eat improve or worsen my health? Do my sleep and exercise habits improve or worsen my health?

Which habits of mine are detrimental to my health and my life? And how do my current health habits affect other areas of my life?

Once you answer these questions, you will know whether it is time to stop your bad habits or whether it is time to add beneficial habits into your life to support a healthy body and mind to achieve your highest potential.

Think about where you would like to be three, six and twelve months from today concerning your health and take the next logical steps to get you there.

As usual, I recommend writing your answers in the PDF journal.

Affirmation Of The Day

After answering the questions in your journal, repeat this affirmation:

I AM RADIATING HEALTH AND ENERGY.

Repeat this affirmation often. With repetition, it has the power to alter your consciousness so you build a better, happier and more purposeful life.

DAY 97 - BECOMING AWARE OF THE IMPORTANCE OF WEALTH

"Wealth is the ability to fully experience life." ~ Henry David Thoreau

Creating abundance is an intricate part of personal development. You have the right to live abundantly. Creating abundance is a part of reaching your fullest potential. Abundance provides you with more time, as you will have people helping you with things that take up your time but are not very enjoyable for you. This can help you achieve more in less time. Not all people need extreme amounts of money to help them fulfill their true potential and purpose, and feel they have abundance, but you must have enough to not have any form of debt.

Like in all other spheres of life, mindset is key to success in the financial sphere, but the actions you take are just as crucial. You *do* need to become a different person to allow abundance into your life if you do not currently have abundance in your life. What do I mean by becoming a different person? I mean that you will need to put in the effort towards changing yourself to have a radically different mentality, an abundant mentality.

As a minimalist, I live my life very simply and happily. I do not need much to be happy, just a walk in nature, pleasant conversations with other people, and to have my family around me. I'm not too fond of shopping, and I wear very basic clothing, and since the weather permits where I live, I wear flip-flops almost everywhere. I eat a very simple whole food plant-based vegan diet and run daily for my physical activity. I am not saying that a person needs a lot of money to be happy. No. Everyone has different financial needs depending on their dreams. But to be happy, you do need sufficient abundance to pay your bills on time, not be in debt, and not be financially worse off every year while supporting the lifestyle you feel makes you happy and allows you to fulfill your purpose in life. This is what I mean when I state "sufficient abundance" in this lesson.

You need money to support you on the path to becoming the ideal version of yourself. You will need money for education. You need money to surround yourself with beauty since your environment and ecosystem have a significant influence on you, and you also want to live a life that is not full of physical toil day in day out. You also need sufficient money to afford nutritious foods because these are often not subsidized by governments, making the unhealthy subsidized foods much cheaper.

This is unfortunately why many people who earn too little money are precisely those who buy unhealthy foods for themselves and their children, because these foods are much cheaper. But at the end of the day, these are the foods that will make you sick, not allowing you to continue working even at a relatively young age due to health issues, making you dependent on other people.

The choices you want to make are those that will benefit you in the long term. Therefore, you want to make sure that you are spending your hours in a job that is earning you sufficient money to support your and your family's health and all aspects of your life in the long term, so that you can continue working and making a good income for yourself and your family. If you do not earn sufficient money to support yourself in the future, you are leading yourself on a downward spiral towards devastation.

You have to find a job that will allow you to make sufficient abundance and time so you may take on the responsibility for your own health rather than leaving it in the hands of governments or doctors with medications, which also cost money.

A change in mindset must precede the path to abundance if you did not come from an affluent background. I formed my abundance mindset through meditation, reading, learning, and unwavering practice of many teachings, especially from books written by Wallace Wattles, Napoleon Hill, Joseph Murphy, Ralph Waldo Emerson, Charles Haanel, and spiritual books. These changed my life, allowing in abundance.

In this lesson, I will talk about what I learned from my meditations and these books that allowed abundance into my life in a relatively short period. I have prepared this lesson in a ten-step formula that, if followed, will bring you sufficient abundance for sure.

You may use these ten steps for achieving any other goals you have in life, from the smallest to the largest. These steps work. So let's dive into them.

1. Understand that you *should* have abundance. Unfortunately, many people do not believe this and think that wealth is evil or can only be attained in immoral ways. It is your duty to create sufficient abundance. You are doing injustice to yourself and those who depend on you when you do not create sufficient abundance for you to live the life you desire.

   You must have sufficient abundance to fulfill your purpose in life, stay healthy, enjoy life while also giving as much as you can back to humanity and the world while you are here. There is no other way to fulfill your fullest potential and to have the most influence and to adequately support those dependent on you if you do not have sufficient abundance to achieve this.

   It is your duty, just as it is everyone's duty, to have sufficient abundance to support yourself for all days of your life. There is enough for everyone to become sufficiently abundant in this world. Your responsibility is to study how to become sufficiently abundant and do whatever you need to do in a moral way to attain this abundance. Unfortunately neither achieving wealth, nor health is taught in schools and these are both crucial knowledge for living a happy life. Therefore, for the time being, these must be studied independently and they are interconnected.

2. Have faith in the process. There is a precise process that will make you sufficiently abundant, and you must have faith in this process and follow it strictly. Just as you must take on specific behaviors to allow yourself a good and healthy life, the same is valid for attaining sufficient abundance.

   The process begins with knowing that there is a connection between the material and the immaterial world. The immaterial world is vast, unlimited, and eternal, whereas the physical world is limited. Therefore, when you are not where you want to be in any field of life, you are unaware of your true divine nature as a creative force in that field of life.

   There is always a connection between the material and immaterial world. It's similar to that of an umbilical cord connecting mother and baby. The umbilical cord provides the genes, oxygen, and nourishment to the growing baby. It also removes waste products from the baby's blood. But when the baby is growing in the womb, another metaphysical umbilical cord is formed between the baby and the immaterial/spiritual world or infinite intelligence. Spiritually speaking, both umbilical cords are necessary for life.

Nourishment through the metaphysical umbilical cord forms the basis for personal creativity and purpose. Your ideal vision for yourself and your intuitive ideas come to you from the metaphysical umbilical cord. You can be open to these inspirations, ideas, and creativity or closed to them. Either way, you are always connected to the immaterial/spiritual world.

You are also constantly sending ideas and creativity in the form of your thoughts, beliefs, and feelings to the immaterial/spiritual world. What you send through the metaphysical umbilical cord will be nourished back to you and form your reality. This is why what you think, and not what you necessarily desire, is what you get in life.

Since you can choose your thoughts, you should select thoughts of what it is that you want to have in your life. Your thoughts are then passed to the immaterial world through the metaphysical umbilical cord connection.

Your thoughts should be creative and not competitive. There is enough for everyone. Hold creative thoughts that are independent of other people.

3. Hold a clear and definite mental image of the things you desire. For this you must know precisely what you want. You must have a clear and specific mental image of the outcome you desire. For most people, this image is not at all clear, and this is their primary problem. You must know where you are going and have a clear picture of what you will have when you get there. **You must remove all doubt.** When you know what you want, you can create a vivid image of it in your mind.

As I mentioned before, goals must be definite and clear so as not to be sending different and often contradicting messages. This is why so many people fail.

4. Hold the mental image of what you desire in your mind as often as possible, a few times daily. Hold the vision of what you desire while driving, eating, exercising, in the shower, before getting out of bed in the morning, and before falling asleep at night. Any free moment you have, contemplate on the vision of your desires and how you will feel once you have them in your life, just as you would if you had an obsession for something. This should not be so difficult to hold these mental images in your mind since this is what you desire to have. It should come naturally to you to think of what you want, even in an obsessive way. In this way, you are sending your images to the immaterial world, to infinite intelligence.

5. Hold in your mind the vision of whatever you want and not what you don't want to have. Be sure to remove all doubt from your vision. There will always be negative thoughts that creep into your mind, but you must control them. Know that there is only room for one thought in your mind at a time, so if you have a negative thought creeping up, notice it, become aware of it, and replace it with what you *DO* want to have in your life.

Thoughts of what we want easily enter our mind, but then we start to rationalize, overthink, doubt, and suddenly we find ourselves in a downward spiral of negative thoughts and "what if's." These must be stopped immediately so that you will not move these negative visions to the immaterial world, which is creative by nature, so eliminate all doubt and uncertainty and hold good thoughts in their place instead.

6. Maintain a mindset of gratitude. The more you feel gratitude for what you have, the more favorable your outlook will be, so the more positivity is sent through the metaphysical umbilical cord, the more positivity will fill your life. The depth of your gratitude for what you

have now will bring you happiness, and when joy is sent through the metaphysical umbilical cord to the immaterial world, more happiness will come to you.

Hold a mindset of gratitude for the abundance that is available to you always. Persist in feeling deeply grateful, knowing that all is working out in your favor.

7. Have patience. Things are not created from thin air. There is a natural process of creation in the material world. Just as a seed most often does not become a full-grown tree with fruits after one year, all things have their natural cycle of growth and development.

Things take time and must follow the natural growth pattern and order of things.

In this growth period, you must keep your faith in the process high. No matter how much time it takes, you must continue believing, having gratitude, and envisioning the ideal future. Things need time to blossom and develop. Know that things are being created in the immaterial world even if you do not see growth. It does not mean that nothing is not growing underneath the surface if something is not yet seen.

Your thoughts, beliefs, and feelings are creative and will bring about what you focus upon most. Thoughts, beliefs, and feelings are your creative power. You can create through your connection to the immaterial world or create in the material world with much more effort. If your thoughts are positive, the creative energy comes from your connection to the immaterial/spiritual world and will provide you with many blessings in life.

Maintain your faith in the process, and persist with patience. Don't ever let what's in front of you now discourage you from believing and creating a vision in your mind of what could be and what you would like to have in your life.

8. Use your days for action. Do more than you previously did. Do all that you can do every single day.

Many people skip this step. They keep persistent thoughts and feelings of where they desire to be, and their thoughts and feelings produce their desires in the immaterial world underneath their radar. But the person cannot have access to their desires in the material world if they do not take the right actions to get them. There is a joke about a man who prayed to win the lottery every day of his adult life. He planned exactly what he would do with the money when he would win and saw everything just as it would be had he won, but he never won the lottery. Then he died and came before God in heaven and asked, "I prayed so much to win the lottery; why did you not grant me this wish not even once in my lifetime?" And God's reply was, "I would have gladly granted you your wish had you filled out a lottery ticket even once in your lifetime."

So although things are created for you after you've impressed your thoughts onto the immaterial world's creative energy, you will only get your desires when you take the right actions in the direction of your vision in the material world.

9. Give away more value than you desire in return. This step is essential because you will never have guilt or self-sabotage your success. Instead, you will persist with assertiveness towards your goals, and your self-esteem will increase. You will feel deserving of all the abundance that comes to you.

People will part with their money when they believe they are getting more value than paying for it. For example, I buy real estate only when I know that the value I pay for the property is less than the value it will be worth for me once I'm done renovating.

Giving more value in the form of service connects you to a mindset of abundance. You cannot provide others what you believe you do not have to begin with. Therefore, to be in a state of giving is also to be in a state of knowing that you have. You will get riches when you bring more life to others because you bring more life to yourself at the same time. When your desires bring more progress and life for you and others, everyone wins.

10. Choose your steps towards realizing your goals with your intuition. To know the subsequent actions to take every day, you must listen to your intuition which you receive from your connection to the immaterial world. When you connect to the immaterial/spiritual world, you connect to the creative force that binds us all. Then you can draw ideas to achieve your goals and understand your next best steps effortlessly.

Now take action and do what needs to be done persistently and with faith and gratitude.

You can follow all ten of these steps for every goal you wish to attain, not only wealth-related goals.

Anybody can attain wealth and riches from wherever they are currently in life through awareness of your connection to the immaterial world and your ability to influence it through belief and impressions. Today the internet is so full of opportunities, and internet access is cheap that there is really no excuse but to find the time to learn.

It is your duty to have sufficient abundance and not be in debt so you do not limit yourself and your dreams. Follow these ten steps laid out for you, and you will get the abundance that you desire in any field of life.

You can and must do whatever you can to start producing the abundance that you deserve and desire. Start today. There is no reason why you should fail.

Questions Of The Day

To end this lesson and help you become financially free, ask yourself:

What are my precise goals for wealth? What can I do today, this week, and this month to move me steadily towards my goals?

I recommend reading the book *Rich Dad, Poor Dad* by Robert Kiyosaki, which offers many ways to build a passive income to support you on the path to financial freedom.

As usual, I recommend writing your answers in the PDF journal.

Affirmation Of The Day

After answering the questions in your journal, repeat this affirmation:

I PUSH MYSELF TO DO BETTER AND IMPROVE DAILY. I RELEASE ALL RESISTANCE AND DOUBT FROM ATTRACTING ABUNDANCE. I AM TAKING THE PROPER STEPS TO REACH FINANCIAL FREEDOM.

Repeat this affirmation often. With repetition, it has the power to alter your consciousness so you build a better, happier and more purposeful life.

DAY 98 - BECOMING AWARE OF A PLATEAU PERIOD

"At some point, you will hit a plateau. If you keep doing same things you did to get to that point, make a change." ~ J.R. Rim

When you are going for long-term goals, there will be many plateau periods when it seems as if nothing is happening on the way to the top. This is a special period, the plateau period. This is the time when you can look back at your successes as stepping stones on your way to your dreams, but also look at what can be changed to move you forward.

Many people choose to stay in their plateau state, where they are now, more comfortable than when they started, but have still not reached their end goals. They get too comfortable to move forward.

I reached such a plateau a few years ago. I had made enough money from my entrepreneurial adventures to be comfortable for the rest of my life. I kept working for the fun of it, but I lost my motivation to work for money. I was too comfortable. I did not reach the goals I dreamed of reaching, but I was comfortable enough. It is understandable why you can be stuck in a comfortable plateau that may be far from your real dreams but comfortable enough to stay there.

However, during these plateau phases, it is actually time to rock the boat if you want to reach the life of your dreams and the achievements of your dreams. When you do reach a plateau phase on your way to reaching any goal, it is then time to celebrate what you have achieved up to this point. Look back at your achievements. What have you learned? What have you changed as a result to get to where you are today? What new habits did you adopt to get you to where you are today? It is vital to acknowledge your forward movement.

Prepare a timeline of where you were in the beginning in terms of skills and all else that has to do with each area of your life. At the end of the timeline, write down how you see this area of your life when it is perfected, in its ideal form. Also, make a note of where you currently are on this timeline on the path to your dreams. Write down your current situation in that area of life. Do this for all areas of your life, your relationships, your career, your finances, your home, your peace of mind, your social life, your health and fitness, and your life vision.

Now you can celebrate your successes in each area and enjoy your plateau period for a while. I strongly recommend stating exactly how long you plan to enjoy your new plateau whereby you maintain your new skills and habits but do not make any progress forward. Two weeks up to three months is sufficient for a plateau period, but no more. If you want to live a life that you will be happy with and proud of, do not stop progressing towards your dreams for too long, even if the forward movement is minimal.

Don't stop getting better at what you want to be better at. There may be people in your life who may say that what you've reached is good enough. Yes, it may be good enough for them, but is it really good enough for you? People may not be happy with your growth. They may see it as a threat to them. Many people do not like to see their friends or spouses grow beyond what they can handle because they may feel insecure from this growth. They may feel that their own life needs improvement, and they don't like that feeling. They may not be willing to do the work and prefer to stay small. And if you listen to them, you will fall into their plan of life for you, not exactly the life you have planned for yourself.

Whenever you reach a plateau phase in any area of life, you have two choices: falling back or rising up. This is when you can see your commitment to the life of your dreams. Will you quit, or will you continue until you reach the finish line? This is up to you.

It's challenging to keep working at something when you must renew yourself every time to progress. But as I mentioned before, you cannot be the same person you were when you set your goals and dreams. You need to become a different person to achieve them. You need to have other habits, skills, and a different mindset than what you had before you started in order to reach your goals. If these skills, habits, and mindset were part of your life beforehand, then you would already have the things that you desire in life.

When you reach a plateau phase, although you may feel good and enjoy life momentarily, you stop making real progress towards your goals. And since progress equates with happiness for most people, you will not be happy for long by continuing to plateau.

However, progress does not necessarily continue linearly; there are regular spikes of change and plateau periods. This is part of any progress and development. This plateau is also a part of any health and fitness challenge.

You need to adjust your diet to your new weight every time you make advancements. For fitness, you need to change your workout routine to continue to grow muscle mass or improve endurance.

These are small examples that explain what needs to be done to overcome a plateau. To overcome a plateau, you will need to learn and follow different or more dedicated efforts. Dedicated effort can be learning new skills, changing something about yourself, trying new ideas, or even just putting in more effort than previously was needed.

When you reach a plateau phase, you have to decide whether you will stay committed to your goals and your ideal life or are you going to stay in your newfound comfort zone and say that you have enough. It is your choice. Put everything on a scale and decide. Can you live with this level of satisfaction? This is yours to decide because it is your life. You are the one making the decisions, and you are the one who will need to live with the consequences.

Questions Of The Day

To end this lesson and help you overcome a plateau phase after celebrating your successes, please ask yourself:

Where in my life am I currently at a plateau of progress? What are the next steps I need to take to make progress possible? Am I committed to reaching the next level?

As Beyonce says in her song, "Level Up", "Thank God I never settled, this view is so much better."

As usual, I recommend writing your answers in the PDF journal.

Affirmation Of The Day

After answering the questions in your journal, repeat this affirmation:

I CHOOSE TO BE THE RARE ONE WHO GOES BEYOND THE PLATEAU AND CONTINUES ON THE PATH TOWARDS MY DREAMS NO MATTER WHAT.

Repeat this affirmation often. With repetition, it has the power to alter your consciousness so you build a better, happier and more purposeful life.

DAY 99 - BECOMING AWARE OF THE IMPORTANCE OF TIME OUT

"The world is a book, and those who do not travel read only a page." ~ St. Augustine

Vacations are an excellent way to reduce stress and increase the immune system's function. It lowers your chances of becoming ill in the coming months after your holiday, and it reduces the chances of heart disease and helps lower blood pressure for the coming months after a relaxing holiday. A vacation also helps improve your outlook on life. When you return from holiday after having some introspection time, you will be more motivated and inspired to follow through with your goals and have the energy to do what is required to move you forward towards a better life for you. Holidays inspire us and may lead us to see where we are off track and not headed to where we desire to be. They give us time and space to step back and see the bigger picture.

When you take time out of the rat race, you have time to think and see if you are headed in the right direction for yourself. This is why I recommend taking one real vacation a year so that you still have the continuity of life but with some added spice to inspire you.

People who take regular, relaxed, or adventurous vacations are much more likely to be more creative and productive and less stressed and burned out. When we burn out due to constant stress, we alter our brain to make it more likely for us to suffer from depression, anxiety, overwhelm, and prefer to stay in our comfort zone.

When I was raising my elder daughters after divorce under the pressures of poverty, no sleep, high levels of stress at work, and the difficulty that came with their special needs, without ever taking a break, every day seemed like a week. It felt as if I would have a breakdown. For six years, I did not take any vacation or time off because I lacked time and money. But money or time should not be a consideration. You can still take time out on a weekend by putting your children with a caretaker or your parent or family member and sleeping in a tent in nature. In fact this can be a very powerful, intimate vacation.

I was chosen to take part in a reality show. Out of 20000 applicants, they chose ten of us, and off we went to sleep in tents in the freezing weather of winter. But for me, it was like going on holiday. The difficulties in the reality show were dwarfed by the difficulty in my day-to-day life. I enjoyed the experience as if I was on an amazing holiday, and this outlook led me to win first place.

After the show aired, the production crew sent my future husband and me on holiday to the French Alps for a skiing vacation. It was amazing. We learned to snowboard and had a wonderful time. I returned from the holiday full of energy and with a new perspective on life, so powerful was this holiday adventure for me that after we came back, I found the courage to open my own clinic. This was twenty years ago.

Spending time with friends, family, or our significant others while enjoying life together strengthens these bonds. A study also showed that women who took regular holidays with their partners were more satisfied with their marriages.

Even planning the holiday will improve your mood and lower stress levels weeks before the holiday even begins.

So as you can see, there are many benefits, both physical and emotional, to taking a holiday.

Motivation, inspiration, and even self-esteem will increase.

When you visit new places and overcome the discomfort of being away from your comfortable everyday life, your self-esteem grows, and you become more courageous and strong. You see yourself as more independent and more powerful, allowing yourself to lead a more effective and happier life. You are also more capable of dealing with the difficulties that inevitably arise in life.

Life goes like the tide, and there are times when we work harder, we produce much, and we are full of energy to squeeze the most out of every waking minute. Yet, there are also times when we need solitude and quietness. Time to seek answers from within to our questions about our life and future.

Taking time out is excellent for revealing aspects of your life with which you have become dissatisfied. You will realize how satisfying your life *can* become if you are willing to make the changes that need to be made.

It is a pleasant time to analyze where you are in life and what is important for you. It is a time to allow your intuition to guide you. Time to reflect, research, and gain the faith to believe that things are going your way.

This is a time to slow down and to plan your next moves in a natural direction. This slowdown will help you see the finer and often overlooked details of your life to determine the best next steps for you.

When we stop the constant stress that we have in life and take the time to relax and be at ease with ourselves, we can reach more profound levels of awareness. From this quiet, peaceful perspective, you will find ways to change what you do not like.

Time off *supports* focus for your mission in life and prevents burnout. It is a time to reset yourself mentally. This prevents your creativity from drying up. Your mood improves, and you become more productive and refreshed when you return.

This freedom to allow your thoughts to wander without a tight schedule can do wonders for your life and future.

Questions Of The Day

To help you take a productive, enjoyable break from the day to day responsibilities and commitments while making you more focused and stronger, ask yourself:

When will I take some time off to spend time with my friends or family and take time for myself, for introspection, fun, and gratitude for what I have in my life? Can I find the time this week to plan my future holiday? Now start to enjoy the process of planning your next holiday.

As usual, I recommend writing your answers in the PDF journal. Plan your next vacation if you haven't already done so.

Affirmation Of The Day

After answering the questions in your journal, repeat this affirmation:

I ALLOW MYSELF TO TAKE TIME OFF AND ENJOY THE GIFTS OF LIFE WHILE ALSO PLANNING FOR THE FUTURE I DESIRE.

Repeat this affirmation often. With repetition, it has the power to alter your consciousness so you build a better, happier and more purposeful life.

DAY 100 - BECOMING AWARE OF YOUR WORTHWHILE LIFE

"Life is worthwhile when you walk on a path aligned to your purpose." ~ Gift Gugu Mona

To sum up these past 100 days, I would like to go over what a worthwhile life truly is about and ensure that you leave this challenge with an overall understanding of how to live the life you truly desire. So let's get into the summary of what a worthwhile life is really about.

You now know that life must have meaning to feel worthwhile, and life can only have meaning when you have:

1. Growth or progress
2. Contribution to other people's lives in some way by making their lives better, happier, and fuller, even if for only one person.
3. Expression of your true self. It is not that difficult to lead a worthwhile life. All you have to do is grow continuously—personally, through a business, or your children, and show your true light to the world in a way that benefits other people's lives.

Albert Einstein, said, "Only a life lived for others is a life worthwhile."

Some older people volunteer in different charities because they want to contribute more to this world and its people before leaving. They still desire progress, and they feel that they are expressing their true self through a commitment to a worthy cause.

So how do you live life for others in a way that will give you joy? Here is a summary of a how to ensure a worthwhile life for yourself:

1. Learn from life experiences. You also read or learn from other people's experiences and the lessons they learned. Integrate these lessons and tools into your own life. This is part of your hero's journey. You must keep learning and growing continually to give your wisdom or other gifts to people who need it.

   You want to learn more about yourself. Recognize your limiting beliefs, and then master your mind so that it works for you and not against you. Your mindset can lead you to a life of joyful experiences or a life of ongoing struggle. You have a choice of what you choose to be and become every moment of your life. Will you be happier or more depressed? Will you be fearful, stressed, and lack faith, or will you live from courage, faith, and belief? Will you be involved in purposeful activities, will you overcome addictions, will you be more responsible for your life, or will you be lazy, victimized, and a slave in life? Will you be self-absorbed, or will you make others your main focus?

   Once you acknowledge the power in your hands, you can steer your life to a better place and become an inspiration for others to do the same.

   Victimhood or heroism is unnecessary. You're not here to be less than or better than anybody else. You are here to be you and to serve your highest potential. You will always have people who need your gifts in this world. Trust in yourself and follow the calling of your intuition.

2. Ensure that you have put in your best effort. All people who have lived a worthwhile life have given life their all. They went all in. They did their best, and they gave their best.

   Do and give your best! Do not do a mediocre job. Do not live a mediocre life. *You* know the truth about your actions. You know whether you gave them your all or you were lazy and scared. It is only you who knows whether you gave something your all or not. Only you know if you did what you could have done, under the circumstances you were in.

You learned that you do not need to be the best at everything. There is no need to run after more and more achievements. There is no need to do things just for the sake of doing more to validate your worth and to feel that you've earned the approval of others. You are already worthy. You were born worthy. Do what you feel an urge to do to show your light to the world in a meaningful way in the present moment.

To experience the present moment, you must also enjoy what you are doing. When you enjoy what you are doing, love will flow from you, affecting you and everyone positively. This is what a worthwhile life really is.

You now understand that you do not need to feel accepted by everyone, but you do need to follow your bliss and spread your gifts to the world.

The happier you get, the more you will achieve, and also, the more content you become, the more you spread positivity in the world, which will make you feel that you've lived a worthwhile life. This is truly what the world needs today, more happy people.

Gandhi said, "Satisfaction is in the effort, not in the attainment." So total effort = total success. The results don't matter when you try and give it your best, and you persist until the end.

3. Go after your dreams. You will not feel that your life is worthwhile if you did not even try to go after your dreams. There are things that you may succeed at, and there are other things that you may not succeed at, but it is the fact that you tried to go after your dreams and did your best that will make you feel that your life was worthwhile, even if you did not get everything you desired.

   By now, you also know that when you blame others, or give excuses, and complain about not reaching your goals, dreams, or the life that you desire without putting in the effort, you are giving away your power to be in a position to change your circumstances. Stay connected with your authentic essence and make your decisions from your soul without the influence of trends or public opinion.

4. Complete what you start. If you start something and complete the task, then you have achieved something you wished to achieve. You have made progress and became wiser. You can now use what you gained to be the foundation for further improvement and help or give other people who have less than you in this particular field of life.

   Jim Rohn said there is no point in building one foundation after another without building the rest of the house. Aim to complete any task that you still find worthy enough of your time.

   Only through the things that you will finish and go all the way with will you feel that you did your best and feel that your life is worthwhile.

   It is easy to stop in the middle when the going gets tough, and it will at some point be challenging, but how will you feel after you quit? How would Barak Obama or any other president if they did not go all the way to become presidents of the USA?

   These people went all the way. They did their best and tried to get as far as they could. And because they tried and persisted with courage, they also succeeded in the end.

   Never stop trying. When you try to do your best it brings meaning to your life. This prevents feelings of stagnation, depression or being overwhelmed, and allows feelings of meaningful progress in your life.

Life can feel confusing at times. During such times it is good to review your goals and desires. Ensure you are still doing what you need and want to get you to the vision you desire. Keep refining yourself and keep improving. When everyone improves themselves, the whole world becomes a better place.

Work towards something meaningful for you. Be creative. Life is not only to fulfill your duties. Use your imagination and creativity to create the life of your dreams. You must keep your responsibilities, but you must also be the creator of your life.

Yes, you now understand that there will be setbacks and unexpected events on the way towards any achievement. See these as learning opportunities, direction, and support for self-refinement. If need be, design a new path towards any goals that YOU believe are worthwhile for you.

5. Follow your heart and do what you love so that you can serve others effortlessly. Don't worry about the outcome. As I mentioned, when you are selfishly attached to the results you desire, you become their prisoner. It is what you give to others through inspiration, ideas. love, and understanding that will stay with them and transform their lives, and this will make you aware of how worthwhile your life indeed was. Love yourself and follow your heart. Understand your value, and your unique gifts, and all that you can offer the world, and then use your heart to be of service to others who need you.

6. Be around those who make you better and not those who bring you down. We know that there are people who you cannot remove from your life, and you may even not want to remove them from your life, but perhaps, their unhealthy mindset can have a negative influence on you. Keep these people at a healthy distance. You may wish to keep certain people closer to you because they help, support, and push you forwards, even if they have a negative disposition, but being aware of this is of significant importance. You know which people are stealing your power away and who are empowering you.

Surround yourself with people who appreciate you and your gifts. Think about Jesus before he was crucified. He only had a few followers around him who believed in him. You only need a few people who believe in you and support you and your gifts and help you spread the love within you.

Questions Of The Day

Ask yourself: Am I learning, improving, and progressing? Am I trying and doing my best? Am I completing what I start? Am I going after my dreams? And am I giving my gifts to society?

If yes, then great! But if not, ask yourself, What is holding me back? Is it the people around me, or is it my mindset?

As usual, I recommend writing your answers in the PDF journal.

Affirmation Of The Day

After answering the questions in your journal, repeat this affirmation:

I LIVE MY LIFE WITH INTENTION, AND I WILL USE MY GIFTS TO MAKE MY LIFE WORTHWHILE.

Repeat this affirmation often. With repetition, it has the power to alter your consciousness so you build a better, happier and more purposeful life.

A WORD OF DEPARTURE

Use this book to constantly improve yourself and move towards the life of your dreams. Every time you read this book, new lessons will come to your attention. It's here to guide you through life and should be looked at as an owner's manual.

Go through the lessons; there will always be something new to gain from rereading this book.

Take it with you on holiday and when you have time for introspection. Delve into it until the lessons are embedded in your being and your ideal life reveals itself before you.

You are ready, you deserve this. You are in the perfect place to continue your hero's journey and, at the end of it, you will reveal the true hero within you to the world.

With love, joy, and wonder,

Dr. Galit Goldfarb

Printed in Dunstable, United Kingdom